FRAGILE DEMOCRACIES

Twenty-five years after the fall of the Berlin Wall, the democratic ascendency of the post-Soviet era is under severe challenge. While fragile democracies in Eastern Europe, Africa, and East Asia face renewed threats, the world has witnessed the failed democratic promises of the Arab Spring. What lessons can be drawn from these struggles? What conditions or institutions are needed to prevent the collapse of democracy?

This book argues that the most significant antidote to authoritarianism is the presence of strong constitutional courts. Distinct in the Third Wave of democratization, these courts serve as a bulwark against vulnerability to external threats as well as internal consolidation of power. Particular attention is given to societies riven by deep divisions of race, religion, or national background, for which the courts have become pivotal actors in allowing democracy to take root.

Samuel Issacharoff is the Reiss Professor of Constitutional Law at New York University School of Law. A pioneer in the field of law of the political process, he is the author of more than 100 articles, books, and other academic works, including the seminal *The Law of Democracy* casebook (with Pamela Karlan and Richard Pildes, 4th ed., 2012). Issacharoff is a Fellow of the American Academy of Arts and Sciences.

To Miraya.
Gracias por venir a una
discusión de los asuntos del
día.

Sam Issacharoff

CAMBRIDGE STUDIES IN ELECTION LAW AND DEMOCRACY

Recent developments have pushed elections scholarship in new directions. As a result, interdisciplinary work has flourished and political scientists and law professors have developed a more sophisticated sense of the relationship between law and politics. This series seeks to create an intellectual roadmap for the field, one that systematically examines the issues confronting both mature and emerging democracies. It will chart those new intellectual paths to spur interdisciplinary work, to identify productive ways in which scholars' research agendas connect to policy makers' reform agendas, and to disseminate this body of work to the growing audience interested in the intersection of law, politics, and democracy.

Books in the Series

Fr   s

CONTESTED POWER   ERA
OF CONSTITUTIONAL COURTS

SAMUEL ISSACHAROFF

New York University School of Law

CAMBRIDGE
UNIVERSITY PRESS

CAMBRIDGE
UNIVERSITY PRESS

32 Avenue of the Americas, New York NY 10013-2473, USA

Cambridge University Press is part of the University of Cambridge.

It furthers the University's mission by disseminating knowledge in the pursuit of education, learning and research at the highest international levels of excellence.

www.cambridge.org
Information on this title: www.cambridge.org/9781107654549

First published 2015

A catalogue record for this publication is available from the British Library

Library of Congress Cataloguing in Publication data
Issacharoff, Samuel, author.
Fragile democracies : contested power in the era of constitutional courts /
Samuel Issacharoff, New York University School of Law.
    pages   cm. – (Cambridge studies in election law and democracy)
ISBN 978-1-107-03870-7 (hardback) – ISBN 978-1-107-65454-9 (paperback)
1. Constitutional history.   2. Democracy.   3. New democracies.
4. Constitutional courts.   I. Title.
K3161.I84   2015
347´.035–dc23   2014047370

ISBN 978-1-107-03870-7 Hardback
ISBN 978-1-107-65454-9 Paperback

Contents

Preface

About a decade ago I began to redirect a significant part of my academic focus away from the study of the law of American democracy. My new attention was the product of a renewed sense of common enterprise across democracies that emerged from two critical events. The first was the contested presidential election of 2000; in particular, the failure of the Florida electoral machinery to produce a clear result and the subsequent intervention of the Supreme Court in *Bush v. Gore*. The second was the emergence of difficult national security decisions within the United States following the attacks of September 11. Each represented a significant challenge to the structure and integrity of American democracy, each exposing a characteristic vulnerability of democracy either to process failure from within or to external enemies.

In the aftermath of these events, I began to wonder more systematically about how other democracies deal with such challenges. American democracy is no doubt exceptional in its duration and in its constitutional pedigree. But it has also had the benefit of a relatively stable political order and geographic isolation (or insulation) from potential military threats. What if the workings of democracy in this country were themselves challenged? Or, what if the War on Terror forced a recalibration of the delicate balance between liberty and security?

If American democracy were suddenly more vulnerable, perhaps the experiences of other democracies would help in thinking about the resulting challenges. This inquiry assumes no universalism of law, no sense that a foreign consensus should obligate a response in American law – although it does not presume either that informed judgments from abroad should be rejected per se because of their foreign origins. Rather, comparative assessments sometimes help to illuminate certain characteristics of domestic difficulties that might otherwise be obscured by their apparent intimate relations to our lived experiences.

The results of this decade-long inquiry have emerged in a series of articles in journals in law and political science and in book chapters. This book draws from these prior publications but brings them together more synthetically around a single concern: How is it that democracies manage conflict, and what are the institutional preconditions for democracies to be able to perform this function? Much as the central organization of the work is new, it is nonetheless important to acknowledge the earlier versions of work from which I have drawn here.

The part of this inquiry addressing democratic responses to antidemocratic forces, as well as the title of this book, is based heavily on an earlier work of mine, *Fragile Democracies*, which appeared in the Harvard Law Review in 2007. The part addressing the perils of what I term *one-partyism* draws most heavily from another earlier work, *Constitutional Courts and Democratic Hedging*, which in turn appeared in the Georgetown Law Journal in 2011. Some of the themes have also appeared in a series of articles that look more broadly at the relation between democracy and constitutionalism, most notably *The Enabling Role of Democratic Constitutionalism* and *Constitutionalizing Democracy in Fractured Societies*, which appeared in the Texas Law Review in 2003 and 2006, respectively; *Democracy and Collective Decisionmaking*, which appeared in 2008 in the International Journal of Constitutional Law; *The Democratic Risk to Democratic Transitions*, which appeared in Constitutional Court Review in 2015; and *Constitutional Courts and Consolidated Power*, which appeared in the American Journal of Comparative Law in 2014.

A project of this scale demands great research assistance to try to make sense of subtle developments in political and legal systems around the world. I have tested many of the hypotheses and observations in many settings over the past decade and have most benefited from the ability to hear responses in numerous national settings. While all the institutions are too numerous to mention, I have profited from great exchanges in Argentina, Australia, England, France, Germany, India, Israel, Italy, Mexico, Peru, South Africa, Spain, Switzerland, and the United States. I received wonderful backing from the NYU School of Law and my deans while here, Richard Revesz and Trevor Morrison, and the added benefit of a year at the Straus Institute where these themes were pursued in a great collegial setting. I also received support for the book manuscript from the Rosenthal Lectures at Northwestern Law School and from the Filomen D'Agostino and Max E. Greenberg Research Fund at the NYU School of Law. Special thanks to Bonnie and Richard Reiss, who created the chair I occupy at NYU and who have been wonderfully supportive of my ventures.

Many colleagues have been sounding boards for the ideas presented here over the years, and while not saddling them with responsibility for what follows, I do thank Giovanni Capoccia, Sujit Choudhry, William Forbath, Pamela Karlan, Brendan O'Leary, Pasquale Pasquino, Richard Pildes, and Wojciech Sadurski.

In addition, over the years that I have been engaged in this project I have had a number of great research assistants and they should be thanked: Yotam Barkai, Matt Brown, Kirti Datla, Thad Eagles, Nathan Foell, Philip Fortino, Camden Hutchison, Anna Morawiec Mansfield, Swapna Maruri, Jeremy Peterman, Maria Ponomarenko, Aaron Kates Rose, Peter Ross, Ian Samuel, Zach Savage, Josh Stillman, Daniel Suleiman, Alec Webley, and Josh Wilkenfeld. This list includes four former research assistants who are now colleagues in the academy: Chris Brummer, Erin Delaney, Ari Glogower, and Teddy Rave. Finally, special thanks to Matthew Holbreich and Mitchell Stern for tremendous labor in helping get the final manuscript in shape.

Finally, behind every work that allows contemplation of broad themes there are those who make life go on and give meaning to our daily engagements. For me they are my wife, Cindy, and my children, Jessica and Lucas.

Introduction: The Burden of Modern Democracy

A quarter century has passed since the fall of the Berlin Wall. The initial throes of the twentieth-century defeat of communism and fascism invited the triumphant claim that the sweep of democracy was indeed upon us. As even the Arab protesters from Cairo to Tunis would show, seemingly impervious autocratic regimes could succumb to long nascent aspirations for popular governance. The wave of embryonic democratic transitions that began with the fall of the Soviet Union was indeed a heady time. History may not have ended with the fall of democracy's ideological rivals. But the arc of history appeared decisively tilted toward democracy.

Today the assessment is more mixed. Democracy turns out to require more than just holding an initial election for head of state. The rule of law cannot be commanded by a text but needs institutional guarantors. Political parties need to learn the give and take of electoral coalitions and the difficult translation of a party platform into a program for governance. There must be confidence that the rules of the game are relatively fair and that the losers of today can emerge as the potential winners of tomorrow. Perhaps most of all, there has to be some assurance that there will be a chance to reconsider tomorrow, that the winners of today will be willing to surrender office tomorrow as the tides of public opinion and electoral support may shift.

To look around twenty-five years after the end of the Soviet Union is sobering. The initial flirtations with democracy in the former Soviet republics of Central Asia collapsed into autocratic rule. The Green Revolution in Iran was suppressed, as was the Bahraini uprising. The civil war in Syria, at the time of this writing, rages on. In Egypt mass protests, street violence, ethnic conflict, and political instability continue, with the military now once again in power. Libya remains a cauldron of political unrest with even rudimentary public authority deeply contested. Of the inspiring Arab Spring, only Tunisia holds on to its democratic aspirations. Even countries of great democratic mobilization, such as Ukraine, spiraled down into an insidious form for strong-man politics and are now a sad recreation of Cold War lines of division.

While the Arab Spring may have sputtered out, the aspirations and practical problems of these democratic movements have followed closely upon the explosive opening of what has been appropriately termed the Third Wave of democratization.[1] We can confidently say that with the fall of the Soviet Union, the world embarked on a far-flung experiment in democracy. Newly minted governments tried their hands at the uncertain project of letting the people select their governors through elections. These unlikely democracies are now found not only in the former reaches of the Soviet empire, but in postapartheid South Africa, pluralist Mexico, and post-authoritarian South Korea. The past quarter century has yielded the largest surge of new constitutional democracies since the end of the colonial period after the two world wars. As with any sudden development, it comes as no surprise that the results have been mixed, the machineries of voting frequently imperfect, the commitment to accompanying liberal values problematic. Yet it seems that no new country can avoid some aspect of democracy if it is to claim a place at the table of legitimate governments.

What renders these efforts at democracy truly an experiment is the difficult national contexts in which they emerge. The demise of an authoritarian regime highlights the frailty of the very idea of a nation. Many, if not all, of these societies face the problems of religious and ethnic fracture. Without an established sense of nationhood, the form of governance would appear a secondary consideration. Peculiarly, the process of consolidating a nation and the efforts at creating the institutions for democratic governance arise together, particularly in the post-Soviet world. Much historic uncertainty attaches to the question of whether elections, the indispensable touchstone for democratic rule, actually further the accompanying aims of securing a manageable nation.

The problem of creating democratic institutions and culture out of the ashes of authoritarianism, and in a fractured society, is that fragile democracies must navigate a dilemma at the heart of all successful liberal democracies: they must enable majority rule while also institutionally limiting it. The mechanism of enabling majority rule is invariably elections. An autocrat falls, and the cry for elections is heard all around. Elections have become the hallmark of democratic transitions. But they are hardly sufficient. Elections

---

[1] SAMUEL HUNTINGTON, THE THIRD WAVE: DEMOCRATIZATION IN THE 20TH CENTURY 3–6 (Norman: University of Oklahoma Press, 1991) (defining the "Third Wave" as democratization between 1974 and 1990).

alone do not foster political stability across time, protect vulnerable minorities against politically powerful majorities, address historic ethnic grievances, ensure tolerance, or even guarantee political legitimacy.

A successful democracy requires the capacity to win and to lose, the ability of the losers of today to reorganize and press for gains in elections tomorrow. The experience in postcolonial Africa, for example, shows that it was far easier to hold the first election than the second. The history of failed democracies fleshes out the intuition that stable democracy requires more than just rushing to hold an election. Too often the holding of an election becomes the forum for the attempt to cement power in the hands of a dominant majority followed by a demoralizing descent into one-party rule and show elections.[2] To the words of the cynical and oftentimes culpable ex-colonialists, this was one-man, one-vote, one-time.[3]

Moreover, elections alone often serve to recreate and rekindle ethnic conflict. Imagine a society historically divided between groups of peoples, each of whom has perpetrated grave violence on the other over centuries of tumult. Take as an example a poor country such as Moldova, a country locked in Eastern Europe and having just emerged from decades of Soviet oppression. Its peoples share neither a language nor an intuitive sense of a common national enterprise. Now, suddenly, the Soviet behemoth collapses and the country is thrust into political uncertainty. In such conditions of instability, with claims of historic injustices reasserted and with the risks of communal violence reemerging, what possible chance could there be for a tolerant democratic culture to emerge through elections alone? What guarantee is there that a momentary claim to being a democracy will not be merely a chance for the dominant ethnic group to capture the state apparatus through the apparent legitimating process of an election, treat itself preferentially, and force a minority group to submit to its will?

Take South Africa, where the first elections held after apartheid would no doubt permit the black majority to wield power. What confidence should the newly politically powerless white minority have that the historic need to redress injustice will not lead to outright expropriation and oppression

---

[2] *See* DONALD L. HOROWITZ, A DEMOCRATIC SOUTH AFRICA? CONSTITUTIONAL ENGINEERING IN A DIVIDED SOCIETY 97 (Berkeley and Los Angeles: University of California Press, 1991) (providing examples of "polarizing elections" leading to authoritarian regimes).

[3] This unfortunate pattern prompted the phrase "one man, one vote, one time," attributed to former Assistant Secretary of State and U.S. Ambassador to Syria and Egypt Edward Djerejian. *See, e.g.,* Ali Kahn, *A Theory of Universal Democracy,* 16 WIS. INT'L L.J. 106 n.130 (1997). Djerejian's cynicism was founded in fact: between 1967 and 1991, for example, no country in Africa experienced power passing from one elected government to another.

of the former apartheid rulers? Or imagine India, where the awakening of political extremism amid the dominant Hindu majority leads with distressing frequency to assaults on the Muslim minority. There too, what confidence should the minority population have when the exponents of Hindu triumphalism emerge as the dominant political party after national elections?

In all of these circumstances, the basic question returns: What possible reason is there to trust the future leadership of the country to the outcome of an election? Is it not perfectly predictable that an election, even if fair, would be a referendum on which group would hold power to the possible detriment and exclusion of others? The fact of being a majority in a fair election, or even just getting more votes than anyone else, cannot possibly legitimate the settling of historical scores, even if the redrawing of the historic balance sheet takes advantage of duly enacted laws used to exploit historic adversaries. To rekindle historic grievances, the laws of a fractured society need not build on the overt racialism and menace of apartheid or, even worse, the Nuremberg laws of Nazi Germany – which, it must be recalled, were also duly enacted through the operation of compromised democracies. We need not invoke cataclysmic events to address the fears that minorities must have in any context where a well-defined majority has power. There are far too many simpler mechanisms, some seemingly quite innocuous, that may prove capable of representing communal oppression, including designating the national language of government, decreeing the materials for instruction in the public schools, or even deciding where to locate a capital.[4]

Democracy may forge a collective, national identity, but it may also have just the opposite effect. There is in fact reason to believe that elections inflame ethnic conflict as politicians seek to mobilize their constituents by appealing to their partisan ardor. New democratic orders need to channel popular passions into democratic engagement. But the attendant risk is that the freedoms and ambitions unleashed by popular sovereignty will "intensely politicize all areas of organized collective existence," as Pratap Mehta duly cautions in his wonderful work on Indian democracy, from which this introductory title borrows its theme.[5] The lead-up to an election is a jolt of adrenaline to the political passions of a society. As with any disabled or diseased individual, the exercise that keeps the vibrant strong may prove fatal to the weak. The weaker

---

[4] The commanding study of the relationship between linguistic claims and allocations of governmental benefits is: Sujit Choudhry, *Managing Linguistic Nationalism Through Constitutional Design: Lessons from South Asia*, 7 INT'L J. CON. LAW 577 (2009).

[5] PRATAP BHANU MEHTA, THE BURDEN OF DEMOCRACY 6 (New Delhi: Penguin Books, 2003).

the institutions of democracy and the more fixed the societal divisions, the more likely it is that the lines of partisan dispute will reproduce the historic fault lines of the society. Under such circumstances, the reality of democratic "choice" is likely to be the retribution of victor's justice against the defeated minority. Elections are the shorthand for other factors that we think characterize democratic life, but they are unfortunately not always the pathway to a more tolerant society. Just as likely, elections in a fractured society will serve as the rallying point for intolerance.

The formal mechanisms of democracy by themselves ensure neither tolerance nor legitimacy. Elections simply tally up who is the majority and who is the minority. By themselves they neither guarantee civility nor the subsequent accountability of the victors to their subjects. In country after country – be it with the beleaguered Turkish minority in Bulgaria, or the Bosniaks in Bosnia-Herzegovina, or the formerly dominant whites in postapartheid South Africa, or even black citizens in the United States – no election is really needed to distinguish historic minorities from the majority population. An election does not quell the sense of injustice of a minority subjected to such perceived majoritarian tyranny by speciously legitimating majority rule. An election all too often lends a fictitious air of legitimacy to what is merely, in the words memorialized by Alexis de Tocqueville from the American founders, the "tyranny of the majority."

A brief tour of political thinking reveals just how extraordinary is the idea that democracy, elections, or political contests would ever emerge as a way of managing core conflicts in a society. Elections historically were thought to presuppose a settled form of governance, and that in turn presupposed a culturally defined *demos*. The idea of democracy without a demos, to borrow from Joseph Weiler's account of the European Union, is a concept without resonance in historic liberal thought. Indeed, and pushing the idea more deeply, the notion that democracy cannot exist without cultural homogeneity has deep roots in republican political thought, from the small city-state lauded in Rousseau's Social Contract to the rural, homogeneous, agrarian regime trumpeted by the Anti-Federalists.[6] Even classical liberals expressed skepticism that democratic government was possible in a fractured society. John

---

[6] *See* Brutus, No. 1, 18 Oct. 1787 ("In a republic, the manners, sentiments, and interests of the people should be similar."). For a discussion of the dominance in the history of political thought of cultural and political unity as the bedrock of the free or good regime, *see* NANCY ROSENBLUM, ON THE SIDE OF THE ANGELS: AN APPRECIATION OF PARTIES AND PARTISANSHIP (Princeton, NJ: Princeton University Press, 2008).

Stuart Mill, the central proponent of liberty as the desired end state of human affairs, thought that:

> Free institutions are next to impossible in a country made up of different nationalities. Among a people without fellow-feeling, especially if they read and speak different languages, the united public opinion, necessary to the working of representative government, cannot exist.[7]

Alexis de Tocqueville, Mill's correspondent and another champion of nineteenth-century liberalism, echoes Mill's doubt that a society of diverse languages, ethnicities, and cultures can maintain the proper political culture required for liberalism.[8] Even in an age of pluralism and multiculturalism, prominent political thinkers still wonder whether democracy is possible in societies riven by core division over identity.[9]

Yet the democratic experiment of the modern period turns time and again to the mechanism of election to augur in an era of stability following wars, conflicts, or the demise of authoritarian rule – or at least to attempt to do so. Clearly elections serve as a shorthand, a code for a more robust political agenda. Elections are the sine qua non of democracy, but as with all conditions that are necessary but not sufficient to ensure a desired end, there are a host of institutional and cultural factors that define democratic life, independent of the ultimate act of casting a ballot. We cannot conceive of democracy without political party rivalry, robust public debate, and the heat of dispute all culminating in a decisive election contest. But elections alone are insufficient.

Fragile democracies also need limitations on majoritarian power. Societies with chronic fractures along religious or ethnic lines need a commitment to pluralist power that might temper the divisions. As efforts at democratic governance spread to the former colonies, state planners and political scientists turned to the national experiences in European countries such as Austria, Belgium, the Netherlands, and Switzerland to find models that would reconcile democracy with a divided society. From these examples came the claim that democracy should be limited by formal power sharing that would make all the rival groups stakeholders in shared governance. Under the rather cumbersome term "consociational structures" emerged the belief that divided societies could forge a national integration of rival elites that would in turn yield a politically stable democracy before the divisive process of voting was

---

[7] JOHN STUART MILL, ON LIBERTY, AND, CONSIDERATIONS ON REPRESENTATIVE GOVERNMENT 292 (New York: MacMillan Co., 1947).

[8] *See, e.g.,* 1 ALEXIS DE TOCQUEVILLE, DEMOCRACY IN AMERICA 27–44 (Harvey C. Mansfield & Delba Winthrop, eds., trans., Chicago, IL: University of Chicago Press, 2000) (1835).

[9] SAMUEL HUNTINGTON, WHO ARE WE?: THE CHALLENGES TO AMERICA'S NATIONAL IDENTITY (New York: Simon and Schuster, 2005).

engaged.[10] Arend Lijphart authored the pathbreaking study that identified the critical elements of the consociational experiment:

(1) government by a grand coalition of all significant segments;
(2) a mutual veto or concurrent-majority voting rule for some or all issues;
(3) proportionality as the principle for allocating political representation, public funds, and civil service positions;
(4) considerable autonomy for various segments of the society to govern their internal affairs.[11]

The key to the consociational model was that power would be allocated across competing interests in the society independent of the political process. Thus, elections in consociational democracies can decide which among the candidates of a particular ethnic or racial group will hold an office that was predetermined to be assigned to that particular group; whether a particular group or interest should hold office is decided outside the electoral process through the formation of what Lijphart terms the "grand coalition."

Strikingly, despite the fact that new democracies almost invariably fit the pattern of fractured societies, the democracies of recent vintage rejected the simpler model of formally dividing power, as with reserving half the seats in the Lebanese national parliament for the Maronite Christians and half for the Muslims, to use the old Lebanese power-sharing arrangement as an example. In part, the disappearance of formal power sharing as the preferred conflict-management model reflects a recognition of how much more sophisticated the world has become since the simple consociational models that were supposed to yield stability in Lebanon[12] or Sri Lanka[13] or Cyprus[14] or the Ivory Coast.[15] In larger part, the reason

---

[10] *See* AREND LIJPHART, DEMOCRACY IN PLURAL SOCIETIES: A COMPARATIVE EXPLORATION 1 (New Haven, CT: Yale University Press, 1977) (discussing how consociational democracy explains the "political stability" of Austria, Belgium, the Netherlands, and Switzerland).

[11] *Id.* at 25.

[12] *See, e.g.*, Richard H. Dekmejian, *Consociational Democracy in Crisis: The Case of Lebanon*, 10 COMP. POL. 254 (1978) (describing how the 1926 constitution and National Pact of 1945 provided for a six to five ratio of Christians to Muslims in the Chamber and an even division in the cabinet); ANTOINE N. MESSARRA, THÉORIE GÉNÉRAL DU SYSTÈME POLITIQUE LIBANAIS (Paris: éditions Cariscript, 1994).

[13] *See* H. E. Chehabi, *The Absence of Consociationalism in Sri Lanka*, 11 PLURAL SOCIETIES 55 (1980) (accounting for the lack of consociationalism in Sri Lanka).

[14] Lijphart, *supra* note 10, at 158–61 (discussing the failure of consociationalism in Cyprus); AREND LIJPHART, DEMOCRACIES: PATTERNS OF MAJORITARIAN AND CONSENSUS GOVERNMENT IN TWENTY-ONE COUNTRIES 184 (New Haven, CT: Yale University Press, 1984) (noting that the 1960 constitution of Cyprus provided for separately elected communal chambers for the Greek majority and Turkish minority).

[15] *See, e.g.*, Connie de la Vega, *The Right to Equal Education: Merely a Guiding Principle or Customary International Legal Right?*, 11 HARV. BLACKLETTER L.J. 49 (1994) (discussing Ivory Coast's equal protection guarantees).

that new democracies have turned away from formal power-sharing accords is the tragic fact that each of the early signature claims for consociational success soon descended into fratricidal civil war. Invariably, the new democracies had to look elsewhere.

The rejection of formal consociationalism in most democracies of recent vintage is a sad recognition of the stakes in truly fractured societies. The unfortunate lesson of history is that stable civilian governance is most likely to emerge from post-conflict societies when one ethnic group has accomplished clear dominance over or destruction of the other.[16] Even with the introduction of more aggressive international peacekeeping, the key issue in nation building remains the creation of an integrated political authority claiming legitimacy beyond an ethnic or racial or sectarian religious base.[17]

In place of the formal limitations associated with consociationalism, the latest waves of democratizations have turned to an assertive form of constitutional democracy. Consociationalism sought to constrain democracy by removing the ultimate issue of power allocation from competitive democratic elections. Constitutionalism of the modern sort is also a system of constrained democracy, only now the system of broader democratic choice is constrained by constitutional limitations on what political majorities may do rather than how they are formed. Much as the terms "constitutional" and "democracy" are linked in the definitions of a just, liberal society, the two embody antagonistic impulses in organizing the body politic. Democracy vests decision making in majorities; constitutionalism removes from immediate popular control certain significant realms of politics.

Some aspects of constitutional constraint seem unremarkable. At some level, there must be a set of fixed ground rules for any democratic process. The rules of governance and selection have to be set independently of any particular election, in just the same way that a sports event requires prior acceptance that a soccer goal may not be scored with the hand, or that the bases in baseball are run counterclockwise. In this fashion, constitutionalism may be thought of as a particularly strong form of regulation of the terms of democratic engagement culminating in elections. But, constitutions do more. They impose a normative vision of rights and structural arrangements that resist the

---

[16] *See* Roy Licklider, *The Consequences of Negotiated Settlements in Civil Wars, 1945–1993*, 89 AM. POL. SCI. REV. 681 (1995) (finding that in so-called identity civil wars "negotiated settlements are less likely to be stable than military victories").

[17] *See* S.C. Res. 1378, U.N. SCOR, 56th Sess., 4415th mtg., at 2, U.N. Doc. S/RES/1378 (2001) (proclaiming that a transitional government in Afghanistan should be "broad-based, multi-ethnic and fully representative of all the Afghan people").

intrusion of ordinary political preferences. Even if only aspirationally, they mandate that political power be exercised with an eye toward a higher set of societal obligations.

The tension between political democracy and constitutional constraints requires a mediating institution capable of imposing that restraint. None of the new democracies of the recent period has chosen to follow a Westminster model of ultimate parliamentary sovereignty. Not only have many chosen to divide power between a president and a parliament, but they have further rejected the Westminster model of Parliament itself being the ultimate judge of the limits of parliamentary conduct. The critical question for this book is how those constraints are exercised, and how there can be credible commitments in countries without an established track record of democratic governance.

While political power will always be contested in the elected branches of government, the new democracies of the Third Wave have focused great attention on a new governmental actor to enforce the constraints on the majoritarian political branches. In country after country, the transition to democracy is eased by the creation of a court system specifically tasked with constitutional vigilance over the exercise of political power. All the new democracies have either created constitutional courts or endowed supreme courts with ample power of judicial review to enforce the democratic commands of the constitution. What is striking, and perhaps distinct, about the Third Wave of democratization is the central role assumed by these apex courts in sculpting democratic politics.

Indeed, the signal feature of the constitutional democracies of the modern wave is precisely this creation of a new set of strong constitutional courts. As typically constructed, these are courts that stand aside from the normal chain of command of the national judiciary and instead act as guardians of the democratic order. It is not simply that a constitution serves as a limitation on either antidemocratic groups or self-aggrandizing rulers, it is that a constitution performs this process of limitation through enforceable institutional constraints. The ability of a constitution to impose such limitations in turn presupposes the ability of the designated institutions – the courts – to serve as a credible force either in legitimating the drawing of democratic boundaries or in intervening to constrain the governing powers.

The lodestars of scholarly literature either failed to predict, or severely underestimated, the rise of constitutionalism and independent judiciaries that have been the hallmark of recent waves of democratization. Samuel Huntington's classic *The Third Wave* not only does not discuss at any length constitutionalism and the judiciary as important vehicles of democratic transition and consolidation, but this new institutional actor is barely mentioned.[18] Arend Lijphardt, writing well into the latest surge of democracies, only more recently amended his account of the failings of pure majoritarian systems to include the "absence of judicial review."[19] The implication in Lijphardt's subsequent writing is that an independent judiciary bearing the constitutional authority to proscribe legislation was a necessary limitation on the risks of untrammeled majoritarianism. That role for the judiciary was conspicuously absent in the earlier accounts of consociationalism, which instead focused on the nature of the grand coalitional bargain among political elites and the corresponding assignment of authority within the political branches. The introduction of a judiciary bearing independent constitutional authority is a significant shift in the thinking over how to stabilize democratic rule in divided societies. However, the stabilizing impact of courts exercising constitutional review remains rather underdeveloped and something of an afterthought in these theories.

This book fills that gap. It is an examination of the challenges that fragile democracies face. While the inquiry as to how democracies are sustained sounds in the methodology of political science, this is a book about legal institutions and the role of law in the structure of constitutional democracy. It is about law and the legal institutions that have emerged as a hallmark of the recent wave of democratizations, and particularly about the contested concept of "constitutional democracy." The thesis is that the use of constitutionalism, and the accompanying institution of constitutional courts, has emerged as a primary means of managing conflict in the difficult national settings of so many of the world's democracies and of doing so in the service of state building. This judicial task is undertaken in what are almost invariably deeply fractured societies, meaning societies that are characterized by persistent racial, ethnic, or religious animosities in which cross-racial, ethnic, and religious political institutions are either poorly realized or simply do not exist.

The title of this book invokes the concept of "fragility" to identify constitutional democracies, usually recently enabled, whose political institutions and supporting groups from civil society are insufficient for managing conflict. Such a definition, without more, risks descending into a tautology whereby the problem defines the category, and the category in turn is established by the problem as such. What characterizes the modern fragile democracies is that they typically inherit political authority from the collapse of an authoritarian

---

[18] Huntington, *supra* note 1, at 270–80.
[19] ArEND LIJPHART, PATTERNS OF DEMOCRACY: GOVERNMENT FORMS AND PERFORMANCE IN THIRTY-SIX COUNTRIES (New Haven, CT: Yale University Press, 1999).

regime, and in turn have to confront recrudescent societal divisions that were suppressed or exploited by strong-arm governments. These democracies essay to manage conflict, stabilize governance, and inculcate the values of popular sovereignty, all at the same time. They do so among a population that frequently has only a fleeting attachment to conceptions of citizenship or shared enterprise. And they often do so in the face of determined foes, both within and without, for whom the contestation inherent in democratic governance is an inviting sign of weakness.

For purposes of this book, I do not wish to explore the full dimensions of what is meant by either democracy or constitutionalism. Instead, I accept initially a rather spare definition of *democracy* as a system through which the majority, either directly or through representative bodies, exercises decision-making political power,[20] and I use the term *constitutionalism* only to refer to the creation of a basic law that restricts the capacity of the majority to exercise its political will.[21] For these purposes, it does not matter whether the restraint is an absolute, as with the non-amendable provisions of the German Constitution,[22] or simply the "obduracy" of Article V of the American Constitution,[23] or the temporal constraints requiring successive parliamentary action for constitutional reform, as in some European countries. Under any such system, the constitution serves as a limitation on what democratic majorities may do.[24]

[20] *See, e.g.*, Jon Elster, Introduction to CONSTITUTIONALISM AND DEMOCRACY 1 (Cambridge, England: Cambridge University Press, 1988), 1 (arguing that democracy is "simple majority rule, based on the principle 'One person, one vote.'"); ROBERT A. DAHL, HOW DEMOCRATIC IS THE AMERICAN CONSTITUTION? 50–51 (New Haven, CT: Yale University Press, 2001) (explaining that governmental units in a democratic system derive authority from majority rule).

[21] Frank Michelman captures this tension well in defining democracy as ultimately "popular political self-government" and constitutionalism as "[t]he containment of popular political decision-making by a basic law." FRANK I. MICHELMAN, BRENNAN AND DEMOCRACY 5–6 (Princeton, NJ: Princeton University Press, 1999). *See* also Richard H. Pildes, Constitutionalizing Democratic Politics, in A BADLY FLAWED ELECTION: DEBATING BUSH V. GORE, THE SUPREME COURT, AND AMERICAN DEMOCRACY 155, 156 (New York: New Press, 2002) (defining *constitutionalization* as subjecting the "fundamental structure of democratic processes and institutions to constitutional constraint").

[22] *See* Donald P. Kommers, *German Constitutionalism: A Prolegomenon*, 40 EMORY L.J. 846 (1991) (discussing the "eternity clause" of German Basic Law, which bars amendments tampering with German federalism or basic political principles).

[23] *See* John Ferejohn and Lawrence Sager, *Commitment and Constitutionalism*, 81 TEXAS L. REV. 1930, 1954 (2003) (casting constitutions as self-restraints against "blatant majoritarian expropriation").

[24] *See* Douglas Greenberg et al., Introduction to CONSTITUTIONALISM AND DEMOCRACY: TRANSITIONS IN THE CONTEMPORARY WORLD xxi (New York: Oxford University Press, 1993) (describing modern constitutionalism as a "commitment to limitations on ordinary political power").

Unlike efforts to divide power formally, democratic constitutionalism offers a different avenue of nation building. Rather than securing national unity through formal power sharing along the major axes of social division, constitutionalism tends to impose limits on the range of decisions that democratically elected governments may take. The test is whether constitutional constraints allow the emergence of a democratic politics, as opposed to the simple notion of an elected head of state. Democratic politics requires institutions of political contestation, most notably oppositional political parties, and the capacity of the losers of today to emerge as part of a victorious coalition tomorrow. The measure of the effectiveness of constitutional democracy is whether that indeed happens, whether the rulers of the day can be made to cede office to the shifting will of the electorate.

WHY COURTS?

To the hammer, the world looks like a nail. There is of course a risk that to a constitutional lawyer, the world of democracy will similarly be constructed out of constitutions and courts. Democracy requires innumerable institutions, many from the nongovernmental domain of civil society. It is not simply the formal separations of governmental power among coordinate branches, or even the divisions along federalist lines between the center and the provinces. As Tocqueville observed about the young American republic, democracy requires the intermediary forms of civic engagement that allow the far-flung citizens to have a voice in the project of self-governance.

Yet this is a book that looks heavily to the recent emergence of constitutional courts as an important actor in embattled democracies. The focus on courts is not to gainsay the importance of other attributes of democracy. But the attention to courts does highlight an important institutional shift in the structuring of new democracies, and one that has received insufficient attention to date.

On my account, constitutional courts serve two primary roles. First, they provide a critical process limitation on the exercise of democratic power. For example, Part I of this book addresses how democracies, particularly those that I group under the rubric of fragile democracies, respond to electoral challenges presented by antidemocratic groups. The image of the Nazi takeover within the debilitated Weimar democracy is a looming reminder that democracies must have a militant resolve to withstand being undermined from within. Nonetheless, any intervention to bar certain individuals or parties from the political arena risks compromising the integrity of the electoral process. Every time a candidate or party is prevented from running for office, the state intervenes to remove a choice from the electorate. As will be developed later, the difficulty of clearly defining the substantive limits for democratic competition requires rigorous procedural oversight, something that is provided primarily by the judiciary.

Second, courts serve as important forces in easing the transition to a new democratic order. Part II looks extensively at the emergence of democracies in South Africa and post-Soviet Eastern Europe to discern the curious role played by constitutional courts in the initial bargain for a democratic state. In societies riven by historic divides, the consequences of an election may well be a continuation of historic battles, but with one side now adorned with the uniforms of state authority. Some assurances must be given to minorities who are likely losers in initial elections that the resulting grant of state power to their historic adversaries will not simply unleash a retaliatory use of governmental power. As most clearly evident in the negotiations for a postapartheid South Africa, the creation of a constitutional court can postpone agreement on contested allocations of power while at the same time offering some solace to the likely minorities in government that there will be an institution that can aid in resisting majoritarian excess.

This second role as a constraint on the exercise of consolidated power is all the more important in countries where the initial stages of democracy yield a dominant political party, seemingly impervious to electoral challenge. To begin with, in many countries strong constitutional courts have served as a stopgap against efforts of the rulers of today to manipulate the powers of governmental authority to secure their permanence in office. Democracies prove vulnerable not only to assault from without, as with the electoral efforts of antidemocratic parties, but to erosion from within by dominant parties with a democratic mandate. When democracies are confronted with strong parties with an inherited mandate – such as the Partido Revolucionario Institucional (PRI) in Mexico, or the Peronists in Argentina, or perhaps the African National Congress (ANC) in South Africa – the risk is that control over the bureaucracy, the dispensation of patronage, and the domination of the electoral apparatus will yield what I term "one-partyism," and that the demise of accountability through electoral competition will follow.

These roles of constitutional courts in legitimizing the exclusion of antidemocratic groups and in preserving the accountability of the leaders of today add an ingredient to the contemporary efforts to stabilize democracy through elections in seemingly inauspicious settings. Viewing constitutionalism as the enabling ground rules for democratic governance provides an insight into the need for a strong constraint on the exercise of power by electoral majorities, particularly with the first post-conflict regime. This book argues that there is the need for such constitutional constraint in stabilizing democratic governance in fractured societies. The argument is that constitutionalism emerges as a central defining power in these societies precisely because of the limitations it imposes on democratic choice.

For constitutionalism to become effective, it must rise from the desks of its authors and take form in the governing institutions of a society. The result is a species of constrained democracy in which the dominant constraint has been a strong set of constitutional limitations on political power, and with constitutional courts emerging as the major institutional enforcers of the bargained for constraint. The major concern of this book is not so much the political science account of the institutional role of courts, but the constitutional lawyer's concern for what courts should do when called upon to play this limiting role. In what follows, I examine some of the different forms of constitutional restraint on democracy that have been employed in fractured societies from the vantage point of constitutional review of the resulting institutional structures. Examined from this perspective, it is possible to ask, "What features of constitutionalism serve best to address the problems of fractured societies?" Or, put another way, "What constitutional restrictions on majoritarian power appear conducive to the emergence of stable democratic governance?" If the object of constitutional democracies in these fragile states is to manage conflict, the question becomes how this is done.

This is a book primarily about law. The objective is not simply to provide an institutional account of the role played by strong constitutional courts in the modern era. The inquiry pushes further to ask how courts actually discharge that function. Courts playing the role of democratic safeguards develop a jurisprudence corresponding to that role. Some of the cases may seem familiar as they correspond to claims sounding in civil liberties or human rights. But viewed against the background of the frailties of democracy, these judicial interventions take on a different cast. Examining these first-order cases about the structuring of the political process is the central undertaking of this book.

PART I

Militant Democracy

1

The American Paradox

In 2010, retired Justice Albie Sachs of the South African Constitutional Court was giving a series of lectures on his recently published autobiography, *The Strange Alchemy of Life and Law*. As part of that series, Justice Sachs came to New York University School of Law, where I teach, for a public event on the role of a constitutional court with my colleague Jeremy Waldron and myself. Our inquiry was on the role of a court in the transition from an unjust to a just regime, and on how a court addresses the question of the frailties of an emerging democratic society. Jeremy Waldron is famously protective of the dignity of the legislative process and critical of judicial review of legislative enactments. My views, as will be evident from this book, are notably different, and I defend the importance of judicial oversight of some of the characteristic vulnerabilities of democratic rule.

The discussion with Justice Sachs grounded the divide in the role of courts in the South African experience. The South African Constitutional Court has actively engaged the political process during the transition process and beyond, a theme I develop in subsequent chapters. Alone among courts any-where in the world, the constitutional court was tasked with assessing the first draft of the constitution for its conformity with core democratic principles, and indeed found the draft wanting. This was the world's first unconstitutional constitution.

While Justice Sachs strongly defended the active role of the South African court in the transition from apartheid to multiethnic democratic rule, he was cautious about the relation between the emerging South African jurisprudence and American constitutional doctrines. According to Justice Sachs, it was diffi-cult in any new democracy to resist the gravitational pull of American consti-tutional law, particularly for an English-language constitutional court. It was not simply the longevity of American democracy and the U.S. Constitution, but the commanding language and arguments honed by the U.S. Supreme

Court over centuries of constitutional debate. Certainly, the South African court could select – and has in fact charted – an independent course, but it does so with frequent reference to the American court's doctrines and with self-awareness of when those doctrines are rejected as incompatible with the needs of South African constitutional law.

Justice Sachs's comments on the strong pull of American doctrine serve as a cautionary note in the initial exploration of the role of "militant democracy"; that is, the ability of democratic regimes to restrict forms of debate, political organization, or political participation that pose an existential threat to democracy itself. The American First Amendment tradition is the standard-bearer for freedom of political expression and association the world over. Yet, as we shall see, it is a standard that corresponds poorly to what democracies the world over actually do when faced with threats to their existence. Accordingly, our point of departure is to curb the temptation in readers to view democratic survival through the prism of American First Amendment law.

In the spirit of the cautionary warning on American television that "viewer discretion is advised," it is best to give the historical antecedents of both the American marketplace of ideas concept and the European embrace of more forceful responses to domestic threats. To the American part of the audience, however, much of this discussion will seem completely antithetical to core First Amendment principles in American law, and it is likely that American courts would not tolerate most, or perhaps any, of the measures discussed and endorsed in the following chapters.

The central focus of this chapter, however, is on dissuading the American part of the audience of the utility of the clear and present danger model as defining the only permissible boundary on free expression in the political arena. By contrast, other democracies have responded with a different set of doctrines to a subset of the threats they face – as with armed insurrectionist parties and military splinter groups, for example. While the terminology may be similar, it is vital to understand the limits of the parallels between the threats that democracy faces in the United States and in other countries. It is also important to recognize several characteristics of the twentieth-century legal landscape in which the clear and present danger test was promulgated. While it may seem that American formal law is much less tolerant of preemptive acts of self-protection in the political arena, historical events that preceded and followed the test's formulation present a more nuanced picture of even American regulation of political participation.

AMERICAN EXCEPTIONALISM

American constitutional law justifiably trumpets its commitment to liberty of expression for despised speakers and repugnant ideas, and even proclamations of the desire to rise up against the state. As formulated by the Supreme Court in *Brandenburg v. Ohio*, a state may not "forbid or proscribe advocacy of the use of force or of law violation except where such advocacy is directed to inciting or producing imminent lawless action and is likely to incite or produce such action."[1] *Brandenburg* itself concerned a rally called by the Ku Klux Klan in southern Ohio to mobilize against the claimed government suppression of "the white, Caucasian race." The Ohio courts had convicted Brandenburg, a local Klan leader, under the state's criminal syndicalism law, a conviction set aside by the Supreme Court as antithetical to the guarantees of freedom of speech. Under the test articulated in *Brandenburg*, there is a heavy presumption in favor of free expression, a presumption that is overcome only by the imminence of direct harm:

> "[T]he mere abstract teaching ... of the moral propriety or even moral necessity for a resort to force and violence, is not the same as preparing a group for violent action and steeling it to such action." A statute which fails to draw this distinction impermissibly intrudes upon the freedoms guaranteed by the First and Fourteenth Amendments.[2]

The *Brandenburg* test for the imminence of actual upheaval draws from the historic dissents of Justices Oliver Wendell Holmes[3] and Louis Brandeis[4] that together defined the emergence of robust First Amendment protections in twentieth-century American constitutional law. Indeed, so influential were Justices Holmes and Brandeis that the First Amendment standard is still popularly referred to by its pre-*Brandenburg* formulation: the "clear and present danger" test. The namesake language can be traced to Justice Holmes's opinion in *Schenck v. United States*, which framed the constitutional inquiry as "whether the words used are used in such circumstances and are of such a nature as to create a *clear and present danger* that they will bring about the substantive evils that Congress has a right to prevent."[5] That opinion also contains

---

[1]   395 U.S. 444, 447 (1969) (per curiam).
[2]   *Id.* at 447–48 (alteration in original) (citations omitted) (quoting *Noto v. United States*, 367 U.S. 290, 297–98 (1961)).
[3]   *See, e.g., Abrams v. United States*, 250 U.S. 616, 624–31 (1919) (Holmes, J., dissenting).
[4]   *See, e.g., Gilbert v. Minnesota*, 254 U.S. 325, 334–43 (1920) (Brandeis, J., dissenting).
[5]   *Schenck v. United States*, 249 U.S. 47, 52 (1919) (emphasis added) (citations omitted).

what has become the most famous limitation on any claimed freedom to speak: "The most stringent protection of free speech would not protect a man in falsely shouting fire in a theatre and causing a panic."[6]

As Justice Holmes subsequently elaborated in dissent in *Abrams v. United States*, the import of the clear and present danger test is to limit the regulatory reach of the government in matters concerning expression of ideas, particularly in the domain of public discourse. "It is only the present danger of immediate evil or an intent to bring it about that warrants Congress in setting a limit to the expression of opinion where private rights are not concerned. Congress certainly cannot forbid all effort to change the mind of the country."[7] The great free speech opinions of Justices Holmes and Brandeis combine rhetorical force with the sense that their authors had not succumbed to the war-inflamed passions of the times. Although not initially embraced by the Court, these opinions came to dominate American law, as carefully chronicled by Professor Geoffrey Stone.[8]

But what of speech that does constitute a clear and present danger? Even in American history, there have been imminent incitements to violence by all sorts of groups, and certainly plenty of violence that has ensued. Whether it is an anarchist's assassination of the president, or nightriders of the KKK terrorizing a Southern black community, even the U.S. commitment to freedom of speech is tempered by a realization that speech may be too closely integrated with conduct that threatens the body politic at a fundamental level. The United States may be an outlier in protecting hate speech, such as the ability of latter-day Nazis to march through the streets of Skokie, Illinois. The unfurling of swastikas in the heart of an American refuge was a deep wound to the large Jewish community that had resided there since the end of World War II.

Let's be honest, however. The Nazis in Skokie were there as a repugnant and hurtful symbol, not as a threat to unleash a strike against the aging Holocaust survivors. Skokie was symbolic speech, hateful as it might have been. No one imagined that the self-preservation of a democratic society was on the line when history's remnants reenacted a cartoon version of Nazism in central Illinois. Unfortunately, the tragic history of the twentieth century does not allow the indulgent belief that fascist street mobilizations are purely acts of symbolism. Nor, unfortunately, does American history, despite all the romanticizing of free speech.

---

[6] *Id.*

[7] *Abrams*, 250 U.S. at 628 (Holmes, J., dissenting).

[8] *See, e.g.,* GEOFFREY R. STONE, PERILOUS TIMES: FREE SPEECH IN WARTIME 395–411 (New York: W. W. Norton, 2004) (describing the centrality of the clear and present danger test in *Dennis v. United States*).

What is distinct about the United States is the constitutional prohibition on regulating speech as speech. Current American doctrine was created in reaction to the defining period of the communist scare after World War II. This period combined a doctrinal commitment to the First Amendment and a perceived fear that the United States was under assault.

Notably, in the controlling precedents from the McCarthy era, with the central example being *Dennis v. United States*,[9] the question of unprotected speech came to the Supreme Court in the context of criminal cases. The Supreme Court did not engage speech in the abstract form of a prohibition on ideas, but through the prosecution of the proponents. The Communist Party cases of the postwar period centered on the relation between ideas and the criminal law. *Dennis*, for example, involved charges against eleven leaders of the Communist Party for advocating the violent overthrow of the government. The chief evidence was the revolutionary tracts published by the Communist Party rather than any overt acts of insurrection or violence. In effect, the ideas became the advocacy and the advocacy became the criminal act.

Dennis collapsed the distinction between the type of political agitation that could be *prohibited* and the type that could be *criminalized*. The assumption in the clear and present danger test is that there should be no margin between the criminal code and state-imposed restrictions on political speech. If the danger is not imminent, then speech is protected from any and all forms of government restraint under First Amendment doctrines. If the speech does present an imminent danger, it is because the underlying conduct or threatened conduct must fall within the scope of the criminal law. The range of ensuing criminal laws extends from the direct prohibition on violence to the growing body of inchoate crimes of criminal conspiracy, including the material support to terrorism statutes of the post–September 11 period.[10]

The assumption that speech is either protected or criminal, with nothing in between, covers a broad spectrum of the constitutional discourse in the United States. For example, in his criticism of *Dennis*, Professor Stone chastises the Court for allowing the Communist Party to be subjected to legal restraints that should not have been permitted under the standards of the criminal code: "[T]o the extent there was criminal conduct, the individuals ... should have been investigated and prosecuted for their crimes. That is quite different from prosecuting other people – the defendants in *Dennis* – for their advocacy of Marxist-Leninist doctrine."[11]

---

[9]   341 U.S. 494 (1951).
[10]   18 U.S.C. § 2339A (2012) ("Providing Material Support to Terrorists"); 18 U.S.C. § 2339B (2012) ("Providing Material Support or Resources to Designated Foreign Terrorist Organizations").
[11]   Stone, *supra* note 8, at 410.

THE STRUCTURAL DIMENSIONS OF DEMOCRATIC STABILITY

Much as American law follows from the "criminal or protected speech" paradigm, the weight of American constitutional authority – as Justice Sachs noted – confronts other national courts as well in addressing the problem of antidemocratic incitement. Strikingly, other constitutional courts have resisted the clear and present danger test, for entirely defensible reasons. Before turning to the how and why of other constitutional doctrines, it is worth examining how the clear and present danger test in the United States is a response to some underappreciated features of American law. The aim here is not to reargue the cases from the Palmer Raids after World War I, or the McCarthy period of the early Cold War. Rather, it is to put these clearly in the context of three distinct features of American law.

First, the divide between the criminal law and any effort at regulating directly the political process goes back to the origins of the American republic, beginning with the Alien and Sedition Acts of 1798. In a case largely unimaginable today, Republican congressman Matthew Lyon was convicted under the Sedition Act for criticizing Federalist president John Adams as possessing "an unbounded thirst for ridiculous pomp, foolish adulation, or selfish avarice."[12] Lyon then served a four-month prison sentence for an offense that would today hardly get airtime on Fox News or MSNBC. Yet even in the earliest days of the republic, a divide was drawn between the domain of criminal law and the ability to engage in the political process. Much as Lyon's incarceration for rhetorical flourishes strikes modern sensibilities as bizarre, it is equally noteworthy that the conviction had no effect on Lyon as a political figure. Remarkably, Lyon was reelected to Congress while still in prison, and continued serving in Congress once he was released.

While the initial enactment of the Alien and Sedition Acts was a short-lived embarrassment to American democracy, expiring following the election of Thomas Jefferson in 1800, the use of the criminal law as a primary mechanism for policing the boundaries of democracy continues. As a result, freedom of political expression has become inextricably bound up with the standards for criminal prosecution, including burdens of proof and heightened specificity requirements. Critics of American constitutional treatment of free speech have focused on this central feature of American law without fully appreciating how

---

[12] *See generally History of the Federal Judiciary: The Sedition Act Trials – Historical Background and Documents*, FEDERAL JUDICIAL CENTER, http://www.fjc.gov/history/home.nsf/page/tu_ sedition_narrative.html. The trial famously featured Lyon calling presiding justice William Paterson as a witness to ask if Paterson could testify about any "ridiculous pomp and parade" at President Adams's Philadelphia home.

distinct it is on the world stage. For example, Professor Martin Redish declares that *Dennis* "clearly was, as one historian has described it, little more than 'a trial of ideas,' something more appropriately associated with a totalitarian society than what is supposedly a constitutional democracy."[13] The assumed but not articulated baseline is that speech regulation, even in the electoral context, must be accomplished primarily through criminal prosecution.

Before sweeping quite so broadly, it is worth pausing to consider how susceptible to generalization the American cases have been. A great deal of the doctrinal work under the First Amendment's treatment of political speech stems from the specific question that is typically presented in American courts: whether the speech in question is sufficiently inciteful of criminal conduct to sustain a criminal prosecution. The landmark cases in this area have tended to be criminal cases, such as *Brandenburg*, which involved a prosecution under an Ohio anti-syndicalism law, and *Cohen v. California*, which featured a lone antiwar protester wearing a jacket that said "Fuck the Draft" in a state courthouse.[14] Even in civil cases, like the Supreme Court's landmark libel decision in *New York Times v. Sullivan*,[15] the analogy to a criminal prosecution remains the analytic point of departure. For Professors Frederick Schauer and Richard Pildes, "the quick judicial assimilation of all content-based regulations to the criminal law prohibition model" tends to preempt the field outside the context of what might be criminal incitement, and forecloses the possibility that "different modes of regulation structure might justify different First Amendment responses."[16] The result is that regulations distinctly aimed at the electoral context are quickly swept up in a legal framework imported from the conditions necessary for putting a speaker in jail. Drawing again from Schauer and Pildes, perhaps when regulations "do not take the form of criminal prohibitions, courts should not deploy doctrines whose purposes are not actually implicated by the particular context of regulation."[17]

Second, there is a structural dimension to the American response to marginal antidemocratic groups that needs to be weighed in the balance. The American

[13] MARTIN H. REDISH, THE LOGIC OF PERSECUTION: FREE EXPRESSION AND THE MCCARTHY ERA 97 (Stanford, CA: Stanford University Press, 2005) (footnote omitted) (quoting PETER L. STEINBERG, THE GREAT "RED MENACE": UNITED STATES PROSECUTION OF AMERICAN COMMUNISTS, 1947–1952, at 157 (Westport, CT: Greenwood Press, 1984)).
[14] 403 U.S. 15, 16 (1971).
[15] 376 U.S. 254 (1964).
[16] Frederick Schauer & Richard H. Pildes, *Electoral Exceptionalism and the First Amendment*, 77 TEX. L. REV. 1803, 1833 (1999); *see also New York Times*, 376 U.S. at 277 ("What a State may not constitutionally bring about by means of a criminal statute is likewise beyond the reach of its civil law of libel.").
[17] Schauer & Pildes, *supra* note 16, at 1833.

system of districted legislative elections and independent presidential selection is not the norm in democratic societies. None of the recent democracies created in the aftermath of the collapse of the Soviet empire has attempted to replicate American-style governance. Some form of proportional representation is the standard in new democracies and many new democracies divide executive functions between a formal president and a prime minister who is the actual head of government. Nor did the United States try to impose the complete package of American governance structures such as single-district congressional elections or a territorial senate or a state-based electoral college in seeking to establish democratic regimes in regions over which it maintained military control, as in Germany, Japan, and Iraq.

The forms of elections do make a difference regarding the disruptive potential of antidemocratic groups. Over the years, I have resisted the easy claim that proportional representation systems are inherently unstable or were even responsible for the rise of fascism, a claim that has made its way even into Supreme Court discussions of the extent to which the two major parties may be protected from electoral competition.[18] Certainly, the exceptional characteristics of American democratic practices should dictate some caution before proclaiming these practices to be superior as a general matter, let alone preferable in all circumstances under a one-size-fits-all rationale.

Whatever my reluctance on this score, I have now come to the conclusion that there is indeed something in non-parliamentary, nonproportional representation political systems that provides a buffer against antidemocratic forces, perhaps explaining why American law is decidedly directed to the truly marginal behavior that might rise to the level of a criminal offense. There is a well-trodden path in political theory – running through Harold Hotelling,[19] Anthony Downs,[20] and Maurice Duverger[21] – explaining the propensity of single-seat, single-winner elections to produce two (and only two) relatively stable, relatively centrist parties. Third parties – including fringe parties, to the

---

[18] *See, e.g., Timmons v. Twin Cities Area New Party*, 520 U.S. 351, 367 (1997) ("The Constitution permits the Minnesota Legislature to decide that political stability is best served through a healthy two-party system.").

[19] Harold Hotelling, *Stability in Competition*, 39 ECON. J. 41 (1929) (introducing the "spatial markets" theory of how firms compete for the center).

[20] ANTHONY DOWNS, AN ECONOMIC THEORY OF DEMOCRACY 115–22 (New York: Harper and Row, 1957) (applying the spatial market approach to describe competition for the median voter as the key to winning two-party elections).

[21] MAURICE DUVERGER, POLITICAL PARTIES 217–28 (Barbara North & Robert North trans., rev. ed., London: Methuen, 1964) (1951) (introducing "Duverger's Law," which states that in first-past-the-post elections there will be exactly two relatively centrist parties).

extent they gain electoral traction – tend to tip the scales to the major party farthest from them, thereby dissuading even the polar supporters of the major parties from joining spoiler efforts. Think of Ross Perot in 1992 and Ralph Nader in 2000 for recent shorthand versions of the sophisticated political theory underlying this insight. The Tea Party might pillory the concessionism of mainstream Republicans, and minority voters might bemoan the lack of responsiveness to their needs from the Democrats. But neither is likely to bolt from its party to form an independent group for fear of delivering the election to its customary opponents.

Because districted elections force the prospective governing coalitions to form before the election and to run as political parties, the inclusion of extreme candidates discredits the entire slate and forces such candidates to the margin. As a result, truly extreme candidates face formidable hurdles to attaining legislative office, even with the heightened levels of polarization evident in contemporary American politics. The inability of legitimately antidemocratic groups to gain legislative office means that their representatives do not readily achieve the immunity from criminal prosecution for incitement that comes with parliamentary office. It also means that fanatical parties do not have access to state funds for their political crusades and are denied meaningful access to political debates formed around the question of who should govern. To the extent that extreme parties try to use the electoral arena, the structural barriers to their participation marginalize them. Their contributions to the public debate are duly set off on local public access stations (or their modern substitute, low-traffic political blogs). In the sphere of marginal debate, political extremists must compete for time with the purveyors of the conspiracy trade, who continue to obsess over fluoridation of the water supply, the latest permutation of the Kennedy assassination, "proof" that September 11 was an inside job, the real location of Obama's birth, and other marginal deviations from mainstream political engagement.

A further buffer is created by presidential rather than parliamentary governance. Even if an extremist party were to find its way into Congress, its ability to disrupt governance would be limited. Marginal parties in the legislature in a presidential system cannot command a bloc of votes that, in a parliamentary system, could be used to bring down a shaky coalition government through no-confidence votes or other parliamentary devices. Thus, unlike the National Socialists in Germany before Hitler's rise to power, marginal political groups would be far less able to wear down the government by disruptive tactics in parliament. Further, unlike fringe parties in many proportional representation

systems, Israel being the prime example,[22] they would not be able to leverage
their small presence in parliament into significant demands on public policy.
Presidentialism puts the choice of head of state in the hands of the national
electorate, rather than relying on fractured parliamentary leadership to forge the
governing coalition and, in turn, to accommodate the last holdouts necessary to
put them over the top. There are many reasons to be wary of presidentialism,[23]
but it does serve as a buffer to the threat posed by marginal parties' ability to
insinuate themselves into parliament and disrupt governance from within.

Third, and finally, there is the unmistakable stability of politics in the
United States, a stability that perhaps leads Americans to underestimate the
need to protect democratic processes elsewhere from real threats, even those
masquerading as contenders for democratic election. For the United States,
the twentieth century witnessed significant turmoil: two world wars, at least
four regional wars, a protracted standoff with a major foreign power, four presidents who died in office (two of whom were assassinated), a major depres-
sion followed by a significant overhaul of the administrative state, and a major
upheaval in race relations. But through it all, the same two political parties
remained in charge. Despite hard-fought elections and periodic social unrest,
changes in governance were incremental, and the electoral system remained
intact at all times. Indeed, perhaps uniquely among democratic states, the
United States has held regularly scheduled elections during wartime, even
during the Civil War. The short of it is that the United States has been a
remarkably stable political system since Reconstruction.

IMPOSING DEMOCRACY BY FORCE

The clear and present danger test of Justices Holmes and Brandeis merges
seamlessly with the concept of democratic politics as a marketplace of ideas.

---

[22] *See* Steven G. Calabresi, *The Virtues of Presidential Government: Why Professor Ackerman Is
Wrong to Prefer the German to the U.S. Constitution*, 18 CONST. COMMENT. 51, 60–61 (2001)
(describing leverage of small religious parties under the Israeli proportional representation
system).

[23] For an overview of the propensity in Latin America toward overconcentration of power
in the executive, *see* Matthew Søberg Shugart & Scott Mainwaring, *Presidentialism and
Democracy in Latin America: Rethinking the Terms of the Debate, in* PRESIDENTIALISM AND
DEMOCRACY IN LATIN AMERICA 12 (Scott Mainwaring & Matthew Søberg Shugart, eds.,
New York: Cambridge University Press 1997). Another leading treatment of this issue is found
in Juan J. Linz, *Presidential or Parliamentary Democracy: Does It Make a Difference?, in* THE
FAILURE OF PRESIDENTIAL DEMOCRACY 3 (Juan J. Linz & Arturo Valenzuela, eds., Baltimore,
MD: The Johns Hopkins University Press 1994). For advocacy of parliamentarism to replace
the independent selection of the president in the United States, *see* Bruce Ackerman, *The New
Separation of Powers*, 113 HARV. L. REV. 633, 643–44 (2000).

According to Justice Holmes, the Constitution embodies the idea that "the ultimate good desired is better reached by free trade in ideas – that the best test of truth is the power of the thought to get itself accepted in the competition of the market."[24] Justice Brandeis similarly argued that the power of the government to limit the expression of opposing viewpoints was confined to situations where the "suppression of divergent opinion is imperative; because the emergency does not permit reliance upon the lower conquest of error by truth."[25] Absent criminal incitement, the give-and-take of interest against interest, idea against idea, must be the American norm.

Run the clock back a half century from the time of the Holmes and Brandeis dissents and a different picture emerges. America in the nineteenth century was no stranger to a root threat to the ability to govern its territory, nor to a military rejection of its sovereignty. When faced with a military threat not an ocean away but within the United States, many of the normal precepts of governance fell under the strain. Much attention is now given to the emergency powers claimed by President Lincoln during the Civil War itself, including the delay in calling Congress to action following the first Confederate act of war against Fort Sumter, and the unilateral suspension of habeas corpus. But the postwar period also reflects a muscular reaction to the attempted secession, and a response that brings to mind the militant democracy concepts of post–World War II Europe.

When the United States emerged from the existential challenge of the Civil War, confidence in the orderly exchange of ideas was at low ebb. Hundreds of thousands of war dead, an exhausted population, broad sections of the country in tatters, and an uncertain path toward the integration of the freedmen required structural repair. The United States after the Civil War, especially in the occupied South, looked more like the emergent democracies after the fall of the Soviet empire than the comfortable image of a vibrant democracy able to absorb noncriminal political discord. The resulting reintegration of the Confederacy is aptly termed by Professor Alexander Kirshner as "America's first attempt to impose democracy by force."[26]

The Reconstruction administration that followed the end of the Civil War made clear that the debates over slavery were over. The strenuous debates of the Reconstruction period were over the means and extent of the social reorganization of the slave South and the duration of federal military oversight

---

[24] *Abrams v. United States*, 250 U.S. 616, 630 (1919) (Holmes, J., dissenting).
[25] *Gilbert v. State of Minn.*, 254 U.S. 325, 338 (1920) (Brandeis, J., dissenting).
[26] Alexander S. Kirshner, A Theory of Militant Democracy: The Ethics of Combatting Political Extremism 142 (New Haven, CT: Yale University Press, 2014).

over the transformation. There was no ambiguity about the political mandate of Reconstruction, nor any question of allowing the marketplace of ideas alone to handle any attempted restoration of Southern resistance. At the same time, one of the interesting legacies of the Civil War was that the attempt to impose a Reconstruction political order after the cessation of hostilities would largely fall outside the confines of the criminal law. The exclusion of political agitation on behalf of the old Confederacy did not await conduct that rose to the level meriting criminal punishment.

During the war, the Union promulgated the first official set of doctrines for the conduct of war, known as the Lieber Code after its drafter, Francis Lieber. The Lieber Code specified that the "municipal laws," as the normal civilian power was termed, of the belligerent sides would not be the norm of conduct for armies facing one another.[27] Soldiers were held to the norms of conduct becoming warfare and not, for example, the regular civilian rules prohibiting intentional killing. Under the Lieber Code, normal legal prohibitions on ordinary citizens had no vigilance over warfare, nor could they be applied to captured soldiers. To the extent the criminal law did apply to wartime conduct, it was not directed at insurrectionary Confederates but at Union soldiers for desertion or misconduct, or at citizens of the border states for treason.[28]

The Lieber Code introduces the modern efforts at a law of armed conflict, reflected most prominently in the Geneva Conventions. The Code begins with the recognition that a soldier is not a criminal but an honorable individual, and that the conduct of war requires acts that would ordinarily be criminal – the most obvious being the intentional killing of others. Although modern laws of war generally apply to international warfare, with a more complicated reach in domestic conflicts, President Lincoln wisely chose to treat the U.S. Civil War as "warfare" and to give captured Confederate soldiers treatment befitting prisoners of war.

The treatment of the Confederacy as a defeated military enemy rather than as a criminal conspiracy extended all the way to the top and provided the basis for the postwar treatment of the defeated Confederacy. At Appomattox, General Lee surrendered to General Grant, but did not surrender into custody.

---

[27] Article 41 of the Lieber Code provides, "All municipal law of the ground on which the armies stand, or of the countries to which they belong, is silent and of no effect between armies in the field." See Francis Lieber, Instructions for the Government of Armies of the United States in the Field 34 (Gov't Printing Office 1898) (1863), *available at* http://www.loc.gov/rr/frd/Military_Law/pdf/Instructions-gov-armies.pdf.

[28] See generally John Fabian Witt, Lincoln's Code: The Laws of War in American History 268–69 (New York: Free Press, 2012).

In exchange for laying down their arms, the Confederate troops and officers were allowed fully to resume their civilian lives. Under the terms of the surrender accord, Grant offered that "each officer and man will be allowed to return to their homes, not to be disturbed by United States authority so long as they observe their paroles and the laws in force where they may reside."[29]

Nonetheless, the absence of criminal liability for the Confederacy did not end the inquiry. If the South was to be reintegrated, the end of the three-fifths compromise meant that, paradoxically, the South's congressional representation – and the corresponding number of Electoral College votes – would increase as a result of the full citizenship status of the former slaves. The fact that the Confederacy was not tried criminally, from its highest reaches to its foot soldiers, did not mean that those who engaged in rebellion simply reacquired full rights in the restored Union and could presumably exercise the franchise to attempt to restore what they had lost militarily. The return to democratic norms required not only the guarantee of the black franchise under the Fifteenth Amendment and its enforcement by federal voting registrars, but further limitations on political options for the South.

For the Republicans who controlled Congress in the decade following the Civil War, the political reintegration of the South required a meaningful guarantee that the Confederacy would not be permitted to claim through the ballot box that which had been denied by force of arms. Congress accordingly conditioned both the terms of Southern reintegration into the Union and the rights of political participation that would follow. With the exception of congressmen from Tennessee, the individual representatives of the former Confederate States were denied any ability to reclaim their seats in Congress. Readmission to the Union was conditioned upon ratification of the Fourteenth Amendment, which famously prohibited states from "deny[ing] to any person within its jurisdiction the equal protection of the laws."[30] Significantly, the commands of the Fourteenth Amendment reached beyond the formal norms of equal protection and due process and restricted political eligibility for the leaders of the rebellion.

Political exclusion of enemies of the Union was an express condition of reintegration, and it did not stop at former members of Congress. The Fourteenth Amendment expressly forbade the holding of any governmental office by anyone who had ever sworn an oath of allegiance to the United States as a

[29] Letter from Ulysses S. Grant to Robert E. Lee (Apr. 19, 1865), *in* THE CIVIL WAR MEMOIRS OF ULYSSES S. GRANT 474 (Brian M. Thomsen, ed., New York: Forge Books, 2004).

[30] U.S. Const., amend. XIV § 1.

condition of office and then "engaged in insurrection or rebellion against the same, or given aid or comfort to the enemies thereof."[31] The result was the removal from the body politic of individuals deemed disloyal to the new public order, as established by prior impermissible affiliation.

In the twentieth century, the selective social and political incapacitation of former members of an authoritarian regime was a standard remedy of the transition to democracy. Following the fall of the Soviet empire, the term *lustration*, derived from the Latin for Roman purification rituals, was applied in Eastern Europe to the removal from office and political exclusion of former Soviet officials. These individuals were neither imprisoned nor, most often, criminally charged, but were nevertheless excluded from holding political office.

By its express terms, the Fourteenth Amendment embraces an American version of what would now be termed lustration – the exclusion from public office of individuals compromised by association with a legally unacceptable past authority. The exclusion of such individuals was a matter of law, not something left to the judgment of the electorate. Tellingly, it was also not a matter of criminal law, unlike the prohibitions envisioned by the modern First Amendment tradition.

PREEMPTIVE POWER

As a general matter, fragile democracies react to threats to their existence more like the United States during and after the Civil War than like the idealized vision of political give-and-take of First Amendment romance. The political stability from which the American clear and present danger test emerged was not jeopardized by the extreme turmoil abroad, no matter what its domestic repercussions. There was never a direct threat to the United States being overrun militarily or toppled by domestic enemies. The great crises of the twentieth century emerged in the context of wars fought on distant continents with only secondary direct impact on the United States. American First Amendment law did not exist when the fight for survival of the American

---

[31] Section 3 of the Fourteenth Amendment provides that:

No person shall be a Senator or Representative in Congress, or elector of President and Vice President, or hold any office, civil or military, under the United States, or under any state, who, having previously taken an oath, as a member of Congress, or as an officer of the United States, or as a member of any state legislature, or as an executive or judicial officer of any state, to support the Constitution of the United States, shall have engaged in insurrection or rebellion against the same, or given aid or comfort to the enemies thereof. But Congress may by a vote of two-thirds of each House, remove such disability.

republic took place at home against fellow countrymen challenging the core existence of democratic governance. Other new and frail democracies have shied away from the American commitment to no prior restraints on political organization and speech. Potential criminal conduct by marginal groups is only a subset of the threats faced by democracies, particularly in far less stable national settings. Such democracies either cannot or do not believe they must await the immediacy of the threat of unlawful activity before reacting.

At the same time, if democracies are to claim the power to act preemptively to ward off threats from noncriminal actors, where does that power stop? If the first impulse of power is to preserve itself, cannot any opponent of the incumbent regime be cast as a threat to democratic stability? How democracies walk that fine line is the subject of the chapters that follow.

2

The Boundaries of Democracy

What are the boundaries of democratic tolerance? Of necessity, elections require the engagement of ideas, disagreements over policy, mobilizations of adherents, and fraught exchanges spilling over into core challenges frequently beyond the border of insult. Even while proclaiming its wide-open quality, democratic engagement presupposes some baseline accords on mutual tolerance and respect for rights across the spectrum, as well as the ability of democratic majorities to assess the past, make new political commitments, and alter the course of government. What of those who reject the core tenets of democratic governance, those whose participation exploits the porousness? This question leads to the precarious state of what may be termed *democratic intolerance;*[1] that is, the intolerance that democratic governments must exhibit toward antidemocratic actors in the name of preserving the fundamental democratic character of government.

While much of the discussion that follows draws upon the tragic inability of Weimar Germany to withstand the Nazi attack from within, we can begin with a more contemporary example. The 2006 controversy surrounding the Danish cartoons mocking Islam provides an illuminating window into the problem of challenges to core democratic values. At issue were cartoons appearing in a secondary Danish publication that were deemed sacrilegious by religious adherents. Although the political maneuverings and machinations surrounding the protests were no doubt multifaceted, the controversy centered on Islamic fundamentalist demands that Denmark be held responsible for its failure to censor the publication of a series of cartoons perceived as blasphemous attacks on the Prophet Mohammed.[2]

---

[1] The term is loosely adapted from a major contribution to this debate. Gregory H. Fox & Georg Nolte, *Intolerant Democracies*, 36 HARV. INT'L L.J. 1 (1995).

[2] *See, e.g., Protesters Burn Consulate over Cartoons,* CNN.com, Feb. 5, 2006, http://www .cnn.com/2006/WORLD/asiapcf/02/05/cartoon.protests/index.html (detailing the foreign minister of Denmark's denials of official responsibility for the publication of the cartoons).

In commenting on the publication of these cartoons, my late colleague Professor Ronald Dworkin provocatively asserted a right to insult as a precondition for political engagement. In so doing, he made a moral and instrumental argument requiring weak or unpopular minorities to tolerate social insult as a condition of making a claim on the majority for protective antidiscrimination legislation. "If we expect bigots to accept the verdict of the majority once the majority has spoken, then we must permit them to express their bigotry in the process whose verdict we ask them to accept."[3]

Professor Dworkin's idea that there is a limit to claims by the intolerant – in this case, the Muslim protesters – for accommodation by a tolerant society resonates with core liberal principles. John Rawls, for example, posits that the individual's "right to complain is limited to violations of principles he acknowledges himself. A complaint is a protest addressed to another in good faith."[4] The intolerant may complain of the insult felt and of the norms of civility that should be honored, but, per Dworkin, the fear of insult cannot be thought to "justify official censorship."[5] Resisting censorship is therefore part and parcel of ensuring the civil liberties that make robust political exchanges and democratic politics possible.

At bottom, Professor Dworkin's argument is an intriguing rallying call for democracies to stand fast against the demands by intolerant groups that democracies lend their governmental authority to the cause of silencing offending speech. Posed as a question of whether democratic regimes should enlist their arsenals of coercion in the suppression of unpopular, discordant, or simply intemperate speech, the civil liberties answer seems inescapable. Just as a liberal democratic state, such as Denmark, would no doubt refuse to engage in such censorship itself, so too no legitimate claim could be made that it should enlist its state resources toward such aims on behalf of others. In short, democratically tolerant governments should not succumb to demands for censorship made by less tolerant groups.

The Danish example is more germane here than the much graver attacks on the French satirical weekly *Charlie Hebdo*. Although the perceived offense in cartoon depictions of the Prophet Mohammed was pretty much the same, the response in the French setting transgressed any norms of politics and moved directly into murderous rage. Twelve journalists were killed, as well as four individuals at a kosher supermarket. No society could, or should, tolerate such murders or the underlying spirit of fundamentalist rage and anti-Semitism.

3   Ronald Dworkin, *The Right to Ridicule*, N.Y. REV. BOOKS, Mar. 23, 2006, at 44.
4   JOHN RAWLS, A THEORY OF JUSTICE 217 (Cambridge, MA: Harvard University Press, 1971).
5   Dworkin, *supra* note 3.

By contrast, the Danish events were largely a demand for a *political* solution in which the Danish government would assume the responsibility of shutting down speech deemed offensive.

Alter the facts of the Danish protests a bit and the central issue for this chapter emerges. Imagine once again that a Danish newspaper publishes a cartoon containing a visual depiction of the Prophet Mohammed. Denmark again does not censor the publication. Both there and around the world, Muslims decry the image as blasphemous and highly offensive, insisting that Denmark be brought to task. This time, however, the efforts to suppress speech in Denmark take a different form. Instead of – or perhaps even in addition to – the street protests and the burning of Danish flags in various locations around the world, the Muslim protesters and their supporters create a political party in Denmark. The party promotes itself like any other, vying for state authority through the democratic process – that is, through elections. It does so, however, in order to impose speech codes and other forms of repressive legislation, with the ultimate goal of rooting out all traces of blasphemy in Danish society (of which there are, doubtless, quite a few). Suppose further that the Danish parties presently in power choose to respond by using state authority to ensure that the new political party does not become the platform for leading an assault on its liberal democratic society.

This is no abstract inquiry. If we return to the rise of fascism in the heart of Europe between 1915 and 1935, we find that democratic processes were not only incapable of resisting the antidemocratic onslaught, but actually facilitated its ascent. Hitler's ultimate acquisition of power occurred within the confines of Weimar democratic processes, something that allowed Joseph Goebbels tauntingly to remark, "This will always remain one of the best jokes of democracy, that it gave its deadly enemies the means by which it was destroyed."[6]

Nor were the Nazis the last antidemocratic force to lay siege from within the confines of the electoral process. Algeria witnessed the capture of a commanding electoral victory by antidemocratic forces, prompting a seizure of power by the military to forestall an elected Islamic party from assuming power and carrying out its program of dismantling multiparty democracy.[7] An interesting recent variant is found in the curious letter sent by former Iranian president Mahmoud Ahmadinejad, himself elected in apparently legitimate elections,

[6] Fox & Nolte, *supra* note 1, at 1 (quoting Karl Dietrich Bracher et al., *Introduction* to NATIONALSOZIALISTISCHE DIKTATUR 16 (Karl Dietrich Bracher et al. eds., Bonn, Germany: Bundeszentrale fur Politische Bildung, 1983)).

[7] *See id.* at 6–9.

to President George W. Bush articulating the claim that recent developments in U.S. foreign policy in the Middle East and elsewhere had shown the ultimate failure of "[l]iberalism and Western style democracy" itself.[8] "In the context of full-fledged mass democracies,"[9] might it be then, to paraphrase one of Goebbels's contemporary adversaries, that the only thing democracy has to fear is democracy itself?

The inquiry, like the Danish hypothetical, becomes a variation on the initial theme, examining the resistance of democracies to the use of their electoral arenas as platforms for religious or other socially destructive forms of intolerance. In other words, can democracies act not only to resist the conscription of state authority to the cause of intolerance, but also – under certain circumstances – to ensure that their state apparatus is not captured wholesale for that purpose? If so, what parties or activities constitute sufficient threats to democratic institutions to justify government intervention? And what tools are available to a democratic state for self-defense?

POLICING THE DEMOCRATIC PROCESS

In post–World War II European debates, the terms "militant"[10] or "intolerant"[11] democracy are the shorthand for the programs employed by democratic regimes to avoid incubating the celebratory Goebbels of tomorrow. The ability of extremism to find its way into the protective crevices of a liberal democratic order requires anticipatory defenses to resist capture – in one form or another – by antidemocratic forces. The aim is to prevent the institutions of democracy from being harnessed to achieve what may be termed "illiberal democracy."[12]

The problem of democratic intolerance takes on special meaning in deeply "fractured societies,"[13] in which the electoral arena may serve as a parallel or even secondary front for extra-parliamentary mobilizations. With regard to

---

[8] Letter from Mahmoud Ahmadinejad to George W. Bush (May 2006), available at http://news.bbc.co.uk/1/shared/bsp/hi/pdfs/09_05_ 06ahmadinejadletter.pdf.

[9] Giovanni Capoccia, *Militant Democracy: The Institutional Bases of Democratic Self-Preservation*, 9 Ann. Rev. L. Soc. Sci. 207, 210 (2013).

[10] Karl Loewenstein, *Militant Democracy and Fundamental Rights* (pts. 1 & 2), 31 Am. Pol. Sci. Rev. 417, 638 (1937).

[11] Fox & Nolte, *supra* note 1, at 6.

[12] Fareed Zakaria, The Future of Freedom: Illiberal Democracy at Home and Abroad 17 (New York: W. W. Norton & Co., 2003).

[13] Samuel Issacharoff, *Constitutionalizing Democracy in Fractured Societies*, 82 Tex. L. Rev. 1861, 1863 (2004) (describing societies riven by ethnic or religious divides, in which political alignments are largely a reflection of prepolitical allegiances based on kinship of some kind).

the rise of religiously infused political parties in the Middle East, for example, Professor Noah Feldman captures well the futility of assuming that democratic politics is the sole or even the primary arena of struggle: "The model of Islamist organizations that combine electoral politics with paramilitary tactics is fast becoming the calling card of the new wave of Arab democratization."[14] For Professor Feldman, "[t]he fact that Hamas and Hezbollah pursue democratic legitimacy within the state while also employing violence on their own marks a watershed in Middle Eastern politics."[15]

Democracies are not powerless to respond to the threat of being compromised from within. At the descriptive level, the prime method of response is the prohibition on extremist participation in the electoral arena. Although the tools vary, the practice exists with surprising regularity across democratic societies. The regulatory devices range from prohibitions on forms of speech, to bans on certain parties, to ideological acceptance of the bases of the democratic state, to the exclusion of individuals from eligibility for public office.

Thus some states restrict speech within the electoral arena, as India has done with its prohibition on any campaign appeals to religious intolerance or ethnic enmity.[16] Other states forbid the formation of parties hostile to democracy, as Germany has done in banning any successors in interest to the Nazi or Communist Parties and in more recently banning an Islamic fundamentalist movement, the Califate State.[17] Still others impose content restrictions on the views that parties may hold, as with the long-standing requirement in Turkey of fidelity to the principles of secular democracy as a condition of eligibility for elected office.[18] Similarly, Israel, through its Basic Law, excludes from the electoral arena any party that rejects the democratic and Jewish character of the state, as well as any party whose platform is deemed an incitement to racism.[19] Other states specifically ban designated parties, as evidenced by the practice in several of the former Soviet republics of barring their local communist parties from seeking elected office. Yet others ban individuals

---

[14] Noah Feldman, *Ballots and Bullets*, N.Y. TIMES, July 30, 2006, § 6 (Magazine), at 9.

[15] *Id.*

[16] The Representation of the People Act, No. 43 of 1951, § 125, INDIA CODE, *available at* http://lawmin.nic.in/legislative/election/volume%201/representation%20of%20the%20people%20act,%201951.pdf.

[17] *See* Peter Niesen, *Anti-Extremism, Negative Republicanism, Civic Society: Three Paradigms for Banning Political Parties* (pts. 1 & 2), 3 German L.J. No. 7, 4, 8, 46 (2002), http://www.germanlawjournal.com/article.php?id=164 (pt. 1), http://www.germanlawjournal.com/article.php?id=169 (pt. 2).

[18] Turkish Constitution of 1982, art. 68 cl. 5.

[19] *See* Basic Law: The Knesset § 7A, *translated in* ISRAEL'S WRITTEN CONSTITUTION (6th ed., Haifa, Israel: A.G. Publications, 2009).

compromised by association to the prior regime, as did the United States through the Fourteenth Amendment's prohibition on eligibility for federal office by former Confederate officials. Finally, some states prohibit parties that are deemed fronts for terrorist or paramilitary groups. Thus, Spain has banned Batasuna, a political party sharing the objectives of the Basque separatist ETA insurgents, from any participation in Spanish or European parliamentary elections.[20]

The list of types of restrictions could go on at some length, and the scope of these restrictions has expanded, most recently, in the aftermath of September 11 and the growing salience of Islamic militancy.[21] The key point, however, is not the ubiquity of the prohibitions but the rationale for them. Each of these societies recognizes that the electoral arena is not simply a forum for the recording of preferences, but a powerful *situs* for the mobilization of political forces. These restrictions stand apart from the clear and present danger test and its presumptive use of a criminal law template as the guide to legitimate state interference with the give-and-take of exchange in the marketplace of ideas. All of these restrictions are anticipatory and depend on judgments about ideology, proclivities, status, and a host of considerations that are foreign to the retrospective assignment of blame for concrete acts under the criminal law. To the extent that a criminal law template is imported into the domain of regulating politics, it will fail.

Instead, militant democracy begins with the insight that elections are not only a form of selection of governors, but also a forum for political mobilization. Elections serve to amplify the ability of all political forces to disseminate their views. They also provide a natural opportunity to raise partisan passions and to provoke frenzied mob activity. The capacity to advocate antidemocratic aims extends beyond the electoral period. If elected to parliamentary office, even fringe extremist groups typically enjoy parliamentary immunity for incitement from the halls of power. Under most national laws, they can command official resources for their electoral propaganda and for their parliamentary activity.[22] And, as with the fascist rise to power in Europe, under the right institutional conditions, and with sufficient seats in parliament, fringe groups can use their positions in parliament to cripple

[20] *See* Víctor Ferreres Comella, *The New Regulation of Political Parties in Spain, and the Decision to Outlaw Batasuna, in* MILITANT DEMOCRACY 133, 133–34 (András Sajó ed., 2004).

[21] *See* Patrick Macklem, *Militant Democracy, Legal Pluralism, and the Paradox of Self-Determination,* 4 INT'L J. CONST. L. 488, 493–94 (2006) (giving examples of post-1989 limitations on political party formation).

[22] *Comparative Data,* ACE ELECTORAL KNOWLEDGE NETWORK, http://aceproject.org/epic-en/CDMap?question=PC015 (last visited Jan. 9, 2015).

any prospect of effective governance, destabilize the state, and launch themselves as successors to a failing democracy.

DEMOCRATIC CONSTRAINTS

Whatever the inherent difficulties in the use of state authority to enforce codes of democratic exchange, the problems are presented most acutely in the electoral arena. Seemingly, the world has learned something from the use of that arena as the springboard for fascist mobilizations to power in Germany and Italy. Perhaps as well, the world has learned that appeals to communal intolerance in countries like India, even if conducted from within the safe harbor of democratic processes, lead almost invariably to communal violence in which election rhetoric is a rostrum from which antidemocratic forces rally the faithful. At some level, all these countries grapple with an intuition that democratic elections require, as a precondition to the right of participation, a commitment to the preservation of the democratic process.[23]

At the same time, limiting the scope of democratic deliberation necessarily calls into question the legitimacy of the political process. When stripped down to their essentials, all definitions of democracy as an organizing principle for a real-world state rest ultimately on the primacy of electoral choice and the presumptive claim of the majority to rule. It is of course true that this thin definition of democracy cannot stand alone, for all electoral systems must assume a background set of rules, institutions, and definitions of eligible citizenship that serve as preconditions to the exercise of any meaningful popular choice. Moreover, all democracies of the modern era have constitutional constraints that cabin, through substantive limits and procedural hurdles, what the majority may do at any given point, with such constraints emerging even in the remaining Westminster states in Britain, Australia, and New Zealand.[24] However, a distinct set of problems emerges whenever a society decides that certain viewpoints may not find expression in the political arena, and that

[23] An interesting example is the argument by Israeli justice Aharon Barak that restricting a party's ability to register is more suspect than banning a party from electoral activity altogether because the latter is more easily understood as a state-protective move. PCA 7504/95, 7793/95 *Yassin & Rochley v. Registrar of the Political Parties & Yemin Israel* [1996] IsrSC 50(2) 45, 66–67. This point is discussed further in Chapter 4.

[24] *See* STEPHEN GARDBAUM, THE NEW COMMONWEALTH MODEL OF CONSTITUTIONALISM 31 (New York: Cambridge University Press 2013) (arguing that these nations now sit at "intermediate positions" which are distinct from both "traditional parliamentary sovereignty" and "judicial or constitutional supremacy").

the exponents of those viewpoints may never be considered as contenders for popular support.

At a more theoretical level, the need for such restrictions on democratic participation is acknowledged, albeit uncomfortably, even at the core of liberal theory. To return to Rawls, one finds a basic recognition that constraining the freedoms of intolerant groups may be justified when the freedoms of the society as a whole are at risk: "just citizens should strive to preserve the constitution with all its equal liberties *as long as liberty itself and their own freedom are in danger.*"[25] Under "stringent" conditions, in which there are "considerable risks to our own legitimate interests," Rawls felt restrictions on the intolerant may be necessary, even while disfavored.[26] He hoped that in a stable, well-ordered society, this would not often be necessary, for "[t]he liberties of the intolerant may persuade them to a belief in freedom."[27] But where the practical and theoretical benefits of democratic tolerance fail, societies find themselves in "a practical dilemma which philosophy alone cannot resolve."[28]

Liberal political theory generally seeks refuge from the hard normative issues involved in suppressing speech in two arguments, which, although certainly important, are insufficient. The first is the traditional understanding that the best antidote to bad speech is more speech. The core tradition of free expression,[29] brought to American law forcefully in the famous opinions of Justices Holmes and Brandeis, is that good speech will prevail in the marketplace of ideas.[30] On this view, suppression of speech is not only ineffective, but also likely counterproductive. Only a threat of tremendous immediacy justifies suppression: "If there be time to expose through discussion the falsehood and fallacies, to avert the evil by the processes of education, the remedy to be applied is more speech, not enforced silence."[31]

The second argument is a quietism: ultimately, not much can protect the people from their doom if that is their charted course. Justice Holmes famously argued that judicial invocation of the Constitution cannot thwart a pronounced desire of society to do itself in. The classic expression is found in his dissent in *Gitlow v. New York*: "If in the long run the beliefs expressed in

---

[25] Rawls, *supra* note 4, at 219 (emphasis added).

[26] *Id.* at 218–19.

[27] *Id.* at 219.

[28] *Id.*

[29] The classic account is found in ALEXANDER MEIKLEJOHN, FREE SPEECH AND ITS RELATION TO SELF-GOVERNMENT (Clark, NJ: The Lawbook Exchange, 2014) (1948).

[30] *See, e.g., Whitney v. California*, 274 U.S. 357, 372–80 (1927) (Brandeis, J., concurring); *Abrams v. United States*, 250 U.S. 616, 624–31 (1919) (Holmes, J., dissenting).

[31] *Whitney*, 274 U.S. at 377 (Brandeis, J., concurring).

proletarian dictatorship are destined to be accepted by the dominant forces of the community, the only meaning of free speech is that they should be given their chance and have their way."[32] As Justice Holmes elaborated in claiming that it was not the job of the judiciary to stand in the way of popular sentiment, "if my fellow citizens want to go to Hell I will help them. It's my job."[33] This fatalism is also found in a broader claim by the American Framers that control of the basic structures of democracy was a matter of democratic entitlement. Hence, Alexander Hamilton proclaimed forcefully that a "fundamental principle of republican government" would reserve a right to the people to "alter or abolish the established Constitution whenever they find it inconsistent with their happiness."[34]

In the realm of jurisprudence, the risk posed by intolerant groups has not been a major concern of liberal theory of late. By and large, contemporary liberal theory draws its animating principles from the relation of the individual to the state, primarily through the rights-based defenses that the individual may invoke against state authority. In Professor Ronald Dworkin's famous formulation, rights are "political trumps held by individuals" and "individuals can have rights against the state that are prior to the rights created by explicit legislation."[35] Secondarily, contemporary liberal theory focuses on the claims of justice that individuals may assert for just rewards from – and dignified treatment by – the society as a whole.[36] There are, of course, conflicts that emerge when rights claims by some individuals would impose burdens on others,[37] but these too are limitations on the rights claims of individuals against the state.

---

[32]   268 U.S. 652, 673 (1925) (Holmes, J., dissenting).

[33]   Letter from Oliver Wendell Holmes to Harold J. Laski (Mar. 4, 1920), in 1 HOLMES-LASKI LETTERS 249 (Mark DeWolfe Howe ed., Cambridge, MA: Harvard University Press, 1953).

[34]   *See* THE FEDERALIST No. 78, at 468 (Alexander Hamilton) (Clinton Rossiter ed., New York: The New American Library, 1961).

[35]   RONALD DWORKIN, TAKING RIGHTS SERIOUSLY, at xi (London: Gerald Duckworth & Co., 1977). Indeed, on most accounts, liberal thought "is a heritage which prizes individuality." JEREMY WALDRON, LIBERAL RIGHTS 1 (Cambridge: Cambridge University Press, 1993). For a fuller discussion of the role of rights as trumps in liberal theory, see the exchange between Richard H. Pildes, *Dworkin's Two Conceptions of Rights*, 29 J. LEGAL STUD. 309 (2000), and Jeremy Waldron, *Pildes on Dworkin's Theory of Rights*, 29 J. LEGAL STUD. 301 (2000).

[36]   *See* Rawls, *supra* note 4, at 75–83; *see also* Frank I. Michelman, The Supreme Court, 1968 Term – Foreword: On Protecting the Poor Through the Fourteenth Amendment, 83 HARV. L. REV. 7 (1969).

[37]   *See, e.g.*, JOSEPH RAZ, THE MORALITY OF FREEDOM 203 (New York: Oxford University Press, 1986) ("It is difficult to imagine a successful argument imposing a duty to provide a collective good on the ground that it will serve the interests of one individual.").

Generally missing from contemporary liberal discourse are the prerogatives and obligations of the state as such, acting as the guardian of the broader democratic well-being. It is not that the question of enforceable terms of political interaction is unknown to liberal theory. Professor Jeremy Waldron, for example, finds it useful to frame some fundamental dignitary rights claims as species of "public goods," concluding that "there should be no difficulty at all in expressing them as human rights, no problem accommodating them to the idiom of that particular discourse."[38] Rather, it is simply that the juxtaposition between state and individual is where the action is and has been. Further, it is clear that even the language of human rights has come to embrace an individual right of democratic participation within the core values of political liberty. Once again, the effect is to place the individual in opposition to the state in terms of democratic values.[39]

There are, of course, areas where liberal theorists are eager for the state to restrain democratic freedoms in the name of greater principles of democratic integrity. A particularly salient example in the United States is the area of campaign finance regulation, in which there is widespread support from many liberal quarters for limitations on both contributions and expenditures. Notably, however, the first move in this area is necessarily to deny the rights claim on the other side of the equation, following in one form or another the admonition of Judge Skelly Wright that "money itself is not speech."[40] Only then is there a demand that the state act to control access to the political process. It is hard to make a comparable move in the area of prohibitions on participation in the electoral arena. No matter how circumscribed the view of rights protections might be, there is no higher plane for protection of expression than in the domain of pure politics and in the ability to present ideas about the governance of society and advocate on behalf of candidates committed to those ideas.[41]

---

[38] Waldron, *supra* note 35, at 354. Professor Waldron argues that such communal goods should not be expressed as individual rights, but leaves open the question of whether they should be expressed as rights belonging to a society or government.

[39] *See, e.g.,* Thomas M. Franck, *The Emerging Right to Democratic Governance,* 86 AM. J. INT'L L. 46, 88 (1992) ("States' nonaggressiveness ... depends fundamentally on domestic democracy.").

[40] J. Skelly Wright, *Politics and the Constitution: Is Money Speech?,* 85 YALE L.J. 1001, 1019 (1976). For examples of arguments denying this rights claim, see OWEN M. FISS, THE IRONY OF FREE SPEECH 5–26 (Cambridge, MA: Harvard University Press, 1996); CASS R. SUNSTEIN, DEMOCRACY AND THE PROBLEM OF FREE SPEECH 93–119 (New York: The Free Press, 1993); Ronald Dworkin, *The Curse of American Politics,* N.Y. REV. BOOKS, Oct. 17, 1996, at 19, 23.

[41] *See, e.g.,* Robert H. Bork, *Neutral Principles and Some First Amendment Problems,* 47 IND. L.J. 1, 26–28 (1971) (defining a limited core of First Amendment rights focused on ideas of self-governance).

Nonetheless, my aim here is not to engage directly the jurisprudential foundations for the responsibility to maintain the vitality of the democratic process. In much of my writing in this area, I have been drawn to analogies between the political process and economic markets.[42] It does not seem too fanciful a notion to imagine that even the night watchman state has an obligation to maintain the openness of the instrumentalities of political competition in much the same way as the state must protect the integrity of economic markets from theft, fraud, and anticompetitive behavior. One could derive from the principle of political competition a robust role for the state as guardian of the vitality of the democratic process as a whole.

If elections are seen as a marketplace for political competition, and if the state does indeed hold a public trust for ensuring the capacity of the citizens to choose their governors, there is still the critical question of what kinds of restrictions may be utilized to protect the viability of democratic competition, as well as what procedural and substantive protections should be put in place to protect against misuse of those restrictions. My concern in the coming chapters, therefore, is with the institutional considerations that either do or should govern restrictions on political participation, with particular attention to how these have been assessed by reviewing courts.

As an initial matter, it will be useful to outline three sets of questions that courts and legislatures have grappled with in trying to set the parameters of democratic participation, from the most general to the most institutionally specific:

(1) May a state draw a boundary around participation in the democratic process, excluding from the right of participation those who fall on the wrong side of the boundary?

(2) If so, where does that boundary lie? Is it based on the ideological positions of the excluded actors, or must it turn on the immediacy of the danger they present?

(3) How are the boundaries to participation policed? Must there be an independent body to implement exclusion or review the boundaries to avoid – if nothing else – the temptation toward political self-dealing or the settling of scores?[43]

---

[42] *See, e.g.,* Samuel Issacharoff, *Gerrymandering and Political Cartels,* 116 HARV. L. REV. 593 (2002); Samuel Issacharoff & Richard H. Pildes, *Politics as Markets: Partisan Lockups of the Democratic Process,* 50 STAN. L. REV. 643 (1998).

[43] In the context of militant democracy, this book's addition to its namesake article is the shift in focus from the legislatively defined "outer bounds of the right of participation" to the importance of constitutional courts in policing *any* circumscription on participation in the democratic political process.

THE LESSONS OF WEIMAR

Militant democracy cannot be understood without reference to the failure of the Weimar Republic and the immediate postwar response. The rise of Nazism within the heart of European democracy is the touchstone for every debate on the vulnerability of democracy to antidemocratic assault. "The memory of some particularly traumatic experiences from precisely the inter-war European experience, most of all the fall of Weimar, has substantially influenced how reactions to extremism have evolved in later years, both in Europe and elsewhere."[44] Indeed, the very term "militant democracy" owes its existence to Karl Loewenstein,[45] himself a German academic who immi-grated to the United States after witnessing Hitler ascend to power in his home country.

The Nazi regime "came to power in Germany without clearly violating the strictures of a democratic constitution."[46] Yet the rise of the Nazi Party was attributable as much to the inability of the democratic state to protect itself as to electoral inevitability. The Nazis were the single strongest party in Germany in January 1933, when Hitler was appointed chancellor. But the Nazi Party had actually lost seats in the Reichstag over the previous six months, garnering less than one-third of the popular vote in the election immediately preceding the appointment.[47] The party still did not capture a clear majority in the March 1933 elections, despite electoral intimidation by the Nazi Sturmabteilung (paramilitary "storm troopers"). Nonetheless, later that same month the Reichstag passed the Ermächtigungsgesetz (Enabling Act) by an overwhelming majority, granting full legislative authority and extra-constitutional powers to Hitler and his Nazi-controlled cabinet.[48]

Germany's inability to defeat the Nazi challenge is only half the equation. Although the concept of military democracy emerged from the Nazi debacle, the interwar period includes cases of both "democratic breakdown" (Germany being the prime example) and "democratic survival."[49] As Giovanni Capoccia

---

[44] GIOVANNI CAPOCCIA, DEFENDING DEMOCRACY: REACTIONS TO EXTREMISM IN INTERWAR EUROPE 240 (Baltimore, MD: The Johns Hopkins University Press, 2005).

[45] Loewenstein, *supra* note 10.

[46] Fox & Nolte, *supra* note 1.

[47] *See id.* at 10 nn.33–34 ("Before Hitler's appointment as Chancellor in January 1933, the Nazi high water mark occurred in the elections of July 31, 1932 when the party received 37.4% of the popular vote.") (citing A. J. NICHOLLS, WEIMAR AND THE RISE OF HITLER 136–37 (3rd ed., New York: St. Martin's Press, 1991)).

[48] *Id.* at 11 ("Although it is possible to raise technical objections to the constitutional validity of the Ermächtigungsgesetz, the requisite two-thirds majority of deputies in the First Chamber had clearly consented to its passage." (footnote omitted)).

[49] The quoted terminology is borrowed from Capoccia, *supra* note 44, at 3, 4.

points out in a systematic review of the European response to fascism, Czechoslovakia, Belgium, and Finland faced interwar crises not unlike those seen in the Weimar Republic, yet only in Germany "did the outcome of the crisis put the system on a different historical path."[50] Examining the key differences, Capoccia observes:

> In essence, the analysis of the interwar experience showed that successful reactions to extremism essentially consisted of a three-step process: first, the antisystem challenge was recognized and perceived as such; second, significant defection from the prosystem front was avoided or blocked and extremists were politically isolated; third, actual strategies of short-term defense, normally a mix of repression and accommodation, were enacted.[51]

The postwar constitutions and the Allied occupation of Germany reflect a commitment to prohibiting certain kinds of advocacy and banning threatening political organizing.

The Potsdam Conference on the fate of Germany after the war was convened jointly by President Truman, Generalissimo Stalin (as he was termed in the conference protocols), and Prime Minister Atlee (who replaced Winston Churchill after the 1945 British elections). In reference to the means by which Hitler rose to power and the apparent democratic legitimacy of Hitler's regime, Potsdam Conference's Report noted that the electorate had "openly approved and blindly obeyed" the Nazis.[52] This shorthand account both underestimated the importance of institutional failure in Weimar and overestimated the claimed electoral approbation of Nazi rule. Nonetheless, the historical misassessment usefully allowed the victorious powers to close the postwar electoral arena to any efforts at Nazi resurrection. The major Allied heads of state committed themselves not only to the restoration of democracy, but to the complete elimination of the Nazi Party from German political life, a move seen as a precondition to any claim of legitimacy for postwar democracy:

> German militarism and Nazism will be extirpated and the Allies will take in agreement together, now and in the future, the other measures necessary to assure that Germany never again will threaten her neighbors or the peace of the world.

---

[50] *Id.* at 229.

[51] *Id.* at 234.

[52] *Report on the Tripartite Conference of Berlin, in* 2 FOREIGN RELATIONS OF THE UNITED STATES: DIPLOMATIC PAPERS: THE CONFERENCE OF BERLIN (THE POTSDAM CONFERENCE): 1945, at 1499, 1501 (Gov't Printing Office, 1960), *available at* http://digital.library.wisc.edu/1711.dl/FRUS.FRUS1945Berlinv02 (follow Final Documents hyperlink).

It is not the intention of the Allies to destroy or enslave the German people. It is the intention of the Allies that the German people be given the opportunity to prepare for the eventual reconstruction of their life on a democratic and peaceful basis. If their own efforts are steadily directed to this end, it will be possible for them in due course to take their place among the free and peaceful peoples of the world.[53]

This idea was embodied in the terms of the Potsdam Agreement, which included among the purposes of the Allied occupation:

(iii) To destroy the National Socialist Party and its affiliated and supervised organizations, to dissolve all Nazi institutions, to ensure that they are not revived in any form, and to prevent all Nazi and militarist activity or propaganda.

(iv) To prepare for the eventual reconstruction of German political life on a democratic basis and for eventual peaceful cooperation in international life by Germany.

The reconstruction of a new democratic order required excluding any move at a reactionary restoration of the past. The Allies famously held some Nazi leaders criminally accountable at the Nuremburg trials. But the main effort at German reconstruction was not through the prosecution of all Nazis, a task of impossible dimensions. Rather, most former Nazi officials, and certainly the great bulk of the Nazi military, were to be drawn back into democratic society.

Instead, the control on Nazism was largely a matter of political limitation rather than an application of the criminal law. This puts the postwar German experience in the same framework as the conditions imposed on the post–Civil War South by the Reconstruction Amendments. There is another parallel as well. Like the South, Germany's reabsorption of democratic governance occurred under military occupation. In this respect, Germany enjoyed a relative advantage in its formative years as compared to many other fledgling democracies. Unlike most of the other nations discussed throughout this book, which effectively had to go it alone, Germany was occupied by foreign forces committed to the reestablishment of democracy on terms that did not risk a return to the past. There was simply no chance that the occupying Allied powers were going to allow Nazis to reclaim control of Germany.

The commitment to democratic governance was not merely abstract. The Allies demanded that the repudiation of the past be included in specific provisions of German constitutional law. Concretely, this included the

---

[53] *Id.* at 1501–02.

requirement that the German Basic Law, which would serve as the German postwar constitution, be approved by the Allied Control Council of military governors before it could take effect, and that it enshrine institutional protections of democratic Germany.[54]

All constitutions entrench provisions beyond the reach of ordinary legislative politics. But the German Basic Law went a step further in not allowing any revision at all to certain of its core provisions, what are termed the eternity clauses.[55] Such unamendability, the inevitable dead hand of the past weighing down on the present, raises difficult questions of democratic legitimacy as time passes and the distance increases between the enacting past generation and the present active political generation.[56] In the German case, however, the force of the constitution was its repudiation of the immediate Nazi past, and its implementation was as much an outgrowth of military surrender as was the South's acquiescence to the Fourteenth Amendment.

Article 1 of the German Basic Law opens with a forceful, although hardly unique, commitment to basic human rights: "Human dignity shall be inviolable. To respect and protect it shall be the duty of all state authority."[57] What is distinct is the coupling of the definition of human rights with an affirmative duty for state authorities to enact "provisions that are meant to ensure that the enemies of democracy will never again be able to exploit the freedoms inherent in democracy."[58] The Basic Law then adds some particular provisions whose operational force is far removed from the clear and present danger test of American design, despite American oversight of the German constitutional

---

[54] Erich Hahn, *U.S. Policy on a West German Constitution 1947–1949, in* AMERICAN POLICY AND THE RECONSTRUCTION OF WEST GERMANY 1945–1955, at 21–44 (Jeffry Diefendorf et al. eds., Cambridge: Cambridge University Press, 1993).

[55] Article 79(3) of the German Basic Law provides, "Amendments to this Basic Law affecting the division of the Federation into Länder, their participation on principle in the legislative process, or the principles laid down in Articles 1 and 20 [preserving human dignity, human rights, democracy, and rule of law] shall be inadmissible."

[56] The West German constitution anticipated the possibility of a new constitutional arrangement once reunification occurred, although no such effort has been made in the post-1989 period. Article 146 provides that "This Basic Law ... shall cease to apply on the day on which a constitution freely adopted by the German people takes effect." Accordingly, while the main purpose for which Article 146 was drafted – German reunification – was accomplished by other means, it is open for a constitution approved by a referendum to do away with the Basic Law. *See* PETER QUINT, THE IMPERFECT UNION: CONSTITUTIONAL STRUCTURES OF GERMAN UNIFICATION (Princeton, NJ: Princeton University Press, 2012) 48–55 (discussing Article 146).

[57] GRUNDGESETZ [GG] [Basic Law] art. 1(1). BASIC LAW FOR THE FEDERAL REPUBLIC OF GERMANY (Christian Tomuschat & Donald P. Kommers eds., Christian Tomuschat & David P. Currie trans., 2010), *available at* https://www.btg-bestellservice.de/pdf/80201000.pdf.

[58] DONALD P. KOMMERS & RUSSELL A. MILLER, THE CONSTITUTIONAL JURISPRUDENCE OF THE FEDERAL REPUBLIC OF GERMANY 285 (3rd ed., Durham, NC: Duke University Press, 2012).

process. The dangers may have been clear and past, once Allied forces moved into Germany, but the Basic Law takes no chances.

German constitutional law does not wait for the moment of imminent criminal threat, but instead prohibits groups "whose aims or activities contravene the criminal laws, or that are directed against the constitutional order or the concept of international understanding."[59] Furthermore, associations and individuals may forfeit their basic rights (such as those of free association and assembly) if they misuse them "in order to combat the free democratic basic order."[60] In protecting democracy, the German Basic Law empowers any German "to resist any person seeking to abolish this constitutional order, if no other remedy is available."[61] Most important, at least for present purposes, is the inclusion of specific provisions concerning political parties: "Parties that, by reason of their aims or the behaviour of their adherents, seek to undermine or abolish the free democratic basic order or to endanger the existence of the Federal Republic of Germany shall be unconstitutional."[62]

The German Basic Law shifted the terms of debate. Prior to World War II, the question seemed to be whether democracies could muster the wherewithal to withstand the totalitarian challenge from within. The unamendable provisions of the Basic Law answered that question by placing the militant democracy rationale at the heart of the new constitutional order. With new democracies being created out of the remnants of failed authoritarian regimes, the question is not so much whether democracies can respond to antidemocratic forces, but how. Democracies may seek to wall off the appeal of extremism through inclusive social policies, but there is little confidence, at least in the short run, that such approaches are sufficient. Instead, there must be some mechanisms specifically aimed at "rising extremist challenges that threaten to lead to democratic breakdown or at least to paralyze a government's ability to respond to extremism."[63]

SAFEGUARDING CORE DEMOCRATIC PRINCIPLES

All constitutions constrain the options available to majoritarian choice. However, they vary in the degree of "obduracy" of their provisions.[64] Some

---

[59] GRUNDGESETZ [GG] [Basic Law] art. 9(2).

[60] *Id.* art. 18.

[61] *Id.* art. 20(4).

[62] *Id.* art 21(2).

[63] Capoccia, *supra* note 9, at 217 n. 18.

[64] LAWRENCE G. SAGER, JUSTICE IN PLAINCLOTHES: A THEORY OF AMERICAN CONSTITUTIONAL PRACTICE 81–82 (New Haven, CT: Yale University Press, 2004).

allow change by supermajority; others require that approval be demonstrated over an extended period of time.[65] Many also have unamendable provisions that are intended to define the society indefinitely and are not subject to review absent a complete overhaul of the society. Examples of unamendable provisions include Articles 1 and 20 of the German Basic Law and Article V of the U.S. Constitution (as to both the mechanics of amendment and the specific prohibition on any state being denied its representation in the Senate). Other constitutions take the basic form of governance off the table, as with Article 139 of the Italian Constitution, which prohibits any amendment altering the republican form of government, or Article 112 of the Norwegian Constitution, forbidding amendments that "contradict the principles embodied in the Constitution."[66]

Which provisions are off the table for internal change generally reflects the birth pangs of that particular society. The concept of a constitution as addressing the contested politics of a government at its moment of formation is hardly new, going back at least to Aristotle.[67] What is distinct is the frequency with which modern constitutions assume the right to restrict from politics matters that threaten the core divides of the society.

Whether through the numerous protections of slavery in the original U.S. Constitution, or the tormented recognition of the Nazi period in the German postwar constitution, such provisions shore up the weak points in the social order that cannot bear direct political conflict. In turn, many countries prohibit political participation by parties that do not share the fundamental aims of the constitutional order. Thus, it is not surprising to find provisions in the (West) German Constitution that later formed the foundations for a ban on the descendants of the Nazi and Communist Parties,[68] or to see a

---

[65] *See, e.g.*, FIN. CONST. art. 73 (providing that a constitutional amendment introduced in one parliamentary session may only be approved after an intervening parliamentary election); 1958 FR. CONST. art. 89 (requiring that amendments be approved by two successive assemblies and then by a referendum).

[66] *See* GARY JEFFREY JACOBSOHN, THE WHEEL OF LAW: INDIA'S SECULARISM IN COMPARATIVE CONSTITUTIONAL CONTEXT 138 (Princeton, NJ: Princeton University Press, 2003) (quoting ITALY CONST. art. 139; NOR. CONST. art. 112). For a fuller discussion of constitutions as precommitment pacts against current majoritarian preferences, see Samuel Issacharoff, *The Enabling Role of Democratic Constitutionalism: Fixed Rules and Some Implications for Contested Presidential Elections*, 81 TEX. L. REV. 1985 (2003).

[67] *See* ARISTOTLE, POLITICS §1296b10, *reprinted in* ARISTOTLE, THE POLITICS AND THE CONSTITUTION OF ATHENS 9, 109 (Stephen Everson ed., Cambridge: Cambridge University Press, 1996) (asserting that constitutions must be measured by what is best in relation to actual conditions).

[68] *See Socialist Reich Party Case*, Bundesverfassungsgericht [BVerfG] [Federal Constitutional Court] Oct. 23, 1952, 2 Entscheidungen des Bundesverfassungsgerichts [BVerfGE] 1 (F.R.G.), *translated in part in* Kommers & Miller, *supra* note 58, at 286; *Communist Party Case*, BVerfG

corresponding early prohibition of communist parties in Ukraine and other former Soviet-controlled countries. As expressed by the Czechoslovakian Constitutional Court in a 1992 decision upholding that country's lustration law against a constitutional challenge, "A democratic State has not only the right, but also the duty to assert and protect the principles on which it is based."[69]

But the prohibition goes significantly further in many countries, defining the permissible bounds of democratic deliberation and banning outright parties that raise claims outside these limits. Common examples are found in the banning of parties that challenge the country's territorial integrity (resulting in prohibitions on electoral participation by separatist movements) or that seek to reconstitute society along religious lines. Here, the best examples are found in a series of decisions by the Turkish Constitutional Court upholding bans on parties advocating Kurdish independence or fidelity to sharia – campaigns that were deemed violative of the constitutional commitment to the integrity of Turkey as an organic secular state.[70] These are complicated cases that will be discussed more fully later in this book. But the principle of drawing the boundaries of where democratic deliberation and democratic politics end is a generalized phenomenon across democratic societies.

Most democratic countries appear to draw some form of protective line around the legal status of the political party. This protection means that the constitutional definition of the permissible scope of democratic politics is also the defining boundary for the right to organize a political party. For example, German (formerly West German) constitutional law grants significant protections to the ability of political parties to form and operate effectively in the electoral arena.[71] Nonetheless, that protection is granted only to those parties that are entitled to legal status as proper actors in a democratic society.

Aug. 17, 1956, 5 BVerfGE 85, *translated in part in* Walter F. Murphy & Joseph Tanenhaus, Comparative Constitutional Law 621 (New York: Palgrave Macmillan, 1977).

[69] 3 Transitional Justice: How Emerging Democracies Reckon with Former Regimes 346, 350 (Neil J. Kritz ed., Washington, DC: United States Institute of Peace Press, 1995) (presenting edited translation of Czech and Slovak Federal Republic Constitutional Court Decision on the Screening Law, Nov. 26, 1992). For a discussion of the comparable Hungarian treatment of lustration issues, see Gábor Halmai & Kim Lane Scheppele, *Living Well Is the Best Revenge: The Hungarian Approach to Judging the Past, in* Transitional Justice and the Rule of Law in New Democracies 155, 171–78 (A. James McAdams ed., Notre Dame, IN: University of Notre Dame Press, 1997). The corollary problem of lustration of former officeholders after a transition away from authoritarian rule is discussed in the second half of this book.

[70] *See* Dicle Kogacioglu, *Dissolution of Political Parties by the Constitutional Court in Turkey: Judicial Delimitation of the Political Domain*, 18 Int'l Soc. 258 (2003).

[71] *See, e.g.*, Kommers & Miller, *supra* note 58, at 269–84 (translating, in part, the *Party Finance* cases and describing the role of political parties in the (West) German constitutional order).

As noted earlier, prohibited by Article 21(2) of the German Basic Law are "[p]arties that, by reason of their aims or the behaviour of their adherents, seek to undermine or abolish the free democratic basic order or to endanger the existence of the Federal Republic of Germany."[72]

This now raises the next piece of the puzzle. It is all well and good to proclaim the ability of democracies to police their boundaries, but how are such determinations to be made? The power to place dissident views beyond political discourse is a power asserted by all authoritarian states who claim the need for social order or social harmony as a rationale for suppression of challenges to the regime. A similar power in the hands of an elected government is too great an invitation to decreeing oppositional views beyond electoral tolerance.

Here again, the post–World War II experience of Germany sets the model for the late twentieth-century round of democratization. While Germany allows for the banning of parties from the boundaries of democratic engagement, it at the same time takes that power out of the hands of incumbent political officials. The German Basic Law places the determination of a party's constitutionality with the constitutional court, and no attempt to ban a party can go into effect until the court has exercised its power of review.[73] In the early days of the Federal Republic, the constitutional court did in fact twice exercise its authority under Article 21 to declare parties unconstitutional: in 1952, in the *Socialist Reich Party Case*,[74] it declared a neo-Nazi party unconstitutional; and in 1956, in the *Communist Party Case*,[75] it declared the Communist Party of Germany (KPD) unconstitutional. In each case, the basis for the party banning was the constitutional limitation on the scope of permissible political advocacy in Germany. The court created symmetry between what could properly be advocated to the electorate and the organizational boundaries on what could constitute a legal political party.

While there are different modes of implementation, these party prohibitions are all premised on the idea that the aims of political parties and their form of organization place them either within or without the democratic process.[76]

[72] GRUNDGESETZ [GG] [Basic Law] art. 21(2); *see also id.* art. 9(2) (prohibiting "[a]ssociations whose aims or activities … are directed against the constitutional order"); *id.* art. 5(3) ("The freedom of teaching shall not release any person from allegiance to the constitution.").

[73] *Id.* art. 21(2) ("The Federal Constitutional Court shall decide on the question of unconstitutionality.").

[74] BVerfG Oct. 23, 1952, 2 BVerfGE 1, *translated in part in* Kommers & Miller, *supra* note 58, at 286.

[75] BVerfG Aug. 17, 1956, 5 BVerfGE 85, *translated in part in* Murphy & Tanenhaus, *supra* note 69, at 621. For a general discussion of the case, see Kommers & Miller, *supra* note 58, at 290–93.

[76] *See* Paul Franz, *Unconstitutional and Outlawed Political Parties: A German-American Comparison*, 5 B.C. INT'L & COMP. L. REV. 51, 63 (1982) (noting that under German law,

If their aims are sufficiently antithetical to core democratic principles, they may be banned. The substantive grounds for the bans diverge from country to country, although in most democracies the authority for banning of a political party is derived from the constitution directly. France is exceptional in this regard, relying on a 1936 statute regulating the existence of private militias.[77]

Some constitutional prohibitions are quite open-textured, as with Article 49 of the Italian Constitution, which enjoins parties from violating the "democratic method."[78] Most are more specific, as with Article 21 of the German Basic Law, which guarantees the right of free formation of political parties but dictates that "[t]heir internal organization must conform to democratic principles" and flatly prohibits parties that "seek to undermine or abolish the free democratic order or to endanger the existence of the Federal Republic of Germany."[79] Nonetheless, the flipside to the inquiry is that if parties are not banned, they enjoy plenary rights of free expression; according to the German court, "[t]he Basic Law tolerates the dangers inherent in the activities of such a political party until it is declared unconstitutional."[80]

The concept of banning parties as a means of throwing off the vestiges of a recently deposed regime has gained attention in the post-Soviet period. In the volatile national settings where new democracies are perilously found, party banning is designed to cement the break from the authoritarian past – as was the case in postwar Germany. In Ukraine, within days of the declaration of independence from the Soviet Union in 1991, a special committee of the new legislature issued a pair of decrees banning the Communist Party of Ukraine and seizing its assets.[81] Similarly, the first order issued by the Coalition Provisional Authority in Iraq – led by the United States – eliminated Saddam Hussein's Baath Party, banned the four highest ranks of Baath Party members from holding government jobs, and removed all party members from government.[82] The lustrations were often problematic in their scope,

parties "are to be free from government discrimination and governmental intervention as long as the Constitutional Court has not found the party to be unconstitutional").

[77] *See* Yigal Mersel, *The Dissolution of Political Parties: The Problem of Internal Democracy*, 4 INT'L J. CONST. L. 84, 92 n.41 (2006) (contrasting French statutory authority with constitutional provisions in Croatia, Italy, Germany, Poland, and Spain).

[78] Niesen, *supra* note 17, at 19 (quoting ITALY CONST. art. 49).

[79] GRUNDGESETZ [GG] [Basic Law] art. 21(1)-(2).

[80] *Radical Groups Case*, BVerfG Feb. 14, 1978, 47 BVerfGE 198, *translated in part in* DONALD P. KOMMERS, THE CONSTITUTIONAL JURISPRUDENCE OF THE FEDERAL REPUBLIC OF GERMANY 224, 227 (2d ed., Durham, NC: Duke University Press, 1997).

[81] *See* Alexei Trochev, *Ukraine: Constitutional Court Invalidates Ban on Communist Party*, 1 INT'L J. CONST. L. 534, 535 (2003).

[82] Amit R. Paley & Joshua Partlow, *Iraq's New Law on Ex-Baathists Could Bring Another Purge*, WASH. POST, Jan. 23, 2008, http://www.washingtonpost.com/wp-dyn/content/article/2008/01/22/AR2008012203538.html.

especially in Iraq, but the principle of using prohibitions to dismantle prior authoritarian power is well established.

Perhaps nowhere is the use of and accompanying danger of party banning more evident than in Egypt, where a series of coups d'état after the Arab Spring has resulted in repeated oscillations in party status. Following the resignation of President Hosni Mubarak in February 2011, an Egyptian court disbanded his National Democratic Party (NDP), and ordered all of the party's assets be turned over to the government.[83] The following presidential election in 2012 was won by Mohamed Morsi of the Muslim Brotherhood, despite the Supreme Constitutional Court ruling two days before the elections dissolving parliament and permitting the participation of Mubarak's former prime minister, Ahmed Shafik.[84] After Morsi's ouster in 2013, however, an Egyptian court banned the Muslim Brotherhood and ordered the seizure of its assets.[85] The Muslim Brotherhood had attempted to include language in Egypt's new constitution that would have banned leaders of Mubarak's former party from government for ten years, but the provision was eliminated during the amendment stage. Subsequently, in July 2014, the Cairo Appeals Court for Urgent Matters held that NDP leaders could run for office in Egypt's upcoming elections.[86] Most recently, at the time of writing, the Supreme Administrative Court banned the Freedom and Justice Party (FJP), the political arm of the Muslim Brotherhood. The court also called for the confiscation of all assets of the FJP. Although the party "can no longer compete in the next parliamentary elections," the former members of the FJP "can run either as individual candidates or form a new political party."[87]

CONTEXTUAL ASSESSMENTS

Somewhere between the stability of postwar Germany and the reassertion of military control in Egypt lies a proper path for democracies. As will be set

---

[83] *Egypt Dissolves Former Ruling Party*, Al Jazeera English, Apr. 16, 2011, http://www.aljazeera.com/news/middleeast/2011/04/201141612505188931.html.

[84] David D. Kirkpatrick, *Blow to Transition as Court Dissolves Egypt's Parliament*, N.Y. Times, http://www.nytimes.com/2012/06/15/world/middleeast/new-political-showdown-in-egypt-as-court-invalidates-parliament.html (June 15, 2014).

[85] *Egypt Shuts Down Headquarters of Muslim Brotherhood Newspaper*, Reuters, Sept. 25, 2013, http://www.reuters.com/article/2013/09/25/us-egypt-brotherhood-newspaper-idUSBRE98O07B20130925.

[86] *Egypt: Mubarak Leaders Can Run for Elections*, SEATTLE TIMES, July 14, 2014, http://seattletimes.com/html/nationworld/2024067687_apxegypt.html.

[87] *Egypt Court Bans Muslim Brotherhood's Political Wing*, BBC News, Aug. 9, 2014, http://www.bbc.com/news/world-middle-east-28722935.

forth in the following chapters, the challenges to democratic authority vary across national settings, as do the tools considered legitimate to contain those challenges. The effort to define with precision the exact ideas or advocacy that should be proscribed is unlikely to be fruitful. If advocating overthrow is prohibited, then it is easy to advocate for resistance – and if that too is banned, then the language of choice might be freedom. A corresponding threat exists on the side of state authority, where impermissible aims become an invitation to censor disagreement with those in power.

Where formal legal rules are unlikely to be sufficiently sensitive to nuanced situational particulars, there needs to be some authority to apply the general to the specific. This is the familiar regulatory divide in law between rules and standards. Rules are regulations of fixed application (such as stop at the red light) that require precision in their creation (there must be a functioning streetlight), but can be applied relatively mechanically once in place. By contrast, standards are easier to promulgate (an instruction to drive prudently is near costless to issue), but require more difficult after-the-fact assessments when they fail to avert some harm. The more precise the rule, the more its implementation and enforcement is a matter of bureaucratic application. By contrast, the more expansive the standard, the more likely the assessment of rights and wrongs will require judicial oversight; that is, the use of an arbiter capable of making independent value assessments of all the circumstances in the particulars of an individual case.

Policing the boundaries of democratic politics almost invariably requires contextual assessments. Well before there are armed militias pouring into the capital, modern states will attempt to forestall political mobilizations, even if the initial rallying cries are issued in the name of a political party and are voiced during the course of an election campaign. This necessitates some consideration of the types of threats that democracies face and the legitimate tools available to address them. This is the subject of the following chapters. Beyond the substantive and procedural protections invoked by democracies is the question of institutional design. As with all acts of suppression of ideas and organizations, there is the risk that democracy will end with the end of political ferment. At the end of the day, strong institutions taking the form of modern constitutional courts need navigate the precarious path between "the Scylla of Weimar" and "the Charybdis of McCarthyism."[88]

---

[88] ALEXANDER S. KIRSHNER, A THEORY OF MILITANT DEMOCRACY: THE ETHICS OF COMBATTING POLITICAL EXTREMISM 3 (New Haven, CT: Yale University Press, 2014).

3

Types of Threats

Banning political parties is not the desired end state of democracy. Rather, it is a prudent act to ward off an existential threat not yet realized. It is always possible that driving a party underground will harden its cadres, or gain them public sympathy as romantic figures of the Che Guevara sort. These are questions of prudence and tactics that can only be answered pragmatically. The question of principle is the justification for the ban, not whether it is wise under the particular circumstances.

Nor is it an objection to say that a party facing a ban is still weak. How much wiser to remove surgically a cancerous tumor when it is small rather than large. The wisdom of the incision depends on the proper diagnosis, not whether the patient is at death's door. Indeed, allowing an antidemocratic movement to mature into a mass party renders intervention quite unlikely to succeed.

The initial question of principle is therefore to identify the conditions that require democracies to assume a defensive posture against threats to their continued existence. In turn, this requires identifying the types of risk that democratic states consider to require removal from political participation. By and large, these party prohibitions fall into one of three categories, each of which raises a separate set of concerns.

First, there are prohibitions that result from groups having a terrorist or insurrectionary component based either domestically or abroad. The paramilitary side of these groups is independently subject to criminal prosecution or defensive military operations. Yet there is often a political wing that seeks to operate publicly and may serve as a legal or propagandistic front for terrorist or insurrectionary groups. A ready example is the complicated relationship between the Irish Republican Army's military wing and the Sinn Féin political branch. Whether it is wise to ban the political exponent – Britain chose never to move legally against Sinn Féin – is separate from the question of whether organized political propaganda on behalf of paramilitary groups may be legitimately suppressed.

Second, there are prohibitions on parties that have some sort of separatist or nationalist self-determination element, such as supporting regional independence movements based on religious or ethnic divides, or taking a political stance opposing the continued territorial integrity of the country. Such prohibitions are inherently problematic because the claims for autonomy are usually raised in the name of a disfavored, often oppressed, group. In some instances, as with the Kurdistan Workers Party (known as the PKK), the claims for autonomy may spill over into paramilitary activity.

Third, there are bars to parties that challenge the country's core democratic values – usually as they are manifested in the status quo or are described in the established constitutional order – through use of the established electoral processes. This group consists of mass-based political forces that advance their aims through the give and take of electoral competition, but ultimately seek to terminate the premises of democratic tolerance or, sometimes, electoral accountability altogether. The distinguishing feature of this third category is that there is a serious effort to achieve political power through majoritarian elections.

In the real world, the lines between the three categories are often blurred. The Hezbollah platform in Lebanon arguably contains elements of all three, while Turkey has justified its suppression of parties supporting Kurdish nationalism on the ground that they engaged in or supported guerrilla actions against the government. In the American context, the Confederacy could be considered both a separatist group and a threat to core democratic values. The same could be said of the Batasuna Party in Spain, which was banned not for seeking Basque independence from Spain as such, but for its close ties to the terrorist group ETA.

Regardless of the inability to seal off hermetically one type of banned group from another, the three archetypes help to define the nature and severity of the challenges they present. The first two categories, insurrectionary and regional independence parties, represent minority attacks on the polity. These groups seek to use the electoral arena to erode the will of the broader society to resist attacks on the core organizational structure of the state. Each poses different problems for democratic societies, particularly because political platforms of the regional independence parties are likely to be heavily infused with legitimate claims concerning discriminatory treatment of national or ethnic minorities within the broader society. But it is the third category that is the most problematic, and the most dangerous. The strategy for gaining power employed by parties in this category was the one used by the Nazis, as reflected in Goebbels's chilling quotation that democracy can be conquered from within its own structures. It is this form of mass challenge that has been so dispiriting for the hopeful champions of democracy in the Middle East, as clericalist Islamist parties and others that reject the fundamental premises of democracy use the electoral platform to claim power.

INSURRECTIONARY PARTIES

Within democracies, there is almost always a category of parties that seek to participate in the electoral process for the purpose of propagandizing their views, but without any real prospect of seriously competing for political office. This category describes many minor parties around the world, currently including all third parties in the United States, all parties in South Africa outside the African National Congress (ANC), and – until at least the 1990s – all Mexican political parties outside the Partido Revolucionario Institucional (PRI). Even if they are not viable candidates for electoral victory, these third parties are critical components of the political order. They challenge incumbent officials and appeal for political change at the time citizens are most focused on politics: elections.

At times, however, participation in electoral politics by groups without hope for winning can be a matter of more than just airing minority views. Despite their lack of political capital, these parties can cause problems for the political order if they use the electoral arena as an organizing forum for insurrectionary attacks on the state or as an outlet for defending illegal activities.

The most pressing threat to fragile democracies emerges from parties that have goals of insurrection, regardless of the imminence of their threats, and for whom electoral politics is a propagandistic side note. These parties fall outside the realm of ordinary politics, defined by Nancy Rosenblum – in her defense of political parties – as a sphere for citizen engagement with democracy. By their nature, such insurrectionary groups reject the democratic precondition that "conflict is restricted to the regulated rivalry of obtaining political office and influencing laws and policy by peaceful, electoral means."[1] Thus, even a staunch defender of political parties such as Rosenblum concludes that "militant democracy justifiably proscribe[s] 'fundamentalism in power and chauvinism with an army.'"[2] As with any restriction on political parties, claims of

---

[1] NANCY L. ROSENBLUM, ON THE SIDE OF THE ANGELS: AN APPRECIATION OF PARTIES AND PARTISANSHIP 423 (Princeton, NJ: Princeton University Press, 2008).

[2] *Id.* (quoting MICHAEL WALZER, POLITICS AND PASSION: TOWARD A MORE EGALITARIAN LIBERALISM 64 (New Haven, CT: Yale University Press, 2008)).

insurrectionary ambitions easily turn into a pretext for enabling a "lockup" of the political process – a scenario in which incumbents entrench and immunize themselves against electoral challenges.[3] The question is not whether party prohibitions against insurrectionists are ever appropriate, but rather what constitutes (sufficient) evidence of antidemocratic intent and who is the ultimate arbiter of the prohibition.

Part of the evidence comes from the confederates of insurrectionary parties. These parties are often tied to paramilitary-style organizations that threaten the state monopoly on force and put pressure on domestic tranquility. The category can include drug cartels[4] and other criminal organizations, as well as parties with loyalties to hostile foreign entities.

Specific examples help to elaborate the shapes these parties can take and the issues they raise about the boundaries of the electoral systems. Here again the era of contemporary militant democracy is heavily shaped by the experiences of pre–World War II Europe. Thus, the best and most troubling paradigms are often drawn not from the electoral efforts of drug cartels, but from the communist and fascist parties within various democracies.

Prewar Czechoslovakia was confronted with the emergence of the Sudentendeutsche Heimatfront (SHF), a Sudeten German party devoted to the integration of the German-speaking parts of Czechoslovakia into Germany. Despite the SHF's "political camouflage" of public expression of loyalty to democratic values, the party became intimately tied to the Nazis in Germany, who in turn were a mainstay of the party's funding.[5] The SHF grew to be the largest parliamentary force in the German regions of Czechoslovakia, from which it agitated not only for separation, but to destabilize the government. The party agitated for the Volksschutzgesetze, a bill that would transform each nationality into an ethnically based corporation, where each corporation would elect its own representative to government. That representative was responsible only to the national constituency, and could not be removed by any government powers nor otherwise held accountable by the central government. As Giovanni Capoccia observes, the aim was to compromise the government's sovereignty over several regions within its borders, a goal that was

---

[3] *See* Samuel Issacharoff & Richard H. Pildes, *Politics as Markets: Partisan Lockups of the Democratic Process*, 50 STAN. L. REV. 643 (1998).

[4] In an extreme example, Colombian president Ernesto Samper was charged with accepting $6 million from the infamous Cali Cartel to fund his 1994 campaign. *See* John C. Dugas, *Drugs, Lies, and Audiotape: The Samper Crisis in Colombia*, 36 LATIN AM. RES. REV. 157–74 (2001).

[5] GIOVANNI CAPOCCIA, DEFENDING DEMOCRACY: REACTIONS TO EXTREMISM IN INTERWAR EUROPE 78 (Baltimore, MD: The Johns Hopkins University Press, 2005).

ultimately realized when German troops overran Czechoslovakia, integrated the Sudetenland into Germany, and installed the SHF as the puppet Nazi regime.[6] The prewar Czech government did not ban the SHF or remove it from parliament, choosing instead a policy of accommodation in the hope of maintaining "interethnic coexistence," a policy that failed decisively in the face of German tanks.[7]

On the other hand, the response in Finland to the threat posed by the pro-Soviet communists shows an alternative strategy. Finland claimed independence from Russia in 1917, leading to a short but bloody civil war in which pro-Soviet forces captured the south of the country and sought realignment with the new Soviet Union. With assistance from Germany, the country was able to withstand the Russian military challenge until March of the following year, when the Treaty of Brest-Litovsk ended Russian claims against Finland. Despite Germany's subsequent defeat in World War I, Finland's independence was preserved as the beleaguered Soviets were fighting off an attempted overthrow, including military intervention from Western powers.

With the first parliamentary elections in 1919, Finland confronted two antidemocratic challenges: first from the remnants of the defeated communist movement itself, and second from the right-wing Lapua movement, itself an extremist reaction to the communist hold on the south of the country during the civil war. In the aftermath of the civil war, Finnish communists reorganized into the Finnish Socialist Workers' Party (SSTP) and used their control of the trade union confederation, the Suomen Ammattijarjesto (SAJ), to unleash a strike wave, creating the kinds of parliamentary disruptions more commonly associated with Weimar Germany. Unlike Czechoslovakia before the Nazi threat, Finland responded by suppressing the communist-led groups. A series of parliamentary initiatives struck at the organizational support for the communists, and the courts upheld allowing membership in the Communist Party to be punished as an act of sedition or treason, which in turn led to the arrests of a large number of arrests of communist activists. A corresponding, although less far-reaching set of prohibitions were enacted against the right-wing Lapua movement, which became more significant as World War II approached and the threat to Finnish independence came less from the Soviet side than from militarizing Germany. The takeaway is that unlike Czechoslovakia, which remained relatively passive before the rising Nazi movement in the Sudetenland, Finland secured its newfound

---

[6]   *Id.*

[7]   *Id.* at 90–91, 106–07.

independence and fledgling democracy through strong reactions against domestic antidemocratic groups.

The Finnish model comes closer to the experience of postwar Europe. Germany again sets the standard, and its postwar constitution declares that "parties that, by reason of their aims or the behavior of their adherents, seek to undermine or abolish the free democratic basic order or to endanger the existence of the Federal Republic of Germany shall be unconstitutional."[8] Historically, as will be examined more fully with regard to oversight by the constitutional court, this power was invoked first and most importantly against the remnants of the Nazi Party and against the pro-Soviet Communist Party.

But the question of exclusion of antidemocratic parties persists. For example, several German states recently requested the banning of the National Democratic Party (NPD), a neo-Nazi party whose platform was built on a volatile combination of racism, xenophobia, and anti-Semitism. The NPD has developed an electoral following through its advocacy of removing Germany from NATO and forcing immigrants to leave Germany. Whether the NPD is in fact a sufficient menace to merit exclusion is a topic of ongoing debate in Germany, and the constitution leaves the issue of formal banning to adjudication by the constitutional court, which has not yet ruled.[9]

The German debates over banning the NPD point to the difficulty of actually implementing the militant democracy power to move against antidemocratic parties. In moments of political or economic stress, dissident parties will emerge, sometimes radically dissident parties. In most instances, these marginal groups will fade over time as the rhetoric of anger fails to hold adherents or fails to adjust to the waning of an imminent crisis. But not always.

A reserved power to act against antidemocratic groups is not a strategy for the deployment of that power, and in many instances a formal ban may be counterproductive. While the postwar consensus is that states must have the power to act prophylactically against antidemocratic groups, even in the electoral guise, the question of how and when persists. Where the danger to democratic stability posed by a party rises to the level of an actual threat of extralegal conduct, the normal operations of the criminal law generally suffice. The more difficult question is posed by the support for illegal activity that may define a party but is harder to specify, as with Sinn Féin in Northern Ireland.

As will be developed more fully in the discussion of court oversight of party prohibitions, applying the criteria for banning a party for incitement

8 Grundgesetz [GG] [Basic Law] art. 21(2).

9 Nastassja Steudel, *Second Attempt to Ban Neo-Nazi NPD Under Way*, Deutsche Welle (June 21, 2014), http://www.dw.de/second-attempt-to-ban-neo-nazi-npd-under-way/a-17726217.

looks like a milder version of the clear and present danger test. The German
constitutional court cases that are the judicial wellspring for this area of law
did not turn first to the Nazi remnants and then to the German Communist
Party in the abstract, but in the context of Germany's recent Nazi past and during the heyday of the Cold War threat from the East. Even the current debates
in Germany over the banning of the NPD are infused with the question of the
imminence of the harm, not simply ideology standing alone.

Some test for imminence of the threat is not the same as the clear and
present danger standard from American First Amendment law. What distinguishes the European experience from the Cold War-era Smith Act cases in
the United States is the noncriminal nature of the sanction. American criminal law requires proof of concrete actions, what in the context of inchoate
crimes is defined by the Model Penal Code as "an overt act in pursuance
of such conspiracy."[10] In cases such as *Dennis v. United States*,[11] an inquiry
into specific criminal acts concerning the scope of Soviet espionage was transformed into a prosecution for conspiracy to advocate the overthrow of the
government through force and violence.[12] American courts confused the question of whether the Communist Party was for all practical purposes a stalking
horse for a military challenge to the United States with the distinct question of
whether its leaders could be incarcerated for advocacy without conduct. The
postwar cases on militant democracy have not collapsed the two inquiries.

SEPARATIST MOVEMENTS AND SELF-DETERMINATION THREATS

Separatist parties, on their face, present similar threats to insurrectionary parties. These groups also align themselves with movements whose aims are to
change fundamentally the preexisting form of the state, eschewing any prospect – certainly any realistic prospect – of gaining the adherence of a majority
or even a politically significant minority of citizens in the broad body politic.
Separatist parties often have some sort of paramilitary component or a relationship with armed associations fighting for the same general goals, which
may constitute a threat to the physical security of the state and its residents.
In those instances, of course, any democratic society can claim a compelling
interest in protecting itself against armed insurrection and may seek to prohibit the nonmilitary political party promoting separatist aims.

---

[10] Model Penal Code § 5.03(5).
[11] *Dennis v. United States*, 341 U.S. 494 (1951). See Chapter 1 for a more detailed discussion of
      the case.
[12] *See* GEOFFREY R. STONE, PERILOUS TIMES: FREE SPEECH IN WARTIME 367, 396
      (New York: W. W. Norton & Co., 2004) (discussing *Dennis*).

The distinction lies in the affiliations and aims of each type of party. An insurrectionary party is frequently associated with either a foreign entity or a criminal enterprise within the country. By contrast, the separatist's central objective is alleviating a perceived oppression of a specific ethnic or religious minority or region within the country. In addition to direct ties with the people or place for which it is fighting, in championing the cause of oppressed groups within the broader polity the party may form an uneasy and oftentimes conflicting relationship with armed groups fighting for the same general objectives. The party's claims for democratic rights, including self-determination, may be undermined by allegations of terrorism against the party itself or an associated group, as with ETA in Spain or the PKK in the Kurdish region of Turkey.

Unlike insurrectionary parties, separatist parties usually do not seek control of the entire state. Rather, their primary goal is usually autonomy or independence. Their party platforms include the claim that they are fighting for the rights of the majority of citizens within the oppressed ethnic or religious group or subjugated region of the country in question.[13] Thus, they claim a democratic pedigree as a majoritarian movement within a bounded part of the nation. Because of their identification with a broader claim for the rights of a regionally defined, generally subordinated section of the nation, separatist parties readily invoke the language of self-determination to claim independent democratic grounds for their right to advocate dissolution of the broader polity.[14] The loss or diminution of control over a region or minority group clearly proves threatening to the stability of the country as a whole, especially within an emergent democracy.

Separatist parties are frequent targets for exclusion from the electoral arena for two distinct reasons. First, like insurrectionary parties, they may serve to provide legal cover for attacks on the state through force or violence. This is in effect the story of Batasuna (whose name, somewhat ironically, means "unity") in Spain, as well as that of its affiliated Herritarren Zerrenda

---

[13] There are exceptions that complicate the picture. Israeli Arabs can be expected to chafe at the Basic Law's proclamation of the Jewish character of the Israeli state. The unwillingness of Arab parties in Israel to accept this characterization has led to numerous efforts to ban such parties, which have generally been resisted by the courts absent some tie to the PLO or terrorism. For a comprehensive history of the early bans on Arab parties, see Ron Harris, *State Identity, Territorial Integrity and Party Banning: The Case of a Pan-Arab Political Party in Israel*, 4 SOCIO-LEGAL REV. 19 (2008).

[14] For an examination of the relationship between international law norms and claims of self-determination, see Patrick Macklem, *Militant Democracy, Legal Pluralism, and the Paradox of Self-Determination*, 4 INT'L J. CONST. L. 488, 504–10 (2006) (describing the debate in European law over the scope of claims to self-determination as a core democratic right).

party, which sought to present the same platform in European parliamentary elections.[15] Various Kurdish nationalist parties in Turkey, Sinn Féin in Northern Ireland, and numerous other examples pose the same issues. Second, any state – France, Turkey, Iraq, Israel, and Spain offer ready examples – can declare that its territorial boundaries are beyond the scope of proper political debate.

As a general matter, and for reasons recognized by John Stuart Mill nearly two centuries ago, the less severe the core divisions in a society, the easier is the task of democratization. Thus, in Eastern European states such as Poland or the Czech Republic, the path to post-Soviet consolidation of democratic governance has been generally smoother than in other parts of Eastern Europe where the sectional demands among different ethnic or religious groups have been more pressing.[16] In fractured societies, however, the restoration of democratic governance is likely to lead to an increase in sectional politics (the demise of Tito's Yugoslavia being a clear example), and may even lead to fratricidal conflict reflecting centuries of antagonisms (with the former Yugoslavia again the prime example). Particularly where a new political order has not been reestablished, the press for group political rights often blurs into support for armed separatist forces. Whether in Iraq, Eastern Ukraine, or Bosnia-Herzegovina, the politics of group protection and the mobilization of separatist militias are rarely far apart.

Precisely because separatist parties draw on a core of political grievances that correspond to group disadvantage, these parties are more difficult to manage than purely insurrectionary parties. First and foremost, there is a legitimacy problem. When the British government is accused of oppression in Northern Ireland, a prohibition on the most effective party of the Irish Catholics, Sinn Féin, is unlikely to be seen as anything but a further act of oppression. Absent fairly compelling evidence of violent activity by such a party, any prohibition will be seen as silencing the political activism of the only parties who will voice the grievances of these minority citizens.

Basques

The Basque Batasuna party provides a clear case in point. Batasuna is a pro-independence and socialist political party that has been historically tied

---

[15] *See* Thomas Ayres, *Batasuna Banned: The Dissolution of Political Parties Under the European Convention of Human Rights*, 27 B.C. INT'L & COMP. L. REV. 99, 109 (2004).

[16] *See* Paul G. Lewis, *The "Third Wave" of Democracy in Eastern Europe: Comparative Perspectives on Party Roles and Political Development*, 7 PARTY POL. 543, 558–60 (2001) ("[T]he ethnically homogenous nature of many east-central European states facilitated rapid democratization").

to ETA, the Basque equivalent of the Provisional wing of the Irish Republican Army. ETA began as a militant group fighting for Basque autonomy against the Franco dictatorship. During that period, its targets were police or military officials and the group enjoyed considerable support not only within the Basque region, but also in much of Europe. With the transition to democracy after Franco's death in 1975, ETA paradoxically appeared to have become more violent and was implicated in a number of bombings of public places such as railroad stations and shopping centers that resulted in hundreds of fatalities, including many civilians.

In June 2002, the Spanish Parliament amended Article 9 of the Law of Political Parties, making it illegal for a party to conduct itself in a manner that endangers the democratic principles of the country,[17] but only if done "repeatedly and seriously." After the law was amended, the legislature requested that the Supreme Court of Spain ban Batasuna under the new Article 9. Although initially "brought to trial for failing to condemn the violent activities of the military organization ETA," Batasuna was subsequently characterized by Spain as being "inseparable from ETA, providing the military operation both funding and logistic support."[18]

While most of the immediate charges against the party were related to the Batasuna refusal to censure the ETA for a bombing attack against civil guard barracks that killed two people, the problem was far deeper.[19] ETA, and by extension Batasuna, never accepted the legitimacy of the Spanish state, whether headed by Franco or by democratically elected leaders. ETA was the inspirational force behind Basque independence demands, just as the IRA had been in Northern Ireland during the time of "the Troubles." Batasuna refused to distance itself from the violence of ETA, but so too did Basque public support refuse to reject Batasuna. When the Spanish Supreme Court and then the Spanish Constitutional Court upheld the ban on Batasuna, the Basque regional government decried the prohibition as "unjust" and "criminalizing the majority of the Basques."[20]

The reasoning of the Spanish Constitutional Court highlights the distinction between what suffices as a basis for a criminal conviction and permissible grounds for the banning of the party. The court did not directly associate

---

[17] Ayres, *supra* note 16, at 101–02.

[18] ALEXANDER S. KIRSHNER, A THEORY OF MILITANT DEMOCRACY: THE ETHICS OF COMBATTING POLITICAL EXTREMISM 90 (New Haven, CT: Yale University Press, 2014).

[19] Leslie Crawford, *Spain Set to Decide on Banning Basque Party*, Fin. Times Ltd., Aug. 23, 2002, at 1.

[20] Elizabeth Nash, *Spain Hails Capture of "Most Brutal ETA Leaders,"* The Indep., Sept. 18, 2002, at 10.

Batasuna with participation in terrorist acts, only with using its political platform to promote the paramilitary activity of ETA:

> The fact that convicted terrorists are regularly appointed to positions of leadership or entered on lists of candidates for election may appear to constitute an expression of support for terrorist methods which goes against the obligations imposed by the Constitution on all political parties. Furthermore, the fact that such a practice can be taken into account only if the convicted terrorists have not "publicly rejected terrorist aims and methods" cannot be interpreted as an obligation to disavow earlier activities. The provision in question [section 9(3)(c)] is of prospective effect only and applies only to political parties which are led by convicted terrorists or whose candidates are convicted terrorists. It lays down as a cause of dissolution the regular use of people who may legitimately be assumed to sympathise with terrorist methods rather than with any ideas and programmes that terrorist organisations might seek to implement.[21]

In turn, the Batasuna ban was upheld by the European Court of Human Rights (ECHR) in 2009 on the grounds that the core values of Batasuna presented a significant danger to Spanish democracy. According to the ECHR, the political advocacy of a lawful political party must respect two conditions:

> [F]irstly, the means used to that end must in every respect be legal and democratic; secondly, the change proposed must itself be compatible with fundamental democratic principles. It necessarily follows that a political party whose leaders incite to violence or put forward a policy which fails to respect democracy or which is aimed at the destruction of democracy and the flouting of the rights and freedoms recognised in a democracy cannot lay claim to the [European] Convention's protection.[22]

Still, while it is true that Batasuna may have been intertwined with ETA's illegal actions, the matter does not end there. Regional autonomy is a serious political issue in Spain, and Catalan independent governance was achieved without recourse to the violence associated with ETA. This necessarily complicates the case for the exclusion of the largest Basque pro-autonomy party from the political arena. The mixture of regional resentment, traditional political mobilizations, and a violent paramilitary wing is not easy to disentangle. As Nancy Rosenblum notes, this raises the difficult question of how to determine the party's level of complicity with and commitment to violence: "When

---

[21] *Herri Batasuna and Batasuna v. Spain*, App. Nos. 25803/04, 25817/04, at ¶ 22 (Eur. Ct. H.R. June 30, 2009) (quoting the decision of the Spanish Constitutional Court).

[22] *Id.* ¶ 79.

are members' actions representative and imputable to the party, and what is the party's responsibility to discipline or expel leaders or members whose actions violate the law?"[23]

Kurds

Turkey provides yet another troubling example. The Turkish Constitution expressly prohibits any challenges to "the independence of the State, its indivisible integrity with its territory and nation."[24] The constitution authorizes the Turkish Constitutional Court to ban permanently any political party that has violated this constitutional clause.[25] As promulgated in Law No. 2820, the criteria for banning political parties include any attempt to eradicate fundamental rights and freedoms, incitement of religious discrimination, or actions that generally endanger the existence of the Turkish republic.[26]

These provisions have been used in the past to enforce a ban on the Turkish Communist Party. The Turkish court found that the party's program "covering support for non-Turkish languages and cultures [was] intended to create minorities, to the detriment of the unity of the Turkish nation."[27] Although the prohibition was subsequently overturned by the ECHR,[28] the efforts to ban the Communist Party show the extreme sensitivity of Turkey historically to any efforts to assert national minority rights.

Of immediate interest is the application of the territorial integrity principle to direct prohibitions on various Kurdish parties. These are difficult cases because, once again, the suppression of Kurdish political advocacy comes very close to the outright repression of a disfavored national minority. In 1992, the government accused the Kurdish Halkin Emek Partisi (People's Labor Party or HEP) of promoting Kurdish separatism "with the aim of destroying the 'inseparable unity'" of the Turkish state.[29] In deciding to dissolve the party, the Turkish Constitutional Court[30] attempted to draw a distinction between

---

[23] Rosenblum, *supra* note 1, at 425.

[24] TURK. CONST. art. 68, *available at* http://global.tbmm.gov.tr/docs/constitution_en.pdf.

[25] *Id.* art. 69.

[26] Law No. 2820 has not been translated from Turkish. The relevant provision, § 78, is translated in *Refah Partisi (The Welfare Party) v. Turkey*, 2003-II Eur. Ct. H.R. 267, 289–90.

[27] *United Communist Party of Turkey v. Turkey*, 1998-I Eur. Ct. H.R. 1, 10.

[28] *Id.* at 39.

[29] *See* Dicle Kogacioglu, *Dissolution of Political Parties by the Constitutional Court in Turkey: Judicial Delimitation of the Political Domain*, 18 Int'l Soc. 258, 263 (2003).

[30] The decision of the constitutional court has not been translated from Turkish. It is thoughtfully discussed by Dicle Kogacioglu. *See id.*

everyday life – where following a distinct cultural tradition is legitimate – and politics, where invoking that same tradition becomes an illegitimate political claim that threatens state unity and public order.[31] The court found that the use of the Kurdish language in the realm of politics was, like other activities of HEP, an indication of a forbidden commitment to "separatism" that threatened to compromise the unity of the state.[32]

The Turkish court's initial rulings in the HEP case were later overturned by the ECHR, which held that dissolving HEP was a violation of the right of free association and fined the Turkish government.[33] However, this was hardly the last word on the issue. The Turkish court again upheld the suppression of Kurdish parties on the grounds that their endorsement of Kurdish national claims and championing of Kurdish grievances violated the territorial integrity of the Turkish state or represented a rejection of democracy as such, decisions that the ECHR overruled in 1999 and 2002.[34]

Yazar v. Turkey,[35] a 2002 case again involving HEP, is particularly instructive. The Turkish Constitutional Court had upheld the banning of HEP on the ground that the party's platform undermined the integrity of the state by "seeking to divide the Turkish nation in two, with Turks on one side and Kurds on the other, with the aim of establishing separate States."[36] This case closely resembles the ECHR's upholding of the ban on Batasuna in the Basque context. A critical factual underpinning was HEP's refusal to denounce the aims of the Partiya Karkerên Kurdistan (PKK), an insurrectionary Kurdish force with a history of terrorist attacks on Turkish targets. According to the Turkish court, HEP referred to the PKK as "freedom fighters" and described the guerrilla fighting as an "international" conflict between distinct national forces.[37]

The ECHR also overturned this prohibition, relying on Article 11 of the European Convention that guarantees basic rights of association and assembly, including the right to form political parties.[38] Article 11 denies states the ability to restrict the right of association except to the extent that such a measure

---

[31] *See id.* at 265.

[32] *Id.*

[33] *See id.* at 271.

[34] *See Yazar v. Turkey,* 2002-II Eur. Ct. H.R. 395; *Freedom and Democracy Party (ÖZDEP) v. Turkey,* 1999-VIII Eur. Ct. H.R. 293.

[35] 2002-II Eur. Ct. H.R. 395.

[36] *Yazar,* 2002-II Eur. Ct. H.R. at 402 (internal quotation marks omitted) (quoting the Turkish Constitutional Court).

[37] *Id.*

[38] The application of Article 11 to political parties originated in *United Communist Party of Turkey v. Turkey,* 1998-I Eur. Ct. H.R. 1.

is "necessary in a democratic society in the interests of national security or public safety ... or for the protection of the rights and freedoms of others."[39] In rejecting Turkey's claim that HEP's propaganda lent tacit support to the PKK, the ECHR appeared particularly solicitous of the right of advocacy on behalf of national minorities, so long as there was no direct advocacy of the use of force or violence and so long as the political party remained faithful to democratic principles.[40] "In the absence of any calls for the use of violence or any other illegal methods," the ECHR decreed:

> [I]f merely by advocating those principles [of national self-determination] a political group were held to be supporting acts of terrorism, that would reduce the possibility of dealing with related issues in the context of a democratic debate and would allow armed movements to monopolise support for the principles in question....
>
> Moreover, the Court considers that, even if proposals inspired by such principles are likely to clash with the main strands of government policy or the convictions of the majority of the public, it is necessary for the proper functioning of democracy that political groups should be able to introduce them into public debate in order to help find solutions to general problems concerning politicians of all persuasions.[41]

The result is that under emerging European law, separatist parties, like insurrectionary parties, are given a broad swath of protection so long as they are not engaged in actual incitement or violent acts against the democratic regime. In the case of separatist parties, the overlay with the claims of an embattled minority should enhance the level of judicial solicitude for these parties and restrict the ambit of permissible state suppression.

Less clear is the apparent distinction between the Spanish and Turkish settings. Likely, there are two sources of demarcation. The first is that Spain in the twenty-first century is a well-established democratic regime that has shown, as with Catalan devolution, a capacity to accommodate nonviolent demands for regional or national minority autonomy. The immediacy and extreme violence of ETA's campaign of terror in the heart of Spain tips the scales of Batasuna away from democratic participation and in the direction

---

[39] European Convention for the Protection of Human Rights and Fundamental Freedoms art. 11, ¶ 2, Nov. 4, 1950, 213 U.N.T.S. 221.

[40] *Yazar*, 2002-II Eur. Ct. H.R. at 413–14; *see also id.* at 413 ("[T]he HEP did not express any explicit support for or approval of the use of violence for political ends. Furthermore, incitement to ethnic hatred and incitement to insurrection are criminal offences in Turkey. At the material time, however, none of the HEP's leaders had been convicted of any such offence.").

[41] *Id.* at 413–14.

of accomplice to violence. In the Kurdish context, the government's aims appeared less tolerant and the threat perhaps more remote. The simpler answer, and at the very least a likely contributing factor, may be that Turkey has received less solicitude from the ECHR than post-Franco Spain. A further complicating fact may be the apparent Turkish eagerness to ban any party showing solicitude for Kurdish national grievances.

The next chapter will address the range of tools that democracies use, showing that the ultimate punishment of prohibition is not the only means available. For example, Belgium does not permit the banning of political parties, but reserves the right to deny state support to parties that "show clearly and repeatedly their hostility toward the rights and freedoms protected in the European Convention on Human Rights and its additional protocols."[42] Alternatively, if the issue is the misdirection of funds to violent organizations, internal audits might serve as a less restrictive means of achieving the same objective while allowing a mechanism for state vigilance. Regardless of the means of disciplining the parties, however, the link to the cause of regional autonomy lends an air of retaliation to the banning of a separatist party, despite its problematic ties to paramilitary activity.

MASS ANTIDEMOCRATIC MOBILIZATIONS

The hardest case for party suppression comes from parties that incite mass antidemocratic mobilizations. This category of parties poses a far more acute threat to a democratic society than the dangers emerging from separatist movements or groups with goals of insurrection. The latter two types of parties, generally, neither want nor have the ability to gain enough control over the national electorate to dismantle the democratic order. Instead, those parties are suppressed when they either are actually involved in unlawful or paramilitary activities, or are sufficiently implicated by association with those that are.

By contrast, the urgency of democratic self-protection against mass-based, electorally significant antidemocratic parties is the historical legacy of the twentieth century. The concept of militant democracy emerges from the response to the Nazis in Germany and the fascists in Italy taking power through internal democratic pathways, as well as from the need to forestall the role that parliamentary disruption played in facilitating the rise of antidemocratic groups. The form of these antidemocratic groups has changed. Today,

---

[42] *See* Gur Bligh, *Defending Democracy: A New Understanding of the Party-Banning Phenomenon*, 46 Vand. J. Transnat'l L. 1321, 1376 (2013) ("Belgium does not have a party-banning regime but does allow for the temporary denial of state subsidies to political [parties].").

they are more likely to be based on religious fundamentalism, as with some Islamist parties, or on ties to a deposed authoritarian regime, as with remnants of the communist parties of Eastern Europe. But regardless of the reigning ideology of the parties, the threat persists from the efforts to use majoritarian democratic processes to dismantle liberal democracy.

Parties that lead or incite mass antidemocratic mobilizations are unique in that they can be – and frequently are – suppressed without regard to their use of violence, relationships to terrorist organizations, or similar activities that threaten to destroy or fracture the existing democratic order. Here, the use of legitimate democratic processes to destabilize democracy within the country complicates the relationship between a party and its prohibition. There is an inherent difficulty with any government being allowed to claim that a group with substantial popular support – one that has had its members elected to influential positions and may even constitute a plurality in government – is a threat to democracy. Removing a party from office or from the electoral slate because of its popular support necessarily raises questions about the democratic legitimacy of the regime invoking the authority to suppress the expressed will of a substantial portion of the population.

At its most calamitous, this tension is illustrated by Algeria's confrontation with a mass antidemocratic movement, which led to civil war, thousands of deaths, and ensuing military rule. The country held its first multiparty election in three decades in December 1991, in which the Islamic Salvation Front (FIS) party ran on a platform of turning Algeria into an Islamic state. At least some FIS candidates were committed to using the ability of a supermajority in parliament to amend the constitution to end democratic elections, while others seemed openly hostile to democracy as such.[43] FIS won 189 seats in parliament in the first round of elections, effectively ensuring that the Islamists would win enough seats in the second round of elections to be able to amend constitutional provisions at their whim.[44] The aim of abolishing democracy was confirmed when, upon the first round victory, some FIS leaders publicly stated that "Islam is light ... darkness is in democracy," a claim that appeared to equate an FIS achievement of complete legislative power in the second election with the transformation of Algeria into an Islamic state without democratic order.[45]

---

[43] Gregory H. Fox & Georg Nolte, *Intolerant Democracies*, 36 HARV. INT'L L.J. 1,6 (1995).
[44] Peter A. Samuelson, *Pluralism Betrayed: The Battle between Secularism and Islam in Algeria's Quest for Democracy*, 20 YALE J. INT'L L. 309, 317 (1995) ("FIS needed only 28 more seats to win an absolute majority in the second round of elections.").
[45] *Id.*

The denouement was no more inspiring. The second round of the election was canceled as the military seized power in January 1992. Not only were all further elections canceled, but the new military rulers also ordered the arrest of FIS members, banned the party, and declared a state of emergency. The FIS was driven underground and Algeria plunged into a drawn-out civil war that left many tens of thousands dead. What was left of the FIS emerged as various armed guerrilla groups whose targets expanded over time from military and police authorities to civilians.

Algeria's military reaction to a perceived mass Islamist threat is an inspiring story for no one. At issue, however, is not militant democracy fighting to protect itself but an unbounded military response to a civilian challenge. Any debate about the relative merits or failings of the FIS and the military rulers takes us outside the framework of this book. The choice was between two forms of terminating any democratic prospects in Algeria. Instead, the issue for democracies under siege is whether a legally constrained response could have salvaged democratic prospects and salvaged democratic governance as such.

In contrast, Turkey provides an example of a nation with at best a troubled democratic tradition responding to Islamist political mobilization under legal oversight generally, and court review in particular.

Modern Turkish history begins with the muscular efforts of Kemal Ataturk to compel rapid Westernization after the collapse of the Ottoman empire. The Turkish Constitution is an extraordinary document, reflecting its origins in the efforts to create a Western liberal society in a country far removed from the European mainstream. The Turkish Constitution's preamble enshrines the principles of Ataturk, "the immortal leader and the unrivalled hero"[46] of the Republic of Turkey: "no activity can be protected contrary to ... the reforms and modernization of Ataturk and ... , as required by the principle of [secularism], sacred religious feelings can in no way be permitted to interfere with state affairs and politics." While all constitutions limit procedurally and substantively what democratic majorities may obtain from ordinary political power, the Turkish Constitution goes a step further in entrenching a set of principles that are far beyond any form of political consensus in that country, and uses restrictions on access to the political process to enforce the underlying constitutional commitment. Thus, based on the Kemalian vision of Turkey as a "democratic, [secular] ... state,"[47] the constitution prohibits political parties from interfering with "the principles of the democratic and [secular] republic"; it also mandates that they "can not aim to support or to

[46] TURK. CONST. pmbl.
[47] *Id.* art. 2.

establish a dictatorship of class or group or dictatorship of any kind, and nor [can] they encourage the commitment of offence."[48]

Against this backdrop, two different bodies – the Turkish Constitutional Court and the military – emerged as the most vigilant enforcers of the Kemalist constitutional order, and particularly its commitment to Turkish secularism. The history of enforced secularism under the Turkish Constitution is complicated, to say the least. When the state has been threatened by the rise of charismatic Islamist politicians or mass-based Islamist parties, the court and the military have emerged as the two institutions most inclined to prevent any kind of Islamic political mobilization. This history includes military interventions both overt and covert, jailing of opposition leaders, and a host of measures beyond the scope of the democratically tolerable.

Both the court and the military have used the preamble's secularism clause as a vehicle to prevent Islamist political mobilization, measures that have not all been confined to lawful acts.[49] However, Turkey moved to greater reliance on the legal arena to constrain the political mobilization of Islamist parties, particularly since Turkey's efforts at integration into the European Union – however futile those may now appear – got under way in the 1990s.

The most significant case, and the one that dominates in this area of law, is that of the Refah Partisi (Welfare Party), a mass-based Islamist group that grew to be one of the largest parties in the Turkish Parliament. By 1996, the party had secured widespread popular support, held a dominating plurality in the Turkish Parliament, and was the central force behind the coalition government it had helped form. The growth of the Welfare Party both established its democratic importance and magnified the risk presented if it were in fact hostile to democratic challenge.

Perhaps because its strong constituency made it the likely head of the next government, secular authorities in the judiciary decided to stage a confrontation. The party was accused of conducting activities that were "contrary to the principle of secularism," charges that would place it outside the bounds of electoral politics in Turkey. The motivation for the charges was likely the fact that most believed that the party would gain outright control of the legislature in the next election because of a coalition agreement with another party. The charges were upheld within the Turkish system, and the Turkish Constitutional Court subsequently ordered that the Welfare Party dissolve,

---

[48] *Id.* art. 68.
[49] For a good overview from the perspective of defending the democratic rights of Islamic parties, see NOAH FELDMAN, AFTER JIHAD: AMERICA AND THE STRUGGLE FOR ISLAMIC DEMOCRACY 105–11 (New York: Farrar, Straus and Giroux, 2003).

that it forfeit all of its assets to the state, and that four duly elected Welfare Party members be removed from the legislature. Further, the court decreed that Refah Party officials were prohibited from holding public office for five years.

The Welfare Party case is steeped in Turkish political history, centering largely on Professor Necmettin Erbakan. In 1970, Professor Erbakan founded the Milli Nizam Partisi (National Order Party or NOP). At the core of the NOP's platform was a plan for what it termed *domestic spiritual overhaul*, which included permitting public exercise of religion and closing secular entertainment venues.[50] After the constitutional court banned the NOP, holding that the party platform promoted "Revolutionary Religion" in violation of the constitution, Professor Erbakan founded a successor party, the Milli Selamet Partisi (National Salvation Party or NSP). The NSP was similarly banned and ordered dissolved by a military regime that came into power in 1980 and – after eliminating all political parties – ordered the Islamist political leaders to stand trial.[51]

Upon the reinstatement of civilian rule, the same minuet resumed. Professor Erbakan founded the Welfare Party, a party little changed from its earlier incarnations. The Welfare Party emerged as the strongest force in parliament and formed a government with two smaller, more centrist parties. When the time came for the Welfare Party to assume control of the government under its coalition agreement, its coalition partners recoiled and the constitutional court dissolved the party, holding that it was a "'centre' … of activities contrary to the principles of secularism."[52] Even allowing for the disputed factual premises of the charges against the Welfare Party, the harder question is how to resolve the tension created by a secularist constitution that is increasingly discordant with mass religious aspirations presented in the democratic process. The fact that the immediate charges against the Welfare Party, and the timing of those charges, may have been pretextual does not avoid the deeper conflict over an asserted national interest in suppressing excessive Islamist politics.

The Welfare Party conflict becomes all the more interesting because Turkey, as a signatory to the European Convention on Human Rights, has accepted the ample jurisdiction of the European Court of Human Rights since at least

[50] See Susanna Dokupil, *The Separation of Mosque and State: Islam and Democracy in Modern Turkey*, 105 W. VA. L. REV. 53, 83 (2002).
[51] See Talip Kucukcan, *State, Islam, and Religious Liberty in Modern Turkey: Reconfiguration of Religion in the Public Sphere*, 2003 B.Y.U. L. REV. 475, 492.
[52] Lance S. Lehnhof, Note, *Freedom of Religious Association: The Right of Religious Organizations to Obtain Legal Entity Status under the European Convention*, 2002 B.Y.U. L. REV. 561, 578 (internal quotation marks omitted) (quoting *Refah Partisi (The Welfare Party) v. Turkey*, 2003-II Eur. Ct. H.R. 267, 276).

1990. This means that the decision of the Turkish Constitutional Court was subject to review by the ECHR to check its conformity with the rights to political organization and expression guaranteed by the International Convention on Civil and Political Rights. For the Turkish Constitutional Court, it was sufficient that Professor Erbakan had made cryptic speeches that could be viewed as a call for religious rule under principles of Sharia: "Refah will come to power and a just [social] order will be established. The question we must ask ourselves is whether this change will be violent or peaceful; whether it will entail bloodshed."[53] But for the ECHR, the fundamental inquiry was whether a Turkish commitment to constitutionally enforced secularism was a legitimate grounds to ban an Islamist party. After all, many of the leading liberal states of Western Europe themselves had an established church, with Great Britain and Denmark being ready examples.

Stated otherwise, the question before the ECHR had two aspects. The first was whether a state could in fact decide, as a matter of constitutional precommitment, that secularism was a compelling state interest. The second was whether the state could take actions to protect its constitutional order from challenge, even by a mass electoral movement that had not engaged in any overt actions against the legal order.

On the first, somewhat surprisingly, the ECHR endorsed secularism as among "the fundamental principles of the [Turkish] State which are in harmony with the rule of law and respect for human rights and democracy."[54] This is a broad claim, but somewhat off the mark. The question is not whether Turkey could commit itself to secularism consistent with a respect for human rights and democracy, but whether Turkey could ban *advocacy* of a different accommodation of church and state by closing its political process to adherents of a different order. Worse yet, the ECHR coupled its holding with a gratuitous swipe at Islam more broadly, stating that "sharia is incompatible with the fundamental principles of democracy, as set forth in the [European] Convention."[55] A difficult case on the boundaries of democratic constraints was thus unfortunately intertwined with a disregard for the ability to integrate Islam into a democratic order – a sweeping claim that was certainly unnecessary to the resolution of the status of the Refah Party. Given the establishment of Christianity in several of the founding states of the European Union, the ECHR's dictum could not avoid being seen as an insult to Islam as such.

[53] See *Refah Partisi (The Welfare Party) v. Turkey*, 2003-II Eur. Ct. H.R. 267, 282 (alteration in original) (quoting part of a speech by Erbakan relied on by the Turkish court as evidence of the Welfare Party's anti-secular activities).

[54] *Id.* at 302.

[55] *Id.* at 312.

Turning to the capacity of the state to act, the ECHR reaffirmed the central tenets of militant democracy. As the court explained, the lack of overt unconstitutional acts by the Refah Party was not dispositive of the state's ability to resort to legal intervention against it:

> [A] State cannot be required to wait, before intervening, until a political party has seized power and begun to take concrete steps to implement a policy incompatible with the standards of the Convention and democracy, even though the danger of that policy for democracy is sufficiently established and imminent.... [W]here the presence of such a danger has been established by the national courts, after detailed scrutiny subjected to rigorous European supervision, a State may reasonably forestall the execution of such a policy ... before an attempt is made to implement it through concrete steps that might prejudice civil peace and the country's democratic regime.[56]

At no point did the ECHR demand proof of the imminence of democracy's demise. The court noted that "Refah had the real potential to seize political power"; however, that was evidence not of the immediacy of the threat posed by its principles, but simply of the fact that the threat could have been realized.[57] There was no suggestion that Refah's program was so imminent as to constitute a direct threat of the sort posed by an insurrectionary party. But, more to the point, what was undertaken in Turkey was not a criminal prosecution of Refah members or leaders, but a disqualification from organizing an electorally based political party to pursue what the courts perceived as intolerant aims.

On first impression, the opinion jars many democratic sensibilities, particularly those formed in the free speech environment of the United States. The condemnation of all sharia was far too sweeping, and the court almost certainly applied a different standard to Islam than would have been applied to any Christian faith. Further, the use of a deferential "reasonableness" standard for the political exclusion of a party with broad popular support gives a great deal of latitude to national determinations that are necessarily problematic. Nonetheless, the effect of the court's ruling seemed the best that anyone could have hoped for. Under the pressure of prohibitions for its proclaimed aim of imposing clerical rule, the Welfare Party fractured.

Unlike the earlier prohibitions, which simply declared the various incarnations of Professor Erbakan's movement illegal through either court action or military intervention, the Turkish Constitutional Court decision upheld by

---

[56] *Id.* at 305 (internal quotation marks omitted).
[57] *Id.* at 307.

the ECHR targeted certain electoral objectives more surgically. The decision left in place a sizeable bloc of the former Refah Party in parliament, still with tremendous authority over national politics. Under these circumstances, the prospect of reintegration into Turkish politics remained present subject to a tempering of the perceived threats to continued democratic order.

The result was that a moderate wing led by former Istanbul mayor Recep Tayyip Erdogan, himself a former protégé of Professor Erbakan, broke off to form the Justice and Development Party, a far more moderate Islamist party. In 2002, Erdogan became prime minister when Justice and Development emerged as the largest bloc in parliament. Under his tutelage, Turkey has pursued its ultimately unsuccessful efforts at EU integration, and emerged as a bastion of moderation in the Middle East.[58] Far from creating an insuperable barrier to an Islamic voice in Turkish politics, the dissolution of the Welfare Party appears to have sparked a realignment in which committed democratic voices from the self-proclaimed Islamic communities found a means of integration into mainstream Turkish political life.

Although the struggle over Islamization continues to dominate Turkish political life, it does so within the confines of electoral battles. The political aspirations of Islamist parties as electoral forces presented, as Professor Nancy Rosenblum argues, an opportunity for democratic integration as "political entrepreneurs come to judge that their ambitions are better served by effectively signaling moderation than by maintaining oppositional poses to preserve 'base' support; and perhaps above all by the iteration of elections and political learning."[59] Looked on ten years hence, the rise of Erdogan was not the last word in the struggle between a constitutional commitment to secularism and significant popular support for Islamist politics. But under the circumstances of a conflict between a constitutional order without popular backing and a rising democratic movement demanding change, it is difficult to imagine a better outcome.

The intervening years no doubt color the assessment of Erdogan's leadership. Secular institutions are embattled, efforts at constitutional reform persist, and the once effective administration of a booming economy has yielded to constant charges of corruption and cronyism. Opponents of the regime are increasingly subject to arrest and criminal charges, and in 2012 and 2013, Turkey had the unfortunate distinction of having more journalists in prison

[58] *See* Thomas Patrick Carroll, *Turkey's Justice and Development Party: A Model for Democratic Islam?*, 6 MIDDLE E. INTELLIGENCE BULL. No. 6–7 (2004), http://www.meib.org/articles/0407_t1.htm.

[59] Nancy L. Rosenblum, *Banning Parties*, 1 LAW & ETHICS HUM. RTS. 17, 74 (2007).

than any other country in the world. As will be discussed in the second part of this book, however, these are the characteristic debilities of a democracy without electoral challenge, not a product of the Islamist orientation of the Justice and Development Party. That Erdogan has been in office too long and without sufficient challenge is distinct from the question of whether the emergence of a reasonably tolerant Justice and Development movement out of the suppressed Refah Party was a step forward for Turkey. At least the bulk of Erdogan's tenure in office indicates that it was.

4

Responses to Antidemocratic Threats

Until quite recently, most scholarly discussions of the restrictions on antidemocratic groups began (and many of them ended) with the question of whether a democracy *ever* has the right to impose viewpoint constraints on extreme dissident views. Professors Gregory Fox and Georg Nolte, for example, in their important contribution to the debate, primarily focused on the possibility of restricting political participation consistent with international law, particularly the guarantees of the 1966 International Covenant on Civil and Political Rights.[1] The responses to Professors Fox and Nolte did not question their analytic framework; instead, they simply challenged the capacity of any society to police the boundaries of something as nebulous as "democracy"[2] and questioned whether the remaining product was worthy of the name:

> If one is to say to the people, in essence, "The fundamental principle of democracy dictates that you can have any government except the one the majority of you presently think you want," there had better be a more compelling argument for democracy than that it enables the people to choose. There is nothing intrinsically valuable about choosing among undesired options.[3]

Although these critiques take a back seat to claims that suppression does not work,[4] all of these arguments tend to lump together the different sorts

---

[1]   Gregory H. Fox & Georg Nolte, *Intolerant Democracies*, 36 HARV. INT'L L.J. 1 (1995).
[2]   *See, e.g.*, Brad R. Roth, Response, *Democratic Intolerance: Observations on Fox and Nolte*, 37 HARV. INT'L L.J. 235, 236 (1996) ("'[D]emocracy' has in recent parlance been transmogrified into a repository of political virtues.... The consequence of this indeterminacy is that 'democracy' becomes identified with whichever choice engages our sympathies.").
[3]   *Id.* at 237.
[4]   *See, e.g.*, Edip Yuksel, *Cannibal Democracies, Theocratic Secularism: The Turkish Version*, 7 CARDOZO J. INT'L & COMP. L. 423, 458 (1999).

of responses that might be deployed against antidemocratic threats. More recently, however, "consensus has emerged on the fundamental principle underlying the theory and practice of militant democracy: Democracies have a right … to limit fundamental rights of free expression and participation – albeit with various qualifications and caveats – for reasons of self-preservation."[5] The idea that *every* political viewpoint is entitled to participate in the political arena "has virtually no supporters today."[6] Even staunch advocates of protecting political parties such as Nancy Rosenblum acknowledge that there are times when, quite simply, "the facts justify banning" a party.[7]

Rather than questioning whether prohibitions of antidemocratic forces are ever possible, it is more fruitful to begin by focusing on what kinds of prohibitions are permissible and under what circumstances. Here, I diverge from American case law, which tends to collapse the question of prohibitions on political parties into the debate over what criminal sanctions on political speech are justified. As set forth in the opening discussion of this part of the book, the point of departure here is the form of political restraint that operates outside the bounds of the criminal justice system. The inquiry concerns the existence of a space between the standards that justify incarceration and those that might suffice to justify a prohibition on electoral participation. Put simply, are there methods to suppress antidemocratic political mobilizations that are distinct from criminally prosecuting their adherents, and can those methods be justified even if we would not tolerate incarceration for those who share the antidemocratic viewpoints?

In rough form, consider three different approaches to antidemocratic mobilizations in the electoral arena that are distinct from criminal prosecutions of the advocates of the underlying positions: first, the proscription of political parties that fail to accept some fundamental tenet of the social order; second, an electoral code governing the content of political appeals; and third, a ban on electoral participation for some political parties, even if they are permitted to maintain a party organization. The first two approaches represent the general range of established responses to antidemocratic agitation, stretching from regulations of electoral conduct to prohibitions on the organization of political parties. The third option – the ban on electoral eligibility but not on

5   Giovanni Capoccia, *Militant Democracy: The Institutional Bases of Democratic Self-Preservation*, 9 ANN. REV. L. SOC. SCI. 207, 210–11 (2013).

6   *Id.* at 211.

7   NANCY L. ROSENBLUM, ON THE SIDE OF THE ANGELS 414 (Princeton, NJ: Princeton University Press, 2008). For a recent, forceful defense of militant democracy, see ALEXANDER S. KIRSHNER, A THEORY OF MILITANT DEMOCRACY: THE ETHICS OF COMBATTING POLITICAL EXTREMISM (New Haven, CT: Yale University Press, 2014).

party formation – is less established as a form of party regulation. Nonetheless, this intermediate form of regulation offers an intriguing, less restrictive means of addressing the unique problems of antidemocratic mobilization through electoral activity.

PARTY EXCLUSION

Party exclusion has come to represent the typical response to antidemocratic threats. The formal recognition of party exclusion of groups deemed fundamentally hostile to democracy comes from the German postwar constitution. Where a group is identified with a clear threat to democracy, as with pro-Nazi groups in Germany after 1945, the question of their exclusion under now conventional European law is beyond dispute. There are always evidentiary issues about whether the groups are really as claimed, as well as pragmatic concerns about whether often truly marginal antidemocratic groups are better off ignored. The issue is more problematic, however, when the grounds of party exclusion move beyond the simpler cases of proponents of a totalitarian *ancien régime*, as with neo-Nazis in Germany or Soviet restorationists from the old communist parties of Eastern Europe.

Turkey provides the most developed expression of the emerging European law on party exclusions, starting with the Kurdish cases discussed in the prior chapter. The ultimate difficulty in the Turkish cases comes from the hard lines drawn in the Turkish constitution over Turkish national identity and secularism. Thus, the Turkish constitutional preamble expressly enshrines the territorial integrity of the Turkish nation:"[N]o protection shall be accorded to an activity contrary to Turkish national interests [or] Turkish existence and the principle of its indivisibility with its State and territory."[8] Moreover, the Turkish Constitution goes on to forbid challenges to "the independence of the State [and] its indivisible integrity with its territory and nation."[9] In turn, the Turkish Constitutional Court is empowered to dissolve any political party that threatens the integrity of the state. Law No. 2820, which governs the formation and conduct of political parties, forbids parties that "jeopardize the existence of the Turkish State and Republic, abolish fundamental rights and freedoms, introduce discrimination on grounds of ... religion or membership of a religious sect, or establish ... a system of government based on any such notion or concept."[10]

---

[8] Turk. Const. pmbl., *available at* http://global.tbmm.gov.tr/docs/constitution_en.pdf.
[9] *Id.* art. 68.
[10] Law No. 2820 has not been translated from Turkish. The relevant provision, § 78, is translated in *Refah Partisi (The Welfare Party) v. Turkey*, 2003-II Eur. Ct. H.R. 267, 289–90.

As discussed in the previous chapter, the European Court of Human Rights (ECHR) has upheld prohibitions by the Turkish Constitutional Court against Islamic parties that, in its view, threatened to compromise democratic rights by promising to alter the fundamentally secular nature of the Turkish state. By contrast, the ECHR has repeatedly protected Kurdish political expression in Turkey, and done so by overruling the Turkish Constitutional Court's invocation of its commitment to territorial integrity (as opposed to secularity in the case of the Islamic parties). The contrast between the ECHR's deference to the Turkish national judiciary's treatment of Islamic parties and its strict and exacting review of the prohibitions on the Kurdish parties in Turkey requires some explanation. To begin with, the ECHR in the Kurdish cases relied on a robust application of Article 11 of the European Convention on Human Rights, the basic guarantee of associational rights.[11] Under Article 11, "[e]veryone has the right to freedom of peaceful assembly and to freedom of association with others," and any "restrictions ... placed on the exercise of these rights" must be "necessary in a democratic society in the interests of national security or public safety, for the prevention of disorder or crime, for the protection of health or morals or for the protection of the rights and freedoms of others."[12]

Despite its strong language and seemingly broad scope, Article 11 was not applied to the protection of political parties until the relatively recent case of *United Communist Party of Turkey v. Turkey*.[13] There too the Turkish Constitutional Court had applied the broad powers of party regulation to dissolve Türkiye Birleşik Komünist Partisithe (United Communist Party of Turkey or TBKP) and ban its party leaders from office. According to the constitutional court, the party's program "covering support for non-Turkish languages and cultures [was] intended to create minorities, to the detriment of the unity of the Turkish nation."[14] Such a broad prohibition seemingly contradicted the express guarantees of Article 11 of the European Convention on Human Rights, and only with great difficulty could be fit within the exceptions for national security or the prevention of disorder. Indeed, the prohibition was overturned by the ECHR for just this reason.[15]

The Kurdish party cases are more difficult to assess than the Communist Party case. Whereas the Turkish Constitutional Court had to read into the

---

[11] Convention for the Protection of Human Rights and Fundamental Freedoms art. 11, Nov. 4, 1950, 213 U.N.T.S. 221.

[12] *Id.*

[13] 1998-I Eur. Ct. H.R. 1.

[14] *Id.* at 10.

[15] *Id.* at 39.

Communist Party's platform an implicit rejection of Turkish territorial integrity from the generalized support for recognition of minorities, the Kurdish
parties pushed directly against Turkish authority over the Kurdish region.
At the same time, the Kurdish parties were the public transmission of the
long-standing grievances of the Turkish Kurds on matters ranging from language rights to forms of local governance. As a result, the Kurdish cases contained both a more direct confrontation with a core constitutional tenet of
Ataturk's legacy, and an ensuing outright repression of the political claims
of a disfavored national minority. Unless the ECHR were to condemn the
ability of a member state to protect its boundaries, the Turkish constitutional
commitment to territory did identify a legitimate state interest worthy of protection. Yet the claims of national oppression could not be so easily ignored.

A concrete example comes with the party prohibition of the People's
Democratic Party (HADEP), a party believed by Turkish officials to have links
with the Kurdish terrorist group Partiya Karkerên Kurdistan (PKK). HADEP
was established in 1994, and quickly garnered support among the Kurdish
sector of the electorate. By the time of the 1995 general election, HADEP
amassed more than 4 percent of the total vote, concentrated within the
Kurdish community.[16] Only after HADEP became a viable political party was
it accused of violating Article 69 of the Turkish Constitution, allegedly acting a puppet for the PKK and becoming a "center of illegal activities against
the integrity of Turkey."[17] Under Article 14, "None of the rights and freedoms
embodied in the Constitution shall be exercised with the aim of violating the
indivisible integrity of the state with its territory and nation, and endangering
the existence of the democratic and secular order of the Turkish Republic
based upon human rights." In the course of criminal proceedings, the prosecutor accused HADEP of disseminating propaganda that advocated for a
separatist movement and creating racial tension. For example, one specific
allegation lodged against HADEP by the prosecution was the raising of a PKK
flag and its substitution for the Turkish national flag during a HADEP meeting in 1996. The Turkish Constitutional Court dissolved HADEP for violating
a number of legal provisions including Article 69.

On appeal, the ECHR reversed the party prohibition. It would have been
intolerable to allow Article 14 of the Turkish Constitution to be a per se barrier to the assertion of nationality-based grievances of the Kurdish sections
of Turkey. At the same time, the ECHR had to avoid the freighted question

---

[16] *HADEP v. Turkey*, App. No. 28003/03, ¶¶ 1, 5, 6 (Eur. Ct. H.R. Dec. 14, 2010), *available at*
http://hudoc.echr.coe.int/sites/eng/pages/search.aspx?i=001-102256.

[17] *Id.* at ¶¶ 9, 23.

whether a state could use its defense of territorial integrity to ban political parties in general. Separatist movements abound in Europe and any recognition of a right to regional autonomy as such could compromise the United Kingdom, Spain, and efforts to stabilize the Balkans. Instead, the ECHR ruled narrowly and relied on the perceived insufficiency of the evidentiary record in proving the links between HADEP and the PKK.[18]

Another example is the Turkish attempt to ban the Halkin Emek Partisi (People's Labor Party or HEP), as was described in the previous chapter. Much as in the case addressing in the suspension of HADEP, the ECHR overturned the Turkish Constitutional Court's decision in the HEP case and fined the Turkish government, holding that dissolving HEP violated the party's freedom of association under European law.[19] The Turkish case studies are problematic under European law because the suppression of Kurdish-based political parties brings Turkey far too close to absolute repression of a political minority group. This reveals one of the tensions in employing political party prohibitions as a means of counterbalancing possible antidemocratic mobilizations: the state's response could simply be an illegitimate extinguishment of a minority voice.

At the same time, the party prohibitions enforced or attempted by the Turkish Constitutional Court ultimately led to the emergence of a moderate Islamic political party headed by Prime Minister Recep Tayyip Erdogan, and the 2010 constitutional amendments that sought to close the gap between the hard, nationalist, and secular constitution of Ataturk, and the more pluralist and Islamic demands of a majority of the population. Undoubtedly, the de facto bargain with the increasing Islamic orientation of the broad sectors of the Turkish was unlikely to be a long-term solution to the problem of an aging constitutional order. Specifically, the 2010 amendments permit elected legislators to remain in office even if the Turkish court dissolves their political party, giving a measure of protection against reassertion of court intervention into the political arena. While still too early to assess the results of these amendments, the primary effect should be to permit the parliamentary forum

---

[18] Turkish courts have responded to the ECHR by modulating its response to parties deemed threatening, such as responding to Islamist pressures by withdrawing half the state support from the Justice and Development Party (AKP) in 2008, rather than banning the party outright. BANU ELIGÜR, THE MOBILIZATION OF POLITICAL ISLAM IN TURKEY 269–790 (New York: Cambridge University Press, 2010). Later, the Venice Commission would call this financial strangling its "most controversial and politically intrusive" case. European Comm'n for Democracy Through Law [Venice Comm'n], *Opinion: Constitutional and Legal Provisions Relevant to the Prohibition of Political Parties in Turkey*, Op. No. 489/2008, § 98 (2009), *available at* http://www.venice.coe.int/webforms/documents/default.aspx?pdffile=CDL-AD (2009)006-e.

[19] *See id.* at 271.

to remain open to dissident voices even if the political parties stray uncomfortably into the domain of impermissible activities. Yet another factor that cannot yet be adequately assessed is Erdogan's recent victory as Turkey's first directly elected president, which may portend a diminution in the role of parliamentary sovereignty in Turkey.

POLICING AND REGULATING ELECTORAL SPEECH

Party prohibitions begin from the premise that participation in the political arena carries the privilege of freedom of action. Thus, the sanction for abuse of that privilege is removal from the open political arena through the suspension or dissolution of an offending political party. If we imagine the proscription of a political party to be its death sentence, then surely there must be less draconian sanctions for offenses that transgress the boundaries of what parties may be permitted to do, but do not require the termination of all activity by that party.

The readiest alternative is to discipline not the organization as such but the transgressing conduct, specifically, the political agitation that crossed the line into impermissible threats to the democratic order. The subject of regulation under this alternative approach is not the organizational existence of a political party, but its conduct and, most notably, its speech. While this is a type of sanction less onerous than the outright prohibition of a party, it paradoxically may raise more concerns about state censorship. To oversee directly the message of a party and its forms of communication brings the state into the business of assessing the content of the political message and the viewpoint expressed. For those rooted in the American First Amendment tradition, such content restriction on speech, and most particularly viewpoint restrictions, trigger the highest constitutional concerns and the corresponding greatest levels of judicial scrutiny.

By contrast in India, the world's most populous democracy, restrictions on electoral communications are the prime mechanism to prohibit inflammatory campaign rhetoric and the threat of politically inspired violence. India's constitutional order is built on the birth pangs of the great communal violence of the Partition following independence in 1947.[20] Just as the German postwar constitution cannot be understood except by reference to the legacy of Nazism, so too India's regulation of political debate is incomprehensible without reference to the persistent threat of communal violence.

---

[20] For a thorough account of the role of the Partition in shaping early Indian constitutional debates and its persistent impact, see RAMACHANDRA GUHA, INDIA AFTER GANDHI (London: Macmillan, 2007).

Nor is this an abstract consideration. Political speech in India has on numerous occasions been the trigger for communal violence along the critical fault
line of religion, stirring once again the long-standing tensions between Hindus
and Muslims within the country. Consider the following remarks by the rather
notorious Hindu nationalist agitator Bal Thackeray, made a decade ago during a campaign appearance on behalf of a local candidate of the extremist
Shiv Sena party:

> Hinduism will triumph in this election and we must become hon'ble recipi-
> ents of this victory to ward off the danger on Hinduism, elect Ramesh Prabhoo
> to join with Chhagan Bhujbal who is already there. *You will find Hindu tem-
> ples underneath if all the mosques are dug out.* Anybody who stands against
> the Hindus should be showed or worshipped with shoes. A candidate by the
> name Prabhoo should be led to victory in the name of religion.[21]

While the cultural significance of being shown shoes may not readily cross all
national frontiers, it is hard to dispute that the ideas are rather coarse appeals
to Hindu unity against non-Hindus. Thackeray rose to prominence as a leading political operative in Bombay, a city that he was instrumental in renaming
Mumbai.[22] His claimed sources of political inspiration include, among others,
Adolf Hitler, whom Thackeray exalted as "an artist who wanted Germany to
be free from corruption."[23]

However, the significance of the speech goes well beyond the repugnant
appeals to chauvinism and the call to take offensive measures (showing the
shoes) against non-Hindus. The image of Muslim shrines sitting on the ruins
of Hindu temples is a potent incitement to sectarian violence over contested
religious shrines. The most famous such site is the Babri mosque in Ayodhya
in northern India, a shrine with religious significance and a violent past that is
strikingly reminiscent of the Temple Mount in Jerusalem.[24] Beginning in 1984,
shortly before the speech in question, the hard-line World Hindu Council had
agitated among Hindu followers to tear down the mosque, which, according
to legend, sat atop the birthplace of the Hindu deity Rama.

---

[21] *Prabhoo v. Kunte*, A.I.R. 1996 S.C. 1113, 1118–19 (emphasis added).
[22] *See, e.g.*, Christopher Beam, *Mumbai? What About Bombay?: How the City Got Renamed*,
      SLATE, July 12, 2006, http://www.slate.com/articles/news_and_politics/explainer/2006/07/
      mumbai_what_about_bombay.html.
[23] Larissa MacFarquhar, *The Strongman: Where Is Hindu-Nationalist Violence Leading?*,
      NEW YORKER, May 26, 2003, at 50, 50 (internal quotation marks omitted) (quoting Bal
      Thackeray).
[24] *See generally* Gary Jeffrey Jacobsohn, *The Permeability of Constitutional Borders*, 82 TEX.
      L. REV. 1763, 1798 & n.169 (2004); Daniel Pipes, *The Temple Mount's Indian Counterpart*,
      JERUSALEM POST, Jan. 17, 2001, at 8.

In 1992, agitation turned to reality when a Hindu mob destroyed the mosque and then attacked other Muslim sites and homes in Ayodhya. The ensuing ethnic riots left thousands dead in a wave of communal violence not seen since the initial partition of India and Pakistan in 1947.[25] At the organizational center of the mob assault were the Hindu nationalist political parties, including the most prominent Hindu nationalist party, the Bharatiya Janata Party (BJP). The BJP emerged as a focal point for Hindu nationalist agitation in the state of Gujarat and other parts of northwest India, combining market-oriented rejections of the socialist legacy of the Congress Party with increasingly militant agitation against non-Hindus. The BJP's nationalist agitation, particularly the focus on Ayodhya, was implicated in the Ayodhya communal riots in 1992 and then again in the Gujarat riots of 2002. The BJP itself was able to find mainstream outlets for its electoral aspirations, winning the prime ministership in 1998 and again in 2014, and emerging today as the largest political party in India following the electoral collapse of the Congress Party. But the whiff of communal agitation and violence has not dissipated from its early mobilization in Gujarat, and the threat of communal violence is never far from the forms of on-the-ground political agitation in India. That the 1987 speech by Thackeray did not give rise to a similar conflagration was a matter of happenstance – the ethnic tinderbox was just as much present. Indeed, Thackeray and Shiv Sena did reemerge in 1992 as instigators of the violence in Bombay, the worst carnage following the attack on the mosque in Ayodhya.[26]

The problem of political speech inciting violence between ethnic or religious factions is, of course, hardly confined to India. By way of example, Bosnia and Herzegovina's fragile ethnic peace was similarly threatened by an inflammation of ethnic tensions during an early election campaign after the fragile Dayton Accords. In the words of Christian Schwarz-Schilling, a senior international official in Bosnia:

> Inflammatory rhetoric raises tensions, and this in turn can all too easily escalate into violence in a society where weapons are everywhere, alcohol plentiful and the summer long and hot.... The more abusive the campaign rhetoric now, the more difficult it will be to find the necessary partners to create functioning institutions.[27]

---

[25] See GARY JEFFREY JACOBSOHN, THE WHEEL OF LAW: INDIA'S SECULARISM IN COMPARATIVE CONSTITUTIONAL CONTEXT 129 (Princeton, NJ: Princeton University Press, 2003).

[26] BARBARA D. Metcalf & Thomas R. METCALF, A CONCISE HISTORY OF INDIA 279 (New York: Cambridge University Press, 2012).

[27] Nicholas Wood, *Fiery Campaign Imperils Bosnia's Progress, Officials Warn*, N.Y. TIMES, Aug. 27, 2006, at A3 (quoting Christian Schwarz-Schilling).

As in India, Bosnian democracy emerged from a long period of massive communal violence in the aftermath of the fall of Tito and Soviet power. The ethnic animosities had been held at bay under authoritarian rule and then erupted in the period of political uncertainty that followed. This proves a recurring pattern as political unrest following strong-arm rule propels efforts at both advancement and self-defense along simpler, communal lines of authority. The negotiated solution in Bosnia was one of the few openly consociational efforts at formalized power sharing. Under the terms of the Dayton Accords, political power is carefully divided among the contending ethnic groups, something that highlights the charged ethnic political environment and easily leads campaign rhetoric down the slippery slope to violent incitement.[28]

In these fragile societies, political mobilization easily leads to communal agitation and in turn to ethnic or religious violence, with India being the most significant long-standing democracy to engage this issue directly. Certainly, Indian history does not lack for examples of election agitation leading to scores of deaths. The question is what steps may be taken to permit genuine, even if distasteful, political expression while maintaining public order in the face of likely violent outbursts. As a doctrinal matter, any restriction has to balance the Indian constitutional guarantee of freedom of expression[29] and the reserved constitutional emergency power to protect public order.[30]

In order to quell problems associated with speech-incited violence and stem divisive fractures based on religious affiliation, India by statute restricts electoral speech that propagates hate "between different classes of" Indian citizens "on grounds of religion, race, caste, [or] community"[31] and prohibits appeals to vote for or against a candidate on any basis that might foment sectional antagonisms. As will be evident, the codification of prohibited categories of electoral speech is necessarily open-ended, intended to be applied retrospectively to speech that is deemed excessively inflammatory, rather than as a formalized code of speech terms to be studied prospectively.

[28] *See* Anna Morawiec Mansfield, Note, *Ethnic but Equal: The Quest for a New Democratic Order in Bosnia and Herzegovina*, 103 COLUM. L. REV. 2052, 2054–65 (2003).

[29] INDIA CONST. art. 19, §1.

[30] Id. art. 19, §2 ("Nothing … shall … prevent the State from making any law, in so far as such law imposes reasonable restrictions on the exercise of the right to free expression in the interests of the sovereignty and integrity of India, the security of the State, friendly relations with foreign States, public order, decency or morality, or in relation to contempt of court, defamation or incitement to an offence.").

[31] *See* The Representation of the People Act, No. 43 of 1951, § 125, INDIA CODE, *available at* http://lawmin.nic.in/legislative/election/volume%201/representation%20of%20the%20people%20act,%201951.pdf.

While this is perhaps the least intrusive form of regulation of antidemocratic agitation, it raises the most vagueness concerns in the American First Amendment tradition. India does not attempt to prohibit parties, but to regulate their conduct within the electoral arena. To accomplish this means that India must accommodate a strong constitutional commitment to freedom of expression with a rigid electoral code that proscribes "corrupt practices," which are defined as including an appeal to vote for or against a candidate "on the ground of his religion, race, caste, community or language or the use of, or appeal to, religious symbols."[32] The power to enforce this prohibition is in turn delegated to an Election Commission that has the authority to identify corrupt practices and seek extraordinary remedies, including the exclusion from office of victorious candidates who relied on prohibited speech, subject in turn to exacting judicial review.[33] This is the mechanism by which the Indian government has policed electoral speech as a means of curbing antidemocratic tendencies among its political parties.

Once again, Bal Thackeray provides an insight into the harm to be addressed and the form of the response. In 1987, Thackeray, together with a leading politician, Manohar Joshi, and ten others, was prosecuted for violating section 123 of the Representation of People's Act[34] for campaign activities during state elections in the province of Maharashtra. The case ultimately went to the Supreme Court in *Prabhoo v. Kunte*[35] as a test of the decision of the Bombay High Court to set aside the election of Ramesh Yeshwant Prabhoo to state legislative office in Maharashtra. The setting aside of an election is one of the recognized remedies for the "corruption" of the electoral process by impermissible electioneering. According to the Bombay High Court, Prabhoo's campaign success was in part attributable to the inflammatory rhetoric of Bal Thackeray as part of the Shiv Sena party drive. Consistent with the statutory definition of corrupt practices, the High Court found that the campaign had appealed to Hindus to vote for Prabhoo based on his religion.[36] The appeals to Hindu solidarity were coupled with tirades against the threats posed by Muslim candidates or by any appeasement of Muslims. Thackeray's campaign speeches referred to some Muslims as snakes and used other religious

---

[32] *Id.* § 123(3).

[33] *Id.* § 8A.

[34] The Act "prohibits candidates from any appeal to his or her religion, race, caste, community, or language to further his or her prospect for election or prejudicially affect[ing] the election of any other candidate." Brenda Cossman & Ratna Kapur, *Secularism: Bench-Marked by Hindu Right*, 31 ECON. & POL. WEEKLY 2613, 2613 (1996).

[35] A.I.R. 1996 S.C. 1113.

[36] *See id.* at 1117.

imagery[37] that was understood as a basic call for a Hindu assertion of power to thwart the perceived Muslim threat.

In upholding the High Court's conclusions, including its reversal of the election result, the Supreme Court rejected the claim that only a manifest threat to public safety could justify an electoral prohibition. The narrow basis for the ruling was that the perceived threat to public order allowed for the invocation of the government's reserved constitutional powers to protect domestic order.[38] The court found that the statute prohibited any appeal to vote for or against a candidate based on his religion, regardless of whether the appeal was "prejudicial to the public order."[39] It held the prohibition to be constitutional as a reasonable restriction in the interest of "decency or morality."[40] For the court, "seeking votes on the ground of the candidate's religion in a secular State is against the norms of decency and the propriety of the society."[41] The legality of any particular electoral appeal would thus turn on the nature of the speech itself, not on whether it presented a clear and present danger.

An earlier decision dealing with the aftermath of the chaos in Ayodhya, the *Ayodhya Reference Case*,[42] provided precedential authority in reading the constitutional guarantee of equality of religion to be an affirmative commitment to secularism, in turn described as "one facet of the right to equality woven as the central golden thread in the fabric depicting the pattern of the scheme in our Constitution."[43] Secularism provided the substantive basis for the *Prabhoo* court to restrict campaign speech that threatened significant public disorder. But the court could not place all invocations of religion outside the bounds of electoral politics – the guarantees of free expression would necessarily protect the right to claim discrimination or unequal treatment based on religion. Instead, the court carefully distinguished appeals made to religious bigotry as implicating conflicting constitutional concerns between public order and freedom of religious expression.[44]

Moreover, the court placed particular emphasis on the incendiary nature of the speech in question, noting that "the mere use of the word 'Hindutva'

---

[37] *See id.* at 1119.

[38] *See* INDIA CONST. art. 19, §2.

[39] *Prabhoo*, A.I.R. 1996 S.C. at 1121.

[40] *Id.* at 1126 (quoting INDIA CONST. art. 19, §2).

[41] *Id.*

[42] *Ismail Faruqui v. Union of India*, A.I.R. 1995 S.C. 605.

[43] *Id.* at 630.

[44] Thus, in an earlier case involving two Muslim candidates, it was considered permissible to air grievances of the Muslim community, but impermissible for one candidate, in the last stages of the campaign, to charge his opponent with not being a true Muslim. *See Bukhari v. Mehra* (1975) Supp. S.C.R. 281.

['Hinduness'] or 'Hinduism' or mention of any other religion in an election speech" is insufficient on its own to trigger a violation of section 123.[45] Based in part on this language, *Prabhoo* and two other cases – along with *Joshi v. Patil*[46] and *Kapse v. Singh*[47] – are often collectively referred to as the *Hindutva Judgments*, and have been criticized as "giving a veritable *judicial imprimatur* to political hate speech."[48] This remains a work in progress as the *Hindutva Judgments* are subject to further Supreme Court review.[49]

What is most significant is that the attempt to reconcile freedom of expression for religious grievances and the demands of public order turned uniquely on the combustible electoral context. The court resolved the constitutional conflict by making two distinct findings about the constitutional status of the election period. First, the court reiterated an earlier understanding that the constitution itself expresses a commitment to a democratic political order:

> No democratic political and social order, in which the conditions of freedom and their progressive expansion for all make some regulation of all activities imperative, could endure without an agreement on the basic essentials which could unite and hold citizens together despite all the differences of religion, race, caste, community, culture, creed and language. Our political history made it particularly necessary that these differences, which can generate powerful emotions depriving people of their powers of rational thought and action, should not be permitted to be exploited lest the imperative conditions for the preservation of democratic freedoms are disturbed.[50]

Second, the court found it significant that the prohibition on speech was directed only to the election period itself. The prohibition served not as a generalized speech code but as a commitment to the maintenance of the integrity of the democratic process. The electoral context was both a time of particular vulnerability for the reemergence of communal hostilities, and a heightened period of government interest in acting anticipatorily to thwart social disruption: "The restriction is limited only to the appeal for votes to a candidate during the election period and not to the freedom of speech and expression

---

[45] *Prabhoo*, A.I.R. 1996 S.C. at 1127.

[46] A.I.R. 1996 S.C. 796.

[47] A.I.R. 1996 S.C. 817.

[48] See Saurav Datta, Op-Ed, *Political Hate Speech Flourishes in India*, AL JAZEERA ENGLISH, Mar. 18, 2014, http://www.aljazeera.com/indepth/opinion/2014/03/political-hate-speech-india-201431832847177887.html.

[49] See id.; *see also SC's Seven-Judge Bench to Revisit Hindutva Judgement [sic]*, THE NEW INDIAN EXPRESS, Feb. 2, 2014, http://www.newindianexpress.com/nation/SCs-Seven-judge-Bench-to-Revisit-Hindutva-Judgement/2014/02/02/article2033912.ece.

[50] *Prabhoo*, A.I.R. 1996 S.C. at 1124 (quoting *Bukhari* (1975) Supp. S.C.R. at 288).

in general or the freedom to profess, practise and propagate religion uncon-
nected with the election campaign."[51]

The Indian approach to antidemocratic appeals has two major limitations.
First, in terms of practical effect, it is intended only to address the problem of
accentuation of communal antipathies in the crucible of a contested election
campaign. Parties can easily organize on antidemocratic platforms outside
the electoral arena. To the extent that parties moderate their language for
the election campaign itself – a seemingly inevitable problem with election
statutes that amount to speech codes – the definition of corrupt practices in
India does not regulate their conduct. Thus, for example, the Spanish decision to ban the Basque separatist Batasuna Party might have been difficult to
enforce as a speech ban on a party that promoted the claimed plight of the
Basque people.[52] Even in India, the Electoral Commission has had to push
further, ruling for example that no elections could be held in Gujarat in 2002
after the local BJP government helped instigate anti-Muslim riots that left
more than 1,000 people dead.[53] More aggressive still was the decision of the
Indian Supreme Court upholding the dismissal from office of three state governments on grounds of complicity or acquiescence in mob violence in the
aftermath of the destruction of the Babri mosque in Ayodhya.[54] Recently, however, the Supreme Court of India has asked the Law Commission to "make
recommendations to the Parliament to strengthen the Election Commission
to curb the menace of 'hate speeches' irrespective of whenever made."[55]

Second, and perhaps more significant, the Indian approach would require
setting aside qualms that many – including many educated in the American
First Amendment tradition – might have with governmental speech codes
that lack clear guidance and are largely applied after the fact. It is ironic that
the least restrictive form of electoral prohibition, one that does not require
banning parties or individuals wholesale, is likely to have the most capacity
for as-applied abuse. As with all rules governing the electoral process, any
departure from prospective application means that the application of a rule

---

[51] *Id.* at 1125–26.
[52] Recall that the dissolution of Batasuna was based on the party's refusal to condemn acts of vio-
      lence by ETA, an omission that would not have been reached by a speech code. *See* Thomas
      Ayres, *Batasuna Banned: The Dissolution of Political Parties under the European Convention
      of Human Rights*, 27 B.C. INT'L & COMP. L. REV. 99, 109 (2004).
[53] *See* Edward Luce, *Appeal on Indian Election Ruling*, FIN. TIMES, Aug. 19, 2002, at 6 (detailing
      the Electoral Commission's decision to postpone and the legal appeals that followed).
[54] *See S. R. Bommai v. Union of India*, A.I.R. 1994 S.C. 1918. For a fuller discussion of the politi-
      cal and ethnic dimensions of these decisions, see Jacobsohn, *supra* note 38, at 126–32.
[55] *Sangathan v. Union of India*, 2014 SCC Online SC 221, *available at* http://judis.nic.in/supreme
      court/imgs1.aspx?filename=41312.

will have outcome-determinative effects. This is nowhere as clear as in India where the remedy of recourse is the reversal of the electoral results.

On the one hand, the use of after-the-fact speech codes to reverse an election result could mean removing candidates from office who have a great deal of support in the electorate, undermining the overall democratic process. In *Prabhoo*, for example, the effect was to expel from office a candidate supported by the majority of voters. To the extent that electoral officials and reviewing judges are always at risk of succumbing to political pressures, or at least of being perceived as having done so, any regulatory approach that applies retroactively necessarily raises genuine legitimacy concerns.

On the other hand, precisely because reversing the apparent will of the people is such an intrusive judicial remedy, there is undoubtedly great reluctance in its application. In turn, this reluctance may translate into an unwillingness to invoke the case-specific, after-the-fact assessment of the legitimacy of electoral results. Particularly at a time of political rearrangement in India, as the Congress Party recedes into almost unimaginable minority status and the BJP emerges as the dominant political force, the sad fact is that efforts to police speech in the electoral period may prove an inadequate safeguard against renewed religious fissures in the electoral arena.

Certainly, the use of electoral speech prohibition decisions made by the court has long been decried as allowing too many Hindu-centric declarations to pass through the courts without adequate censure. For example, prior decisions have allowed for an extremely lenient interpretation of "hindutva," "the ideological lynchpin of the Hindu right's efforts to establish a Hindu [state]," as a representation of "a way of life in the subcontinent" and not in itself an electoral violation.[56] Concretely, nearly two decades ago the Supreme Court set aside the judgment of the Bombay High Court that had voided the election of Manohar Joshi to the Maharashtra Legislative Assembly.[57] Joshi, a founder of the BJP, had successfully run for office on the pledge that, through his election, "the first Hindu State will be established in Maharashtra."[58]

The as-applied nature of the rules necessarily forces judges to develop a set of implicit norms that will tack to the prevailing political winds. In the case of the reassertion of Hindu nationalism, courts have struggled to limit abhorrent or overly inciteful speech while allowing provocative campaign speech swaddled in the garb of patriotism. The electoral code, presented in its best light, has sought to moderate interactions between the majority and minority

---

[56] Cossman & Kapur, *supra* note 48, at 2613.
[57] *Joshi v. Patil*, A.I.R. 1996 S.C. 796.
[58] *Id.* at 816.

groups so as to quell violence and disorder. At the same time, the regulation of speech cannot hold back what has in India become an increasingly majoritarian viewpoint invoking a greater degree of Hindu political reassertion.

In practice, however, the Indian approach resembles the effect of the party banning in Turkey prior to the emergence of the first Islamic-oriented government under Prime Minister Erdogan. The BJP's rise to prominence began with agitation for communal claims of Hindus, an agitation often implicated in ensuing violence. Over time, the BJP developed aspirations to govern, first succeeding at the state governor level in 1995, then rising to form two national governments. Along the way, the BJP learned to temper its rhetoric and to tout, as had Erdogan in his rise to national power, its achievements in office in quite old-fashioned good governance terms.

In terms of the role of the courts in applying India's electoral speech regulations, the Indian approach not only invites content and viewpoint regulation of speech, but embraces it. The immersion of the judiciary into speech regulation is quite self-conscious. In the *Ayodhya Reference Case*, for example, Justice Verma invoked Rawls directly to set the secular contours for limiting the role of religion in the electoral and governmental spheres. For Justice Verma, India is a "pluralist, secular polity" in which "law is perhaps the greatest integrating force."[59] His substantive commitment to tamp down religious appeals draws on a "Rawlsian pragmatism of 'justice as fairness'" that in turn permits an "'overlapping consensus' … on fundamental questions of [the] basic structure of society for deeper social unity."[60]

Further, the Indian approach, while committed to maintaining public order during a heated election, exposes a deeper concern in democratic thought about the limits of public decision making and, in particular, uncertainty about voters' motivations in exercising the franchise. There is a lingering concern in democratic theory that base instincts may come to command voters. For example, James Madison was concerned about the descent into the vice of "passion," by which the masses of voters could be swayed by greed or envy of the wealthy to use democratic power for confiscatory aims.[61] The Indian cases

---

[59] *Ismail Faruqui v. Union of India*, A.I.R. 1995 S.C. 605, 630. Here, the court was quoting from "a paper on 'Law in a Pluralist Society' by M. N. Venkatachalia." *Id.*

[60] *Id.* at 630–31. This passage is also quoted from Venkatachalia. *Id.* at 630.

[61] *See* THE FEDERALIST NO. 10 (James Madison), at 78 (Clinton Rossiter ed., New York: The New American Library, 1961) (describing factions, which Madison considered among the foremost threats to the fledging American republic, as "a number of citizens, whether amounting to a majority or minority of the whole, who are united and actuated by some common impulse of *passion* … adverse to the rights of other citizens, or to the permanent and aggregate interests of the community" (emphasis added)); *see also* THE FEDERALIST NO. 49 (James Madison), *supra*, at 317 ("[Such] passions ought to be controlled and regulated by the government.").

applying the electoral speech code contained in the Corrupt Practices Act follow in this tradition, finding a compelling governmental interest in outlawing appeals to base instincts that might, in heated moments, overwhelm the higher aspirations of republican discourse:

> Under the guise of protecting your own religion, culture or creed you cannot embark on personal attacks on those of others or whip up low hard instincts and animosities or irrational fears between groups to secure electoral victories.... [O]ur democracy can only survive if those who aspire to become people's representatives and leaders understand the spirit of secular democracy. That spirit was characterised by Montesquieu long ago as one of "virtue." ... For such a spirit to prevail, candidates at elections have to try to persuade electors by showing them the light of reason and not by inflaming their blind and disruptive passions. Heresy hunting propaganda on professedly religious grounds directed against a candidate ... may be permitted in a theocratic state but not in a secular republic like ours.[62]

There is a disturbing quality to regulating speech in order to protect the electorate against itself. Core foundations of democracy are called into question by the claimed likelihood that the voting public – the demos at the heart of democracy – will submit to its base instincts in the heat of electoral debate. Even so, the specter of communal violence, which is never too far from the surface in heated Indian political battles, yields a constitutional accommodation between civil liberties and public order. It is hard to contest the claim that fewer people have died as a result of a modicum of caution being imposed on politicians lest they be removed from office.

The BJP, after being instrumental in the incendiary storming of the mosque in Ayodhya, subsequently tempered its rhetoric in order to preserve its electoral viability. In its mildly gentler form, the BJP managed to prevail in national elections and put together a fragile governing coalition. Although it initially failed in its efforts at governance – and lost in the subsequent election to a coalition that would select India's first Sikh prime minister – 2014 saw the election of the BJP's Narendra Modi as prime minister, again in clearly tempered form. Lest our narrative fall sway to too much optimism, the BJP's latest Election Manifesto still includes a potentially inflammatory commitment "to explore all possibilities within the framework of the constitution to facilitate the construction of the Ram Temple in Ayodhya,"[63] which is being built at the site of the former Babri mosque.

---

[62] *Bukhari v. Mehra* (1975) Supp. S.C.R. 281, 288, 296.
[63] Bharatiya Janata Party, *Election Manifesto 2014, available at* http://bjpelectionmanifesto.com/pdf/manifesto2014.pdf.

BANNING ELECTORAL PARTICIPATION OF
ANTIDEMOCRATIC PARTIES

In many countries, the exercise of constitutional rights or participation and
expression in the electoral arena is guaranteed to all parties that have organized themselves under the broader constitutional guarantees of freedom of
association or expression. In direct contrast to the Indian approach of regulating the content of electoral speech, the more typical democratic response is to
allow free expression as a dominant constitutional value available to any lawful
participant in the electoral process. For example, the Federal Constitutional
Court in Germany in the *Radical Groups Case*[64] struck down a denial of television and radio advertisement time to left-wing parties on the ground that,
so long as the political advertisements related to the election, "[r]adio and
television stations have no right to refuse broadcasting [time to a party] merely
because its election ad contains anticonstitutional ideas."[65] The controlling
idea – one that is familiar to American law – is that democracies require open
and robust political debate and that nowhere is the right of expression more
important than in matters having to do with self-governance.[66] This principle
follows from the basic approach of regulating the legal status of political parties while granting a broad swath of protection from state interference to those
entities that are legally entitled to form a political party.

As the Indian example demonstrates, however, it is possible to treat conduct in the electoral arena separately from the question of the legal status
of a political party. Indeed, in pursuing less restrictive ways of protecting the
democratic process, it is possible to envision a code of electoral administration
that not only is more supple than the criminal standards at issue in *Dennis
v. United States*, but that also might establish standards for electoral participation on a basis that is distinct from the legal requirements for party formation.

An interesting variation on this approach comes from Israel. The precipitating event was the effort to bar the Kach movement, whose founder, Rabbi
Meir Kahane, had previously been the leader of the Jewish Defense League
in the United States. There is little doubt that Kach promoted racial hostility

---

[64] BVerfG Feb. 14, 1978, 47 BverfGE 198, *translated in part in* Donald P. Kommers, The
Constitutional Jurisprudence of the Federal Republic of Germany 224 (2nd ed.,
Durham, NC: Duke University Press, 1997).

[65] *Id., translated in part in* Kommers, *supra* note 79, at 224, 226 (second alteration in original).

[66] An interesting twist on this argument is provided by then-Professor Bork, who argues against
applying the First Amendment to speech that does not touch on fundamental questions of
political self-governance. *See* Robert H. Bork, *Neutral Principles and Some First Amendment
Problems*, 47 Ind. L.J. 1, 20 (1971).

and ventured sufficiently far to the extreme to be labeled a "quasi-fascist move-ment."[67] Kahane advocated a policy of "Terror Neged Terror" (Terror Against Terror) according to which Jewish vigilante groups would be able to count on the active support of the Israeli government.[68] While Kach purportedly directed itself only to political organization, there seemed little dispute that Kahane's followers engaged in occasional anti-Arab attacks.[69] Further, Kach not only praised specific acts of anti-Arab violence committed by non-Kach Israelis, but also made the perpetrators of violence honorary members of Kach and provided funding for their legal defenses.[70] The exaltation of violence outside the formal boundaries of the Kach organization is reminiscent of the praising of ETA terrorists by Batasuna in Spain, and presumably could have led to the banning of Kach under the same principles.

The first effort to ban the Kach party came on the unilateral initiative of the Central Elections Committee (CEC), an administrative body charged with the conduct of elections in Israel, including verification of the eligibility of political party slates for inclusion on the ballot. The CEC disqualified the Kach party – along with a minor Arab party, the Progressive List for Peace – on the grounds that its platform was antidemocratic and advocated racism. In *Neiman v. Chairman of the Central Elections Committee for the Eleventh Knesset*,[71] the Israeli Supreme Court struck down these independent actions of the CEC on the ground that the CEC's statutory mandate was limited to mechanically checking the petition signatures and other technical qualifica-tions of parties and did not include any political assessment of a party's plat-form. The court rejected the view of then Justice Aharon Barak, expressed in a separate concurrence, that the CEC could ban a political party of its own accord so long as there was appropriate judicial review after the fact.[72] Nonetheless, the court agreed that a party that rejected either the existence of the Israeli state or its democratic character could be banned, although the

---

[67] Ehud Sprinzak, *Kach and Meir Kahane: The Emergence of Jewish Quasi-Fascism I: Origins and Development, in* 19 PATTERNS OF PREJUDICE, no. 3, July 1985, at 15, 16 [hereinafter Sprinzak, *Kach and Meir Kahane I*], *available at* http://members.tripod.com/alabasters_archive/kach_ and_kahane.html; *see also* EHUD SPRINZAK, THE ASCENDANCE OF ISRAEL'S RADICAL RIGHT 80–87 (Oxford: Oxford University Press, 1991).

[68] Ehud Sprinzak, *Kach and Meir Kahane: The Emergence of Jewish Quasi-Fascism II: Ideology and Politics, in* 19 PATTERNS OF PREJUDICE, no. 4, Oct. 1985, at 3, 8, *available at* http:// members.tripod.com/alabasters_archive/kach_and_kahane.html.

[69] *See* Sprinzak, *Kach and Meir Kahane I, supra* note 82, at 18–19.

[70] *See* Ehud Sprinzak, *Extremism and Violence in Israel: The Crisis of Messianic Politics*, 555 ANNALS AM. ACAD. POL. & SOC. SCI. 114, 121 (1998).

[71] EA 2/84, 3/84 IsrSC 39(2) 225[1985].

[72] *See id.* at 304–05 (Barak, J., concurring).

court then split on whether the threat posed by the party had to be a substantial probability, per the lead opinion of President Shamgar of the court,[73] or whether it only had to be a reasonable possibility, as Justice Barak would have had it.[74]

In the aftermath of *Neiman*, Israel amended both its Basic Law governing eligibility for the Knesset and its statutory requirements for the registration of political parties. The immediate aim of the reforms was to provide a sound legal basis for banning parties, which then resulted in the banning of the Kach party in 1988 and 1992 and the banning of its related entity, Kahane Is Alive, in 1992.[75] What is particularly intriguing is not so much the application of the new laws to the Kach militants as the apparent efforts of the reformers to create a gap between the conditions for running for parliament and the conditions for creating a political party.

Under amended section 7A of the Basic Law on the Knesset, no party list may stand for office,

> if the objectives or acts of the list or the acts of the person ... include, explicitly or by implication, one of the following: (1) negation of the existence of the State of Israel as a Jewish and democratic state; (2) incitement to racism; (3) support of armed struggle – by an enemy state or by a terrorist organization – against the State of Israel.[76]

As most recently amended in 2008, unlawful travel to "an enemy state within the seven years before the date for submission of lists of candidates" creates a rebuttable presumption that a candidate's "acts constitute support for the armed struggle [against] the State of Israel."[77]

The language of the party registration law is quite similar but adds an additional necessary condition: whether "any of its purposes or deeds, implicitly

---

[73] *See id.* at 275 (opinion of Shamgar, Pres.).

[74] *See id.* at 315–16 (Barak, J., concurring). The debate on the standard of proof both invoked and was reminiscent of Learned Hand's formulation of the clear and present danger test in the Second Circuit opinion in *Dennis:* "In each case [courts] must ask whether the gravity of the 'evil,' discounted by its improbability, justifies such invasion of free speech as is necessary to avoid the danger." *United States v. Dennis*, 183 F.2d 201, 212 (2nd Cir. 1950).

[75] *See* Raphael Cohen-Almagor, *Disqualification of Political Parties in Israel: 1988–1996*, 11 EMORY INT'L L. REV. 67, 67 (1997).

[76] Basic Law: The Knesset § 7A, *translated in* ISRAEL'S WRITTEN CONSTITUTION 25 (6th ed., Haifa, Israel: A.G. Publications, 2009).

[77] *Id.* Both the 2002 and 2008 amendments appear to have been directly targeted at Dr. Azmi Bishara, the founder and head of the Balad party who had publicly voiced support for Hezbollah. *See* Suzie Navot, *Israel, in* HOW CONSTITUTIONS CHANGE: A COMPARATIVE STUDY 204–05 (Dawn Oliver & Carlo Fusaro eds., Portland, OR: Hart Publishing, 2011).

or explicitly, contains ... reasonable ground to deduce that the party will serve as a cover for illegal actions."[78] Notably, the amended electoral code does not ban the parties that do not meet these conditions, but instead limits their participation in the electoral arena. At least in theory, a ban on running for the Knesset is less draconian than outlawing an entire party. Therefore, the focus on the implicit or explicit direct tie to unlawful conduct in the party prohibition laws can be seen as inviting courts to apply a more stringent standard before a party is outlawed altogether, and a less rigorous standard when a party is simply being disqualified from having its members elected to the Knesset.

Both commentators and the Israeli Supreme Court treat these mild differences in formulation – specifically, the introduction of the reasonable basis for tying a party to illegal activity in the Parties Law – as creating a political space in which it is possible to organize a party around ideas, even if reprehensible ones, while at the same time denying such a party the right of representation in the Knesset. Although there has not yet been any case challenging the distinction between political organization and parliamentary candidacy, President Barak's opinion for the court in *Yassin v. Party Registrar*[79] provided the rationale for treating the two forms of political activity differently. As summarized by Professor Cohen-Almagor:

> Democracy is entitled to defend itself from those who seek to use it in order to destroy its very existence. True, democracy must be tolerant of the intolerant. But in its tolerance, democracy need not allow its eradication. That is the principle of "militant democracy" or "non-tolerant democracy" or, in the words of Justice Sussman, "defensive democracy."[80]

The prospect of parties that are allowed to exist and to recruit members, but are excluded from the electoral arena and by extension from political office, leads directly to the question of whether democracies may regulate the political arena on a basis distinct from that underlying the regulation of speech, association, and assembly generally. Should we be less concerned about restricting expression – under the American First Amendment, for example – when a government imposes a civil penalty against a speaker by denying him access to elective office than when a government imposes a criminal penalty

---

[78] Cohen-Almagor, *supra* note 90, at 92 (translating Parties Law, 1992, S.H. 190).

[79] PCA 7504/95, 7793/95 IsrSC 50(2) 45[1996].

[80] LCA 7504/95 *Yassin v. Party Registrar* 50(2) IsrSC 45, 62 [1995], *translated in part in* AHARON BARAK, THE JUDGE IN A DEMOCRACY 30 (Princeton, NJ: Princeton University Press, 2006). There are no English translations of the full *Yassin* decision.

against that speaker? Do we think differently of a society that, while not incarcerating antidemocratic forces, nonetheless denies them access to the electoral arena as a platform for antidemocratic agitation?[81]

Without a clear template in any country's actual experience, we are left to hypothesize about what it would mean to allow a party to exist but nonetheless to restrict its electoral participation. This is likely not to be a stable arrangement. But the experience of the Turkish Welfare Party and the Indian BJP suggests that even strongly religious or nationalistic parties are coalitions and that their more moderate members (or more electorally ambitious leaders) may temper their ideals to the requirements of democratic life.[82]

It is, of course, unlikely that a prohibition on electoral participation can forestall mass antidemocratic fervor in the long run. It is also true that simply banning Islamic political opponents in the name of an autocratic secular regime, as occurred in Algeria in the 1990s, does little to advance the prospect of continued democratic rule.[83] As the Algerian example demonstrates, by the time electoral politics are commandeered by parties with an express commitment to abolishing civil liberties and cancelling elections, little hope remains. A democracy without a corresponding democratic commitment in the broader society will not survive. At the same time, Algeria offers the caution that in the absence of democratic integrity within the ruling government, any repression of even avowedly antidemocratic elements will resonate as simply another corrupt effort to preserve a failed ruling elite.[84] But such failures of cancerous regimes provide no evidence that a relatively healthy democratic society cannot test the antidemocratic

---

[81] For the importance of the distinction between prosecuting parties criminally and banning them from the electoral arena, see Víctor Ferreres Comella, *The New Regulation of Political Parties in Spain, and the Decision to Outlaw Batasuna, in* MILITANT DEMOCRACY 133, 138–39 (András Sajó ed., Utrecht, The Netherlands: Eleven International Publishing, 2004), in which the author argues that, because the incarceration of individual party members is not at stake, the standards for prohibiting parties administratively may be more relaxed than those used in criminal trials.

[82] *See* Michael S. Kang, *The Hydraulics and Politics of Party Regulation*, 91 IOWA L. REV. 131 (2005) (exploring how different forms of legal regulation empower distinct constituencies in political parties).

[83] *See generally* MICHAEL WILLIS, THE ISLAMIST CHALLENGE IN ALGERIA 107–392 (New York: New York University Press, 1996); Lise Garon, *The Press and Democratic Transition in Arab Societies: The Algerian Case, in* I POLITICAL LIBERALIZATION AND DEMOCRATIZATION IN THE ARAB WORLD 149 (Rex Brynen et al. eds., Boulder, CO: Lynne Rienner Publishers, 1995).

[84] For a related though less favorable account of how expansive constitutional review allows political and economic elites to hold illiberal majorities at bay, see RAN HIRSCHL, TOWARDS JURISTOCRACY 214 (Cambridge, MA: Harvard University Press, 2004).

mettle of its parties by frustrating the electoral ambitions of some. Healthier democracies place constraints upon any curtailment of access to the political process, most critically a strong measure of judicial oversight, rather than allowing exclusion to be a matter of executive fiat. As fraught with the risks of censorship as this approach might be, there is reason to believe that the process may embolden more moderate elements and forestall the use of the electoral arena for the worst antidemocratic ends.

5

Judging Militant Democracy

Extremist groups threaten democracy in terms of both what they might try to do through elections and governmental office and what they might provoke democratic societies to do in order to ward off the perceived danger. The threat is real, from both directions. That there are antidemocratic groups trying to worm their way into governmental positions so as to undermine tolerant, pluralistic, democratic societies is not a new development. What is perhaps new is the increasing likelihood that these groups will be clerically inspired rather than driven by the messianic social visions of communism or fascism. But there is the corresponding threat of excessive intolerance. Democracy thrives on contestation, and suffers if the ambit of democratic deliberation is drawn too narrowly and if the threat to social peace is used to drive out the uncomfortable voices of dissent.

In most circumstances, efforts to silence parties by prohibition are probably ill advised. As nettlesome as the Quebec independence movement may have been for Canada, the national government's ability to channel disputes over Quebec's status through the political process and even the Supreme Court is far preferable to any attempt to drive the party underground.[1] The relative civility and tolerance of debate in Canada, however, is unfortunately not the global norm. So the question becomes what preconditions must exist for the banning of parties or for other restrictions on political expression in the electoral arena. Here I wish to leave to the side the parties alleged to be allied with insurrectionary or regional military forces. With respect to such parties, the directness of the organizational link to unlawful activity and the immediacy of the likely harm serve as workable responses to the problems posed, at least in theory.

---

[1]   *See* Reference re Secession of Quebec, [1998] 2 S.C.R. 217.

In the absence of direct or indirect participation in illegal or violent activity, the starting point for any discussion of the banning of political parties, political participation, or political speech should be that the presumption is in favor of freedom of political expression and association. As set forth in the Guidelines on the Prohibition and Dissolution of Political Parties and Analogous Measures issued by the European Commission for Democracy Through Law, commonly referred to as the Guidelines of the Venice Commission, there must be justification for the banning of a party:

> The right of individuals to associate and form political parties should, to the greatest extent possible, be free from interference. Although there are limitations to the right of association, such limitations must be construed strictly, and only convincing and compelling reasons can justify limitation on freedom of association. Limitations must be prescribed by law, necessary in a democratic society, and proportional in measure.... The broad protection given to the right of individuals to associate requires that political parties also be free from unnecessary interference.[2]

At bottom, prohibiting or dissolving a political party is an exceptional measure in a democratic society. If the relevant state bodies invoke legal authority to ban a political party, there must be sufficient evidence that there is a real threat to the constitutional order or citizens' fundamental rights and freedoms, and that evidence must be marshaled in a manner "prescribed by law," invariably through legal processes culminating in judicial oversight. Developing that evidence is relatively straightforward when the party is implicated in illegal or violent activities such that criminal conduct can be attributed to the party.

The more difficult concern is with parties that genuinely vie for governmental office and even majority status in an effort to unwind liberal democracy. It is easy to imagine what may go wrong with party prohibitions. The ability to cordon off certain areas of democratic deliberation from particular kinds of speech invites censorship or suppression of political opposition, a move that can be utilized to insulate incumbents from electoral challenge or as a pretext to impose the ruling majority's own form of orthodoxy on political exchange. But if history is a guide, excessive tolerance is dangerous as well. We can begin to test the range of permissible state responses to antidemocratic mass movements through the familiar categories of procedural limitations on and substantive definitions of prohibited conduct.

---

[2] European Comm'n for Democracy Through Law (Venice Comm'n), *Guidelines on Prohibition and Dissolution of Political Parties and Analogous Measures*, art. III, § V, ¶ 14 (2010) [hereinafter *Democracy Through Law Guidelines*], *available at* http://www.venice.coe .int/webforms/documents/default.aspx?pdffile=CDL-INF(2000)001-e.

I wish to put to the side two technical objections to this exercise. The first is that democratic suppression will not work: that ultimately it will induce greater antidemocratic mobilization than the free ventilation of all viewpoints. I view this as an empirical claim about what actually works. In the stable framework of the United States, it may well be that reactions to suppress political participation have been overwrought and largely unnecessary. I am far less confident that – as an empirical matter – this is universally true. The decision of India, a country forged in fratricidal religious conflict, to limit inflammatory campaign rhetoric in order to suppress election day incitements likely to engender communal violence is not a move so readily discounted. Turkey's suppression of Islamic extremism, which led its Islamic opposition to mature and develop an appetite for competent governance, is also not so easily cast aside as unwise or ineffectual.[3] Even the most extreme cases, such as the Algerian military intervention to prevent a parliament from forming around a platform of eliminating democracy, are not so readily dismissed as simply counterproductive exercises, despite the resulting military confrontation.

The second objection is that electoral prohibitions tend to be either void for vagueness or unacceptably overbroad. In plain terms, these are objections that the prohibitions can never work because they will either sweep too broadly or be so uncertain as to be impossible to apply on a non-arbitrary basis. The dangers of overreach are ever present in the exercise. But if the claim is that all efforts to bar impermissible viewpoints are likely to be overbroad or vague there must be some reason offered for why this is so. The fact that all laws dealing with intentionality can be cast too broadly or too narrowly does not mean that democratic societies have not found a way of incorporating punishment of conspiracy or intentional harms within the rule of law. The difficulty in drawing lines does not mean that all efforts at suppressing an antidemocratic opposition must, of necessity, reach beyond acceptable parameters. To condemn the entire exercise requires a theoretical reason why all electoral prohibitions must ultimately fail, rather than an individual attack on a

---

[3] Although the subject is too broad for this book, it is important to note that the complex nature of political parties is a factor that interacts with the imposition of legal restraints on certain kinds of activity or expression. Political parties invariably reflect deep internal tensions among their mass bases, their elected officials, and their internal apparatus. This is the basic analysis of political parties developed in the United States, initially in V. O. Key Jr., POLITICS, PARTIES, & PRESSURE GROUPS (New York: Thomas Y. Crowell Company, 5th ed. 1964). *See also* Nathaniel Persily & Bruce E. Cain, *The Legal Status of Political Parties: A Reassessment of Competing Paradigms*, 100 COLUM. L. REV. 775 (2000). For a broader theoretical account of how parties respond to the incentives created by legal regulation, see Michael S. Kang, *The Hydraulics and Politics of Party Regulation*, 91 IOWA L. REV. 131 (2005).

particular law or ruling as having an undemocratic effect. Whatever such a theory might posit, it must be robust enough to counter the risks embodied in the twentieth-century examples of mass antidemocratic mobilizations that successfully toppled democratic governance.

PROCEDURAL PROTECTIONS

Across the range of cases in which democratic regimes have sought to prevent antidemocratic elements from securing the advantages of the electoral arena, three forms of procedural concerns emerge. Although there is no judicial discussion that I am aware of setting out these considerations in comprehensive fashion, taken together they highlight some of the primary protections against the potential misuse of viewpoint-based suppression of political activity.

The first and undoubtedly most significant procedural safeguard is the concentration of the power to suppress away from self-interested political actors. In all the cases in which democratic regimes have formalized the power to ban political parties, the judiciary acts based on the government's petition or the public prosecutor's charges. Regardless of whether the power to proscribe political actors is reserved to apex courts or is part of the ordinary functioning of the courts,[4] the judiciary acts as an independent arbiter of the legitimacy of the government's professed need to suppress an antidemocratic threat.

Independent judicial review takes on particular significance in parliamentary systems. There is a persistent risk in any democratic system that the claimed exigencies necessitating the use of emergency powers, including the power to suppress antagonistic political speech, will become the rule that swallows the exception. Too many putative democracies, particularly in the immediate postcolonial world, have succumbed to one-party rule under the claimed necessity of domestic emergencies. No prescriptive account can safely ignore this threat. The common feature of fledgling democracies that collapse into strongman regimes is the concentration of unilateral power in the executive. Executive authority is at its greatest whenever there is a claimed threat to national security meaning that societies face collapsing into autocratic rule precisely when they are at their most vulnerable.

The threat of executive unilateralism is confined to the extent that there are effective checks on the power of the executive. In the United States, the

---

[4]   "The role of the judiciary is essential in the prohibition or dissolution of political parties.... [T]here can be different judicial bodies competent in this field. In some states it lies within the sole competence of Constitutional courts whereas in others it is within the sphere of ordinary courts." *Democracy Through Law Guidelines, supra* note 5, at art. III, § VI, ¶ 18.

separation between presidential and legislative election allows Congress to play a checking role on claims of unilateral presidential authority, even over the nation's response to military threats. Indeed, the role of the courts in American national security cases has largely been to ensure that the executive not act beyond the scope of congressional authorization.[5] Because parliamentary systems vest executive power in representatives of the legislative majority, such separation of powers is not likely to have the same force as in presidential systems. But separation of powers remains a critical protection in preventing the use of extraordinary powers for quotidian political gain.

Requiring that there be an independent source of legislative authority for the prohibition of a political party and that there be a source of review independent of the executive provides a check on the misuse of this dangerous power. Perhaps the clearest example is the use of international tribunals, such as the European Court of Human Rights, to review party prohibitions. Such cross-national bodies are removed from any immediate accountability to domestic political processes and are unlikely to respond narrowly to partisan or sectional interests. Even at the domestic level, the requirement of independent review of such charged decisions as a ban on a political party may be thought of as a form of "constrained parliamentarianism" that protects democratic integrity by "insulating sensitive functions from political control."[6]

Germany provides the best example of the role of independent judicial review within a national setting, beginning with the seminal cases after World War II. While German (formerly West German) constitutional law safeguards the formation and effective operation of political parties,[7] the right to enter the electoral arena is not absolute. As discussed in Chapter 2, Article 21(2) of the German Basic Law provides: "Parties that, by reason of their aims or the behaviour of their adherents, seek to impair or abolish the free democratic basic order or to endanger the existence of the Federal Republic of Germany shall be unconstitutional."[8]

---

[5]   *See, e.g., Hamdan v. Rumsfeld,* 548 U.S. 557 (2006). For a historical account of the role of the Supreme Court in checking impulses toward executive unilateralism, see Samuel Issacharoff & Richard H. Pildes, *Between Civil Libertarianism and Executive Unilateralism: An Institutional Process Approach to Rights During Wartime,* 5 Theoretical Inquiries L. 1 (2004).

[6]   Bruce Ackerman & Susan Rose-Ackerman, Op-Ed., *Britain Needs a New Agency to Fight Corruption,* Fin. Times, Feb. 2, 2007, at 13.

[7]   *See, e.g.* Donald P. Kommers & Russell A. Miller, The Constitutional Jurisprudence of the Federal Republic of Germany 269–84 (Durham, NC: Duke University Press, 3rd ed. 2012) (translating, in part, the *Party Finance* cases and describing the role of political parties in the (West) German constitutional order).

[8]   Grundgesetz [GG] (Basic Law) art. 21(2); *see also id.* art. 9(2) (prohibiting "[a]ssociations whose purposes or activities … are directed against the constitutional order"); *id.* art. 5(3)

The German Basic Law therefore begins from the premise of both the importance of political parties in a democratic order and the need to ban those that seek to destroy democracy from within, a necessarily perilous line to draw. But the constitutional protections do not end there. Under the German constitution, an important procedural protection for political parties is that only the Federal Constitutional Court can declare a political party unconstitutional.[9]

The court, in the early days of the Federal Republic, twice exercised its Article 21 power to declare parties unconstitutional. First, in finding a Nazi successor party unconstitutional in the 1952 *Socialist Reich Party Case*, the court stated that the framers of the German Constitution, in deciding to limit the freedom of parties that aimed "to abolish democracy by using formal democratic means," had to consider "the danger that the government might be tempted to eliminate troublesome opposition parties."[10] Therefore, the framers committed the decision on unconstitutionality to the Federal Constitutional Court. The court distinguished Article 9(2), which allows the executive to ban "associations whose purposes or activities ... are directed against the constitutional order."[11] Precisely "[b]ecause of the special importance of parties in a democratic state," they could not be banned under the general executive powers of Article 9(2), and could be declared unconstitutional only by the Federal Constitutional Court.[12]

In 1956, in the *Communist Party Case*,[13] the court further declared the Communist Party of Germany (KPD) unconstitutional. What is unique about the two leading German cases is that each involves one of the two ideological enemies of liberal democracy from the twentieth century, fascism and communism. Germany's modern law of political parties was thus

---

(declaring that teaching "shall not absolve [a person] from loyalty to the Constitution"). BASIC LAW FOR THE FEDERAL REPUBLIC OF GERMANY (Christian Tomuschat & Donald P. Kommers eds., Christian Tomuschat & David P. Currie trans., 2010), *available at* https://www.btg-bestellservice.de/pdf/80201000.pdf.

[9] *See id.* art. 21(2) ("The Federal Constitutional Court shall rule on the question of unconstitutionality.").

[10] *Socialist Reich Party Case*, Bundesverfassungsgericht (BVerfG) (Federal Constitutional Court) Oct. 23, 1952, 2 ENTSCHEIDUNGEN DES BUNDESVERFASSUNGSGERICHTS [BVERFGE] 1, *translated in part in* Kommers & Miller, *supra* note 10, at 286, 287.

[11] GRUNDGESETZ [GG] (Basic Law) art. 9(2).

[12] *Socialist Reich Party*, 2 BVERFG 1, *translated in part in* Kommers & Miller, *supra* note 10, at 286, 287.

[13] BVerfG Aug. 17, 1956, 5 BVERFGE 85, *translated in part in* WALTER F. Murphy & Joseph TANENHAUS, COMPARATIVE CONSTITUTIONAL LAW 621 (New York, NY: Palgrave Macmillan, 1977). For a general discussion of the case, see Kommers & Miller, *supra* note 10, at 290–92.

formed against the backdrop of the backward-looking Socialist Reich Party, which sought to invoke in one fashion or another the Nazi past, and the eastward-looking Communist Party, which in turn sought to promote the ascendance of East Germany and the Soviet bloc.

In developing its jurisprudence against the backdrop of a fascist past and an imminent communist threat to its east, Germany provided the critical elements in the modern European law concerning antidemocratic parties. First, the ban is not a criminal sanction but a special form of regulation of the entry into the public political arena. Second, any prohibitions on political assembly and speech must be strictly subject to judicial oversight. Finally, the grounds of party prescription may turn on either the imminence of the threat to democracy or the fundamental ideological rejection of democracy.

Imminent Harm

In reviewing the German party exclusion cases, there is a natural tendency to run together the Socialist Reich Party and Communist Party cases. Indeed, both parties not only had ties to totalitarian ideologies, but both emerged at a time of real vulnerability for West Germany. Additionally, in each case the constitutional limitation on the scope of what could properly be put before the electorate also defined the limits on the organization of a legal political party. But the cases have important dissimilarities as well. The Socialist Reich Party was for all practical purposes a vehicle for destabilizing German democracy in an attempt to recreate Nazi rule. The German postwar constitution was designed to avoid the substance and processes of Nazi rule, and the Socialist Reich Party fell squarely within the constitution's anticipated prohibitions. The German court dealt with that case quickly and without much hesitation, although admittedly not without some analytic difficulties, as will be discussed subsequently.

While the *Socialist Reich Party Case* could be readily handled within the anticipated prohibitions of an anti-Nazi constitution, the same could not be said for the proposed ban on the Kommunistische Partei Deutschlands (KPD), the Communist Party of Germany that emerged in West Germany. The court took six years to issue a complicated, 300-page decision, which focused heavily on the nature of Marxist-Leninist ideology. Although the court easily concluded that the party ideology was antithetical to the democratic order, it struggled to address the constitutional question in the case.

The court had no trouble concluding that the central tenets of the KPD were at odds with the core values of a liberal democracy, and it went even further in concluding that the KPD's brand of Marxism-Leninism was blatantly

antagonistic to the survival of democracy in postwar West Germany. The aim
of this ideology, the court found, was to organize the party's activities under
democracy "as a transition stage for easier elimination of the free democratic
basic order as such."[14]

> Therefore the KPD must actually deny all other parties ... any right to exist
> in the sense of a lasting partnership with equal rights. But precisely such a
> lasting partnership is the prerequisite for the functioning of the multi-party
> principle – and for the struggle for power between several parties – within a
> free democracy.
>
> The same is basically true of the KPD's parliamentary activity. In the par-
> liamentary system of liberal democracy, each party participating in forming
> the popular political will is to be given a chance to come as close as possible
> to achieving its own goals through its activity in parliament. But no party may
> pursue material goals that, when reached, would forever exclude existence of
> other parties.... [T]his is exactly the KPD's goal.[15]

These were hardly conclusions that could be seriously disputed. The difficulty is that the question before the court was not whether the KPD's embrace
of Marxism-Leninism was contrary to or even hostile to liberal democratic
values; that much could be said of Marxist university professors or social activists. Rather, the question before the court was the constitutional legitimacy of
banning a party that advocated ideas that certainly formed part of Germany's
intellectual legacy. The KPD was careful to couch its electoral appeals in
terms of a critique of the treatment of class and other political and social issues
by Germany and its allies, not in advocacy of military conquest by a foreign
power. The court's opinion remains unsatisfying because of its failure to tie
the Communist Party directly to the real perceived threat to German democracy: the Warsaw Pact forces assembled within shooting distance of the West
German border. The opinion repeatedly returns to the party's efforts to dispar-
age all the institutions of West Germany and to agitate against the country's
ties to the United States, leaving unproven the KPD's implicit endorsement of
the other side in the Cold War.

Nonetheless, the opinion does include hints of the need to tolerate *ideas*
about communism outside the immediately perilous setting. For example,
the court added that "[b]anning the KPD is not legally incompatible with
reauthorization of a Communist party were elections to be held *throughout*

[14] *Communist Party*, 5 BVERFGE 85, *translated in part in* Murphy & Tanenhaus, *supra* note 18, at 621, 625.
[15] *Id.*, *translated in part in* Murphy & Tanenhaus, *supra* note 18, at 621, 624 (omissions in original).

Germany,"[16] a clear invitation to revisit the court's holding outside the context of the Cold War – a conflict that seemed neither very distant nor particularly "cold" in Germany in the 1950s. In effect, the court treated the KPD as an organization that was trying to use the electoral system to demoralize and destabilize German politics in order to further the aims of an enemy amassed at the border. The privation that followed World War II and the presence of foreign troops throughout Germany were all too reminiscent of the period following World War I, during which German democracy could not secure its footing. Under these circumstances, the Communist Party became more than an electoral outlier and instead assumed the role of an ally of forces seeking to unwind the German democratic state, not through elections as such, but in conjunction with a real foreign threat.

During the years in which the case was pending, and more so in the following decades, the Communist Party lost its residual appeal. The Party emerged from the postwar period with significant credibility stemming from its opposition to Hitler before and during the war. By the time the opinion was issued in 1956, West Germany had stabilized while the sense of Soviet oppression was undermining any postwar communist aura. The court's opinion followed by a few months the famous "secret speech" of Nikita Khrushchev denouncing the Stalinist legacy, and came on the eve of Soviet tanks invading Hungary. The fading sense of immediacy is likely one of the reasons the opinion does not stand up to exacting review. Moreover, during the same period, the West German economy flourished and the perceived threat from the east diminished. By 1968, when a new organization known as the German Communist Party (DKP) formed, the government took no steps to dismantle it. Indeed, the new DKP "boast[ed] the same program and leadership"[17] as the banned KPD. The party avoided "the Leninist turns of phrase that had been the downfall of its predecessor in 1956," but was hardly discreet in its support for the governing Sozialistische Einheitspartei Deutschlands (SED) [Socialist Unity Party of Germany] in East Germany, "from which it received generous funding."[18]

---

[16] *Id., translated in part in* Murphy & Tanenhaus, *supra* note 18, at 621, 626 (emphasis added).

[17] André Moncourt & J. Smith, *The Re-emergence of Revolutionary Politics in West Germany, in* 2 THE RED ARMY FACTION: A DOCUMENTARY HISTORY 42 (Oakland, CA: PM Press, J. Smith & André Moncourt eds., 2009).

[18] John Sandford, *DKP, in* ENCYCLOPEDIA OF CONTEMPORARY GERMAN CULTURE 152 (New York: Routledge, John Sandford ed., 1999).

Although it is true that the new party had dropped inflammatory invocations of the dictatorship of the proletariat from its official rhetoric, the only genuine difference was the lack of perceived threat – any semblance of a real danger – from a party identified with East Germany and the Soviet bloc. Still, in 1973, just five years after the party's founding, a poll showed that 39 percent of West Germans supported a ban on the DKP.[19] In the early 1990s, Bavarian State Minister for Regional Development and Environment Peter Gauweiler called for the party to be outlawed after documents from the archives of the East German secret police revealed that "DKP members had been trained in East Germany on weapons, explosives, and guerrilla tactics so that they could perform terrorist acts in West Germany in the event of war."[20] But despite the popular outcry, no legal steps were ever taken against the DKP.

The failure to ban the DKP confirms that even with the German constitutional mandate to ban antidemocratic parties, ultimate guidance is found in the need to protect democracy. Despite the ideological overlap between the KDP and the DKP, the perceived threat from the KDP and the lack of such a threat from the DKP is ultimately what explains, on the one hand, the ban on the KPD and, on the other hand, the fact that the DKP has never been subjected to any prohibitions. In cases like the KPD, the court was primarily concerned with evaluating the scope of the insurrectionary or military threat or the degree to which the party was associated with an enemy country, in order to assess whether the party was simply a vehicle for propaganda and recruiting for the adversary.

Following the fall of the Berlin Wall, the DKP not only posed no significant risk to the democratic order, especially as compared to the KPD in the immediate postwar period, but was an inconsequential outlier in German politics. The proposed ban by Bavarian Minister Gauweiler was based on past party conduct and allegiances most likely from the period before the DKP was even formed, and similarly not grounded in any immediate threat posed by the party. Banning the DKP would seem like a senseless act of retribution when there was no longer any semblance of an immediate threat from a party identified with East Germany and the Soviet bloc, and indeed when there was no longer an East Germany or a Soviet bloc.

[19] Barbara Wörndl, *Radicalism*, in WOLFGANG Glatzer ET AL., RECENT SOCIAL TRENDS IN WEST GERMANY, 1960–1990, at 363, 364 (Montreal: McGill-Queen's University Press, 1992).
[20] JOHN O. KOEHLER, STASI: THE UNTOLD STORY OF THE EAST GERMAN SECRET POLICE 24 (Boulder, CO: Westview Press, 1999).

Antidemocratic Ideology

Germany also provides a modern example of party prohibitions that reach beyond an imminent threat. Again, the German Constitution declares, "parties that, by reason of their aims or the behavior of their adherents, seek to undermine or abolish the free democratic basic order or to endanger the existence of the Federal Republic of Germany shall be unconstitutional."[21] If we leave aside for the moment the immediate post-Nazi period, we can see how difficult it is to ban parties solely on the basis of ideology.

In the recent past, the potential to ban parties for "reasons of their aims" has been invoked against the National Democratic Party (NPD), a neo-Nazi party that emerged on the fringes of German politics in 1964.[22] By 2012, however, the NPD had approximately 6,000 members, and could draw about one percent of the national electorate. In December 2012, following a law enforcement crackdown on the NPD that uncovered not only fascist propaganda but weapons, German state officials sought to have the Constitutional Court ban the NPD based on its platform of racism, xenophobia, and anti-Semitism and its goals of removing Germany from NATO and forcing immigrants to leave Germany. The fear over the NPD was exacerbated by the discovery of a seven-year killing spree by a separate "neo-Nazi terror cell," raising serious concern about the reemergence of a far right presence in German politics. In December 2013, the Bundesrat – the German equivalent of an upper legislative body – filed suit with the Constitutional Court seeking the banishment of the NPD.[23]

At the same time, even with neo-Nazis, party banning is still difficult in relatively stable political circumstances. Neither Chancellor Angela Merkel nor the Bundestag (the lower parliament) supported the position of the Bundesrat to ban the NPD and instead have advocated repudiating right-wing extremists in the political arena. This may prove more difficult in light of a recent order of the Constitutional Court striking down the 3 percent voting threshold requirement for parties to be elected to the European Parliament, something that offers a potential platform for groups such as the NPD. For the moment, the issue remains with the German court.

Banning parties for ideological reasons is, and should be, more difficult than moving against a party that is part of an imminent threat. There is little that distinguishes concern over a party's ties to insurrectionary forces or an

---

[21]   Grundgesetz [GG] [Basic Law] art. 21(2).

[22]   *See* Lucian Kim, *Hands off Germany's Neo-Nazi Party*, N.Y. TIMES BLOG (Dec. 18, 2012, 6:46 AM), http://latitude.blogs.nytimes.com/2012/12/18/hands-off-germanys-neo-nazi-party/.

[23]   Nastassja Steudel, *Second Attempt to Ban Neo-Nazi NPD Under Way*, DEUTSCHE WELLE (Jun. 21, 2014), http://www.dw.de/second-attempt-to-ban-neo-nazi-npd-under-way/a-17726217.

external military enemy from a conspiracy or attempt to commit a treasonous or otherwise criminal act. Where the danger to democratic stability posed by a party arises from the threat of extralegal conduct, the imminence and like-lihood of the harm are critical to assessing the likely threat.[24] The imminence requirement serves the same purpose as the *actus reus* (conduct) element of criminal conspiracy statutes. For example, the blanket federal conspiracy law in the United States requires that at least one member of the conspiracy "do any act to effect the object of the conspiracy,"[25] and the Model Penal Code similarly requires "an overt act in pursuance of such conspiracy."[26]

Later cases confirmed the court's exclusive jurisdiction to determine the con-stitutionality of political activity. The reasoning of the German Constitutional Court in the *Radical Groups Case*, which struck down a decision of state radio and television stations denying airtime to radical left-wing parties, is instructive.[27] The court held that so long as an advertisement was related to the election, and so long as the party had not been declared illegal by the court, content-based interference with expression was beyond the power of the broadcast media or the government. An organization acquires rights of expression as a political party, and only the court has the authority to rule on the constitutionality of a party: "The jurisdictional monopoly of the Federal Constitutional Court cat-egorically precludes administrative action against the existence of a political party, regardless of how anticonstitutional the party's program may be."[28]

A similar form of procedural protection emerged in France after World War II, in the Fifth Republic. By contrast to the concentration of power in the legislature under the Fourth Republic, the post-1958 French constitutional order hewed much more closely to a formal recognition of separation of pow-ers in which judicial oversight emerged as an additional source of power[29] – a

---

[24] *See* Shlomit Wallerstein, *Criminalizing Remote Harm and the Case of Anti-democratic Activity*, 28 Cardozo L. Rev. 2697 (2007) (examining application of criminal law principles to anti-democratic incitement).

[25] 18 U.S.C. § 371.

[26] Model Penal Code § 5.03(5).

[27] *Radical Groups Case*, BVerfG Feb. 14, 1978, 47 BVerfGE 198, *translated in part in* Donald P. Kommers, The Constitutional Jurisprudence of the Federal Republic of Germany 224 (Durham, NC: Duke University Press, 2nd ed. 1997).

[28] *Id.*, *translated in part in* Kommers, *supra* note 37, at 224, 227.

[29] For a discussion of the development of judicial review by the Conseil Constitutionnel, see John Ferejohn & Pasquale Pasquino, *Constitutional Adjudication: Lessons from Europe*, 82 Tex. L. Rev. 1671 (2004), which describes the emergence of French judicial review as an "instrument of a 'moderate,' or limited government – a mechanism of the liberal tradition, which guards against potentially tyrannical majorities." *Id.* at 1685 (footnote omitted); *see also* Burt Neuborne, *Judicial Review and Separation of Powers in France and the United States*, 57 N.Y.U. L. Rev. 363, 377–410 (1982).

surprisingly late development in the land of Montesquieu.[30] Perhaps the most significant decision of the Conseil Constitutionnel in establishing the principle of independent judicial oversight came in 1971, precisely in the area of the banning of political parties.[31] The Conseil declared unconstitutional a law that would have vested in the executive branch the authority to prohibit the formation of a political party, a power it had previously denied to the legislature acting on its own accord.[32]

Russia prior to Putin's consolidation of power provides an interesting contrast. In the wake of an unsuccessful military coup in 1991, President Boris Yeltsin issued a series of decrees banning the Communist Party and confiscating its property.[33] The legal prohibition prompted a challenge before the newly formed Russian Constitutional Court.[34] After a politically charged trial, the court in the *Communist Party Case*[35] held that the decree banning the party was constitutional, even in the absence of a state of emergency, because it was rooted in a constitutional provision that "prohibits activity by parties, organizations, and movements having the aim or method of action, in particular, of forcible change to the constitutional order and undermining State security."[36] The difficulty was that the ban had been imposed through unilateral presidential action and in the absence of any established procedures. Even so, the court found the existence of a right of appeal prior to the execution of the ban to be sufficiently protective of the party's rights,[37] and therefore it upheld the ban on the merits.[38]

---

[30] On the difficult relationship between Montesquieu's advocacy of separation of powers, civil codes, and independent judicial review, see Olivier Moréteau, *Codes as Straight-Jackets, Safeguards, and Alibis: The Experience of the French Civil Code*, 20 N.C. J. INT'L L. & COM. REG. 273 (1995).

[31] Conseil constitutionnel [CC] [Constitutional Court] decision No. 71-44DC, Jul. 16, 1971, Rec. 29.

[32] The French cases are discussed at length in Neuborne, *supra* note 39, at 390–93.

[33] *See* 3 TRANSITIONAL JUSTICE: HOW EMERGING DEMOCRACIES RECKON WITH FORMER REGIMES 346, 432–35 (Washington, DC: United States Institute of Peace Press, Neil J. Kritz ed., 1995) [hereinafter Transitional Justice] (translating the presidential decrees).

[34] For more details on the formation and rise of the Russian Constitutional Court and the context surrounding the *Communist Party Case*, see Yuri Feofanov, *The Establishment of the Constitutional Court in Russia and the Communist Party Case*, 19 REV. CENT. & E. EUR. L. 623 (1993).

[35] 3 Transitional Justice, *supra* note 43, at 436–55 (translating, in part, the November 30, 1992, decision of the Russian Constitutional Court).

[36] *Id.* at 442.

[37] *Id.* at 443.

[38] *Id.* at 454.

The second procedural protection derives from the form of governmental action to be taken. Unlike the American Smith Act cases, European militant democracy does not involve criminal sanctions. The typical sanctions include removing members of proscribed parties from legislative office, compelling the disbanding of parties, and seizing the assets of parties. As discussed earlier, the nature of the available sanctions alone diminishes the proof of immediate threat required by the American clear and present danger test. Although the United States has not banned political parties as such, the use of a lesser threshold of evidence for lesser punishment may well fit under prevailing American notions of due process. Even under American constitutional law, the evidentiary requirements for a litigant to satisfy its burden of proof are directly tied to the interests at stake and the potential severity of the punishment.[39]

Finally, lurking in discussions of the ability to thwart antidemocratic elements is the sense that democratic governments must employ the least restrictive means to achieve that objective. This is an unspecified centerpiece of the European cases, and could also be fitted within American constitutional doctrine under the First Amendment. In the ECHR's treatment of a Russian-speaking candidate in Latvia and its analysis of the banning of the Refah Party in Turkey, for example, there was implicit consideration of whether the government's conduct was excessive in light of the perceived threat. Thus, in Latvia, where the government's claimed interest was the ability of the parliament to function in Latvian, the banning of a candidate whose examination in the Latvian language turned into an inquiry into her political views was deemed threatening to the capacity of the Russian-speaking minority to have a voice in the national parliament.[40] In Turkey, on the other hand, the fact that the overwhelming majority of Refah representatives would continue to sit in parliament seemed to provide ample political representation while at the same time disabling the party's organizational commitment to the imposition of clerical law.[41]

A least restrictive means requirement lends considerable support to the Indian and Israeli approaches, which focus on removing certain kinds of agitation from the electoral arena while allowing the political parties that stand behind those views to persist as organized entities. Both of these approaches maintain distinct rules for conduct in the electoral arena, either by regulating speech and agitation in the Indian fashion, or by reserving the right to

---

[39] This is the basic lesson of *Mathews v. Eldridge*, 424 U.S. 319 (1976), and its progeny.
[40] See *Podkolzina v. Latvia*, 2002-II Eur. Ct. H.R. 443.
[41] *Refah Partisi (The Welfare Party) v. Turkey*, 2003-II Eur. Ct. H.R. 267, 315 (citation omitted).

exclude even legal parties from electoral participation, as under Israeli law. This leaves looming the difficult question of "what a democracy should do when it is faced with a party that says it is democratic but in fact looks suspiciously undemocratic."[42] But the focus on campaign conduct and popular proclamations does facilitate the policing of the electoral process on a basis distinct from speech and political organization outside the electoral arena. It bears emphasizing that banning political parties is not a simple matter of withdrawing their registration as an organization. The corollary of banning parties is a willingness to use police authority to prevent like-minded individuals from gathering, agitating for common views, or even protesting governmental conduct that they find objectionable. Party prohibitions are rarely a simple matter of decreeing the conduct illegitimate. The likely result is confrontation and that in turn invites police repression of party activity and party members. If there is indeed something distinct about the electoral arena that magnifies the dangers presented by extremist groups, it is perhaps best to reserve the use of state authority for policing the integrity of the electoral system without reaching deeper into party organization.

Taken together, attention to procedural protections suggests a concept that has thus far been absent, at least as a formal matter, from American law: a distinct electoral arena within which the restraints on the regulatory power of the state over core matters of political speech, assembly, and organization are relaxed. American law has generally resisted treating electoral activity as a separate category, allowing the general First Amendment prohibitions on content and viewpoint discrimination to frame legal oversight of campaigns and political parties. At the same time, even without a deep-seated threat to democracy in the U.S., there is some hint of a distinct administrative period for elections beginning to appear in American law. In passing the Bipartisan Campaign Reform Act of 2002[43] (BCRA), generally referred to as McCain-Feingold, Congress for the first time introduced the concept of a distinct election period for restrictions on what are termed "electioneering communications."[44] As upheld by the Supreme Court in *McConnell v. FEC*,[45] BCRA created specific limitations on campaign funding and distinct disclosure requirements

---

[42] NOAH FELDMAN, AFTER JIHAD: AMERICA AND THE STRUGGLE FOR ISLAMIC DEMOCRACY 111 (New York: Farrar, Straus and Giroux, 2003).

[43] Pub. L. No. 107–155, 116 Stat. 81 (codified primarily in scattered sections of 2 U.S.C. and 47 U.S.C.).

[44] 2 U.S.C. § 434(f)(3). The definition of "electioneering communication" under BCRA – which, if met, triggers special disclosure and contribution rules – is limited to the period sixty days before a general election or thirty days before a primary election. *Id.* § 434(f)(3)(A)(i).

[45] 540 U.S. 93 (2003), *overruled in part by Citizens United v. FEC*, 558 U.S. 310 (2010).

for the periods immediately preceding primary and general elections. The administrative powers granted to an entity like India's Electoral Commission, however, are a far step beyond anything that has been recognized in American law. Even with the U.S. Supreme Court's invalidation of some of BCRA's limitations in *Citizens United v. FEC*[46] and *McCutcheon v. FEC*,[47] the outlines of some attention to an administrative law of elections are beginning to present themselves in the American context as well.

THE SUBSTANCE OF ANTIDEMOCRACY

More challenging than reform in the procedural domain is the effort to define substantively the type of threat to the democratic order that would justify party suppression, an endeavor that will necessarily require much case-specific analysis. Relatively few parties once aware of the potential for being banned will openly announce their antidemocratic objectives. More typically, especially in the case of parties seeking a mass audience, the antidemocratic nature of the party must be inferred from subtle contextual clues, such as the invocation of the imagery of temples buried beneath mosques in India or the insistent claims of the postwar German Communist Party that the newly installed West German government was a corrupt lackey of the Western powers. Absent a strong mooring in the lived domestic context, it is extraordinarily difficult to formulate broad substantive principles that cover the wide range of potential antidemocratic threats within that context.

The *Socialist Reich Party Case* from Germany is again a useful illustration of the difficulty of defining with any precision the nature of an impermissibly antidemocratic party. The Socialist Reich Party (SRP) was as menacing to a democratic order as any party could be. It looked back with unquestioned ardor upon the country's recent Nazi past. It drew its leaders from the ranks of the SS and other notorious forces of the Third Reich, characterized for recruitment purposes as "old fighters" who were "100 percent reliable."[48] Against the backdrop of the disorder and privation of defeated Germany, it looked to tap into the same founts of discontent and hatred as its precursor National Socialist Party had under Weimar.

---

[46] 558 U.S. 310 (2010) (holding BCRA's limits on independent corporate expenditures on electioneering communications violated the First Amendment).

[47] 134 S. Ct. 1434 (2014) (invalidating BCRA's aggregate limits on contributions to political candidates or committees in an election cycle).

[48] *Socialist Reich Party Case*, BVerfG Oct. 23, 1952, 2 BVerfGE 1, *translated in part in* Murphy & Tanenhaus, *supra* note 18, at 602, 604.

Despite the SRP's clear ties to the Nazis, in order to ban the party the German Constitutional Court needed to find, if not an immediate likelihood of overturning democratic governance, at least a concrete intention to realize that objective. A number of considerations were aired, some less convincing than others. For example, the court examined the party's platform and found that "it indulges in platitudes, lays down general demands that are common property of almost all parties or have already become reality, and makes vague, often utopian promises that are hardly compatible with each other."[49] One can only imagine how the court might have analyzed slogans like "Put America First" or "Build a Bridge to the Twenty-first Century" or any of the other mindless sound bites that dominate contemporary American campaigns.

A more interesting approach builds on the German constitutional requirement that parties reflect their commitment to democracy in their internal structures.[50] The court translated this provision into a rule that a political party "must be structured from the bottom up; that is, that the members must not be excluded from decision-making processes, and the basic equality of members as well as the freedom to join or to leave the party must be guaranteed."[51] Although this principle is grounded in the German Constitution, it is difficult to identify the state's interest in controlling so tightly the internal governance of a political party.

The attempt to impose a distinct internal structure on political parties raises paradoxical concerns about the relationship between political parties and the state. As the German court observed in the *Socialist Reich Party Case*, one of the telltale antidemocratic signposts of the SRP was its desire "to impose its own organizational structure on the nation as soon as it has come into power, just as the National Socialist Party did."[52] Indeed, this ambition is characteristic of totalitarian and even authoritarian regimes of the twentieth century. Almost invariably, these oppressive regimes use a disciplined party structure as the basis for governance and seek to collapse any wall between party and state. Thus, for example, several commentators have looked to the role of political parties in forming a democratic polity to argue that the parties themselves must reflect a commitment to just such democratic politics, something that authoritarian parties consistently reject.[53] Yigal Mersel takes this argument

---

[49] *Id.*

[50] GRUNDGESETZ [GG] (Basic Law) art. 21(1).

[51] *Socialist Reich Party*, 2 BVERFGE 1, *translated in part in* Kommers & Miller, *supra* note 10, at 286, 288.

[52] *Id., translated in part in* Kommers & Miller, *supra* note 10, at 286, 289.

[53] *See* Yigal Mersel, *The Dissolution of Political Parties: The Problem of Internal Democracy*, 4 INT'L J. CONST. L. 84, 97 (2006) ("Lack of internal democracy may be seen as evidence of

one step further and claims that because political parties are indispensable to a modern democracy, the parties themselves must be held to the core conditions of democracy in their internal organizational structures.[54]

Premising the right to participate in the electoral arena on internal party organization, however, brings the force of state authority deep into the heart of all political organizations. One reason the banning of political parties is so problematic for liberal democratic thought is precisely that parties are critical intermediary organizations that allow meaningful popular mobilization outside of and against state authority. It is for this reason that the right to organize and maintain political parties is a keystone of modern constitutionalism.[55] Imposing the pluralist values of a democratic society on the internal life of all political parties, however, threatens to compromise parties' political integrity and organizational independence from the state. Under American constitutional law, for example, the state is held to a standard of neutrality on matters of religion, as is indeed the case in many but not all democracies.[56] Does this mean that a Christian Democratic party would have to be banned for violating the state's obligation of neutrality? Clearly not, but the example illustrates the importance of applying different standards to the state than to political parties, even parties that are vying for a position in government.

The problem goes beyond the restrictions on ideological commitments of a democratic state. Political parties play a key role in providing a mechanism for informed popular participation in a democracy precisely because they are organizationally independent of the state. Not only do most modern

---

external nondemocracy."); *see also* James A. Gardner, *Can Party Politics Be Virtuous?*, 100 COLUM. L. REV. 667, 683–85 (2000) (arguing that "broadly inclusive internal procedures" can alleviate democratic concerns arising from party leaders' control over party positions and candidate selection).

[54] *See* Mersel, *supra* note 53, at 96–98 (claiming, as one of several justifications for requiring internal party democracy, that because individuals in a democratic state enjoy rights to equality and liberty, and because political parties are important components of a democratic regime, individuals should enjoy the same rights within the parties).

[55] For an argument that the U.S. Constitution shows its age in its inattention to political parties, see Samuel Issacharoff & Richard H. Pildes, *Politics as Markets: Partisan Lockups of the Democratic Process*, 50 STAN. L. REV. 643, 712–16 (1998). Indeed, the Constitution was supposed to create a political structure without parties, *see id.* at 713–14, an idea that collapsed by the contested election of 1800, see JOHN FERLING, ADAMS VS. JEFFERSON (New York: Oxford University Press, 2004). *See generally* Daryl J. Levinson & Richard H. Pildes, *Separation of Parties, Not Powers*, 119 HARV. L. REV. 2311 (2006).

[56] For a comparison of democracies with and without established churches, see Richard Albert, *American Separatism and Liberal Democracy: The Establishment Clause in Historical and Comparative Perspective*, 88 MARQ. L. REV. 867, 901–23 (2005).

constitutions grant significant autonomy rights to political parties,[57] but even
in the United States a large body of constitutional law has emerged to protect
the independence of political parties from the state, despite the absence of
any textual commitment to such a principle. Thus, for example, the Supreme
Court struck down as a violation of the First Amendment right to freedom of
association a requirement that all voters be able to select the candidates of a
party regardless of prior fidelity to the party or its program.[58] Moreover, the
grounds for striking down such requirements raise questions about the constitutional validity of even more modest attempts to impose the general principle
of full democratic accountability on internal party structure – for example,
the requirement that parties select their general election candidates through
primaries rather than by executive committee.[59]

Any requirement that parties have open and democratic internal structures would put at risk ideological and religious parties that may be organized around certain fixed principles not amenable to internal majoritarian
override. Also at risk would be parties formed around popular leaders, which
might or might not evolve into true mass parties. Historical examples include
early Peronism in Argentina and the creation of Kadima in Israel largely
around the personal authority of then-Prime Minister Ariel Sharon. Precisely
because parties are not the state, membership exit or electoral defeat is a perfectly appropriate response to the hoarding of power by an unrepresentative
central cadre.[60] Furthermore, because parties are not the state, the need for
pluralist competition in a democratic society does not necessarily require the
same pluralist competition within all of the contending parties. By analogy,
we may find a perfectly diverse and competitive set of offerings across a city's
restaurant row, even if each restaurant restricts itself to one particular cuisine.
There appears to be no compelling reason why we should demand that all

---

[57] See SAMUEL ISSACHAROFF, PAMELA S. KARLAN, & RICHARD H. PILDES, THE LAW OF
DEMOCRACY: LEGAL STRUCTURES OF THE POLITICAL PROCESS 215 note a (St. Paul,
MN: Foundation Press, 4th ed. 2012); Richard H. Pildes, *The Supreme Court, 2003 Term –
Foreword: The Constitutionalization of Democratic Politics*, 118 HARV. L. REV. 28, 31–34 (2004).

[58] See *Cal. Democratic Party v. Jones*, 530 U.S. 567 (2000). At issue in *Jones* was the use of a "blanket primary" in which voters were free to vote among Democratic or Republican candidates
on a line-by-line basis – choosing, for example, among Democrats for governor and among
Republicans for senator – regardless of prior identification or enrollment in a particular party.
Id. at 570. The effect was to dampen the distinct identity of each party by allowing the broad
electorate to select the party's standard-bearer. *Id.* at 581–82.

[59] This argument is more fully developed in Samuel Issacharoff, *Private Parties With Public
Purposes: Political Parties, Associational Freedoms, and Partisan Competition*, 101 COLUM.
L. REV. 274 (2001).

[60] The basic argument here draws from ALBERT O. HIRSCHMAN, EXIT, VOICE, AND LOYALTY
(Cambridge, MA: Harvard University Press, 1970).

parties adhere to the same internal structure so long as the ultimate objective is meaningful voter voice and the capacity to vote politicians out of office, a point I will address shortly.

To return for a moment to the *Socialist Reich Party Case* in Germany, the most famous adjudication of a political party ban, what ultimately determined the outcome in that case was neither the SRP's lack of internal democracy nor the platitudinous propensities of its rhetoric. Rather, the key element was the most obvious one: the SRP's direct ties to the country's Nazi past. The court found that the party modeled its uniforms on those of the Hitler Youth and that "[f]ormer Nazis h[eld] key positions in the party to such an extent as to determine its political and intellectual image. No decision [could] be made against their will."[61] The logical conclusion was that dissolution was proper given the party's aim "to impose its own organizational structure on the nation as soon as it has come into power" and "eliminate the free democratic basic order."[62] At the end of the day, the simple, compelling fact was that this was a party of Nazis, complete with a heroic worship of the "Reich," serious elements of anti-Semitism, and a conspicuous refusal to disavow any link to the Hitler government.[63] It was these specifics, in the context of postwar Germany, that placed the SRP outside the bounds of democratic tolerance.

If there were a model for a party that should be banned, it would be a political mobilization of unrepentant Nazi combatants seeking to destabilize and overturn the fledgling German democracy right after World War II. With its worship of the "Führer" and the "Reich," the challenge to democracy posed by the SRP could not have been more clear. Yet the German court's difficulty in crafting principles of general application even in this context should serve as a caution regarding the difficulty of defining with precision the substantive requirements for inclusion or exclusion in the democratic electoral arena.

PRESERVATION OF PLURALIST COMPETITION

Unlike the situation facing the German court a half century ago, there are now many examples of democratic governments' acting to protect the viability of threatened democracies. The general contours of how such bans may be implemented are suggested by democratic countries' experiences prohibiting extremist parties. But these examples also indicate the high level of abstraction

---

[61] *Socialist Reich Party Case*, BVerfG Oct. 23, 1952, 2 BVERFGE 1, *translated in part in* Kommers & Miller, *supra* note 10, at 286, 288.

[62] *Id.*, *translated in part in* Kommers & Miller, *supra* note 10, at 286, 289.

[63] *Id.*, *translated in part in* Murphy & Tanenhaus, *supra* note 18, at 602, 605–06.

needed to describe the exact criteria that justify a prohibition. It is instructive that the efforts of the Venice Commission yielded rather broad commands focusing on the extent to which parties are organized around a commitment to overthrow constitutional democracy, with some secondary sense of the immediacy of the perceived threat:

> [T]he competent bodies should have sufficient evidence that the political party in question is advocating violence (including such specific demonstrations of it as racism, xenophobia and intolerance), or is clearly involved in terrorist or other subversive activities. State authorities should also evaluate the level of threat to the democratic order in the country and whether other measures, such as fines, other administrative measures or bringing individual members of the political party involved in such activities to justice, could remedy the situation.[64]

This brief statement brings together the three core themes identified thus far: the immediacy of the perceived harm, the link to illegal activity, and the generalized antidemocratic commitment of the party to be proscribed.

Typically, the national laws implementing party prohibitions follow the broad outlines suggested by the Venice Commission. These laws combine a concern about potential violence, which takes into account the immediacy of the perceived threat, with a broad hostility toward those who would foment hatred along religious or ethnic lines. For example, as noted in the Venice Commission Report of 1998:

> In France parties may be banned for fostering discrimination, hatred or violence towards a person or group of persons because of their origins or the fact that they do not belong to a particular ethnic group, nation, race or religion, or for spreading ideas or theories which justify or encourage such discrimination, hatred or violence. The situation in Spain is similar, but, in addition to race and creed, sex, sexual leaning, family situation, illness and disabilities are also taken into consideration. Political parties which foster racial hatred are also prohibited, for example, by the constitutions of Belarus and Ukraine, while in Azerbaijan the legislation highlights racial, national and religious conflict. Under Bulgarian law parties may be prohibited both for pursuing fascist ideals and for fomenting racial, national, religious or ethnic unrest. The Russian constitution prohibits the creation and activities of social associations whose aims or deeds stir up social, racial, ethnic and religious discord.[65]

---

[64] *Democracy through Law Guidelines, supra* note 2, art. III, § V, ¶ 15.
[65] *Id.* at app. I, § I.B.b, 5.

These formulations invite the reader to nod in recognition of the problem being addressed. But the generalized sense of accord masks a disquieting abstraction as to how these condemnations play out in the specific. Almost all of these prohibitions have a heavy dose of the "I know it when I see it"[66] principle that is understandably disquieting to First Amendment sensibilities.

Ultimately, in order to address the threat posed by antidemocratic groups there must be a reexamination of the core commitment entailed by democracy. On a very thin definition of democracy, a temporally defined majority must be able to select governors through an election. This definition of democracy addresses the end state of decision making, but lacks the broader conditions of tolerance of democratic society and the institutional framework through which democratic self-governance is exercised. The narrow focus on the end condition of majority selection is insufficient because it lacks the critical element of repeat play, a commitment that the consent of the electorate is being reexamined through the risk of electoral defeat of the prior round's winners. The real definition of democracy must turn on the ability of majorities to be formed and re-formed over time and to remove from office those exercising governmental power.[67] Many deeply antidemocratic groups are willing to vie for power through the electoral arena; few, if any, are willing to give up power that way. The definition of groups that are tolerable within a democratic order must turn, at the very least, on such groups' willingness to be voted out of office should they come to hold power. To take a leading example from India, the question was not whether the BJP could be elected to office despite its past association with religious strife. The key issue was whether the BJP had matured into a political party that could be removed from office, as indeed it now has. The same inquiry would guide the Eastern European countries through their assessment of the reconstituted communist parties, Turkey through its evaluation of the realigned Justice and Development Party, and so forth.

---

[66] *Jacobellis v. Ohio*, 378 U.S. 184, 197 (1964) (Stewart, J., concurring).

[67] This controversial claim roots democratic legitimacy in competition among contending groups for the support of the governed. This view is most notably associated with Joseph Schumpeter's arguments, which define the core of democracy as "that institutional arrangement for arriving at political decisions in which individuals acquire the power to decide by means of a competitive struggle for the people's vote." JOSEPH A. SCHUMPETER, CAPITALISM, SOCIALISM, AND DEMOCRACY 241 (Abingdon: Routledge, 2010) (1942). The concept of competition inheres in most accounts of democratic legitimacy, even ones infused with substantive content. *See, e.g.,* Robert A. Dahl, *Polyarchy, Pluralism, and Scale,* 7 SCANDINAVIAN POL. STUD. 225, 230 (1984) (suggesting that democracy can be understood as "a system of control by competition"), *quoted in* Michael P. McDonald & John Samples, *The Marketplace of Democracy: Normative and Empirical Issues, in* THE MARKETPLACE OF DEMOCRACY 1, 1 (Michael P. McDonald & John Samples eds., Washington, DC: Brookings Institution Press, 2006).

On this view, elections play a central role in democratic theory not because they ensure predetermined substantive outcomes but because they prove to be the best (and likely the only) mechanism for ensuring the consent of the governed. In order for elections to serve this function, however, there must be – in the words of Bernard Manin – "regularly renewed popular consent,"[68] which requires periodic elections in which the governors place their claims to continued officeholding in the hands of the governed. Events over the past decade in Egypt, Iraq, and Afghanistan – to name just a few examples – have shown that holding an election is not the same as creating an enduring system of democratic governance. The experience of "one man, one vote, one time" in postcolonial regimes dictates great caution in assuming that elections and stable democratic governance are necessarily coterminous.[69]

Emphasizing the renewability of consent also illuminates the substantive constraints that guide courts through messy disputes over the boundaries of democratic participation. In order for consent to be meaningfully renewed, the decisions of a majority-supported government bearing on the structure of the political process must be capable of being reversed by subsequent majorities. Hence, a decision to expand the role of religion in the public sphere (as with support to church schools) remains within the realm of a reversible political decision, while a removal of nonbelievers from the political process does not. In this sense, the strongest justification for the holding of the Refah Partisi case turned on the party's efforts to restore a version of the Ottoman millet system, in which each religious community would minister to its own affairs while the dominant Sunni majority alone would attend to the affairs of state. Making political power unaccountable to large segments of the population is just the sort of impediment to reversibility that threatens ongoing democratic governance.

Focusing on renewability of consent further encourages consideration of a broader range of initial constitutional arrangements, particularly in deeply divided societies. Viewing constitutions as documents that facilitate reversible democratic decision making, rather than as fixed arrays of rights, allows more flexibility in constitutional design. As difficult as the inquiry may be, a

---

[68] Bernard Manin, The Principles of Representative Government 176 (1997).

[69] The phrase "one man, one vote, one time" was coined by former Assistant Secretary of State and U.S. Ambassador to Syria and Egypt Edward Djerejian. *See* Ali Khan, *A Theory of Universal Democracy*, 16 Wis. Int'l L.J. 61, 106 n.130 (1997). *See* Donald L. Horowitz, A Democratic South Africa? Constitutional Engineering in a Divided Society 239–40 (Berkeley and Los Angeles: University of California Press, 1991) (noting that power did not change hands through peaceful elections in Africa between 1967 and 1991).

procedural concern for the renewability of consent allows fragile democracies to attend more to the institutional arrangements that best police the borders of democratic participation than to the no-less-contested terrain of which rights must be available in a democratic society.

In order to assess potential threats to subsequent democratic accountability, however, democratic countries need latitude to police the electoral arena in a manner distinct from both the prohibition of particular parties, on one hand, and the imposition of criminal sanctions, on the other. At a minimum, such an approach requires an administrative law of elections, an independent body capable of responding to claims of political retaliation against a disfavored group,[70] and sufficient alternative means of expression to avoid excessively dampening political debate. In several countries, including India, that process of independent administrative review followed by judicial oversight appears to have taken hold successfully. Even in Mexico, a country recently emerging from a lengthy period of one-party rule, an administrative body and electoral tribunal overseeing a tightly contested presidential election has maintained both independence and legitimacy.[71] One reason this approach appears antithetical to the American tradition is that there has been little or no experience here with neutral administration of elections; a complete dearth of administrative review, except for the woefully ineffectual Federal Election Commission; and virtually no recent experience with political agitation being a serious threat to domestic order.[72] Far from being universal, that experience appears to be a distinct outlier on the world stage.

CONCLUSION

It is by now well established that all constitutional orders retain emergency powers, either formally or informally. Justice Jackson's firm admonition that the Constitution is not "a suicide pact"[73] sums up well the sense that even a

---

[70] For an insightful account of the different forms of administrative oversight of elections and their relative efficacy, see Christopher S. Elmendorf, *Representation Reinforcement through Advisory Commissions: The Case of Election Law*, 80 N.Y.U. L. REV. 1366 (2005).

[71] *See* JULIA PRESTON & SAMUEL DILLON, OPENING MEXICO 496–99 (2004); *see also* Jamin Raskin, *A Right-to-Vote Amendment for the U.S. Constitution: Confronting America's Structural Democracy Deficit*, 3 ELECTION L.J. 559, 564 (2004) (describing the key role an independent electoral commission could play in making political change possible and citing Mexico's commission as a successful example).

[72] For an exception, see *Ex parte* McCardle, 74 U.S. (7 Wall.) 506 (1869), in which the Court refused, on jurisdictional grounds, to grant a writ of habeas corpus to the author of incendiary articles.

[73] *Terminiello v. Chicago*, 337 U.S. 1, 37 (1949) (Jackson, J., dissenting).

tolerant democratic society must be able to police its fragile borders. The discussion in the preceding chapters rests on many premises that appear largely alien to the American experience, or at least the past 100 years of it. The starting premise, however, is that the most newly forged democracies are almost invariably deeply fragile, and have political structures that are porous to antidemocratic elements. That porousness requires an ability to restrict the capture of governmental authority by those who would subvert democracy altogether. The next step is to envision a realm of electoral politics with rules of conduct distinct from the rules that apply to broader constitutional rights of assembly, petition, and speech. In order to manage the unique threats that arise from that distinct political realm, fragile democracies need the ability to discipline electoral activity without regard to the imminence of criminal or insurrectionary conduct, the accepted standard for the criminalization of political speech. Finally, independent oversight of the political process is required to prevent the dangerous powers here argued for from being deployed in the name of the self-serving preservation of incumbent political power.

As an empirical matter, it is entirely possible that democracy faces greater dangers from the promiscuous use of police powers than from domestic enemies. This is most likely true with respect to more stable democracies and may point to the centrality of the preservation of civil liberties in times of stress. That reality does little to address the problems faced by societies that are more menaced by the indisputable emergence from time to time of mass-based movements seeking to destroy democratic life.

The international experience also cautions against readily assuming that any restraints in the political process necessarily lead to a collapse of democratic rights or a fundamental compromising of democratic legitimacy. Virtually all democratic societies define some extremist elements as beyond the bounds of democratic tolerance. Despite errors of overreaching, likely inevitable in human affairs, it appears that this power is largely used with restraint and hesitation. With the benefit of hindsight, therefore, the question that needs to be addressed is whether Weimar Germany could have assembled the tools necessary to fight off the Hitlerian challenge within the bounds of democratic legitimacy. One certainly must hope so.

PART II

Competitive Democracy

6

Giving Up Power

When teaching a course on the constitutional law of democracy, it is my custom to open the first day of class with what I describe as a modern-day parable. As presented to the students, the events concern a precipitous and heated confrontation some twenty years ago that I suggest may have escaped their notice. The conflict pitted the head of a large and powerful state against the leader of a small and poorly armed state. As the events unfolded, the tension between the two leaders mounted dramatically. The partisans of the two camps became increasingly divided and braced for what seemed the inevitable showdown. After months of skirmishing, the denouement arrived and the leader of the small state proved victorious. Perhaps most remarkably, the leader of the state of crushingly superior military force turned over his entire arsenal to the newly victorious head of the small state and quietly left office with little concern for incarceration or assassination, contented with nothing more than the equivalent of the palace guards to usher him away.

Now the events in question are, of course, a cartoon rendition of the 1992 U.S. presidential election between the incumbent President George Bush and the governor of Arkansas, Bill Clinton. The shaggy-dog quality of the telling aims to convey just how exceptional it has been, in the course of human history, for power to pass peacefully across a heated partisan divide, particularly when the usually decisive weight of military force rests exclusively in the hands of the displaced incumbent power. The question for the students then becomes to discern the necessary conditions for power to pass in this fashion.

In turn, the chapters that follow examine just this question from the perspective of new democracies. Our modern conception of democracy assumes what Abraham Lincoln termed a "government of the people, by the people, for the people,"[1] in which each election presents a meaningful alternative

---

[1]   President Abraham Lincoln, The Gettysburg Address (Nov. 19, 1863).

between rival sets of candidates, and in which the electors make the choice of who shall govern. By contrast, older conceptions of democracy, notably in ancient Athens, assumed rotation in office among the citizens, not among a group of representatives. As captured by political theorist Bernard Manin, the idea of rotation in ancient democracy "was not that the people must both govern and be governed, but that every citizen must be able to occupy the two positions alternately."[2] In modern representative democracy, "the kind of political equality that was at center stage was the equal right to consent to power, and not – or much less so – an equal chance to hold office."[3]

The critical issue in democratic governance must be whether the political process offers some prospect of removing from office incumbents who have incurred the wrath of the public. In contrast to the Athenian view of elections, in which ensuring the direct participation of all citizens in governance was a prime objective, the modern view turns on the accountability of the governors to the governed. In the words of Joseph Schumpeter, "the primary function of the electorate" in a democracy is not only creating "a government (directly or through an intermediate body)," but also "evicting it."[4]

An unstable democracy may see its first officeholders claim the authority of political processes to ensure their continued unchallenged rule, an extreme variant of the phenomenon that Richard Pildes and I describe in the American context as a "lockup" of the democratic political process.[5] Without clear ground rules that ensure, among other things, that the losers of today can have a fair opportunity to displace the winners in the future, the orderly transfer of governmental authority among competing political factions would be impossible. Particularly in states emerging from authoritarian rule, the critical question is not whether an election will be used to determine the first set of rulers, but whether there will be a second election in which the continued tenure of the heads of state is seriously at issue.

Democracy is a process of electoral consultation with an engaged citizenry. The need for a decision as to who governs must be limited in time and limited in the powers afforded to the dominant majority at any one time. As expressed by political scientist Giovanni Sartori, "democracy is not pure and simple majority rule," but rather "'majority rule' is only a shorthand formula

[2] BERNARD MANIN, THE PRINCIPLES OF REPRESENTATIVE GOVERNMENT 28 (Cambridge: Cambridge University Press, 1997).

[3] *Id.* at 92.

[4] JOSEPH A. SCHUMPETER, CAPITALISM, SOCIALISM AND DEMOCRACY 244 (Abingdon: Routledge, 2010) (1942).

[5] *See* Samuel Issacharoff & Richard H. Pildes, *Politics as Markets: Partisan Lockups of the Democratic Process*, 50 STAN. L. REV. 643 (1998).

for *limited* majority rule, for a restrained majority rule that respects minority rights."[6] In turn, this requires meaningful electoral reaffirmation, both to protect the minority and to ensure the democratic engagement of the majority:

> [U]nless the liberty of minorities is respected, not only would the first electoral test determine, once and for all, those who are free and those who are not; but also the liberty of those who voted for the majority on that occasion would be lost because, in practice, they would not be permitted to change their opinion. Thus, the first election would be, in effect, the only true election. And this amounts to saying that such a democracy dies at the moment of its inception.[7]

A first election, no matter how democratic the participation and how clear the electoral mandate, is not a sufficient hallmark of democracy's inception. For the purposes of understanding modern democratic rule, we may posit that the key to democratic government is not the first election but the second. In other words, the question is not whether the citizenry was consulted on the current head of state, but whether the electorate retains the power to "throw the rascals out."[8] Beyond the fundamental of majority rule based on equal suffrage,[9] democratic governance depends on the ability to review the outgoing government unfavorably and select its replacement. As well captured in 2004 by Indonesian President Susilo Bambang Yudhoyono, the first popularly elected president of that country, in his first inaugural address, "[i]n the democratic transition of any country, the second election is normally regarded as the critical one, the litmus test for the maturity of democracy."[10]

REVOLUTION BY ELECTION

Before turning to these new democracies, however, it is worth recalling just how recent and rare is the ability to reorder power through peaceable election. Invariably, students confronted with the question of why George Bush ceded power to Bill Clinton react with disbelief that the question is even posed.

---

[6] GIOVANNI SARTORI, THE THEORY OF DEMOCRACY REVISITED 31 (Chatham, NJ: Chatham House Publishers, 1987).

[7] *Id.* at 33.

[8] G. BINGHAM Powell Jr., ELECTIONS AS INSTRUMENTS OF DEMOCRACY 47 (New Haven, CT: Yale University Press, 2000).

[9] For a spare definition, see Jon Elster, *Introduction* to CONSTITUTIONALISM AND DEMOCRACY 1 (Jon Elster & Rune Slagstad eds., Cambridge: Cambridge University Press, 1988) (democracy is "simple majority rule, based on the principle 'One person, one vote'").

[10] Susilo Bambang Yudhoyono, president of Indon., Inaugural Address (Oct. 20, 2004), *excerpted in Documents on Democracy*, J. DEMOCRACY, Apr. 2005, at 178, 180.

After all, it has always been thus, hasn't it? In the common law sense of settled practice, the memory of man runneth not to the contrary. Defeated presidents have always yielded power in the United States, and even if there have been only ten defeated after one term, all presidents run for reelection assuming they will depart if the voters tell them to.

The critical question for new contested democracies is how to create the presumption that the winners of today could be the losers of tomorrow, and that the disappointed candidates of today may one day aspire to be electoral victors. Historical practice may provide comfort to political rivals in the United States, but how can other countries get past the first election from which such a history of peaceful transition might be launched? At a minimum, all democracies need to have a confirmed history of power passing as the result of a contested election. Simply put, there has to be a first time, and that first time by definition has no prior moment to rely on, even in the United States.

If the American winners of today routinely depart tomorrow, as in the transition from President Bush to President Clinton, it was not always so. Not until 1800 did an incumbent president face an electoral challenge. George Washington had run unopposed when he was elected in 1789 and reelected in 1792, and had retired from public office after his second term. The election of 1796 was the first contested presidential election in American history, but it had no entrenched officeholder seeking to stay in office against an electoral opponent.

The presidential election of 1800, in which President John Adams lost to Thomas Jefferson, was the first time in modern history that an elected head of state was replaced by his electoral rival. The Athenians had innovated rotation in office, but the rotation in office was among citizens chosen by lot. The Roman Republic had yearly elections for two consuls, who jointly served as heads of state, but they too left office automatically at the conclusion of their one-year term. Neither Athens nor Rome used elections as a means of limiting tenure in office, nor of allowing the electorate a retrospective assessment of the performance in office of the incumbent. The combination of a unitary executive in one person, the president, and of the ability of voters to remove that person from office was unique to the American experiment with republican government.

Whatever may have become routine in the past two centuries could not be assumed in 1800. Unlike the election of 1992, the election of 1800 could claim no constitutional antecedents in which an incumbent president was displaced by a challenger. Nor could the election of 1992, whatever its now-forgotten rhetoric and curious third-party candidacy, match the stakes of the election of

1800, in which the contending parties angrily charged each other with treacherous intent to deliver the young republic to foreign domination by either France or Britain.[11] At issue in the highly charged election of 1800 was, therefore, not only the question of whether presidential power would pass peaceably from the incumbent to the challenger, but whether that could happen under huge partisan strain. Much more so than current partisan divides in the United States, the division between the Federalists and Antifederalists rang to the core of the role of government in American society and to the role of the fledgling republic in the international arena.

Today, the "revolution of 1800,"[12] as Thomas Jefferson immodestly dubbed it, is remembered primarily for the confusion in the counting of votes for president and vice president and the resulting election between Thomas Jefferson and John Adams being thrown to the House of Representatives. The precipitating event in 1800 was a technical defect in balloting for the presidency. In that election, John Adams, a Federalist and the incumbent president; Thomas Jefferson, a Republican and the incumbent vice president; Aaron Burr, a Federalist; and Charles Cotesworth Pinckney, a Republican, were all on the presidential ballot, although Burr and Pinckney were understood to be running for vice president.[13] Jefferson and Burr each ended up with seventy-three electoral votes, Adams with sixty-five, and Pinckney with sixty-four.

Because of a defect in the original constitutional design, which did not distinguish between presidential and vice presidential candidates in the balloting,[14] the election was thrown to the House of Representatives to choose between Jefferson and Burr for president. The fact that Jefferson and Burr received identical numbers of electoral votes necessitated a runoff, even though Burr received his votes as a candidate for vice president. While the Federalists had strategically avoided this potential problem by having one elector cast a vote for John Jay instead of Pinckney, "the Republican managers

---

[11] STANLEY Elkins & Eric McKITRICK, THE AGE OF FEDERALISM 354–88 (Oxford: Oxford University Press, 1993).

[12] Letter from Thomas Jefferson to Spencer Roane (Sept. 6, 1819), *in* 10 THE WRITINGS OF THOMAS JEFFERSON 140, 140 (Paul Leicester Ford ed., New York: G. P. Putnam's Sons, 1899). Jefferson's moniker has stuck for nearly two centuries. *See, e.g.,* THE REVOLUTION OF 1800: DEMOCRACY, RACE, AND THE NEW REPUBLIC (James Horn et al. eds., Charlottesville: University of Virginia Press, 2002).

[13] For a detailed discussion of the election, its electoral vote counting process, and the days leading up to Jefferson's inauguration, see BERNARD A. WEISBERGER, AMERICA AFIRE: JEFFERSON, ADAMS, AND THE REVOLUTIONARY ELECTION OF 1800, at 227–75 (New York: HarperCollins, 2000).

[14] *See* U.S. CONST. art. II, § 1, cl. 3, *amended by* U.S. CONST. amend. XII.

had not made certain that one of their electors 'threw away' a second vote on someone other than Aaron Burr."[15]

The crisis arose because the Federalist Congress still in power was not inclined to vote in Thomas Jefferson, who had beaten the Federalist incumbent, Adams; but to vote in Burr would have made a mockery of the electoral process. In addition, there was still hope on the part of some Federalists that the stalemate between Jefferson and Burr would somehow result in Adams staying in office. Ultimately, however, the crisis passed without violence and the practice of presidential succession took hold in the young republic. After thirty-five fruitless ballots, in which Jefferson received eight votes, Burr received six, and two states did not vote, the Federalists finally relented. On the thirty-sixth ballot, Jefferson carried ten states and became the third president of the United States. Nonetheless, in a messy election with poorly crafted electoral rules, the principle first took hold that electoral victors assume office and the defeated candidate must ultimately stand down.

ROTATION IN OFFICE

While the principle of democratic rotation in office may have taken hold in the United States in 1800, it remains far from established around the world. The simple fact is that, until recently, there have been few such regime changes in history, and even with the growth of constitutional democracies the figure remains quite low. Removal of a head of state by selection of an alternative candidate is still an exceptional occurrence.

In one sense, however, this should not be surprising. Democracies come in many forms, and not all permit the direct election of the head of state by the voters. Many constitutional democracies have a parliamentary system in which the prime minister serves as head of government. Taking the United Kingdom as an example, one could say that no prime minister is ever voted out because the popular vote is limited to the local constituencies that elect only one member of the House of Commons. Alternatively, many countries have a split executive in which a directly elected president serves as formal head of state, but power is concentrated in a prime minister, who is selected by the dominant party or coalition in parliament to be head of government. There too, no formal election allows the public to dislodge directly a disfavored incumbent.

Even with these qualifications, there is no escaping the striking paucity of electoral defeats by heads of state. In Latin America, where a strong form

---

[15]   Weisberger, *supra* note 13, at 256.

of *caudillo* presidentialism is the norm,[16] there were only three instances of elected presidents being voted out of office from independence through 2005.[17] The statistic may need to be qualified as there is a one-term limit on presidents in some Latin American countries. But even so, many countries experience the permanence in office of one-party control of power, as through the rotation in office of the official candidates of the Partido Revolucionario Institucional during its decades-long command in Mexico.

The history of incumbent sinecure is strong the world over, and the displacement of elected presidents remains the exceptional story. Although Africa emerged from colonialism with a number of states with apparent multiparty democracy, by the end of the 1960s, only Botswana, Gambia, and Zambia ever had meaningful multiparty elections.[18] Between 1960 and 1990, there was only one head of state in all of postcolonial Africa who was deposed electorally.[19] In fact, prior to 1990, there appear to have been only eight presidents *in recorded history* outside the United States who have run for office as incumbents and lost, and in three of those cases the newly elected alternative president was then overthrown by the followers of the defeated prior officeholder.

One of the successes of the Third Wave of democratization is precisely the ability in some countries to establish a pattern of defeated incumbents leaving office. There are now more than a dozen incumbents who have been voted out of office outside the United States (and none overthrown between 1990 and 2000). This is in addition to the ten U.S. presidents who have been defeated in attempts at reelection – to which one could perhaps add Lyndon Johnson, whose vulnerability in the primary elections compelled him to withdraw from the general election in 1968.[20]

[16] *See* Juan J. Linz, *Presidential or Parliamentary Democracy: Does It Make a Difference?*, in THE FAILURE OF PRESIDENTIAL DEMOCRACY 3, 6 (Juan J. Linz & Arturo Valenzuela eds., Baltimore, MD: The Johns Hopkins University Press, 1994) (listing features of strongman rule).

[17] Adam Przeworski & Carolina Curvale, *Instituciones políticas y desarrollo económico en las Américas: el largo plazo*, in VISIONES DEL DESARROLLO EN AMÉRICA LATINA 157, 175 (José Luis Machinea & Narcís Serra eds., Santiago, Chile: Comisión Económica para América Latina y el Caribe (CEPAL), 2007).

[18] *See generally* GUY ARNOLD, AFRICA: A MODERN HISTORY 353–54 (London: Atlantic Books, 2005) (describing the politics of postcolonial Africa in the 1960s).

[19] Daniel N. Posner & Daniel J. Young, *The Institutionalization of Political Power in Africa*, J. DEMOCRACY, July 2007, at 126, 131. The only exception was Somalia in 1967, and the winner was quickly overthrown. *See id.*

[20] I am indebted to Adam Przeworski for these data, compiled from his large data set on electoral accountability. These data are limited to presidential systems and do not include either parliamentary regimes or semi-presidential systems, in which the president stands for general election but serves alongside a prime minister who, like the cabinet, is appointed by parliament. *See generally* Maurice Duverger, *A New Political System Model: Semi-Presidential Government*, 8 EUR. J. POL. RES. 165 (1980).

It is tempting to attribute this weak political check on incumbents to the concentration of individual power in presidential regimes versus the control of party authority in parliamentary governments. Looking at the history of presidentialism outside the United States, however, points more to the fundamental difficulties of maintaining democratic rule rather than the attributes of the specific form of democratic governance. The stability of democratic governance appears to be the product of internal political factors rather than the specific form of executive power. Ultimately, the conclusion is that "the fragility of presidential democracies is a function not of presidentialism per se but of the fact that presidential democracies have existed in countries where the environment is inhospitable for any kind of democratic regime."[21]

THE TEST OF TIME

In contemplating the future world of a self-governing republican state, James Madison assumed the central role of a finite tenure in office in a government "administered by persons holding their offices during pleasure for a limited period, or during good behavior."[22] In turn, this leads to a more robust definition of democracy as a government in which "public policies are made, on a majority basis, by representatives subject to effective popular control at periodic elections which are conducted on the principle of political equality and under conditions of political freedom."[23]

The following chapters take up the question of the alterability of political control under democratic rule. First, the historic difficulty in establishing a credible commitment to rotation in office hampers the formation of democratic states in post-authoritarian environments. Second, as will be developed at length, courts are often the only institution capable of resisting the pressures toward consolidation of one-man or one-party rule. The main thesis that follows is that absent meaningful contestation for power, any country's commitment to democracy is at best untested and the temptations toward consolidated, unchecked rule are ever present.

Take for example Botswana, often held out as standard bearer for democracy in Africa, a country that was among the first African nations to hold

---

[21] José Antonio Cheibub, Presidentialism, Parliamentarism, and Democracy 136 (Cambridge: Cambridge University Press, 2007).

[22] The Federalist No. 39, at 241 (James Madison) (Clinton Rossiter ed., New York: The New American Library, 1961).

[23] Henry B. Mayo, An Introduction to Democratic Theory 70 (New York: Oxford University Press, 1960).

multiparty elections,[24] and one hailed by the World Bank as "a developmental success story" and "a mature democracy."[25] To its great credit, Botswana has regularly held elections since independence in 1966 under conditions repeatedly characterized by international observers as free and fair. This record has justly earned Botswana "the reputation of Africa's leading and longest multiparty democracy"[26] and its "oft-used moniker, the African Miracle."[27] Indeed, half a century of free and fair elections is quite an accomplishment and a marked contrast with much of postcolonial Africa. During that time, however, only one party – the Botswana Democratic Party (BDP) – has held power. The BDP has ruled continuously since independence, dominating in every election and rendering the role of the opposition largely ceremonial. What assurance is there that Botswana is indeed responsive to the popular will? Alternatively, does democracy demand a proven capacity for the electorate to replace the government?

As will be discussed in the national examples that follow, one-party dominance leads to a choking of the capacity for effective political challenge. The apparatus of the state consolidates around the political dominance of one party, and often one man. Alongside the absence of political challenge come the uses of the powers of office to reward loyalty to the regime, what I will refer to as the "three C's" of uncontested rule: cronyism, corruption, and clientelism. Where dependence on connections to the incumbent regime becomes the basis for employment or government contracts or social welfare benefits, no opposition can ensure its supporters that disloyalty to the incumbent does not mean isolation and penury. Even where elections are reasonably free and fair, and even where the opposition does not face direct oppression, the suffocating consequences of perpetual rule will be manifest.

Political theorists speak of "renewed popular consent," in Bernard Manin's formulation, as the key to governmental accountability to the public good, and draw the contrast to "a system of election for life [that] leaves voters with no effective means of influencing the actions of their rulers, once elected."[28]

---

[24] *See* ADAM PRZEWORSKI, MICHAEL E. ALVAREZ, JOSÉ ANTONIO CHEIBUB, & FERNANDO LIMONGI, DEMOCRACY AND DEVELOPMENT: POLITICAL INSTITUTIONS AND WELL-BEING IN THE WORLD, 1950–1990, at 23–28 (Cambridge: Cambridge University Press, 2000).

[25] Botswana Overview, THE WORLD BANK, http://www.worldbank.org/en/country/botswana/overview (last visited June 14, 2014).

[26] DAVID SEBUDUBUDU & BERTHA Z. OSEI-HWEDIE, DEMOCRATIC CONSOLIDATION IN SADC 1 (Johannesburg, South Africa: EISA, 2005).

[27] Amelia Cook & Jeremy Sarkin, *Is Botswana the Miracle of Africa? Democracy, the Rule of Law, and Human Rights Versus Economic Development*, 19 TRANSNAT'L L. & CONTEMP. PROBS. 453, 454 (2010).

[28] Manin, *supra* note 2, at 176.

Adam Przeworski and his collaborators have refined empirical tests to assess the prospects for meaningful democratic rule in terms of the proven ability of those out of power to dislodge officeholders through elections. As they formulate the inquiry, "Unless the losers are given political guarantees that their ability to contest future elections will be protected, the mere fact that elections have been held does not suffice to qualify the regime as democratic. Only if the losers are allowed to compete, win, and assume office is a regime democratic." Countries like Botswana simply cannot offer a guarantee that power is really up for grabs: "If the same party or coalition of parties had won every single election from some time in the past until it was deposed by force or until now, we cannot know if it would have held elections when facing the prospect of losing or if it would have yielded office had it in fact lost."[29]

The problem is to distinguish real democratic choice from simply a void in the actual exercise of political power. In newly minted democracies emerging from the collapse of authoritarian rule, as best exemplified by the former Soviet bloc after 1989, there will be uncertainty about who is in charge, who controls the military, who can summon the police, and indeed about whether government can speak on behalf of a functioning state. An initial election may sort out the contenders and identify the party or coalition with the best claim to majority support. But the initial election may or may not serve as the first step toward a robust democracy capable of ensuring popular sovereignty, including the capacity to oust the first set of rulers.

In order to get buy-in from all political factions to the initial democratic project, there must be some commitment that indeed rotation in office is possible. However, young democracies find themselves in the uncertainty of the United States in 1800, not the routine of a contested American election in 1992, let alone the more dramatic 2000 election yielding *Bush v. Gore*.[30] The question then becomes how to offer a credible commitment that democracy does not end with the first election, particularly when the first election has not yet occurred. The modern answer, in part, is a strong institutional constraint in the form of oversight of the political process by a constitutional court. How constitutional courts engage the strong party threat to democratic vitality is the subject that follows.

[29] Przeworski, Alvarez, Cheibub, & Limongi, *supra* note 24, at 18, 23.
[30] 511 U.S. 98 (2000).

7

The Promise of Constitutional Democracy

On November 6, 1985, leftist guerrillas from the Colombian 19th of April Movement overran the Colombian Supreme Court building, taking the justices of the court as hostages. In the ensuing shoot-out with the military, twelve of the judges were killed, along with more than 100 other civilians. The shootings at the court were but the most visible signpost that the country's background of war and strife could overwhelm even the central institutions of state in Bogotá, the capital. Colombia was, for much of the last half of the twentieth century, a state struggling for control of its territory against powerful private militias, and the resulting loss of state authority left open the terrain for one of the highest murder rates in the world, pervasive extreme poverty, and a stubbornly flourishing drug trade.[1] After a civil war that left more than 200,000 people dead during the Gran Violencia of the 1950s, and then the militant uprisings and drug wars of the following decades during which even more succumbed to violence, any prospect of peace and stability seemed nonexistent.[2]

Yet in 1991, in the face of overwhelming odds, a democratically elected constituent assembly promulgated a new constitution that served as part of the "profound constitutional moment throughout the Americas."[3] The fall of military dictatorships across much of South America, most notably in Argentina, Brazil, Chile, and Uruguay, unleashed a democratic revival in the region and a new commitment to limitations on the powers of government. In many ways, the democratic surge in South America paralleled the broader democratic

[1] *See* Manuel José Cepeda-Espinosa, *Judicial Activism in a Violent Context: The Origin, Role, and Impact of the Colombian Constitutional Court*, 3 WASH. U. GLOBAL STUD. L. REV. 529, 532 n.2 (2004).

[2] *See* Centro Nacional de Memoria Histórica, ¡BASTA YA! COLOMBIA: MEMORIAS DE GUERRA Y DIGNIDAD 32 (Bogotáog Centro Nacional de Memoria Histórica, 2013).

[3] Miguel Schor, *An Essay on the Emergence of Constitutional Courts: The Cases of Mexico and Colombia*, 16 IND. J. GLOBAL LEGAL STUD. 1, 12 (2009).

expansion in Eastern Europe and Asia following the fall of the Soviet Union. In each case, central to the desired democratic restoration was the idea of constraint in the exercise of state authority. Authoritarian rule allowed the direct translation of political power into arbitrary and repressive governmental conduct. In response, the democratic revival sought both to restore civilian authority and to enshrine the primacy of a rule of law.

In one sense, Colombia fit well within the movement to create effective democratic governance by focusing not only on securing civil and human rights that had been compromised, but also on the structures of governmental authority used to secure such rights. The constitution sought to overhaul many of the institutions of Colombian government, but none so much as the judiciary. Among the constitutional innovations was the creation of a constitutional court that was "by any measure one of the strongest courts in the world."[4] In the words of then President Cesar Gaviria, the court was integral to the new democratic order: an institution with the "mission of preventing any other powerful authority from hampering the transformations [the constitutional leadership is] encouraging with laws, decrees, resolutions, orders, or any other administrative decisions or happenings ... The new Constitution requires, in order to be adequately applied, a new system of constitutional judicial review."[5]

While Colombia's immediate challenges came from armed opponents of any governing authority, the constitutional court's greatest conflict arose from within the democratic governing order. Indeed, the new Colombian court introduces one of the central themes of the post-1989 new constitutional order. In this period, we find these apex courts again and again confronting excess concentrations of power in emerging and generally weak democratic states. As in Colombia, these constitutional courts emerge from a process of reformation of states in the aftermath of civil strife or the overthrow of authoritarian rule. But they are not merely creatures of the transition process: constitutional courts are created to be central actors in securing the democratic objectives of the transition in the long term.

The model for modern constitutional courts comes from Germany, whose newly created postwar constitutional court oversaw a series of state institutions compromised by Nazism – including the existing judiciary. No country emerging from an authoritarian past is likely to have the human resources to purge from office all individuals tainted by prior association with the deposed

[4] David Landau, *Political Institutions and Judicial Role in Constitutional Law*, 51 HARV. INT'L
     L.J. 319, 339 (2010).
[5] *Quoted in* Cepeda-Espinosa, *supra* note 1, at 550–51.

government. Positions requiring advanced education and professional certi-
fications almost invariably bring individuals into contact with the state and
likely compel either membership in the ruling party or other forms of acquiescence with state authority. Efforts at complete lustration not only would
deplete the society of those with experience in the technical administration of
the society, but would likely force large parts of the society into active opposition to the attempted democratization – as the United States learned to its
chagrin in Iraq.[6]

Judges are no exception to this dilemma. Of necessity, they require legal
training, which brings them into close proximity to the ruling regime, oftentimes no doubt much closer than they truly desire. Yet even authoritarian
regimes need some form of legal regularity in the everyday lives of the citizens.
There are still marriages and divorces, exchanges of goods or services as permitted by law, and the settling of affairs at death. Authoritarian regimes are
typically brutal and self-aggrandizing, but even the worst cling to some form of
order in the commonplace interactions among the citizenry. Inga Markovits
tells a compelling account of the efforts at humanity and decency of East
German family court judges under communism, even in the face of ideological intolerance from above.[7] Undoubtedly, there were moments of party
interference or politically motivated retaliation against disfavored individuals.
As a result, these same judges might be conscripted to enforce laws that no
democratic society could tolerate. But in the great run of cases, the state had
no particular stake in the resolution of the domestic woes of any particular
family, and matters of divorce or child custody had to be resolved with the
accumulation of knowledge and experience that is the judge's craft.

Germany presented both the problem and potential resolution most
clearly. Prewar Germany was home to one of the world's most sophisticated
legal cultures, replete with first-rate legal instruction in its universities and a
centuries-old body of jurisprudence. Few, if any, societies could rival the rec-
titude of German legal proceedings, nor the integrity of the judicial system.
At the same time, German legal doctrine was highly formalistic and boasted a
strong positivistic commitment to the application of the law as the command
of the sovereign, not as reflecting normative aspirational claims. In the familiar

---

[6] Brendan O'Leary, How to Get Out of Iraq with Integrity 7–8 (Philadelphia: University
of Pennsylvania Press, 2009) (describing the "de-Baathification" policy as "thoughtless …
A better policy would have found means to avoid alienating the entirety of the party's active
cadres (many of whom had joined as the sole means to achieve a professional career) which
had reasons to be opposed to [the old regime] as much as the United States.").

[7] Inga Markovits, Imperfect Justice: An East-West German Diary (New York: Oxford
University Press, 1995).

jurisprudential debate on the "is/ought" divide in legal authority, German jurisprudence defined law as that which "is" as commanded by the sovereign, rather
than any transcendent command of a normative "ought" in what laws must guarantee. This formalism was only as strong as the state that backed it: with the
surrender of Germany in the First World War and the establishment of the comparatively much weaker Weimar Republic, judges found themselves implicated
in the social struggle over the "ought" of law with relatively little jurisprudence or
history to guide them. Conservative voices – especially those of the Nazis themselves and of legal philosopher Carl Schmitt – promised a return to positivism,
a claim that found significant support within the judiciary. With the beginnings
of the Third Reich in 1933, the judiciary as an institution, and overwhelmingly
the judges as individuals, allowed their technical expertise to be exploited in the
service of the new totalitarian order.

The relation between the German judiciary and Nazi power is a source
of great controversy, even after more than a half century has passed.[8] Some
judges were notoriously disposed toward the Nazis even in the Weimar period,
as evident in the weak judicial response to the both the Kapp putsch of 1920
(which very nearly brought down the Republic) and the Munich beer hall
putsch of 1923, all of which resulted in little or no sanctions, including for
Hitler himself.[9] Indeed, many of the Weimar judges were holdovers from the
German monarchy and shared the extreme nationalism and anti-Semitism of
the Nazi opposition to Weimar.[10] Further, the weak institutions of the Weimar
Republic led to a breakdown of the positivist consensus undergirding German
legal thought after German unification.[11]

German positivism was shaken by the gradual development of 'natural'
rights norms arising from the Weimar Constitution.[12] The Third Reich built

[8] My thanks to Armin von Bogdandy for commentary on the recent German debates.
[9] INGO MULLER, HITLER'S JUSTICE: THE COURTS OF THE THIRD REICH 12–16 (Deborah
     Schneider, trans., Cambridge, MA: Harvard University Press, 1991).
[10] RICHARD MILLER, NAZI JUSTIZ: LAW OF THE HOLOCAUST 44 (Westport, CT: Praeger, 1995)
     (In the words of one contemporary German liberal: "The [legal] bar was overcrowded, divided,
     frequently anti-Semitic, conservative, wishing they were in uniform ... the last place we would
     have looked to [for opposition to Hitler] would have been the bench and the bar.").
[11] *See* Peter Caldwell, Popular Sovereignty and the Crisis of German Constitutional Law 13-40
     (Durham, NC: Duke University Press, 1997).
[12] *See, e.g.* RICHARD MILLER, *supra* note 10, at 44-46 (describing how a Jewish movie director
     was dismissed on the authority of merely a speech by Goebbels; by 1935 the criminal code
     declared that the "Reich Supreme Court as the highest German tribunal must consider it its
     duty to effect an interpretation of the law which takes into account the change of ideology and
     of legal concepts which the new state has brought about."). *See generally* PETER CALDWELL,
     supra note 11 (analyzing the development of German jurisprudence in the pre-Nazi period
     from positivism to a naturalistic common law ideal).

on these foundations: just as a constitution emanated from 'the people,' the Nazis conceived of law as emanating from the *Volk* (the racialized conception of the German nation) rather than liberal constitutionalism or bourgeois civil-law positivist reasoning.[13] Accordingly judges were required to go well beyond a narrow positivist reading of enacted law to obey their "civil duty" and support the regime.[14] In 1935 this procedure formally entered the criminal code: "The Reich Supreme Court as the highest German tribunal must consider it its duty to effect an interpretation of the law which takes into account the change of ideology and of legal concepts which the new state has brought about."[15] As bluntly stated by Justice Minister Otto Thierack, "Every judge is at liberty to call on me in case he thinks that a law compels him to render a judgment not compatible with real life. In such an emergency it will be my task to provide him with the law he needs."[16]

Certainly the occupying powers saw the legacy of positivism in the Nazi command of the German judiciary. Influential Allies during German Reconstruction saw strict positivism as the principal cause of judicial acquiescence to Nazi rule:

> Contrary to superficial conclusions drawn from Nazi "justice," the German judge is far from being inclined toward arbitrariness. On the contrary, his traditional virtue - which is also his traditional vice - is his unmitigated positivism. Class antecedents and training have accustomed him to administering justice in scrupulous accordance with the law, and the law is what the state commands. Not even the Nazi regime was given to arbitrariness in the sense that the judge could decide as he pleased. The truly exasperating feature of the Nazi legal system lay in the fact that the most arbitrary and unjust of its acts were couched in the form of a statute, decree, or similar enactment, which, because of its formal character as a legal norm, was applied by the judge as "law" regardless of its inherently arbitrary character. The German judge slavishly follows its letter.[17]

Regardless of the tension in the natural law strains of Nazism and the positivist training of the judiciary, in operation a judiciary still had to function, even under totalitarianism. In an advanced country such as Germany, there were

[13] Robert D. Rachlin, *Roland Freisler and the Volksgerichtshof* in THE LAW IN NAZI GERMANY 66-67 (Alan Steinweis & Robert Rachlin, eds., New York: Berghahn Books, 2013).
[14] *Id.* at 70.
[15] Richard Miller, *supra* note 10, at 46.
[16] *Id.* at 50.
[17] EDWARD LITCHFIELD, GOVERNING POSTWAR GERMANY 252 (Ithaca, NY: Cornell University Press, 1953). Litchfield was a special advisor to the U.S. postwar occupying authority.

still contract disputes and accidents yielding injury and all sorts of quotidian legal matters that required equitable resolution. Some might be infected by Nazism, especially if one of the parties was a Jew or was for some other reason a political enemy. But many were not. The great moral dilemma was that almost the entire German judiciary was effectively disciplined by the Nazi regime to resolve these disputes in line with the state's interest; positive law might guide an outcome where the state was not implicated, but a twisted higher "natural law" could be invoked to conform the cases implicating the reigning ideology.[18]

Postwar Germany sought to preserve the judiciary as an institution, even as a handful of the most notorious Nazis in the system were put on trial for their crimes. These few trials changed nothing fundamental. The entire judiciary was compromised as an institution such that any defensible system of moral reckoning would have demanded the removal from office of those who lent any manner of legalistic cover for Nazism. The blunt fact, however, was that after twelve years of fascist rule, there were not enough judges untainted by the past left available to administer the West German legal system.

Germany then was the primary source of a new constitutional model, although the Italian Constitutional Court emerged at the same time. The German solution was to allow the judiciary largely to remain intact, but to create a new constitutional court composed of individuals who had largely been in exile or had in some sense become opponents of the Nazi regime. Unlike the U.S. Supreme Court, which sits as the final appellate chamber for all legal disputes in the United States, the constitutional court model assumed a separation between the ordinary workings of the law and the fundamental guarantees of the democratic order. The first category would attend to contracts, domestic relations, property, and all manner of legal oversight of the daily life of the citizenry. By contrast, the constitutional domain would oversee the exercise of state authority, whether in the form of violations of the rights of individual citizens or the exercise of governmental power beyond that allowed by the constitution.

The German Constitutional Court's structure and considerable power drew from prior experiments within pre-Nazi Germany. Nascent ideas of judicial review (in particular, reviewing subnational laws for compatibility with

---

[18] Tellingly, most judges of the pre-*First* World War German Reich retained their positions in the Weimar Republic, and frequently sided with the Republic's enemies. *See* INGO MULLER, HITLER'S JUSTICE: THE COURTS OF THE THIRD REICH (Deborah Schneider, trans., Cambridge, MA: Harvard University Press, 1991).

federal law) had existed in German law since the late Holy Roman Empire.[19] Judicial review on the basis of constitutional principles rather than pure federalism was established in dicta during the Weimar Republic.[20] The first proposal for an independent, powerful constitutional tribunal was floated in the Herrenchiemsee Conference, a preliminary meeting of experts, largely unconstrained by Allied participation,[21] called to draw up technical proposals for what would become the Basic Law;[22] the conference's proposals for the court were largely adopted by the Parliamentary Council that drafted the finalized document (with some modification of the court's position in the judicial hierarchy).[23]

As a general matter, the Allies had little, if anything, to say about judicial review or a constitutional court in the various agreements or protocols having to do with German reconstruction. Certainly federalism and decentralization, as well as the protection of individual rights, were ironclad requirement laid down from Potsdam onward,[24] but the Western Allies were deliberately circumspect as to the ideal institutional arrangements through which these should be achieved, reserving only the right to veto the final draft of the Basic Law prior to its submission to the states or the people.

As the framers of the Basic Law reacted to the categorical failure of both executive and legislative forces to forestall the rise of Hitler, the Constitutional Court – a new institution, but one with intellectual roots in the pre-Hitler period – was the logical candidate to stand as the ultimate protector of civil liberties and to serve as the check on "arbitrary governmental action" of all

---

[19] DONALD P. KOMMERS & RUSSELL A. MILLER, THE CONSTITUTIONAL JURISPRUDENCE OF THE FEDERAL REPUBLIC OF GERMANY at 4–5 (3rd ed., Durham, NC: Duke University Press, 2012).

[20] *Id.* at 6.

[21] *See* Erich Hahn, *U.S. Policy on a West German Constitution 1947–1949* in AMERICAN POLICY AND THE RECONSTRUCTION OF WEST GERMANY 1945–1955, 33–34 (Jeffry Diefendorf et al., eds., New York: Cambridge University Press, 1994) (noting that the confidential "letters of advice" issued by the Allies, laying out substantive guidance for the Basic Law, were not revealed until the Parliamentary Council meeting that drafted the Basic Law was well under way). The Frankfurt Documents drafted by the Allies, which kicked off the West German constitution-making process, are silent on the structure of the German state save that it be federal and democratic. *See* Dokumente zur künftigen politischen Entwicklung Deutschlands ["Frankfurter Dokumente"], 1. Juli 1948, *available at* http://www.1000dokumente.de/index .html?c=dokument_de&dokument=0012_fra&object=translation&st=&l=de.

[22] Kommers & Miller, *supra* note 19, at 7.

[23] *Id.* at 8.

[24] *Id. See also* U.S. DEPT. OF STATE, GERMANY 1947–49: THE STORY IN DOCUMENTS 49 (Washington, DC: U.S. Department of State, 1950) (Potsdam Conference communique insisting that Germany was to be a federal country); *id.* at 77 (London Conference communique requiring decentralization and protection of individual rights).

kinds.[25] Toward that end, the initial selection of constitutional court judges favored "persons who not only failed to join the Nazi Party but who went into exile or temporary retirement during the Third Reich," or even someone whose anti-Nazi credentials were burnished by involvement in the plot to assassinate Hitler on July 20, 1944, such as Judge Fabian von Schlabrendorff.[26]

No set of formal requirements could cement the break from the past. Nonetheless, the composition of the constitutional court became an immediate concern even when the Basic Law was still in draft, as the German Parliamentary Council deleted a proposed clause that would have preserved a number of seats on the Constitutional Court for existing judges.[27] The people selected to sit on the court likewise received close attention as Parliament drafted the Constitutional Court Act.[28] The parliamentary recruiters sought justices who were "clean" and "untainted by Nazism," and informally they sought to ensure that "a portion of the seats was to be assigned to persons of Jewish ancestry."[29] Ultimately, the twenty-four justices included individuals who had been in exile, or had resigned from official positions for unwillingness to embrace Nazism, or had eschewed public positions during the Nazi period, or held minor positions during that period. The message was clear: a constitutional court for a new democratic order needed to signal a clear break from the authoritarian past, a demand that could not be directed at the judiciary as a whole. A significant part of that signal was to be conveyed by the composition of the court itself.

The division of the application of the laws from the oversight over democracy allowed Germany to retain an experienced judiciary, despite its complicity in the Nazi horrors, including in the application of the Nuremberg laws on racial ordering. The ordinary judiciary could continue to apply the laws of the new democratic order, which would have to be purged of remnants of Nazi rule, even if the judges were not. At the same time, these holdover judges could not be trusted to be the ultimate arbiters of laws that touched on the bedrock qualities of the new political order. Instead, these judges operated under the oversight of a democratic reorganization of law, including the ability of their decisions to be reviewed by the Constitutional Court on questions

---

[25] Taylor Cole, The West German Federal Constitutional Court: An Evaluation after Six Years, J. Pol., May 1958, at 281–82.

[26] Glenn N. Schram, *The Recruitment of Judges for the West German Federal Constitutional Court*, 21 Am. J. Comp. L. 691, 701 (1973).

[27] Kommers & Miller, *supra* note 19, at 7.

[28] Donald P. Kommers, Judicial Politics in West Germany: A Study of the Federal Constitutional Court 120 (Beverly Hills, CA: Sage Publications, 1976).

[29] *Id.*

of fundamental liberties. The independence of the Constitutional Court from both the stains of the past and the normal working operation of the laws served as a bastion against any threatened return of the authoritarian regime.

CONSOLIDATING LIMITED DEMOCRACY

If we move to the post-1989 period, the German experience looms large. Although no country in this period could claim a judiciary as sophisticated as Germany's, each faced the same core dilemma as Germany in the postwar period. The post-authoritarian judiciary needed to fulfill two roles. There was a need for the capable and predictable administration of a legal system such that private ordering could take hold in a secure environment. Without a dependable legal system that can enforce bargains, protect expectations, and offer recompense in case of negligent injury, private parties must assume the burden of protecting themselves amid a world of diminished expectations. A legitimate state relieves the citizenry of this Hobbesian threat, and its judiciary is the guarantor of a meaningful life under the rule of law. Such guarantees require trained judges capable of handling the technical demands of the post. No less so than in Germany, such individuals are invariably in short supply and no society can afford simply to dismiss from public service everyone with any association with the past regime. The brute fact is that just as no one could rise in the judicial hierarchy without some form of engagement or affiliation with the Nazi Party, no one in the Soviet world could rise very far without membership or some form of institutional engagement with the Communist Party.

At the same time, the judiciary needed to constrain governmental excesses in the new constitutional order. That task, unlike the ordinary administration of the daily application of law to largely private disputes, could not be entrusted to judges who had already shown themselves capable of being compromised in the service of an illegitimate political order. The German model provided an elegant solution by separating the ordinary judiciary from the oversight powers entrusted to a special constitutional court. In turn, these constitutional courts saw their charge as the guarantee of a liberal democratic order against governmental excesses. A bifurcated judiciary spotlights the distinct role of the constitutional courts as a limit on the powers of ordinary politics, as reflected through the enactment of legislation. The ensuing strong-form constitutionalism is a self-conscious constraint upon the potential for excess in democratic governance, and the new constitutional courts become the enforcement mechanism for constitutional reins on any simpler conception of democracy as simply the realization of majoritarian preferences.

Before turning to a broader review of how the post-1989 constitutional courts have operated, a specific example from Colombia helps ground the discussion in a rather remarkable setting. Colombia may appear an unlikely candidate for an exemplary use of a new constitutional court to protect democratic authority, compared to the many states emerging from the end of authoritarianism. The creation of a constitutional court in Colombia did not correspond to any great social transition, unlike postwar Germany (the defeat of the Nazi regime), South Africa (the end of apartheid), and Eastern Europe (the fall of communism) – governments that command attention in the coming chapters. In such countries, the constitutional court served as a protection against the reestablishment of an authoritarian state power that had been successfully deposed.

Protecting against historic state excesses was hardly the problem faced in Colombia in 1991. Rather, Colombia was if anything a weak state in which the new constitutional order was at best aspirational, a hope that state authority could be wrested from the armed bands and drug lords that dominated much of the country. Yet even without a functioning consolidated democracy, the Colombian constituent assembly attended to the creation of a new constitutional court with claims to guarantee democratic rule.

The Colombian experiment in constitutional democracy turned first and foremost on the ability to consolidate order across the war- and gang-ravaged country. Prospects for governance improved dramatically after President Álvaro Uribe took office in 2002 and dedicated his administration to "democratic security."[30] Uribe proved capable of marshaling poorly functioning and compromised state institutions to recapture the basic forms of governance, in no small measure militarily. Government exertions against insurgent forces stemmed the tide of violence and stabilized civilian authority over almost the entirety of Colombia. Normalcy returned to the cities and the countryside as crime and violence abated.

Not surprisingly, the security gains were wildly popular with an embattled population that suddenly was able to reclaim the public spaces of towns and cities for civilized life. As kidnappings and murders receded, and as a prosperous normality blossomed, Uribe's popularity soared. The requirement that Uribe would have to retire at the end of his term left Colombians with the prospect of a loss of stable civilian rule. The obstacle was not democracy, but the constitutional mandate of only one term in office.

---

[30] *See* Ann Mason, *Colombia's Democratic Security Agenda: Public Order in the Security Tripod*, 34 SEC. DIALOGUE 391, 396–98 (2003).

In the confrontation between a democratically popular president and the rigidity of the constitution, democracy prevailed. The constitution was amended in 2004 to permit Uribe to seek a second term as president, a departure from the Latin American norm of single-term presidencies. The constitutional court readily upheld the constitutional amendment allowing Uribe to seek a second term, finding that it was procedurally and substantively valid, notwithstanding the unprecedented length of Uribe's tenure in office. Unsurprisingly, Uribe won easily,[31] marking the first time in Colombian history that a chief executive had won a second term in office. Uribe's eight years in office would become the longest period any chief executive remained in power since Colombia gained its independence in 1819.[32]

As Uribe consolidated power, the trappings of excess began to appear. Democratic security, the greatest conquest of the Uribe administration, itself began to tarnish. The military leaders were compromised by association with paramilitary groups who had moved in as local lords of power when the drug gangs and guerrillas were dislodged. The paramilitary groups and the government itself developed a propensity for retaliation against all enemies, insurgent or not. Corruption and wiretaps of political enemies filled out the picture of democracy ceding to strongman rule. Increasingly, the new democratic order narrowed to the person of the president. As power consolidated in Uribe's second term, presidential authority ran once again into the constitutional barrier of term limits. Again the president's political mandate forced a constitutional confrontation, although this time without the same sense of public approbation that had met the initial effort to keep Uribe in office. Perhaps not surprisingly, Uribe rallied his supporters, pressured his opponents, and forced a reluctant Congress to permit him to once again amend the constitution to allow him to run for a third term as president.

The stage was set for the greatest constitutional confrontation in Colombia's history. A third term raised the specter that Colombia would succumb to the Latin American tradition of rule by *caudillos*, the strongmen who hold on to power indefinitely and become the gravitational center of political life. Democracy recedes when entrepreneurial sectors "depend on close personal relationships with the government to obtain permits or public contracts,"[33] and when state institutions, even outside the executive, are staffed entirely by individuals who depend on the incumbent president for their appointment.

[31] *See* INT'L CRISIS GROUP, *Uribe's Possible Third Term and Conflict Resolution in Colombia*, 31 ICG LATIN AM. REP., Dec. 2009, at 8.

[32] Eduardo Posada-Carbó, *Colombia after Uribe*, J. DEMOCRACY, Jan. 2011, at 137, 138 (2011).

[33] *See* Int'l Crisis Group, *supra* note 32, at 2.

Incumbent power tends to feed on itself, creating an expanding state bureaucracy with ever greater control of the economy. The pathology of clientelism
then rewards incumbent politicians for an expansion of the public sector in a
way that facilitates sectional rewards to constituent groups. The phenomenon
was described by Mancur Olsen in his classic work on the pressures toward
the growth of both the size and complexity of government.[34] Politics becomes
not a matter of electoral contests for power but of connections to government.
The ensuing clientelism, the organizing of power to protect incumbent sinecure by dispensing state benefits and contracts to loyal followers, suffocates the
opposition. Politics becomes no longer a contest of parties or ideologies, but
of access to control of state resources, a battle in which incumbent authority
is paramount. The concentration of executive power benefits those with connections to the state. The greater the scale of government enterprise, the more
it rewards those who can master its byways in a process that is non-transparent
to the public and that resists either monitoring or accountability.

The mobilization of the state under Uribe was the perfect medium for a still
popular elected president to pull up the gangplanks of electoral accountability. Yet Colombia defies easy characterization. Uribe's efforts to obtain a constitutional mandate meant that the formalities of law were honored, certainly
in form. This was no military coup of the classic Latin American sort. Uribe
sought power before the Congress and the voters. There was no escaping the
fact that the constitutional reform allowing Uribe a third term was approved
by a constitutional plebiscite and by Congress, seemingly as mandated by the
text of the constitution itself.

Given Uribe's continued popularity, the people's approval was hardly surprising. Nonetheless, Uribe's victory was not simply a moment of popular
endorsement of the manifest improvement of daily life in Colombia. The ability of Uribe to mobilize popular support overwhelmed the opposition of the
weak Congress. The prospect of a presidential third term was a painful confirmation of the failure of democratic restraints to take hold. Despite efforts
to block the amendment legislatively, Congress did ultimately succumb and
passed this second constitutional amendment extending the time that Uribe
could potentially serve as president.

Under these circumstances, the constitutional court emerged as the sole
check on the prospect of increasingly unilateral executive power. The difficulty was that the judiciary had no independent democratic mandate,
particularly as compared to a popular ruler such as Uribe. Nor could the

---

[34] Mancur Olson, The Rise and Decline of Nations 69–71 (New Haven, CT: Yale
University Press, 1982).

constitutional court intervene in the name of a narrow procedural limitation on governmental power; from a technical point of view, the procedures taken to permit a third term seemed unassailable. Instead, as David Landau sustains, any judicial intervention had to draw on a more deep-rooted conception of the reconstitution of civilian rule after decades of violence: "[t]he public [saw] the Court, rather than the legislature, as the best embodiment of the transformative project of the 1991 constitution."[35] While not a democratic mandate in the electoral sense of the term, the court could assert itself as the guardian of a popularly accepted constitutional order that had to restrain the momentary desires of popular majorities, perhaps even if expressed in constitutional amendment. In one of its earliest decisions, the court explained its constitutional role along these lines:

> The difficulties deriving from the overflowing power of the executive in our interventionist state and the loss of political leadership of the legislature should be compensated, in a constitutional democracy, with the strengthening of the judicial power, which is perfectly placed to control and defend the constitutional order. This is the only way to construct a true equilibrium and collaboration between the powers; otherwise, the executive will dominate.[36]

Claiming such broad authority to check the exercise of executive power put the Colombian court in a situation outside the boundaries of the typical conflicts facing immature constitutional courts. A contrast with Germany provides a telling example. Recall that the mandate of the German court was primarily as a check against incipient forms of authoritarianism, defined by the Nazis in the past and by the Soviets to the east. The early defining cases of the German court involved either remnants of Nazi political organizations or the German Communist Party itself. In neither case was a constraint being imposed on incumbent state authority in the name of the court's constitutional mandate. Although the German court is now renowned, famously so, for its sophisticated proportionality test in assessing the legitimacy of state conduct, this was not always so. As Niels Petersen has well chronicled, the proportionality form of review, weighing the significance of the state's objective against the private harm ensuing and the efficacy of the means chosen to realize that objective, developed slowly.[37] Early proportionality cases involved constitutional court review of adjudications between private parties in which the conduct at risk

---

[35] Landau, *supra* note 4, at 344 (footnotes omitted).

[36] *Id.* at 346.

[37] Niels Petersen, *Balancing and Judicial Self-Empowerment: A Case Study on the Rise of Balancing in the Jurisprudence of the German Federal Constitutional Court*, 4, GLOBAL CONSTITUTIONALISM 49 (2015).

of constitutional overhaul was that of the ordinary judiciary, not the political branches. Indeed, in the famous *Luth* case that heralded proportionality, the parties were a social critic seeking to denounce a filmmaker as a former Nazi, and the filmmaker seeking freedom of expression without condemnation – in other words, two private parties disputing the meaning of the Nazi legacy.[38]

Moreover, as the German court developed its jurisprudential moorings and its authority, the fate of Germany was never at issue. West Germany remained under the oversight of the Allied powers, whose sizeable military presence would quickly be brought to bear against any overt efforts to restore Nazism or invite occupation by the troops of the Warsaw Pact.

Not so in Colombia in 2009, when the role of the self-proclaimed judicial power under the constitution was put to the test. With the approach of the end of Uribe's second term in 2010, the court was called upon to review the constitutional amendment allowing a third presidential term. In a surprisingly short opinion, the court cited numerous procedural defects in the congressional vote and in the endorsing popular referendum. None of these defects alone was of sufficient magnitude to justify overturning what appeared a clear popular mandate. The problem was the substance of the changed constitutional rule on presidential term limits, not the manner in which the change was implemented. The court then announced its judgment in strikingly cursory form given the momentous stakes of the decision:

> The Court finds that [the proposed amendment] ignores some of the structural axes of the Political Constitution, such as the principle of separation of powers and the system of checks and balances, [and] the rule of alternation in office according to preestablished time periods.[39]

The court, to its credit, recognized the need to reach beyond the momentary issues of how the processes of constitutional amendment were achieved. Standing alone, such considerations would likely not have justified overturning the formal processes of amendment nor the apparent popular will. Instead, the court reached further and struck down as unconstitutional the proposed constitutional amendment on the basis of deeper commitments to the base requirements for democratic rule. The reasoning may be unspecified,

---

[38] Bundesverfassungsgericht [BVerfGE][German Constitutional Court] Jan. 15, 1958, 1 BvR 400/51 (Ger.), available in translation at http://www.utexas.edu/law/academics/centers/transnational/work_new/german/case.php?id=1369.

[39] Corte Constitucional de Colombia, No. 09 Comunicado 26 de febrero de 2010, available at http://www.corteconstitucional.gov.co/comunicados/No.%2009%20Comunicado%2026%20de%20febrero%20de%202010.php (translation by author).

or fragmentary, but the invocation of base concerns for democratic viability is manifest. Yet there is something deeply disturbing about a court acting in such a freighted political environment and not sensing a need to explain its actions, to offer a justification that could convince Colombian citizens that their revealed electoral preference for a third Uribe term should nonetheless be set aside.

Despite the absence of any compelling judicial reasoning, and notwithstanding his strong popular mandate, Uribe acceded to the court's decision and immediately withdrew his candidacy for office – to his great credit and to the benefit of the prospects of further democracy in Colombia. Uribe's acceptance of the court's judgment was by no means preordained. Courts are at their weakest when it comes to the enforcement of their decrees. In a direct confrontation with the executive or parliament, a court injunction threatens to remove legitimacy from the exercise of power by the political branches, but the court is otherwise without the means to enforce directly its mandate. Yet President Uribe, with fairly consolidated control over the forces of government, ceded to the court just the same. As we shall see, some leaders accept the new role of the apex courts, and some resist. The willingness of any popular leaders to accede to the directives of new constitutional courts is itself a fascinating issue, and one that will be addressed in subsequent chapters.

More problematic immediately is the paucity of reasoning in the opinion denying Uribe a third term. What exactly was the constitutional or democratic deficit that doomed the enactment of the constitutional amendment through prescribed mechanisms, or at least largely so? The principles of separation of powers, and the importance of checks and balances may well be desirable, indeed indispensable, in a stable democracy. Nonetheless, much more work needs to be done before these translate into something as concrete as holding a particular reform unconstitutional. The United States well survived three terms and a fourth election of Franklin Roosevelt as president with its democracy intact, even strengthened, in the face of overwhelming military challenge. A subsequent U.S. constitutional amendment limited the presidential term of office,[40] but no claim could be made that this particular amendment was mandated by deeper democratic requirements in the American context. Perhaps there is a difference between Roosevelt standing for repeat election under the existing rules of the game, and a sitting president changing the rules to extend his mandate. If so, the constitutional significance of the fact of changing the electoral rules would still have to be explained.

[40] *See* U.S. CONST. amend. XXII.

Missing in the Colombian context was not only an account of the structural role of the Colombian court in securing democratic governance, but the deeper jurisprudential wellsprings that would justify its role. Before turning to the elaboration of that jurisprudence in many national settings as newly formed apex courts confront structural weaknesses of democracies, it is useful to turn to an elaboration of a judicial theory of democracy.

Confronting Politics

Colombia is hardly the first country to confront constitutionally the boundaries of democracy in its infancy. Indeed, we can turn back to the United States to show the pervasiveness of the problem, and indeed, the difficulty of the solution. In fact, the United States offers what is likely the first judicial confrontation with democratic power of any country in the world. As with the well-developed body of American law on clear and present danger addressed earlier, however, the United States offers at best a limited model for constitutional courts in newly minted democracies.

The American story begins with the limited acceptance of the terms of the Constitution itself. The State of Rhode Island opposed any prospect of abandoning the Articles of Confederation in favor of a new constitutional order with a more powerful central government. The State had conspicuously not agreed to participate at the Philadelphia Constitutional Convention and did not send delegates to Philadelphia. Under the unanimity requirement of the then reigning Articles of Confederation, this should have blocked all attempts to change the form of governance. By refusing to attend, and by not ratifying the proposed adoption of the Constitution, Rhode Island could prevent any change of government under the formal rules that created the Articles of Confederation. Ultimately, the Convention decided to abrogate the rules of governmental reform and create a new, ad hoc procedure for the new constitutional compact. The Convention enlisted a new institution – the state constitutional conventions – as the ratifying bodies, and then created a mere supermajority requirement for constitutional approval, thereby eliminating the unilateral shutdown capacity of any individual state under the unanimity requirement of the Articles of Confederation.

While Rhode Island grudgingly accepted the new constitution, as it had previously accepted the fact of independence from Britain, its internal political practices changed little. Even after independence, Rhode Island continued to be governed by the 1663 colonial charter granted by Charles II to create the colony of Rhode Island and Providence Plantation. Among its questionable provisions, this charter limited suffrage to property-owning white male adults, amounting to only 40 percent of the adult white male population of the state well into the nineteenth century.[41] Further, the charter included no provisions for amendments, perhaps leaving that to royal decree even after the Revolution.

The restriction on suffrage was particularly galling as universal adult white male suffrage became the norm in the United States. The demand for suffrage led to the assembly of a "People's Constitutional Convention," which drafted a "People's Constitution" that would extend suffrage to all white males, and then submitted it to the public for adoption. Based on the expanded suffrage of the new state constitution, elections were held and Thomas Dorr was elected governor. In effect, Rhode Island underwent a constitutional coup enshrined by the extension of the franchise.

The Charter government responded with legislation "to make all attempts to enforce the People's Constitution subject to criminal sanctions"[42] and declared martial law to stem the challenge of the newly proclaimed state government. The suffragists took up arms in what is known as the Dorr Rebellion of 1841–42. Ultimately, the Charter government prevailed militarily, Dorr's forces were routed, and Dorr himself was forced to flee the state.

One of Dorr's disciples – named Martin Luther, no less – was arrested by a state official, Luther Borden, for his part in the uprising. Luther was subject to an order from the Rhode Island Charter government directing government officials to "arrest and take the said Martin Luther, and, if necessary … to break and enter the dwelling-house of said Luther."[43] This led to a classic legal confrontation when Luther sued Borden for trespass, claiming that Borden had no authority to enter his home and that the entry into his home therefore violated Luther's right to enjoyment of his personal property. Borden's defense was that he was acting as a state official and therefore entitled to immunity for official conduct, a claim that Luther contested by challenging the claimed authority of Borden as a state official. According to Luther, any office holding under the authority of the royal charter would be inimical to the American constitutional guarantee of republican representation. This argument had constitutional mooring under Article IV, section 4 of the federal Constitution, by which the federal government guarantees that each state in the union shall

[41] GEORGE M. DENNISON, THE DORR WAR: REPUBLICANISM ON TRIAL, 1831–1861, 13–14 (Lexington: University Press of Kentucky, 1976). *See also* Note, *Political Rights as Political Questions: The Paradox of* Luther v. Borden, 100 HARV. L. REV. 1125, 1128–29 (1987).
[42] John Schuchman, *The Political Background of the Political-Question Doctrine: The Judges and the Dorr War*, 16 AM. J. LEGAL. HIST. 111, 118 (1972).
[43] *Luther v. Borden*, 48 U.S. (7 How.) 1, 10 (1849).

enjoy a "republican form of government" (known as the "guarantee clause").
The common law claim of trespass was thereby enveloped in a first-order constitutional question about whether Rhode Island's Charter government satisfied the constitutional commitment to popular sovereignty.

Boiled down to its essentials, the question that went all the way to the U.S.
Supreme Court was which of two rivals for power was the legitimate constitutional government of Rhode Island. If the Charter government was indeed
sovereign in Rhode Island, despite a form of election that was inimical to the
spirit of the American Revolution, then the normal protections of the governing prerogatives of the state would bar any suit for civil damages as a result of
restoring order against the Dorr insurgents. On the other hand, if the Charter
government was a usurper, a prerevolutionary throwback that could not order
the arrest of Luther nor the entry into his private residence, then the immunities that are granted to the exercise of sovereign state power would dissolve
away. As formulated in Luther's legal argument, the Charter government was
"*ipso facto*, dissolved"[44] by the claimed enactment of the new state "People's
Constitution," thereby rendering void the declaration of martial law and eliminating the defendants' proffered defense for the trespass.

Once transposed to the legal setting, the pivotal issue in *Luther v. Borden*
turned essentially on the constitutional legitimacy of the government of Rhode
Island. Whatever the electoral claims of the Charter government might be,
ultimately its mandate flowed from the constricted franchise bequeathed by
the English crown. Martin Luther's challenge was that the young constitutional republic owed its citizens a richer set of democratic protections than the
formal staging of elections. *Luther v. Borden* was the first judicial engagement
on record with the consolidation of democratic governance in a divided and
fragile republic. In effect, the U.S. Supreme Court faced the same daunting
question that confronted the Colombian Constitutional Court more than a
century later: Was there a deeper constitutional commitment to democracy
than a simple procedural check on whether the preexisting parliamentary and
electoral rules had been followed?

Like many courts later confronted with such first-order questions of constitutional governance, the U.S. Supreme Court ducked. In the first instance,
the Court looked to the actions of Congress and the president to determine
whether the other branches of the federal government considered the Charter
government as legitimate or as a usurper. Although President Tyler did not
send troops to Rhode Island in response to the Charter government's request in

---

44 *Id*. at 21.

1842 to help restore order, President Tyler nonetheless treated this as a proper request for assistance rather than as the act of a constitutional usurper.[45] More significantly, the Court read the constitutional guarantee of republican government as directed to Congress and not the courts.[46] "For as the United States guarantees to each State a republican government, Congress must necessarily decide what government is established in the State before it can determine whether it is republican or not."[47] In admitting representatives and senators from a state to sit in Washington, Congress is thereby recognizing the legitimacy of the government that appointed them.[48]

Luther v. Borden bequeathed the "political question" doctrine, which controlled in American jurisprudence for more than a century. As expressed by the Court: "Much of the argument on the part of the plaintiff turned upon political rights and political questions, upon which the court has been urged to express an opinion. We decline doing so."[49]

Although the political question doctrine remained a mainstay of American constitutional law, its wellspring remained obscure in the Court's presentation. Certainly, the Court could invoke strong prudential considerations. A court, like any institution, must at times husband its resources and determine whether a matter that could be submitted to legal resolution need be so entertained at any particular time or under any particular circumstances. Cast in such a light, the political question doctrine stood as one among many prudential doctrines in American law that limited the involvement of federal courts, including considerations of the ripeness of the dispute for resolution, the standing of the particular parties before the court, or the exhaustion of inferior remedial options in the state courts or administrative agencies.

So cast, the political question doctrine became one of what Alexander Bickel famously referred to as the "passive virtues" of courts fending an imprecise constitutional path amid a volatile political terrain.[50] Avoidance is not a strategy but a necessary tactic to preserve the limited resources of the judiciary. As Bickel further explained, "the Court wields a threefold power." It may invalidate legislation, it may validate and thereby legitimate legislation, "[o]r it

[45] *Luther*, 48 U.S. (7 How.) at 44.
[46] Rachel Barkow, *More Supreme than Court? The Fall of the Political Question Doctrine and the Rise of Judicial Supremacy*, 102 COLUM. L. REV. 237, 255 (2002).
[47] *Luther*, 48 U.S. (7 How.) at 42.
[48] *See id.*
[49] *Id.* at 16.
[50] Alexander M. Bickel, *The Supreme Court 1960 Term – Foreword: The Passive Virtues*, 75 HARV. L. REV. 40, 74–79 (1961).

may do neither ... and therein lies the secret of its ability to maintain itself in the tension between principle and expediency."[51]

As the political question doctrine matured over the century after *Luther*, the doctrine became more entrenched and more recognizable. As case-based examples accumulated, use of the doctrine became increasingly predictable, especially as regards the Court's conclusion that the guarantee of republican government could not be enforced in the courtroom. By 1912, when an Oregon phone company brought a guarantee clause challenge to a state tax that was enacted through a statewide popular initiative, the Court was prepared to dismiss it out of hand. "We premise by saying that while the controversy which this record presents is of much importance, it is not novel."[52]

Over time the political question doctrine evolved from a deeply fact-based inquiry into a jurisdictional bar. Either the case presented a political question and thus rendered the controversy beyond judicial competence, or it did not. As conceptualized in *Luther v. Borden*, that both the Congress and the president had also had to pass on the legitimacy of the Rhode Island Charter government meant that the case at bar was not an occasion for the Court to decide which constitutional actors were best positioned to make the difficult evaluation of Rhode Island political *bona fides*. Rather, the mere existence of congressional and presidential constitutional duties with respect to Rhode Island became transformed into a categorical obstacle to any Court involvement, no matter the delicacies of the particular moment or controversy.

Cast as a jurisdictional bar, the political question doctrine was a yes-no trigger that turned on the presence of the other branches in the process of decision making. On this formalist reading, discretion was not part of the Court's constitutional arsenal: "the only proper judgment that may lead to an abstention from decision is that the Constitution has committed the determination of the issue to another agency of government than the courts."[53] The political question legacy in the United States became that if other constitutional actors could lay claim to authority over the matter, the courts simply had no warrant to intervene.

Even when the Supreme Court finally curtailed the political question doctrine in *Baker v. Carr*[54] and the famous reapportionment cases of the early

---

[51] ALEXANDER BICKEL, THE LEAST DANGEROUS BRANCH: THE SUPREME COURT AT THE BAR OF POLITICS 69 (Indianapolis, IN: Bobbs-Merrill, 1962).
[52] *Pac. States Tel. & Tel. Co. v. Oregon*, 223 U.S. 118, 133 (1912).
[53] Herbert Wechsler, *Toward Neutral Principles of Constitutional Law*, 73 HARV. L. REV. 1, 9 (1959).
[54] 369 U.S. 186 (1962).

1960s, it did so by evasion rather than confrontation. These cases addressed the refusal of state legislatures to redraw congressional and state legislative lines to allow for equal representation of the urban parts of the country, and for their increasingly foreign-born citizens. But the Court chose not to reconsider the political question doctrine in the operation of the political process as a whole, but to craft instead an awkward individual right to equality of representation.[55] The new equal protection of the 1960s sidestepped any confrontation with political malfunction in ways that avoided updating the seemingly categorical prohibition on judicial entanglement in what Justice Frankfurter famously termed the "political thicket."[56] The Court created an elaborate set of individual claims to rights of participation, all the while eschewing any direct reassessment of the political question doctrine or of the dimensions of the Constitution's textual commitment to a republican form of government.

Courts around the world subsequently seeking guidance confronting structural deficits of democracy therefore need to look elsewhere. The U.S. Constitution is among the oldest of the written constitutions, and the U.S. Supreme Court conjured up the power of judicial review out of a curious combination of political reasoning and constitutional voids. Yet the concern over the "countermajoritarian dilemma" in the United States, to return to another of Bickel's famous formulations, inhibited the ability to elaborate a constitutional doctrine of democracy as such. The U.S. Constitution is conspicuously silent on democracy itself and on its constituent institutions, most notably political parties. Like all constitutions, it is a product of its founding political compromise. In a republic divided between slave and free states, and with a need to guarantee that control of the federal government would not upset that dreadful balance, the U.S. Constitution basically excluded the central government – including the federal courts – from passing on fundamental questions of democracy. If the U.S. Supreme Court could determine the legitimacy of the franchise in Rhode Island, and adjudicate among pretenders to political power, could not South Carolina be next?

---

[55] The most influential assessment of a need for judicial intervention based on the integrity of the political process came with JOHN HART ELY, DEMOCRACY AND DISTRUST: A THEORY OF JUDICIAL REVIEW (Cambridge, MA: Harvard University Press, 1980). Ely built on the influential *Carolene Products* footnote that posited that "prejudice against discrete and insular minorities may be a special condition, which tends seriously to curtail the operation of those political processes ordinarily to be relied upon to protect minorities, and which may call for a correspondingly more searching judicial inquiry." *U.S. v. Carolene Products*, 304 U.S. 144, 152 n.4 (1938).

[56] *Colegrove v. Green*, 328 U.S. 549, 556 (1946).

The constitutions of the twentieth century operated differently. Most began with a constitutional court specifically charged with judicial oversight over the political branches. Almost invariably, these constitutions give express textual protection to democratic processes and to the institutions of democratic politics, first and foremost political parties. Finally, as the following chapters will describe, these constitutions frequently impart to the judiciary a direct administrative role in ensuring the integrity of the electoral process, even apart from controversies presenting themselves in the form of litigation. The political question doctrine thus poorly captures the challenge faced by constitutional courts under modern constitutional commitments to democracy.

Constitutionalizing Democratic Limits

The Colombian dilemma returns this book to its central inquiry. When the Colombian court had to confront the proposed constitutional amendment, the characteristic disabilities of uncontested rule, even when backed by elections, had become manifest. Without rotation in office, as noted in the previous chapter, the "three C's" of consolidated power take hold: clientelism, cronyism, and corruption. These are the characteristic disabilities of weak democratic governments.

These weak new democracies lack institutions with a credible commitment to "policies that serve the general welfare."[57] In particular, they lack political parties, nongovernmental organizations, and other elements of civil society that allow politics to rise above persons and perquisites. Immature democracies lack developed political parties that represent a series of interests and balance among them within a coherent vision of governance. As Nancy Rosenblum develops, it is the need to explain "why 'we' are 'on the side of angels' and deserve to govern, and 'they' do not," that lends a transformative air to mature party politics.[58] Underdeveloped political parties, by contrast, cannot organize politics beyond the immediate advancement of narrow economic claims upon the state; indeed, "the shaky state of political parties contributes significantly to the inadequate aggregation and representation of interests which is such a debilitating problem in so many new and struggling democracies."[59]

[57] ETHAN V. Kapstein & Nathan CONVERSE, THE FATE OF YOUNG DEMOCRACIES, at xviii (New York: Cambridge University Press, 2008).
[58] NANCY L. ROSENBLUM, ON THE SIDE OF THE ANGELS: AN APPRECIATION OF PARTIES AND PARTISANSHIP 342 (Princeton, NJ: Princeton University Press, 2008).
[59] THOMAS CAROTHERS, POLITICAL PARTY AID: ISSUES FOR REFLECTION AND DISCUSSION 4 (2004) (unpublished manuscript), *quoted in* Kapstein & Converse, *supra* note 59.

In this context, the Colombian court stepped up to maintain democratic accountability, even if it could not elaborate a theory of its constitutional mandate. What President Uribe had delivered to Colombia was the reassertion of legitimate legal governance. Nothing should gainsay that tremendous achievement. What remained undeveloped was any lasting sense of democratic accountability for the exercise of state power. With a supine Congress and no effective political parties, Colombia was primed for further descent into one-man rule, with its attendant cronyism and compromise of governmental function. The stakes were high given the poor prospect for any long-term democratic stability under the authority of a single, maximum leader.

Nonetheless, for the Colombian court to repudiate the apparent popular will was a radical judicial intervention, holding the constitution to a higher, unspecified standard of democratic principle that trumped the formal structures of constitutional amendment. Such an assertion of principle over formal procedure seemingly required a more elaborated account of why such judicial intervention was justified. Certainly, a principled account could not be fashioned from courts constrained by fear of engagement with political questions. However, rather than any inspiration from the United States, the Colombian Constitutional Court could have looked to another apex court with a more robust account of the protection of democracy as falling within its mandate. Perhaps the best jurisprudential account is found in the work of the Supreme Court of India, whose democratic jurisprudence extends as well to the striking down of constitutional amendments that threaten the basic underpinnings of democratic contestation.

Contemporary Indian constitutional history begins shortly after the 1950 ratification of the constitution, when early populist governments sought to use legislative majorities to limit certain rights guarantees, most notably the commitment to just compensation for expropriation of private property.[60] In a series of early cases, the Supreme Court obstructed land redistributions without recompense to the owners, invoking its authority as guardian of constitutional commitments to individual rights. Article 19(1)(f) of the original Indian Constitution identified as a "fundamental right" the ability to "acquire, hold and dispose of property." At the same time, other constitutional provisions gave the national and state governments authority to enact reasonable regulations of property. The court's early property rights decisions thwarted efforts by the Nehru government to redistribute land from the big estates known as

[60] Nick Robinson, *Expanding Judiciaries: India and the Rise of the Good Governance Court*, 8 WASH. U. GLOBAL STUD. L. REV. 1, 29–31 (2009).

zamindari to the broad mass of destitute Indians without compensating the prior owners. The court's claimed authority prompted a confrontation in a 1967 case, *Golak Nath v. State of Punjab*,[61] in which the court declared that the primacy of the constitutional right to property is a fundamental right that trumped repeated efforts at redistribution.

While the early property rights cases set up a significant confrontation with the elected government, these decisions were limited in scope and the Indian court did not attempt to interfere more broadly in the exercise of political power in the founding days of Indian democracy. As a result, the Indian court played a secondary role in the early years of Indian democracy and constitutional law had little independent traction in defining the political powers of India. In large part, this reflected the Indian court's inability to break from its jurisprudential attachment to the Westminster tradition of parliamentary supremacy and its concept of narrow procedural review of government action. But, in still larger part, the court operated in a world without strong traditions of judicial review of the political process, the American experience at that time being no exception.

This began to change when the Indian court was faced with repeated efforts to amend the constitution of India to restrict constitutional commitments to property rights and judicial review. For all the inherited traditions of Westminster, the fact was that India operated under a written constitution with fairly specific guarantees to citizens and limitations on government. At the same time, under Article 368 of the Indian Constitution, a liberal amendment process required only a majority vote in both houses of parliament with two-thirds of its members present[62] – a comparatively easy standard internationally where the amendment process typically requires either a supermajority or concurrent majorities over successive sessions of the legislature. Moreover, the Indian Parliament invoked a unique constitutional device of designating a portion of the constitution to be immune from judicial review, what was termed the "Ninth Schedule," and placing controversial enactments within that Schedule; at present there are 284 distinct pieces of legislation shielded from judicial scrutiny in the Ninth Schedule.

The broad use of the Ninth Schedule to immunize acts from judicial oversight reflects the problem of easy constitutional amendment. Indian debates over the role of constitutional judicial scrutiny were influenced by a series of lectures and articles by a German academic, Dietrich Conrad, who highlighted the parallels between the easy amendment process under the

---

[61] (1967) 2 S.C.R. 762, 819.
[62] INDIA CONST. art. 368.

Indian Constitution and similar provisions under the Weimar Constitution that had been exploited to pave Hitler's rise to complete power.[63] Conrad and others looked to some form of judicial limitation on pure parliamentarism as a means of giving teeth to constitutional constraints. The direct constitutional confrontation between the Supreme Court and the government dates from the court's ruling in 1967 that the Indian Parliament's power to amend the constitution was limited, and that parliament could not abridge any fundamental rights inherent in the substantive provisions of the constitution.[64] In broad strokes, the emergence of a substantive doctrine of democratic protection allowed the assertion of power by the Indian Supreme Court. Previously the court has assumed a deferential role in the development of Indian democracy after independence and had effectively stood by through the increasing use of emergency decrees as the central form of governmental authority.[65] The distinct feature of the new constitutional doctrine crafted by the court was not the role of judicial review as such, something already well established in India, but rather a substantive assertion of "the court's regulation of the scope of Parliament's constitution amending power."[66]

With the rise of Indira Gandhi's government, the property cases prompted an early confrontation between the Indian Supreme Court and an assertive expansion of executive authority. The immediate conflict was over the court's rulings protecting property holdings against confiscation. These rulings had become major electoral issues that, in turn, strengthened the government's claimed authority for constitutional change. In a 1975 decision, the Court examined both the process limitations on constitutional amendment and the substantive limits on property redistribution. In an opinion reminiscent of the shrewd politics of Chief Justice Marshall in declaring judicial review in *Marbury v. Madison*, a case upholding governmental conduct yet denying any relief against the government, the Indian court refined its vision on constitutional limitations on even the amendment process while delicately avoiding a direct confrontation with the government.

---

[63] Sudhay Krishnaswamy, Democracy and Constitutionalism in India: A Study of the Basic Structure Doctrine xxvi–xxvii (New Delhi: Oxford University Press, 2009).

[64] *See I. C. Golak Nath v. State of Punjab* (1967) 2 S.C.R. 762, 815 (India). For a discussion of the limitations on amendment trenching on structural protections in the Indian Constitution, see Madhav Khosla, *Addressing Judicial Activism in the Indian Supreme Court: Towards an Evolved Debate*, 32 Hastings Int'l & Comp. L. Rev. 55, 93–94 (2009).

[65] *See* S. P. Sathe, *Judicial Activism: The Indian Experience*, 6 Wash. U. J. L. & Pol'y 29, 43–49 (2001).

[66] Krishnaswamy, *supra* note 65, at 191.

In *Kesavananda Bharati v. State of Kerala*[67] the Indian Supreme Court overturned its own decision in *Golak Nath* and rejected the presumed inviolability of all constitutional rights guarantees, property included. The court held that core rights, including property security, were amenable to constitutional amendment. However, the court reserved a category of the "basic structure" of constitutional rule that stood apart from the normal legislative processes of constitutional amendment. Unlike the unanimity achieved in *Marbury*, however, the Indian court did so with a bench of thirteen justices issuing eleven distinct opinions. Over the course of these fractured opinions that together ran more than 1,000 pages, the court laid the foundation for a constitutional doctrine of basic structures that has garnered worldwide attention.

The effect of the basic structure doctrine was to temper the ease of amendment under the Indian Constitution with an unspecified commitment to core democratic values that was beyond the competence of the legislature to condition. The court did not identify either the source of the basic structure concept or its dimension, at least not initially. But the declaration of a judicially enforced limitation on procedurally proper legislative enactments set the stage for a confrontation with an increasingly assertive Congress Party government.

The critical moment came in the aftermath of the landslide victory by the Congress Party in 1971 when Indira Gandhi's party pushed through the Twenty-Fourth Amendment, purporting to vest constitutional supremacy in the legislature and eliminating the right of constitutional judicial review.[68] In one sense, this amendment was consistent with the English colonial tradition of parliamentary sovereignty and the absence of judicial review of legislation. At the same time, the Twenty-Fourth Amendment was inseparable from the consolidation of increasingly unchecked government authority and the assertion of one-party political power that would ultimately lead to the declaration of the state of emergency of 1975–77.[69]

Modern constitutional jurisprudence in India effectively begins with the state of emergency of 1975–77. It was during this period that the Supreme Court of India emerged as a central force challenging the use of electoral

---

[67] A.I.R. 1973 S.C. 1461.

[68] *See* GRANVILLE AUSTIN, WORKING A DEMOCRATIC CONSTITUTION: A HISTORY OF THE INDIAN EXPERIENCE 500–15 (New Delhi: Oxford University Press, 2014); S. P. SATHE, JUDICIAL ACTIVISM IN INDIA: TRANSGRESSING BORDERS AND ENFORCING LIMITS 68 (New Delhi: Oxford University Press, 2002).

[69] *See* Lloyd I. Rudolph & Susanne Hoeber Rudolph, *To the Brink and Back: Representation and the State in India*, 18 ASIAN SURV. 379, 397–99 (1978).

majorities to consolidate one-party rule, and the basic structure doctrine proved to be the galvanizing judicial doctrine. The court began to intercede much more heavily in the core organization of the Indian political process, no doubt in response to its earlier acquiescence to Indira Gandhi's broad use of emergency powers to shut down internal political opposition.[70] In response, and over a series of highly controversial cases, the Supreme Court gave teeth to the basic structure doctrine, which was read to limit even procedurally proper alterations to the constitution, thereby reining in the emergency decrees.[71] The basic structure doctrine introduced the world to the idea of unconstitutional constitutional amendment, a domain of values so central to democratic governance that alteration was beyond even the power of the constitutional amendment process.

In many ways, the decisive moment came with *Minerva Mills Ltd. v. India*, a case that expressly struck down amendments attempting to curtail the courts' power of judicial review.[72] At issue was a state administrative determination under the Sick Textiles Nationalization Act of 1974 that the state needed to confiscate a particular enterprise because it was "managed in a manner highly detrimental to the public interest." Key to the Indian court's approach was the idea that even constitutional amendments could not alter the deeper commitment to democratic governance. It did not help that the formal issue under review was whether judicial review was itself constitutionally inviolate. Part of the commitment to deeper basic structures could unfortunately be seen as a desperate effort at self-protection by the judiciary. The actual application of the basic structure doctrine, as opposed to its mere articulation, came with legislative attacks on the power of the court itself. In this context, it is perhaps not surprising that the court would include within assaults on the

[70] As well formulated by Upendra Baxi, "[j]udicial populism was partly an aspect of post-emergency catharsis. Partly, it was an attempt to refurbish the image of the court tarnished by a few emergency decisions and also an attempt to seek new, historical bases of legitimation of judicial power." Upendra Baxi, *Taking Suffering Seriously: Social Action Litigation in the Supreme Court of India, in* JUDGES AND THE JUDICIAL POWER 289, 294 (Rajeev Dhavan et al. eds., London: Sweet & Maxwell, 1985). The emergence of the Indian Supreme Court, although no doubt a direct response to the emergency period, also corresponds to the increasing delegation of governmental authority outside the traditional division between courts, legislatures and the executive. *See generally* Bruce Ackerman, *The New Separation of Powers*, 113 HARV. L. REV. 633, 688–90 (2000) (putting forth the need for "functional specialization" as part of the constitutionally constrained exercise of parliamentary authority).

[71] Manoj Mate, *Two Paths to Judicial Power: The Basic Structure Doctrine and Public Interest Litigation in Comparative Perspective*, 12 San Diego Int'l L.J. 175, 185 (2010).

[72] *Minerva Mills Ltd. v. India* (1981) 1 S.C.R. 206, paras. 22, 59–61 (India).

basic functioning of democracy constitutional amendments that restricted the ambit of judicial review of the application of new legislation.[73]

Even if the judiciary was backed into a corner by the attempt to remove judicial review as such, the basic structure doctrine struck a deeper chord. The concurring opinion of Justice P. N. Bhagwati expressly tied the idea of structural limitations on governmental power, existing beyond the formalities of the procedural requirements for constitutional amendment, to the role of judicial review in enforcing those limits. According to Justice Bhagwati, "the limited amending power of Parliament is itself an essential feature of the Constitution, a part of its basic structure, for if the limited power of amendment was enlarged into an unlimited power the entire character of the Constitution would be changed," and the result would be to "damage the basic structure of the Constitution because there are two essential features of the basic structure which would be violated, namely, the limited amending power of the Parliament and the power of judicial review with a view to examining whether any authority under the Constitution has exceeded the limits of its powers."[74]

As Professor Mate well argues, the effect of the basic structure doctrine was to "entrench" the Indian Constitution as a blueprint for democratic governance: "Through the development and entrenchment of the basic structure doctrine, the Court helped assume a 'guardian' role in protecting and preserving basic features of the Constitution from being altered by political majorities."[75] The object is far different from Bruce Ackerman's theory of American constitutional moments, in which a confluence of political demands unfolds a process of constitutional adaptation to new political realities, as with the rise of the modern administrative state. Instead, the Indian court held itself out as a bulwark against excessive majoritarianism that threatened to overwhelm India's fragile state institutions. That power of constitutional review by now extends to the amendment process itself,[76] in effect recreating a Basic Law of democratic governance as has emerged in other countries, notably Germany and Israel.

This then takes us back to the dilemma faced by the Colombian Constitutional Court in facing down President Uribe's aspiration for a third term. A "basic structure" approach, modeled on the Indian Supreme Court's doctrine, could potentially have provided the Colombian court a structural

---

[73] See Gary Jeffrey Jacobsohn, *An Unconstitutional Constitution?: A Comparative Perspective*, 4
    INT'L J. CONST. L. 460, 483 (2006).

[74] *Id.* at para. 3.

[75] Mate, *supra* note 73, at 190.

[76] *See, e.g., I. R. Coelho v. State of Tamil Nadu* (1999) 2 Supp. S.C.R. 394, 396–98.

lever for evaluating the effect of a third term of office for President Uribe. Such a theoretical account would have given the court a deeper doctrinal foundation for its otherwise compelling account of the vulnerability of Colombia's new democracy to descend into single-party political consolidation, if not outright single-person command. While the basic structure doctrine could have provided deeper constitutional mooring for the jurisprudence of limiting presidential tenure, the Colombian dilemma demands further examination of the relation between court-centered constitutionalism and democratic governance.

8

Transition in South Africa

The modern wave of democracies would have been inconceivable without the collapse of the Soviet Union. Most apparently, the removal of the Soviet armed presence allowed the mobilization of democratic forces without the threat of the invasions of Hungary in 1956 and Czechoslovakia in 1968. The impact of the demise of Soviet power reaches much further, however. The easy divide of the world along the Cold War lines of demarcation ended, with far-reaching consequences. The American patrons of right-wing regimes reexamined their commitment to nondemocratic rulers once freed from the need to maintain the anticommunist alliance. Similarly, client states of the Soviet Union from outside the Soviet bloc found their benefactor and, oftentimes, financier suddenly unresponsive. For the Cubas and El Salvadors of the world, one on each side, the realignment forced a recalibration of authoritarian rule in a seemingly post-authoritarian world.

Realignment was not limited to those holding state authority. The end of the Cold War also commanded the agenda of those contesting the lockhold on power of the client regimes of the major powers. For every military regime in Central America counting on American support there was at least one guerilla group drawing sustenance from the Soviet Union or its regional proxy, Cuba. For every Soviet satellite in Africa or Eastern Europe there was a corresponding challenge from some group funded directly or indirectly by Western sources. The prompt toward democracy after 1989 did not need to be triggered by the sudden withdrawal of Soviet troops. It could as easily have been the product of the collapse of the corresponding Cold War patrons and the need for national accommodation of competing political factions.

No country seems more removed geographically from the Cold War struggle than South Africa. The National Party (NP) government was no mere American puppet, and in its final stages, the apartheid state had to withstand increasing economic sanctions from its Western allies. Certainly as well, the insurrectionary African National Congress (ANC) was no simple Soviet ploy, despite its decades-long collaboration with the South African Communist Party. The struggle against apartheid was many-fronted and the ANC struggled to be the big tent in which the diverse opposition elements could rally toward a collective end. Even so, the end of the Cold War removed from the ANC its longtime association to Soviet backing and removed from the National Party its last remaining international card as part of the Western anticommunist alliance.

Negotiations toward the transition from apartheid began in earnest in 1987, before the fall of the Soviet Union, but when the cracks in the Soviet empire were starting to emerge. The first public acknowledgment came from the English-speaking industrialists in South Africa, the part of the population that fought rule by the Dutch speakers in the Boer Wars, but ultimately lost political power to the Afrikaner-led National Party. In 1987, the largest of the English-owned industrial enterprises, the Anglo-American mining conglomerate, began urging multiracial governance under the slogan, "negotiate or be doomed." Two meetings in Zambia, in 1987 and 1989, opened a process of formal dialogue between the ANC and representatives of business interests and set the stage for subsequent negotiations with the NP government itself.

The negotiations proceeded along many fronts. Part of the focus was necessarily economic. The industrialists wanted an easing of the capital controls that the NP had imposed on the more cosmopolitan and distrusted English entrepreneurs. Many sought to diversify their enterprises (and their holdings) outside South Africa, an exit option not necessarily shared by the more locally rooted governing Afrikaners. In addition, the mining sectors, in which the English upper classes were heavily invested, sought relief from the strikes led by the ANC sympathizers leading the black miners' unions. On the other side of the equation, the ANC wanted to use negotiations to open a wedge in the white ruling class. Negotiations with the English-speaking industrialists also allowed the ANC to put on the table the question of redistribution to the impoverished black population, and in turn press the freighted question of land redistribution.

Economic considerations were no doubt a central concern of the pacted transition from apartheid. But the key to the transition lay in the domain of the political. The parties looked to institutional mechanisms and governmental authority to guide the transition and ultimately to allow the abandonment of apartheid to be realized through ordinary legislation of the South African Parliament. As in any negotiations, there were conflicts in ambitions and some irresolution as to how the ultimate objectives were to be obtained. Thus, the negotiations granted security to property rights, even as the mass of the population pressed for a more just distribution of the nation's riches. The concern over the boundaries of economic distribution leads to the focus here on the political dimension of the negotiated transition from apartheid and on the emergence of a constitutional court as a critical component of that process. This aspect of South Africa provides the clearest example for the central inquiry of this book.

SOUTH AFRICA AND THE PROMISE OF
CONSTITUTIONAL FORMATION

Constitutional courts fit uncomfortably within most established legal regimes, and South Africa was no exception. Prior to the dismantlement of the apartheid state, South Africa operated under a Westminster-style parliamentary system, which ensured legislative supremacy without significant separation of powers. The head of government was the prime minister, who in turn owed his selection to the dominant party or coalition in parliament. Further, the legislature served as the highest adjudicative body, as with the House of Lords historically in Britain. This meant there was no independent judicial body capable of imposing constitutional hegemony.

The inherited governing arrangement was thought unsatisfactory in the transitional period for two distinct reasons. First, given the numerical vulnerability of the still-entrenched white minority, unbridled parliamentarism was unlikely to offer sufficient guarantees of the security of person and property in a transition to a majoritarian-based democracy. The need for an independent branch of government capable of protecting rights against a parliamentary majority compelled the creation of an independent judicial authority.

Second, the struggle against apartheid had long been waged in the universalist language of human rights and the rule of law. The international conventions on human rights that followed from the end of World War II created a robust international law of relations between states and their citizens. All of the democracies created in the late twentieth century necessarily internalized the rights commitments, at least formally. Even in states with horrific human rights records, there is generally a formal legal commitment to rights protections for the citizenry. Almost inescapably, the enshrinement of rights commitments also pushes toward the creation of an independent judiciary.

Although some argued that formal parliamentary power sharing could allow minority vetoes and other legislative devices to stabilize minority protections, this view did not prevail for a variety of reasons. First, critics of the application in South Africa of formalized power sharing, what is termed "consociationalism" in the political science literature, responded that the basic black-white divide and the small size of the white minority (estimated at roughly 14 percent a decade ago and now nearing 10 percent) would inevitably yield an overwhelming pressure to simple majoritarianism.[1] Thus, even though the apartheid rulers of the NP sought some form of express minority veto over any future governmental action, they did not focus their negotiation demands on formalized power sharing of the sort envisioned through consociationalism.

On the other side of the table, the ANC had little sentimental or political attachment to the inherited political arrangements of the apartheid state. Formalized power sharing would have to allocate representation in government on the basis of race or ethnicity, a reintroduction of the woeful racialism of apartheid. The ANC sought the overthrow of the existing order and did not seek to build a new formal coalition within the confines of preexisting governmental structures. The end state of the antiapartheid struggle could not be a reallocation of power among the inherited divides of white, black, and colored. Indeed, it was the ANC that proposed both the creation of a constitutional court as part of the Interim Constitution and the formal abolition of Westminster-style parliamentarism.[2]

Much to the ANC's surprise, the National Party ultimately agreed. Despite holding out against human rights claims when it was in government, the NP gravitated toward a formal institutional protection of rights through judicial review, and even pushed hard to make all court appointments the exclusive authority of the executive. The NP likely assumed that it would ultimately have some formal role in the executive and that, in turn, judicial appointments could serve as a bastion of the protection of minority rights.[3] Whatever the complicated political calculations of the NP and the ANC, the role of the constitutional court became an integral part of the negotiations leading to the end of apartheid and marked one of the most significant alterations to the inherited South African political institutions.[4]

---

[1] The most prominent of these criticisms is found in DONALD L. HOROWITZ, A DEMOCRATIC SOUTH AFRICA? CONSTITUTIONAL ENGINEERING IN A DIVIDED SOCIETY 137–45 (Berkeley and Los Angeles: University of California Press, 1991).

[2] *See* Makau wa Mutua, *Hope and Despair for a New South Africa: The Limits of Rights Discourse*, 10 HARV. HUM. RTS. J. 63, 80 (1997) ("The Constitutional Court, which was proposed by the ANC ... can exercise judicial review, a power that the previous Supreme Court lacked under the parliamentary supremacy model of apartheid.").

[3] *See* SIRI GLOPPEN, SOUTH AFRICA: THE BATTLE OVER THE CONSTITUTION 230 (Aldershot: Dartmouth Publishing Company, 1997) (suggesting the failure of the NP to win a share in the executive power, its "primary objective," debilitated its ability to achieve its agenda through the courts).

[4] *See* RICHARD Spitz & Matthew CHASKALSON, THE POLITICS OF TRANSITION: A HIDDEN HISTORY OF SOUTH AFRICA'S NEGOTIATED SETTLEMENT 191–209 (Johannesburg, South

South Africa is a particularly salient example of the new form of constitutionalism that emerged after 1989. Most of the new democracies emerged in states bearing deep historic divisions along lines of race, ethnicity, religion, or language. In some countries, such as Yugoslavia, the divisions had largely lain dormant during the period of authoritarian rule. In others, such as South Africa or the Baltic republics under Soviet rule, the prior regime exercised power based on the supremacy of one group over the others. In all such countries, achieving buy-in from the various constituencies was a critical feature in the stabilization of democratic governance.

Rather than the formalized consociational power sharing that dominated the emergence of new democracies after World War II and the fall of colonialism, the post-1989 period saw a dampened enthusiasm for the formal allocation of political power as a mechanism for protecting vulnerable minorities. Instead, the Third Wave of democratization substituted an institutionalized set of checks on majoritarian power enshrined in a strong form of constitutionalism combined with an empowered independent judiciary. The well-documented transition in South Africa serves as the most visible of the constitutional allocations of power in a new democracy, but it is hardly unique in using constitutional governance to address the fundamental divides in a nascent democracy.

The phases of governance after apartheid well illustrate the contrast between what we may term power sharing and constitutionalism. In the immediate period after apartheid, South Africa was ruled by an interim government that used formalized power sharing to ensure all groups a mutual veto over contested governmental action – precisely the formula for consociationalism identified by Lijphart and other proponents of this approach.[5] The Interim Constitution provided detailed power arrangements, along with its critical list of 34 Constitutional Principles of democratic governance – to which I shall return.[6]

The primary mechanism of initial power sharing was the election of a parliament by proportional representation and the assignment of the position of

Africa: Witwatersrand University Press, 2000) (detailing the negotiations over the structure and functions of the constitutional court).

[5] *See* AREND LIJPHART, DEMOCRACY IN PLURAL SOCIETIES: A COMPARATIVE EXPLORATION 1 (New Haven, CT: Yale University Press, 1977).

[6] *See* HEINZ KLUG, CONSTITUTING DEMOCRACY: LAW, GLOBALISM AND SOUTH AFRICA'S POLITICAL RECONSTRUCTION 108 (Cambridge: Cambridge University Press, 2000) (noting that the development of a set of constitutional values while at the interim Negotiating Forum provided a means to avoid irreconcilable conflict during the later making of the final constitution).

deputy president to the representatives of each party holding at least 80 of the 400 seats in the National Assembly.[7] The creation of a multiple executive is a standard tool in power-sharing arrangements, particularly if the representatives of each subgroup are given an effective veto over action deemed inimical to the interests of that group. Among the powers conferred in South Africa as a result of this representation in the executive was the ability to participate in the selection of some of the justices of the constitutional court, a power reserved to the executive branch and requiring consent of the various members of the executive.[8]

Formal power sharing at the executive level, including in the selection of the constitutional court, was insufficient standing alone to protect the interests of the white minority. The ultimate threat to white minority interests came from the legislative branch, the dominant institution of government under Westminster-style arrangements. Whatever the participatory mechanisms formally adopted, there was no escaping the fact that the ANC would control the parliament and that as a result Nelson Mandela would serve as head of state. Without a credible mechanism to protect against legislative overreach, there could be no long-term guarantee of minority rights.

Constitutionalism was designed to provide that guarantee. Just as critical to the success of the interim constitutional arrangement as the power sharing was the fact that this was an interim arrangement designed to last no more than five years. Within that time period, the interim government was required to cede power to a more formal constitution that could only be implemented if deemed faithful to the original 34 Principles.[9] Moreover, the National Assembly,[10] the selection of which Principle VIII of the Interim Constitution required through proportional representation, would also serve as the formal drafting body for the final constitution.[11] As a result, the final constitution would have two critical features. First, it would bear a democratic legitimacy that could not be claimed by a negotiated compromise among political leaders, no matter how much de facto authority they could muster. Second, the Principles of the Interim Constitution, rather than the formalities of power sharing, could serve to assuage minority concerns over the limits of majoritarianism.

---

[7]   S. AFR. (INTERIM) CONST., 1993 ch. 6, § 84(1).
[8]   S. AFR. (INTERIM) CONST., 1993 ch. 7 § 97.
[9]   S. AFR. (INTERIM) CONST., 1993 ch. 5, § 71.
[10] S. AFR. (INTERIM) CONST., 1993 sched. 4, Principle VIII.
[11] S. AFR. (INTERIM) CONST., 1993 ch. 5, § 68.

There was of course great historic irony in the first constitutional constraints on democracy being imposed on the incipient majority government, rather than the dominant apartheid rulers. Albie Sachs caustically noted that South African apartheid was purely majoritarian among the enfranchised white minority, but that "[n]ow that the majority is going to be black, South African whites suddenly believe majority rule is a terrible thing … Now that the majority stands to change color, you no longer hear people talking about majority rule but 'majoritarianism,' which sounds worse than Marxism-Leninism."[12]

The power-sharing interim arrangements were critical to the sense of order in the transition process. These accords were the product of intense and largely secret negotiations among the major political groups in South Africa, primarily the governing NP and the ANC,[13] yielding what is known as the Kempton Park accords. All participants in these negotiations understood that formal attempts to divide political power through express racial or ethnic guarantees could not be the basis for long-term governance in the new South Africa. As noted, such racialist policies would hearken too closely to the despised regime of apartheid. But the failing was further. The campaign against apartheid had been largely waged in the name of human dignity and human equality. It was simply impossible not to enshrine these inspirational values in a political system based on fundamental treatment of all individuals as repositories of basic civil rights.

At the same time, formalizing individual rights, including the right to property, was seen as a limitation on the future transformation of the society. Once such individual rights enter the domain of constitutionally protected liberties, any future state will be constrained. The transition from Westminster-style parliamentarianism to formalized constitutional rule implied more in the South African context than altering the content of apartheid rule or providing for expanded eligibility for the franchise. Strong constitutions of the modern era take aim at majoritarian prerogatives, fearing the characteristic democratic disability of the "tyranny of the majority," as it was termed by John Adams and later popularized by Alexis de Tocqueville.[14] Concerns about the tyranny of

---

[12] Horowitz, *supra* note 1, at 98 (quoting Albie Sachs).

[13] The Inkatha Freedom Party (IKF) originated in what is now Kwa-Zulu Natal. The IKF drew its regional base from the Zulu population. Through its leader, Mangosuthu Buthelezi, the IKF participated in the negotiations and in the government of national unity that emerged, but then boycotted the final process of constitutional ratification. The negotiations are described in detail in Spitz & Chaskalson, *supra* note 4, at 191–209.

[14] *See* 3 John Adams, A Defence of the Constitutions of Government of the United States of America 291 (London: John Stockdale, 1794); 1 Alexis de Tocqueville, Democracy in America 183, 239–64 (Harvey C. Mansfield & Delba Winthrop, eds., trans., Chicago, IL: University of Chicago Press, 2000) (1835).

the majority in the context of the exclusion from political life of the great majority of the population is at best paradoxical.

Not surprisingly, the ANC initially resisted a formal and judicially enforceable bill of rights, something that was seen as inevitably entrenching the privileged position of the white minority. This proved an untenable position that alienated longtime allies of the ANC, concerned that those "who have suffered long outside the protection of the law are now unwilling to see their oppressors brought within the protection of the law."[15] Some members of the ANC, most notably Albie Sachs, conceded the point but argued that if there were to be a bill of rights, there must also be parliamentary control over its interpretation and implementation.[16] This objection failed as well.

Even the NP was surprisingly wary of embracing any sort of formal guarantees of rights. While this is easy to understand in the context of apartheid rule, it is more difficult to comprehend the initial negotiating resistance to enforceable constitutionalism. It was only after what NP chief negotiator Roelf Meyer termed a "paradigm shift" that the white minority embraced the idea of a constitutional court holding the powers of judicial review. Reluctantly, the NP began to see constitutionalism not as means that would compel the end of racial prerogatives, but as a minority-protection device going forward under inevitable black-majority rule.[17] According to Meyer, the "paradigm shift" came about only when a young staffer on the negotiating team pointed out that under any negotiated transition, dominant white political power would come to an end. Sometimes the hardest truths hide in plain sight. Internalizing this seemingly obvious point finally led the NP negotiators to begin looking to other institutional guarantees against perceived excesses of majority power to come.

As a result, rights guarantees became incorporated in both the interim and final constitutions. Both constitutions vested enormous authority in an independent judiciary. It was, as Heinz Klug aptly summarizes, a revolution "represented by the triumph of constitutionalism over parliamentary sovereignty

---

[15] See Klug, *supra* note 6, at 76 (quoting John Dugard, *Changing Attitudes Towards a Bill of Rights in South Africa*, in A BILL OF RIGHTS FOR SOUTH AFRICA 34 (Johann van der Westhuizen & Henning Viljoen eds., Durban, South Africa: Butterworths, 1988)).

[16] Albie Sachs, *Towards a Bill of Rights for a Democratic South Africa*, 12 HASTINGS INT'L & COMP. L. REV. 289, 308 (1989).

[17] Much of the story of the emergence of constitutionalism in the negotiations is recounted in ALISTAIR SPARKS, TOMORROW IS ANOTHER COUNTRY (New York: Hill & Wang, 1995). For Roelf Meyer's personal account of the circumstances surrounding this "paradigm shift," see Roelf Meyer, *Paradigm Shift: The Essence of Successful Change, A Personal Experience*, available at http://www.incore.ulst.ac.uk/publications/occasional/R_M_Paradigm_Shift.pdf.

and, while its impact was yet to work its way fully through the labyrinth of South African law, its basic premise – a justiciable constitution – was fully guaranteed in the Constitutional Principles which guided the democratically elected Constitutional Assembly."[18]

The debates over enforceable rights guarantees were only the opening wedge of broader debates over the limits of majoritarianism that played out along a series of institutional design questions. There was justifiable outrage at the idea that the transition from racial minority governance could be challenged on the grounds of excessive power given to the oppressed and impoverished black majority. The Kempton Park negotiations only began the process of confronting what consolidated black political power would look like. In terms of institutional design, the inevitability of ANC rule was as contentious as it was certain.

Here one cannot escape the tremendous intellectual influence of Albie Sachs over the constitutional debates in South Africa, at least on the ANC side. Not only did Sachs actively reject any possible formal racial assignment of political power, but it was Sachs who staked out the contours of constitutionalism as the arena for postapartheid political struggle. As he wrote in 1986, "the struggle for self-determination takes the form of a struggle within the frontiers of South Africa to create a new constitutional order."[19] While rejecting any form of racial power sharing, Sachs's view of the constitution served primarily as a way of organizing majority political power. Any rights guarantees were secondary to the overarching aim of ensuring that democracy was the means by which the black majority could exercise its political dominion.

Democratic governance is compatible with a number of distinct forms of state organization. Beginning with Montesquieu, democratic theory has gravitated toward separation of powers as a bedrock protection against state excess. Liberty would be enshrined by impeding the consolidation of excessive state authority, primarily through fractionating the organization of authority. In turn, divided power would create institutional friction among various governmental bodies that did not share the same constituencies or interests. While this is the familiar commitment to separation of powers among most democratic governments, it is not the only way of arranging legitimate political authority. There is no reason that democracy cannot be premised on parliamentary supremacy following the British model. Nor does democracy necessarily require enabling a strong judiciary with the power of judicial review of

---

[18] Klug, *supra* note 6, at 115.
[19] Albie Sachs, *Towards the Constitutional Reconstruction of South Africa*, 2 LESOTHO L. J. 205, 205 (1986).

the acts of parliament. That may be the direction of development even in the classic parliamentary democracies in the United Kingdom, and its former colonies such as Australia and New Zealand,[20] but nothing mandates that this is the sole form of democratic design.

For those seeking to ease the consolidation of majority political power, there was no obvious reason to embrace fractionated authority. One example that would later emerge as key to the judicial assessment of the first proposed permanent constitution was Sachs's rather categorical rejection of federalist constraints on centralized power. For Sachs, federalism:

> is a way of depriving majority rule in South Africa of any meaning ... This would prevent the emergence of national government, keep the black population divided, prevent any economic restructuring of the country and free the economically prosperous areas of the country of any responsibility for helping develop the vast poverty stricken areas.[21]

As one commentator noted, the focus on the ability of a majority to rule effectively was, for Sachs, "not only the crux of the idea of democracy, but absolutely essential if South Africa is to become a more just society."[22] Despite the strong advocacy of majoritarian prerogatives, Sachs was attentive to the risk of governmental oppression, although perhaps more in terms of the risk of political despotism than unbridled majoritarian power. The main risk through the apartheid period remained, quite justifiably, the continued deprivation of political and social rights to the black majority.

The new judicial power extended not only to a future constraint on democratic power, but also formed an integral part of the peaceful transition from apartheid. Beyond the familiar powers of judicial review over the constitutionality of proposed legislation, the South African Constitutional Court had a power that had never before been imparted on any court. As part of the transfer of power rule, the South African negotiators had created not only an interim constitution, but the 34 Principles that defined the transitional pact would in turn form the basis for a final constitution. Under the negotiated provisions of the Interim Constitution, no final constitution could be adopted unless it faithfully adhered in its implementation to these negotiated 34 Principles set out in the Interim Constitution.[23]

---

[20] For a discussion of the evolution of the British-inspired states toward limited forms of parliamentary sovereignty, see STEPHEN GARDBAUM, THE NEW COMMONWEALTH MODEL OF CONSTITUTIONALISM (New York: Cambridge University Press, 2013).

[21] ALBIE SACHS, PROTECTING HUMAN RIGHTS IN A NEW SOUTH AFRICA 152–53 (Oxford: Oxford University Press, 1990).

[22] Gloppen, *supra* note 3, at 63.

[23] *Id.* at 199.

And it was the constitutional court that was entrusted with the power to ensure that the final constitution conformed to the 34 Principles.

LIMITING THE MAJORITY

Despite the breadth of material covered in the 34 Principles, it is worth focusing on what may be subsumed under the category of anti-majoritarian protections. As a general matter, these take three forms. First, there is an elaborate set of rights guarantees that protects individuals against adverse state conduct. Of particular interest to the wealthy white minority, these individual rights protections extended to the confiscation of property. Although other constitutional provisions decreed that the new government would be devoted to the amelioration of disparities in wealth across racial lines, Principle V provides that "[e]quality before the law includes laws, programmes or activities that have as their object the amelioration of the conditions of the disadvantaged, including those disadvantaged on the grounds of race, colour or gender."[24] In essence, this Principle extends legal protection to the white minority to prevent simple expropriation resulting from the exercise of majority power.

Second, there are restrictions on the exercise of state authority that limit the concentration of power in the central government. The draft constitution balanced powers not only by cabining the scope of authority of the legislative majority within the national government but by adopting principles of federalism designed to further impede the overconcentration of political might at the national level. These limitations include the requirements of formal lawmaking (Principle X)[25] through a multiparty legislature (Principle VIII),[26] separation of powers (Principle VI),[27] an independent judiciary (Principle VII),[28] and a multiparty representative government based on proportional representation (Principle VIII).[29] More unique are the constitutional guarantees to the provinces and local governments to be able to claim an "equitable share" of national resources (Principle XXVI),[30] and the creation of a Public Service Commission and Reserve Bank independent of legislative control (Principle XXIX).[31]

---

[24] S. Afr. (Interim) Const., 1993 sched. 4, Principle V.
[25] *Id.* Principle X.
[26] *Id.* Principle VIII.
[27] *Id.* Principle VI.
[28] *Id.* Principle VII.
[29] *Id.* Principle VIII.
[30] *Id.* Principle XXVI.
[31] *Id.* Principle XXIX.

Third, the draft constitution specifically targeted the ease of legislation in certain critical areas. Unlike the Weimar Constitution and the Indian Constitution, the draft in South Africa sought to limit what simple majorities could legislate in areas of fundamental rights and basic constitutional guarantees. Thus, supermajorities were needed to amend the constitution, requiring not only a two-thirds vote in the upper house of the national parliament but approval by a majority of provincial legislatures (Principle XVIII).[32]

The 34 Principles sought to facilitate the transition to democratic rule by assuring the white minority that democratic rule would not simply be an invitation to majoritarian retribution.[33] Whatever the historical merits of retribution, and whatever the grave injustices of apartheid rule, the fact remained that without some formal guarantee of security, power would never have been ceded by the militarily dominant white minority except on the closing end of a bloody civil war. The mechanism for enforcing security would be the newly crafted constitution, but its drafting and implementation presented two key problems, which are best set out in the words of the Constitutional Court of South Africa:

> The first arose from the fact that [the architects of the constitutional compromise] were not elected to their positions in consequence of any free and verifiable elections and that it was therefore necessary to have this commitment articulated in a final constitution adopted by a credible body properly mandated to do so in consequence of free and fair elections based on universal adult suffrage. The second problem was the fear in some quarters that the constitution eventually favoured by such a body of elected representatives might not sufficiently address the anxieties and the insecurities of such constituencies and might therefore subvert the objectives of a negotiated settlement. The government and other minority groups were prepared to relinquish power to the majority but were determined to have a hand in drawing the framework for the future governance of the country. The liberation movements on the opposition side were equally adamant that only democratically elected representatives of the people could legitimately engage in forging a constitution: neither they, and certainly not the government of the day, had any claim to the requisite mandate from the electorate.[34]

---

[32] *Id.* Principle XVIII.

[33] *See id.* Principle XIV ("Provision shall be made for participation of minority political parties in the legislative process in a manner consistent with democracy.").

[34] *In re* Certification of the Constitution of the Republic of South Africa, 1996 (4) SALR 744, 779 (CC) (S. Afr.).

In effect, this is the problem of all contested moments of constitutional formation. The "constitutional moment" is rarely the "democratic moment." As a practical matter, a negotiated transition from authoritarian rule to democracy will require meetings, draft proposals, negotiations, and compromise. The very nature of a "pacted transition" requires a small group of negotiators capable of making deals across divergent interests. In the context of any kind of authoritarian rule, at least some of the negotiating parties will lack any kind of democratic mandate from their constituencies. Following the fall of the Soviet Union, for example, the negotiations in the satellite countries took place among parties that typically had no mechanism for an organized political existence in the prior regime. Even the NP in South Africa could claim an electoral mandate only for governance in the apartheid regime; the translation of that governance mandate to the dismantling of white rule would be problematic, at the very least.

Nor is this a new problem. Recall that the American constitutional founders met in Philadelphia under the command of the Articles of Confederation, whose amendment processes the delegates could not claim to follow. Not only did the Philadelphia gathering lack authority for a new constitutional order under the terms of the Articles of Confederation, but the refusal of Rhode Island even to attend meant there was no hope that the new constitutional charter could claim the unanimity of support needed for altering the basic structure of the Articles. The Philadelphia convention had to contrive a new process of gauging popular consent through the state constitutional conventions. Other constitutions face greater obstacles to claiming democratic legitimacy, notably the Japanese Constitution, which was imposed by American occupation forces after World War II. Somehow, the combination of after-the-fact approbation and successful democratic governance overcomes the birth pangs of many constitutional orders.

The greatest problem is neither the mechanics of negotiating terms in a closed room nor the contestable claim to after-the-fact approval. A successful constitutional transition requires a credible commitment to the protection of vulnerable minorities. With difficulty, that can be negotiated. But few minorities would readily entrust their fate to the electoral discretion of a cohesive majority voting bloc. The initial pact has to make some commitment that certain choices will be off the table for subsequent modification by the electorate, which under conditions of democratic participation would necessarily be dominated by the majority.

Ultimately, a successful constitutional order requires buy-in by the citizenry. If a constitution is to enshrine democratic principles, it must command popular acceptance. The example of Japan shows that even a constitution compelled upon a defeated and exhausted nation may prove itself, over time, a suitable framework for the realization of democracy and prosperity. With that extreme example aside, the reality is that a constitution that repeatedly resists the mass desires of the population is likely unstable. The Kemalist constitution in Turkey, discussed earlier in this book, imposed a Westernized, secular vision of a modern society on an increasingly religious population. Inevitably, the democratic aspirations of significant parts of the country would come into conflict with the prescribed constitutional order.

South Africa innovated in two significant ways. First, it separated the process of negotiating the political accords from the final step of constitutional adoption. In some real sense, the functional constitution of South Africa was the 34 Principles that emerged from the Kempton Park negotiations. These Principles represented the negotiated accord and enshrined not only the transition from apartheid but the political and institutional protections demanded by the NP negotiators. As such, they allowed for representatives of the various groups to sign off on them. Second, the transition accords required a process of popular engagement in creating the exact form of constitutional governance through a popularly elected constituent assembly. That resulting draft was broadly communicated to the public prior to its presentation to President Mandela for signature. The two phases of the process were tied together institutionally by the constitutional court. No final constitution could go into effect without popular ratification, and even then, not until and unless the court certified that it was true to the previously negotiated 34 Principles.

While the tension between a negotiated accord and popular approval of a constitution was hardly a new problem in South Africa, the use of the nascent constitutional court was a novel solution. The negotiating parties agreed to the minimum baselines of protection of the interest of all parties. The subsequent process of final constitutional drafting and popular approval would proceed, but only to the extent that the end product met the negotiated commitments of the underlying political accords. The 34 Principles were the agreed-to pact, and the constitutional court was enlisted as the institutional commitment that the agreement would be honored. As the court explained its role:

> The impasse was resolved by a compromise which enabled both sides to attain their basic goals without sacrificing principle. What was no less important in the political climate of the time was that it enabled them to keep faith with their respective constituencies: those who feared engulfment by a black majority and those who were determined to eradicate apartheid once and for all. In essence the settlement was quite simple. Instead of an outright transmission of power from the old order to the new, there would be a programmed two-stage transition. An interim government, established and

functioning under an interim constitution agreed to by the negotiating parties, would govern the country on a coalition basis while a final constitution
was being drafted. A national legislature, elected (directly and indirectly) by
universal adult suffrage, would double as the constitution-making body and
would draft the new constitution within a given time. But – and herein lies
the key to the resolution of the deadlock – that text would have to comply
with certain guidelines agreed upon in advance by the negotiating parties.
What is more, an independent arbiter would have to ascertain and declare
whether the new constitution indeed complied with the guidelines before it
could come into force.[35]

The task of ensuring compliance was given in its entirety to the constitutional
court. In effect, once South Africa emerged as a full constitutional democracy,
the constitutional court would stand as the ultimate arbiter of the constitution,
holding full powers of judicial review. Ironically, however, the constitutional
court would predate the constitution and would serve as the final body approv-
ing the adoption of the constitution itself. Hardly customary, yet innovative,
this arrangement seemed to satisfy the security interests of all parties and was
integral to the peaceful transition to constitutional democracy.

It is of course possible to assail any political arrangement with the remnants
of apartheid. As one critic has noted:

> For the NP, the principles constituted a shield for the protection of the white
> minority and its privilege from the possible redistributive inclinations of a
> black-led government. In other words, the principles were the essential link
> between the past and the present; through them the old order would ensure
> its survival. For the ANC, which ascended to power through persuasion as
> opposed to the defeat of its adversary, rejection of the principles would likely
> have delayed the transition or compounded the crisis of governance then
> destabilizing South Africa. The establishment was willing to transfer some
> powers to an ANC government so long as the resulting state would have sub-
> stantially inferior powers compared with those of its predecessors.[36]

The comparison to the past is entirely apt. The former government was dedicated to racialist domination. To the extent there would be a peaceful transition, and some prospect of democratic, multiracial rule, the criticism that the
incoming government would have less power than its predecessor misses the
mark. Of course it would. Absent such constitutional constraints, a racial civil
war was inevitable. As all parties to the negotiations realized, the ANC could

---

[35] *Id.*
[36] Mutua, *supra* note 2, at 81.

not govern without the inherited administrative bureaucracy of the defeated apartheid regime. Nor could the ANC readily overcome the apartheid rulers militarily. At the same time, the NP could not very well continue to hold off majority rule and believed that international sanctions would have prevented a bloody war of attrition against the majority population.[37] What emerged was precisely the product of a contested negotiation.

DEMOCRACY AND THE CONSTITUTIONAL COURT

The constitutional court's historic moment came in July 1996 when the proposed permanent constitution was submitted for review. While some courts, as with the subsequent ruling of the Colombian Constitutional Court, have had to confront the constitutionality of particular amendments to the national charter, no other court has ever had to pass on the suitability of the entire constitutional project. Two months later, in September 1996, the court handed down its decision, upholding much of the constitutional project, but significantly rejecting a number of key provisions.[38]

Of greatest significance for present purposes are the provisions that were rejected in order to reaffirm limitations on government. These provisions can be grouped under what may be termed an excess of majoritarianism. If a constitution is viewed as a constraint on the preferences of an electoral majority at any given moment, then the ability to strike down parts of the democratically approved constitutional proposal means that there was a prior constitutional order that the court could invoke. In particular, the ability to strike down democratically enacted constitutional provisions necessarily means that the court was acting under the mandate of some prior higher-order law – in this case, the agreed-upon terms of the 34 Principles. What is striking, therefore, about the *Certification* decision is the relation between the political accommodation of the Kempton Park accords and the subsequent democratic process of constitutional adoption.

Viewed in this light, the *Certification* opinion draws a distinction between the domains of specific institutional structures, which were left to the constituent assembly process, and the areas of express commitment to minority protections, which were held to a higher level of judicial scrutiny. In the second group were particular provisions of the 34 Principles that restricted the ability of a democratic majority to act, and hence could not be compromised

---

[37] This is a dramatically condensed version of a long process of realization through negotiations, told forcefully in Sparks, *supra* note 17, at 120–225.

[38] *In re Certification*, 1996 (4) SALR at 744.

in the ratification process. Among the key provisions struck down for an excess of majoritarian control were the attempt to preclude constitutional review from certain categories of statutes, the absence of federalist safeguards on centralized power, and the lack of supermajoritarian protection for certain components of the constitution itself, including the liberty protections of the Bill of Rights.[39] With regard to the latter, the court found a violation of the principles of the Interim Constitution in the failure to "entrench" the rights in question.[40]

In summary form, the court's majestic ruling turns on the following key understandings of permissible constitutional law:

1. **Bicameralism and divided government.** – There was no question that any postapartheid government would be controlled (as it should be) by the enfranchised black majority and that the party of choice would be the ANC. It is one thing to have a popularly selected central government, and quite another to concentrate all power without institutional filters. There are multiple arrangements that serve to fractionate power, creating different institutional constituencies that, in Madison's famous image from FEDERALIST 51, can create buffers against overly concentrated power: "the great security against a gradual concentration of the several powers in the same department, consists in giving to those who administer each department the necessary constitutional means and personal motives to resist encroachments of the others." For Madison, this meant that "[a]mbition must be made to counteract ambition." Ultimately, the American Framers believed that it "may be a reflection on human nature, that such devices should be necessary to control the abuses of government," but central they must be to secure against overly concentrated power.[41]

   The South African court looked especially closely at the institutions that served to divide power. Invoking Montesquieu, the court reaffirmed the importance of checks and balances across the branches of government.[42] The court pointed specifically to the powers granted to an upper house (the National Council of Provinces) that would not be based on

---

[39] This is referred to as the requirement that there be "special procedures involving special majorities" for constitutional amendment and for any alteration of the constitutional guarantees of individual rights. *Id.* at 821.

[40] *Id.* at 822.

[41] THE FEDERALIST No. 51, at 321–22 (James Madison) (Clinton Rossiter ed., New York: New American Library, 1961).

[42] *In re Certification*, 1996 (4) SALR at 776, 788.

equipopulational voting, but on the election of ten representatives from each of the nine provinces.[43] The powers of the upper chamber were thought to be of considerable practical significance. The geographic division of South Africa yielded one province that was majority Zulu (hence outside the political orbit of the ANC) and two others that had large concentrations of white and colored voters, again a less likely constituency for the ANC.[44] The proposed constitution carried forward the requirement that upper chamber support had to be secured from more than six provinces. However, the court denied certification for the powers granted the National Council of Provinces, particularly in light of areas of law in which the popularly elected National Assembly could override an objection from the upper chamber.

2. **Federalism.** – The court strictly enforced Principle XXII ensuring that the national government would not encroach on the powers of the provinces.[45] Thus the court found unconstitutional those provisions that failed to provide the required "framework for LG [local government] structures," as well as the failure to ensure the fiscal integrity of political subdivisions.[46] For the court, the South African Constitution should provide only those powers to the national government "where national uniformity is required."[47] Under both the 34 Principles[48] and the constitution,[49] the court determined that only economic matters and issues of foreign policy met this restrictive definition.

3. **Supermajoritarianism.** – The court also strictly construed Principle XV, which required "special procedures involving special majorities"

---

[43] *Id.* at 865–66.

[44] The commitment to a territorially based upper chamber was of particular significance in keeping the IFP participating in the process of negotiations and in the interim government, although that party did walk out in the final accords. *See* Gloppen, *supra* note 3, at 204, 222–23. For general background on the structure and powers of the bicameral parliament, see CLEMENS SPIESS, DEMOCRACY AND PARTY SYSTEMS IN DEVELOPING COUNTRIES: A COMPARATIVE STUDY OF INDIA AND SOUTH AFRICA 63–69 (Abingdon: Routledge, 2009).

[45] S. AFR. (INTERIM) CONST., 1993 sched. 4, Principle XXII.

[46] *In re Certification* (4) SALR at 861, 911.

[47] *See id.* at 845 (explaining that the constitution mandates that legislative powers should be allocated predominantly, if not wholly, to the national government where national uniformity is required).

[48] *See id.* at 849 (quoting Principle XIX's requirement that "the Constitution shall empower the national government to intervene through legislation" wherever such intervention is necessary for "the maintenance of economic unity ... [and] the maintenance of national security").

[49] *See id.* at 846 (noting that the constitution expressly "requires that the determination of national economic policies, the promotion of inter-provincial commerce and related matters should be allocated to the national government").

for constitutional amendments.[50] According to the court, the purpose of
this provision was to secure the constitution "against political agendas
of ordinary majorities in the national Parliament."[51] Various provisions
of the proposed constitution requiring supermajoritarian action were
nevertheless struck down for failing to create special procedures outside
the framework of ordinary legislation.[52] Thus, for example, a provision
allowing a two-thirds majority of the lower house to amend parts of the
constitution failed because "no special period of notice is required; constitutional amendments could be introduced as part of other draft legislation; and no extra time for reflection is required."[53] Similarly, the court
found that allowing the Bill of Rights to be amended by a two-thirds
majority of the lower house failed the "entrenchment" requirement
of Principle II,[54] which, the court ruled, required "some 'entrenching'
mechanism ... [to give] the Bill of Rights greater protection than the
ordinary provisions of the [Constitution]."[55]

4. **Judicial review.** – The rejection of judicial review for certain categories of statutes was found to violate the commitment to constitutional
supremacy in Principle IV and the jurisdictional guarantees for judicial
power contained in Principle VII.[56]

5. **International law.** – Although not a central issue in the ultimate
approval of the constitution by the court, Article 39 of the final constitution provides that, in construing the Bill of Rights, a court "must consider international law."[57] Most observers will note only the valorization
of international human rights norms. But the incorporation of a basis
of law beyond the control of the parliamentary majority again serves
to constrain majoritarian prerogatives by providing an independent,
non-parliamentary source of authority for courts to enforce.[58] Thus, in

---

[50] S. Afr. (Interim) Const., 1993 sched. 4, Principle XV.
[51] In re *Certification*, 1996 (4) SALR at 821.
[52] *See, e.g., id.* at 822 (striking down a provision that required approval of a two-thirds majority of
the lower house for any constitutional amendment for failing to dictate "special procedures"
for ratification in addition to supermajoritarian assent).
[53] *Id.*
[54] S. Afr. (Interim) Const., 1993 sched. 4, Principle II.
[55] In re *Certification*, 1996 (4) SALR at 822–23.
[56] *Id.* at 820.
[57] S. Afr. Const. ch. 2, § 39(1)(b).
[58] For example, section 35 of South Africa's Interim Constitution provides: "In interpreting the
provisions of this chapter a court of law shall promote the values which underlie an open and
democratic society based on freedom and equality and shall, where applicable, have regard
to public international law applicable to the protection of the rights entrenched in this chapter, and may have regard to comparable foreign case law." S. Afr. (Interim) Const. ch. 3,
§ 35(1).

construing the obligations of the constitution, the court found an obligation to protect those rights recognized in open and democratic societies as being "inalienable entitlements of human beings."[59] While the court recognized that no consensus exists as to what entitlements are inalienable, the court required the constitution, at a minimum, to guarantee those rights that have achieved a wide measure of international acceptance.[60] Thus, according to the court, in aggregating the fundamental rights of other societies, South Africa's proposed constitution established a set of rights "as extensive as any to be found in any national constitution."[61]

6. **Minority party security.** – Beyond the protections of proportional representation, the constitution contained an "anti-defection" principle in which a member of parliament would have to resign if he or she attempted to switch parties.[62] This provision later proved a lightning rod, as will be discussed in more detail in Chapter 11. For present purposes, it is significant that this measure was included in the constitutional draft and addressed by the court.

The legal claim, embodying a long tradition going back at least to Edmund Burke's famous Speech to the Electors of Bristol in 1774, was that any imposition of party discipline could restrict expression of beliefs by legislators. As expressed by Burke, a representative should seek to be as one with his constituents.

> But his unbiased opinion, his mature judgment, his enlightened conscience, he ought not to sacrifice to you, to any man, or to any set of men living. These he does not derive from your pleasure; no, nor from the law and the constitution. They are a trust from Providence, for the abuse of which he is deeply answerable.[63]

Whatever the merits of an appeal to conscience, the role of individual defections by individual legislators presents a different consideration in the context of a dominant political party. Where one party controls all legislative positions, there is an overriding concern that minority

---

[59] In re *Certification*, 1996 (4) SALR at 790.
[60] *Id.*
[61] *Id.* at 791.
[62] *See id.* at 829 n.136 and accompanying text (considering whether the anti-defection principle was unconstitutional).
[63] Edmund Burke, Speech to the Electors of Bristol (Nov. 3, 1774), *in* 1 THE FOUNDERS' CONSTITUTION 392 (Philip B. Kurland & Ralph Lerner eds., Chicago, IL: University of Chicago Press, 2000), *available at* http://press-pubs.uchicago.edu/founders/print_documents/v1ch13s7.html.

legislators could be induced to sway from their constituents' interests to support majoritarian policies. Because by definition there are fewer minority than majority representatives, any single minority defection would have a more severe impact on the representation of the minority population than the defection of a majority legislator would have on the representation of the majority. Such defection to the majority is not only more costly, but also more likely. Minority caucuses are unlikely to be able to offer the same personal opportunities or chances for local blandishments as is the majority. In rejecting the civil liberties challenge to the anti-defection clause, the court noted that anti-defection clauses were found in the constitutions of Namibia and India and were therefore entirely consistent with democratic governance.

CONSTITUTIONAL DEMOCRACY

The Constitutional Assembly then revised the constitutional draft to meet the court's concerns in October 1996, and following a second round of judicial scrutiny, the new constitution was signed and implemented by President Nelson Mandela in December 1996. The new constitution drew much fanfare, particularly among those taken with its ample guarantees of not just political rights, but also the sort of economic rights that had frustrated American courts even in the most expansionist Warren Court era. The new constitution even assures South African citizens the right to "an environment that is not harmful to their health and well-being."[64] Cass Sunstein seized upon this feature of the South African Constitution to declare it "the most admirable constitution in the history of the world."[65] For many champions of activist courts, the broad recognition of judicial authority in implementing constitutional principles combined with the sweeping rights guarantees sparked expectations that post-enactment cases would usher in an era of active judicial engagement with the process of dismantling the legacy of apartheid.

Consistent with its origins as the handmaiden to constitutional democracy, however, the court in the initial period of democratic consolidation played a circumspect, pragmatic role, refusing to develop a broad mandate of rights jurisprudence.[66] Thus, much criticism was directed at decisions

[64] S. AFR. CONST. ch. 2, § 24(a).
[65] CASS SUNSTEIN, DESIGNING DEMOCRACY: WHAT CONSTITUTIONS DO 261 (Oxford: Oxford University Press, 2001).
[66] For a summary of the criticisms of the South African Constitutional Court and a defense of institutional pragmatism, see Mark S. Kende, *The Fifth Anniversary of the South African Constitutional Court: In Defense of Judicial Pragmatism*, 26 VT. L. REV. 753 (2002).

such as *Republic of South Africa v. Grootboom,* in which the court distinguished between the rights guarantees of the constitution and the deference that should be accorded the government in crafting policies to achieve those objectives.[67] *Grootboom* pressed the tension between respect for preexisting property rights and the demands of the impoverished black majority for improved conditions of basic existence. At immediate issue was the claim for the constitutional guarantee that "everyone has the right to access to adequate housing." The claim for housing was pressed by a group of destitute black citizens, some of whom had been waiting seven years on eligibility lists for as yet nonexistent state housing. They finally left the dilapidated conditions in which they found themselves and built a shantytown from makeshift supplies. When that community was shut down, the now homeless claimants illegally occupied some private land. The court confronted what it termed "the harsh reality that the Constitution's promise of dignity and equality for all remains for many a distant dream." The court largely sidestepped the most difficult issue by requiring through a declaratory judgment that the government attend to the needs of the black majority in its programs, but without compelling any particular resolution to the immediate controversy. For those who saw in the broad constitutional commands an invitation to a court-driven rights jurisprudence that would, in effect, drive political outcomes, *Grootboom* was a grave disappointment.

To my mind, critics of the court largely fail to appreciate the true significance of the South African constitutional process and of the role played by the court in that process. Although many will be taken by the ample rights domain in the South African Constitution, and no doubt its constitutionalization of environmental and labor-organizing protections will feature prominently in future comparative law treatises, the constitutional processes in South Africa served primarily as a success story in constituting democratic rule. The use of an interim constitution defused the pressure to resolve deeply contested governance questions on a once-and-for-all basis while providing a sense of security to minority constituencies. The Interim Constitution, together with the authority entrusted to the constitutional court, allowed for transitional

---

[67] *See* 2001 (1) SALR 46, 68 (CC) (S. Afr.) (indicating that the constitution's guarantee of a right of access to adequate housing did not prevent the court from deferring to "reasonable" measures taken by the state to provide such housing). For a thoughtful account of this tension, see Heinz Klug, *Five Years On: How Relevant Is the Constitution to the New South Africa,* 26 Vt. L. Rev. 803 (2002) (analyzing the conflict over the extent of the constitution's mandate on specific policies in the context of litigation over efforts to require the government to provide nevirapine to prevent mother-to-child HIV transmission).

democratic organization of parties and constituencies and also for a participatory legitimacy to the drafting and ratification of the final constitution. Having helped create a fledgling democracy in a deeply divided and still violent society, the court's reluctance to substitute decrees for democratic deliberation and compromise seems well in keeping with the ambitious mandates of the transitional process.

This leads to some final observations on the generalizability of the South African experience. South Africa entered the constitutional period with a developed industrial base, a well-functioning market economy, and strong institutions of civil society both inside and outside the market arena.[68] Throughout the transitional period, state power remained intact and the Interim Constitution could be implemented by the outgoing regime as ordinary legislation.[69] Both the NP and the ANC were Western-oriented and secular. Even so, the democratic experiment in South Africa remains fragile. What nonetheless emerges is the use of limitations on majority power as a mechanism for stabilizing democratic governance without the reinforcement of ethnic and racial divides created by formal power sharing.

---

[68] This point is further elaborated in Gloppen, *supra* note 3, at 271.
[69] I am indebted to Frank Michelman for this point.

9

The Era of Constitutional Courts

In conversations over the years with justices from the South African Constitutional Court, and with South African scholars, I always come back to a question of historical uncertainty. By the time the South African court entered its famous decision in the *Certification* case, the transition to post-apartheid governance had been largely completed. Now secure in his role as head of state, President Mandela had control of the police and the military, had a formidable legislative majority, and possessed an overwhelming sense of authority as the unquestionably dominant figure in South African politics. The constitution that emerged from the constituent assembly process may have had defects, but at bottom it was just not that bad. It more or less honored the initial agreements, and where it erred on the side of too much unconstrained political power, it did so mildly. In other words, the initial constitutional effort was by no means an affront to the basic values that animated the South African transition, nor would it have been challenged as fundamentally unacceptable in any democratic country.

The question I then ask is why Mandela did not simply disregard the constitutional court. As the future architect of the U.S. Bill of Rights once rhetorically inquired, what reason do we have to think that "parchment barriers" are of any use "against the encroaching spirit of power?"[1] Mandela might have echoed Joseph Stalin's rejoinder to disapproval from the Vatican: "How many divisions does the Pope of Rome have?" Perhaps more gently, Mandela could also have claimed shared constitutional authority with the court, a nascent form of the "popular constitutionalism" claims that briefly entertained American constitutional law at the time. Or, most simply, why not just thank

---

[1] THE FEDERALIST No. 48, at 308 (James Madison) (Clinton Rossiter ed., New York: New American Library, 1961).

the court for its efforts and get on with the fraught task of governing the still fractured republic?

To ask such a question is to invite a bewildered look of incomprehension. To begin with, Mandela's personal trajectory – notably his long legal battles against his incarceration on Robben Island – left him with a surprisingly deep respect for the rule of law. The first president of the constitutional court was Arthur Chaskelson, who served as Mandela's personal lawyer during the years of incarceration and was a regular visitor to Robben Island. Indeed, the first time I had the temerity to ask this question it was directed to President Chaskelson, who reacted politely in disbelief that the question could be posed.

Yet the question needed to be asked. Why would political power cede to the first assertion of judicial supremacy? After all, in the American context, Chief Justice Marshall's opening salvo on judicial review in *Marbury v. Madison* strategically took the form of using judicial authority to buttress rather than defy executive authority – a pattern repeated in Germany and India, to name two of the most powerful courts that might be emulated, when they developed their signal doctrines of proportionality and basic structures review. By contrast, South Africa's court used its power of judicial review initially to confront the political branches over the draft constitution that they had promulgated. This sort of frontal engagement with the political branches, a pattern that would later be repeated in countries like Colombia, demands an answer as to why courts could get away with this. Particularly, in the South African context in which the constitutional court undertook the unprecedented role of reviewing the constitution itself, some explanation is necessary.

Certainly, part of the answer had to be President Mandela himself. Few figures in recent history filled the historic demands for leadership, insight, and decency in such remarkable measures. There is something awe-inspiring in watching an individual rise to the demands of history, and all the more so after years of imprisonment and isolation. Yet the answer must be more than just the person of Mandela. For in country after country in the post-1989 era we see courts playing this role, and fractured polities frequently bending to judicial commands. With great certainty, we can safely say that there were all too few Mandelas on the world stage in that difficult period. Leadership matters, but the pattern seemed quite universal in the first stages of democratization.

Ultimately, the answer cannot be Mandela alone. During the period of constitutional court ascendancy following 1989, the striking result is that ruling leaders in country after country acceded to the assertion of muscular judicial oversight. In the remainder of this chapter, and in the one that follows, the subject is what in fact these courts were doing and why political leaders might have acquiesced to it. In this chapter, I describe a number of archetypical situations in which constitutional courts intercede in order to preserve newly founded democracy through independent, active constitutionalism. In describing each political circumstance, the potential role of constitutional courts in third-wave democracies becomes crystalline: these courts can fill gaps of legitimacy and limitation in an emergent democracy that cannot otherwise be resolved by other bodies within its political structure.

DIVIDED POWER

Samuel Huntington aptly summarized the Catch-22 facing nascent democracies: "lacking legitimacy, they cannot become effective; lacking effectiveness, they cannot develop legitimacy."[2] Characteristically, the fledgling democracies have weak or simply corrupt political parties[3] and poorly defined governmental institutions. Frequently in the post-Soviet settings, the prior authoritarian regime effectively shut down all efforts at maintaining non-state forms of organized citizen engagement. There were no independent political parties, no functioning trade unions, not even an operational church structure. In rushing to fill in the void once the Soviet Union fell, these countries did not have time to develop the precarious balance between governmental and nongovernmental institutions that keeps democracies operating.

Nor is there any reason to believe that all the institutions will develop in tandem. New democracies from post-Nazi Germany to post-Soviet Eastern Europe to post-Mubarak Egypt may curb or prohibit the participation of the mandatory political party of the prior authoritarian regime, as discussed in the early chapters of this book. We can now think of these parties not simply as inheritors of an antidemocratic past, but as hypertrophied institutions within the body politic, engorged by the privileged accumulation of experience and cadres under the *ancien régime*. These parties are the mobilizing force of the prior repressive state, not the vehicles of democratic politics.

It is not just the political parties, however, but also the institutions of government that may develop unequally, in part reflecting the authoritarian past. In many cases, it may be easier to reconstitute an executive power based

---

[2] SAMUEL P. HUNTINGTON, THE THIRD WAVE: DEMOCRATIZATION IN THE LATE TWENTIETH CENTURY 258 (Norman: University of Oklahoma Press, 1991).

[3] *See* ETHAN P. Kapstein & Nathan CONVERSE, THE FATE OF YOUNG DEMOCRACIES 25 (Cambridge: Cambridge University Press, 2008) (reporting a study by the Carnegie Endowment for International Peace that concluded, "citizens of almost every struggling or new democracy are deeply unhappy with political parties ... [which] are perceived as corrupt, self-interested organizations that relentlessly work to maximize their own welfare with no real concern for ordinary citizens.").

on control of the police or military. In other cases, it may be the legislature that emerges as the strongest power. A dominant parliamentary bloc may be able to consolidate power quickly as a reconstituted form of the dominant organization of the prior regime, as with the remnants of the former communist parties.

In turn, uneven development also plagues civil society institutions. Repressive regimes view any source of independent organization as a threat to state dominance, particularly where the state lays claim to a comprehensive ideology for exclusive state authority, as with communism in the Soviet bloc. Some independent organizations, such as religious denominations, may survive in this environment and, as in Poland, may serve as a legitimate oppositional force against authoritarian rule. But organizing congregants on the basis of faith does not translate immediately into democratic political engagement, as most clearly evident in the stillborn democratic experiments of the Arab Spring.

The imbalance in political power frequently defines immediate issues for court review. The problem is easiest to conceptualize with regard to executive power. To recycle an earlier example, Colombia is in many ways typical of the reestablishment of democratic authority through the consolidation of power in the hands of a duly elected president or premier. As a general matter, asserting control of the military and the police powers, backed up by control of the treasury and taxing authority, is a simpler task than creating the give-and-take of parliamentary negotiations and the art of legislating through compromise. Even mature democracies may show difficulties in this endeavor, as attested to by current U.S. congressional dysfunction. The tendency in weak democracies is to have the executive push to exceed its constitutional boundaries, with little effective pushback from the legislature. Again, Colombia is an apt example of a court being drawn into this breach in an effort to maintain constitutional divisions of power.

A curious but illustrative example comes from Mongolia, an unlikely setting perhaps for democratic experimentation, and unlikely also because the threat to divided power came from an excessively strong parliamentary majority. The constitutional conflict in Mongolia arose from the efforts of a dominant parliamentary bloc to control the weak executive – the inverse of what was faced in Colombia. In the early days of democratic governance, a stable parliamentary coalition began to consolidate power and was able to wield complete control over the legislative branch. The cohesive parliamentary majority sought to expand its domain by having important parliamentarians hold cabinet positions as part of the executive. There is nothing particularly novel or shocking about this. Constitutional democracies vary between presidential and Westminster-style parliamentary regimes, with many mixed variants as well. In any pure parliamentary regime, the prime minister is subject not to direct election but to formal selection by the leading party or coalition in parliament. The cabinet is then typically staffed by leading legislators, as, for example, in Britain. Such arrangements do not enshrine formal separation of powers, but they do not necessarily lack for democratic pedigree as a result. Again, Britain remains the chief case in point.

In Mongolia, the parliament sought to force members of its choice into the presidential cabinet. A weak executive could not resist the repeated efforts by the Mongolian Parliament (the State Great Hural) to appoint acting members of the parliament to the presidential cabinet and, as in Colombia, the matter moved from the political realm to the judicial. In a series of rulings, the Mongolian Constitutional Court read the Mongolian Constitution to mandate that members of parliament cannot hold presidential cabinet positions.[4] In so doing, a newly created constitutional court waded into the very heart of the political thicket in the first election that successfully displaced the embedded Mongolian People's Revolutionary Party, the long-standing communist rulers. The constitutional court ruled that such a practice was unconstitutional because it violated a poorly defined constitutional commitment to separation of powers. The court confronted the parliament over this issue twice, first when the matter was brought on petition of a private citizen in 1996, and again by striking down a law passed by the parliament in 1998. The issue of parliamentary control of executive functions continued to dominate Mongolian legal disputes in the early years of noncommunist rule until 2000, when the political parties sufficiently unified in demanding parliamentary authority and the court ultimately backed down.[5]

Although the Mongolian case illustrates the ultimate vulnerability of these new constitutional courts to persistent political pressure, it is nonetheless important to understand the terms of the dispute. Noteworthy beyond the immediate winners and losers in Mongolia was that this was understood by the court as a first-order dispute as to whether Mongolia was a presidential or parliamentary system. Perhaps surprisingly (then again, perhaps not), this question had apparently not been specified in the multiparty and broadly participatory Mongolian constitutional design.

---

[4] Tom Ginsburg & Gombosuren Ganzorig, *When Courts and Politics Collide: Mongolia's Constitutional Crisis*, 14 COLUM. J. ASIAN L. 309, 311–13 (2001).

[5] Stephen Fenwick, *The Rule of Law in Mongolia – Constitutional Court and Conspiratorial Parliament*, 3 AUSTL. J. ASIAN L. 213, 219–20 (2001).

The issue hinged on the interpretation of Article 29(1), which states that members of the parliament "shall not hold concurrently any posts and employment other than those assigned by law."[6] Presumably this clause could be read to prevent private compensation to government officials, to prohibit holding office in different levels of government, or to prohibit holding office in multiple branches of government. Each is a recognizable arrangement in different democratic countries. For example, in the United States, many state legislatures are only in session part of the time as in New York, or only in session every other year, as in Texas, leaving legislators free to pursue other career options – and oftentimes obligated to for those not independently wealthy. Or, in France, it is customary for national government officials to also hold local office in their constituencies. Or, in parliamentary regimes, members of the cabinet continue to serve as members of the legislative branch. The Mongolian clause could be read to limit any one or all of these arrangements.

In order to strike down the proposed dual role of ministers, the court had to first decide that Mongolia was constitutionally obligated to adhere to a presidential system as opposed to a parliamentary system. The court based this on a constitutional commitment to stable governance, a weak reed for such a core matter of governmental structure. This in turn led to the final piece of the analysis that a division of functions between members of the parliament and members of the executive was necessary to maintain both separation of powers and political competition between the branches.

Mongolia may well present the rare case of a court having to resolve the basic structure of democracy, but it is far from the only such case. Courts are critical to establish the boundaries of governmental power in unstable democracies. In Bangladesh, for another extreme example, in order to forestall incumbent manipulation of the powers of state during the elections, a retired judge is required to head a caretaker government during the election period.[7] More representative is the experience of Albania, where the power of judicial review was established in a series of opinions addressing the terms under which an independent constitutional officer, the general prosecutor (the equivalent of the attorney general), could be removed from office by the Assembly and the president.[8] The court there decided that in dealing with an

---

[6] MONG. CONST. art. 29, § 1.

[7] Nick Robinson, *Expanding Judiciaries: India and the Rise of the Good Governance Court*, 8 WASH. U. GLOBAL STUD. L. REV. 1, 66 (2009).

[8] *Decision No. 75 of the Albanian Constitutional Court* 4–5, ACCUEIL, http://www.accpuf.org/images/pdf/cm/albanie/052-jc-autres_jurisp.pdf (translating Gjykata Kushtetuese e Republikës së Shqipërisë [Constitutional Court] No. 76 of Apr. 20, 2002; Gjykata Kushtetuese e Republikës së Shqipërisë [Constitutional Court] No. 75 of Apr. 19, 2002).

independent officer, the political branches were constrained both substantively (only certain offenses suffice to remove such an officer) and procedurally (certain procedures are required for the removal to be valid). As in Mongolia, however, the court ultimately lost out politically as the Assembly then undertook to follow the prescribed procedures and remove the general prosecutor from office. Nonetheless, as noted by Albanian legal academic Agron Alibali, the "case evidenced an important role which Constitutional Courts can play in post-Communist societies ... as a true guarantor of the Constitution and the rights provided therein to their citizens."[9]

Most commonly, courts actively regulate core constitutional commitments to the structural separation of powers, as evident in the Bulgarian context. In 1991, Bulgaria established fundamental principles within its constitution that included separation of powers and a commitment to constitutional supremacy in policing the boundaries.[10] From its inception, the court assumed the power to enforce constitutional supremacy to play an important role in protecting each branch from intrusion by another. For example, the Council of Ministers, a part of the executive branch of government, attempted to alter the Supreme Judicial Council's budget requests before their approval by the National Assembly.[11] The court ruled that the executive branch could not tamper with any budget requests without the authorization of the Supreme Judicial Council, as altering the budget request could effectively change how the Supreme Judicial Council performed its duties. While there is no doubt an element of judicial self-protection here, a frequent concern for the assertion of judicial authority, the form of the response consolidates the judicial role in policing the boundaries of formal separation of powers.

The Bulgarian constitutional court intervened in a similar vein a second time, when the facially neutral Judiciary System Act attempted to entrench former Communists in commanding positions in the judiciary. The Act required all members of the Supreme Judicial Council to have had a minimum of five years of experience as judges, prosecutors, or academics – a seemingly sensible and neutral requirement, save that it could only have been met by holding office during Communist Party rule. The court invalidated this provision as well.

9 *See* Agron Alibali, *Two Landmark Decisions of the Albanian Constitutional Court: The Individual, the Employee, and the State*, 29 REV. CENT. & E. EUR. L. 219, 244–45 (2004).
10 Hristo D. Dimitrov, Note, *The Bulgarian Constitutional Court and Its Interpretive Jurisdiction*, 37 COLUM. J. TRANSNAT'L L. 459, 463 (1999).
11 *See* Albert P. Melone, *Judicial Independence and Constitutional Politics in Bulgaria*, 80 JUDICATURE 280, 283 (1997) (detailing the event).

The American experience provides some sense of the relation between such structural protections and the prospects for democratic self-rule. Under the original constitutional conception, there was no formal bill of rights, but rather a series of structural limitations on power designed to curtail governmental propensity toward excess. "Convinced that direct protection of constitutionally enumerated rights would be futile, the Federalist Framers, led by James Madison, attempted to secure rights *indirectly*, by creating a structure of government that would empower vulnerable groups to protect their interests."[12] Even long after authoring the Bill of Rights, Madison continued to believe that "[t]he only effectual safeguard to the rights of the minority, must be laid in such a basis and structure of the Government itself, as may afford, in a certain degree, directly or indirectly, a defensive authority in behalf of a minority having right on its side."[13]

While the examples of courts acting as guardians of basic structure commitments are numerous,[14] the central theme emerges time and again: fragile democracies are plagued by weak institutions. Courts are called upon to shore up the institutional frailties by imposing, and often creating, a constitutional structure that allows democratic governance to at least have a chance at succeeding. The result is not necessarily a rosy account of democracy always triumphant, but it is a story of an increasingly important constitutional actor in the transition to democracy.

DEEP IN THE POLITICAL THICKET

Since the 1849 case of *Luther v. Borden*, discussed in Chapter 7, the U.S. Supreme Court used the political question doctrine to skirt the fault lines of direct engagement with contested partisan issues, even if imperfectly. The political question doctrine appears most clearly in the constitutional design on the question of impeachment. The U.S. Constitution reserves to the House of Representatives the "sole Power" of impeachment and to the Senate the same "sole Power to try" all impeachments. The judiciary plays no role in the

---

[12] Daryl J. Levinson, *Rights and Votes*, 121 YALE L.J. 1286, 1293 (2012).

[13] *Id.* at 1297 (alteration in original) (quoting James Madison, Speech to the Virginia Constitutional Convention (1829), *in* SELECTED WRITINGS OF JAMES MADISON 355 (Ralph Ketcham ed., Indianapolis, IN: Hackett Publishing Company, 2006)).

[14] *See also* Miguel Schor, *An Essay on the Emergence of Constitutional Courts: The Cases of Mexico and Colombia*, 16 IND. J. GLOBAL LEGAL STUD. 173, 180–83 (2009) (explaining how the Mexican Supreme Court emboldened the transition to competitive democracy by circumscribing the power of the president to impose a series of unilateral budget amendments on the Congress).

removal of federal officials from office, save for the largely ceremonial role of the chief justice in presiding over a Senate trial for the impeachment of a president. Otherwise, the judiciary is removed from participation in a process reserved for the political branches, what Justice Frankfurter once termed the need to avoid becoming ensnared in the political thicket. While the political question doctrine has yielded in the United States as courts assume an increased responsibility over the proper functioning of the political process, the impeachment power remains beyond judicial oversight.

By contrast, new democracies view the role of constitutional courts differently. The creation of a constitutional court necessitates a more circumscribed view of democratic prerogatives. Thus, the constitutions in a number of post-Soviet democracies give constitutional courts the authority to exercise judicial review of parliamentary impeachments prior to any legislative action becoming a final judgment.[15] The recent effort in the Czech Republic to impeach then-President Václav Klaus provides a useful example. In March 2013, the upper house of the Czech Parliament voted the impeachment of Klaus for treason based on his grant of amnesty to 6,000 prisoners and refusal to ratify European Union treaties. Klaus had previously served as the prime minister at the head of a center-right coalition, and had used the largely ceremonial powers of the presidency to further some of his personal agenda items, as most evident in his refusal to sign the Lisbon Treaty on behalf of the Czech Republic. The impeachment for treason was a radical move by the left-dominated Senate, something that would have barred Klaus from future office and dealt a setback to his parliamentary followers, who had lost a close Senate vote on impeachment 38–30. More significantly, the impeachment would escalate the levels of political dispute to a level of outright removal of opponents from the political arena.

Under the Czech Constitution, however, no such impeachment could take effect absent judicial enforcement. No impeachment had ever been attempted in post-Soviet Czech history and the question for the constitutional court was whether the power of impeachment and subsequent exclusion from political life would become internalized in the toolbox of partisan fights, and thereby likely emerge as a central part of Czech politics. Court oversight provided a means to dampen partisan furor and to forestall a permanent poisoning of democratic politics in the Czech Republic. Without ever having to confront

---

[15] *See* Tom Ginsburg, *Ancillary Powers of Constitutional Courts, in* INSTITUTIONS AND PUBLIC LAW: COMPARATIVE APPROACHES 225–44 (Tom Ginsburg & Robert A. Kagan eds., Chicago, IL, University of Chicago Press, 2005) (noting that countries like the Czech Republic and Hungary give such power to their constitutional courts).

the terms of the impeachment itself, the court found a way to defuse the situation and allow Czech politics to return to normal. According to the court, the fact that Klaus's term had expired meant that impeachment was off the table and the justiciable controversy ended when he left office.[16] For that reason, Klaus could never have been convicted of high treason by the constitutional court and thus did not face any of the bars that come with impeachment via treason. More significantly, the charge of treason did not become a toxic feature of political strife in the Czech Republic.

A similar episode in South Korea shows the potential of court scrutiny to dampen a political conflagration that threatens the foundations of democratic governance. In 2003, then-President Roh Moo-hyun took to the hustings to garner support for members of his political party in the upcoming National Assembly election.[17] That in itself would hardly seem surprising in mature democracies where presidents serve as head of state and head of their party. But the South Korean Constitution forbade this role to the president, and President Roh's efforts were perceived as a direct executive challenge to the parliamentary command of the two opposing parties, the Grand National Party and the Millennium Democratic Party. Using their legislative power, they retaliated by seeking the impeachment of Roh on a variety of charges, including a violation of the Public Official Election Act, which prohibits officials from attempting to influence upcoming elections.[18] On March 14, 2004, President Roh became the first president to be impeached in Korean constitutional history, on voting largely following party line divisions.

Not surprisingly, impeachment for engaging in politicking was itself seen as a form of partisan retaliation. In a still weak democracy, such a partisan shock threatened to upend the basic premise of a constitutional democracy: the ability to achieve rotation in office as one winner plays out its term and the defeated party awaits another chance. The partisan divide played out as an institutional contest for power between the legislative and executive branches. However, South Korea also provided for judicial review by the Korean Constitutional Court, which, as in the Czech Republic, found a way to temporize. The court

---

[16] *Current Affairs – Constitutional Court Throws Out Treason Charges against Ex-president Klaus* (Czech Radio 7 broadcast Mar. 28, 2013).

[17] *See* Jonghyun Park, *The Judicialization of Politics in Korea*, 10 ASIAN-PAC. L. & POL'Y J. 62, 68 (2008) (describing the actions of President Roh).

[18] *Id. See also* Youngjae Lee, *Law, Politics, and Impeachment: The Impeachment of Roh Moo-hyun from a Comparative Constitutional Perspective*, 53 AM. J. COMP. L. 403, 411 (2005) ("The motion listed 21 separate counts as grounds for impeachment, ranging from Roh's support of the Uri Party to corruption scandals involving Roh's close aides to Roh's management of the economy.").

upheld the parliamentary finding that Roh was guilty of several constitutional infractions,[19] yet decided that impeachment was nonetheless not warranted.[20] The court openly engaged the question of whether the nascent constitutional order could withstand the partisan dimensions of Roh's removal from office by the Assembly majority. The conclusion was that the ability to remove the president for partisan political activity would undermine effective constitutional rule, even if the acts in question were properly subject to legislative condemnation.[21]

ELECTORAL COMPETITION

Perhaps no impulse is as universal in weak democracies as the efforts of initial political winners to alter the rules of electoral accountability. Jon Elster, in his book *Securities against Misrule*, speaks of the "need to write an enforceable electoral law into the constitution" as being "only a special case of the idea that constitutions are needed to prevent those in power from using their power to keep their power."[22] Elster roots this principle at least as far back as Oliver Cromwell, who spoke of the need to check the propensity of Parliament to generously construe the boundaries of its own power: "That Parliaments should not make themselves perpetual is a Fundamental. Of what assurance is a Law to prevent so great an evil, if it lie in the same Legislature to unlaw it again?"[23] Although Cromwell, perhaps not surprisingly, thought that the checking function must lie with the Lord Protector – the office he held – this well encapsulates the task that has fallen to constitutional courts.

[19] Specifically, Roh violated the law in three ways. First, Roh publicly endorsed Uri Party members for an upcoming parliamentary election in violation of the Public Official Election Act. Second, Roh challenged the National Election Commission's ruling that he violated political neutrality and illegally requested a national referendum, which the court held constituted inadequate respect for the constitution and its bodies. Last, Roh was found by the court to have illegally called a referendum to determine national support and confidence in his abilities as president on the grounds that such a reading of the constitution could lead to an abuse of power.

[20] *See* Jiunn-Rong Yeh & Wen-Chen Chang, *The Emergence of East Asian Constitutionalism: Features in Comparison*, 59 AM. J. COMP. L. 805, 828–29 (2011).

[21] *See* 2004HunNa1(May 14, 2004), *available in English translation at* http://english.court.go.kr/.

[22] JON ELSTER, SECURITIES AGAINST MISRULE: JURIES, ASSEMBLIES, ELECTIONS 192 (Cambridge: Cambridge University Press, 2013) (emphasis omitted) (citation omitted).

[23] Oliver Cromwell, Speech to the Members of Parliament (Sept. 7, 1654), *in* 3 COBBETT'S PARLIAMENTARY HISTORY OF ENGLAND: FROM THE NORMAN CONQUEST, IN 1066 TO THE YEAR 1803, at 1445, 1454 (William Cobbett, ed., London: T. Curson Hansard, 1808), *available at* http://books.google.com/books?id=PJQ9AAAAcAAJ, *quoted in* Elster, *supra* note 22, at 191–92.

Yet, even before descending into the toxic extreme of the first rulers simply seizing power outright and rejecting any further electoral challenge, as
with President Nazarbayeth of Kazakhstan or the bizarre rule of "President
for Life" Saparmurat Niyazov of Turkmenistan, the electoral arena is still particularly susceptible to self-serving manipulations by the first incumbent powers. More than half of the post-Soviet republics give their constitutional court
a formal role in overseeing the political process administratively (a power
also held by the French Conseil Constitutionnel). Even where there is not
a specified form of administrative oversight, the judicial authority over electoral disputes and electoral eligibility resides with the constitutional courts
(as it does in Germany). Prominent cases come from all corners, Ukraine,[24]
Macedonia,[25] and Moldova,[26] for instance. Unifying these cases is the role of
apex constitutional courts assuming the role of superintending electoral procedures and rules.

In 2004, the distinct role of constitutional courts in maintaining the vibrant
competitiveness of new democracies was on display for the entire world to see.
In what came to be known as the Orange Revolution, mass protests resulted
from the efforts of incumbent forces supporting Prime Minister Viktor
Yanukovych to steal the presidential election through fraud and violence, at
least as was widely believed. The Ukrainian Supreme Court derailed efforts to
close off the electoral process in that country and impose Yanukovych as the
victorious candidate. The court declared the election fundamentally compromised by fraud, ordered a revote, and that in turn allowed for election of the
opposition candidate, Viktor Yushchenko. The judicial intervention restored
a period of democratic governance for Ukraine and marked the first effort to
thwart the country being pulled back into the Russian autocratic orbit. While
the Orange Revolution was the high point of the post-Soviet effort to stabilize

---

[24] *See, e.g.*, Rishennia KSU (Konstyutsijnogo Sudu Ukrainy) [Constitutional Court] Jan.
    26, 1998, Nos. 03/3600–97, 03/3808–97, 1–13/98 (Ukr.), *summarized in* European Comm'n
    for Democracy through Law, the Bulletin of Constitutional Case Law 146–48 (Ch.
    Giakoumopoulos et al. eds., 1998) (striking down a prohibition on former judges, public pros-
    ecutors, or state employees running for political office).

[25] *See FYROM Constitutional Jurisprudence, U.br.2/97 off 12.03.1997,* RIGAS NETWORK,
    http://www.cecl.gr/RigasNetwork/databank/Jurisprudence/FYROM/Jur_fyrom.htm (invalidat-
    ing a ban on members of the armed forces, police, and intelligence agencies running for and
    holding positions in local councils or mayoral office).

[26] In Moldova, the constitutional court approved the legitimacy of a bill that called for replac-
    ing the presidential election procedure then in effect with a return to direct elections. The
    court held that the bill did not exceed the revision limitations set forth in the Moldovan
    Constitution. *Moldovan Constitutional Court Rules on Return to Direct Presidential Elections,*
    INTERFAX: RUSSIA AND CIS GENERAL NEWSWIRE, May 4, 2010.

democracy, it was at best a momentary triumph. In 2010, Yanukovych was duly elected president of Ukraine over a now discredited opposition. In 2014, Yanukovych was driven from office by a second mass uprising, only to be followed by direct Russian military intervention in Crimea, the effective partitioning of the country, and the beginnings of civil war in eastern Ukraine.

While the Ukrainian court intervention was the most high profile in the post-Soviet era, it was neither the first such judicial engagement with democratic politics nor, possibly, the most far-reaching. The most aggressive of the early constitutional courts was found in Hungary, where the heavy presence of academics on the court and the ability of direct appeal by any citizen provided an unusually potent form of judicial engagement. *Actio popularis*, as is termed the ability of a citizen petition to reach the constitutional court, removes any institutional filter from cases that can reach an apex court. Whereas some courts restrict standing to minority parliamentary caucuses or to designated government officials, the Hungarian courts were open to any claim that could be framed in constitutional terms, regardless of the identity of the petitioner.

The combination of unrestricted standing and an aggressive view of the court's mandate made the Hungarian Constitutional Court a dominant early actor in defining Hungary's democracy. For example, the court invalidated one-third of all legislation passed from 1989 to 1995.[27] Among the early significant cases was one striking down a categorical prohibition that elected officials of "self governments of social security" (i.e., former Communists) could not be candidates for parliamentary seats.[28] In another series of cases, the court restrained successive popular majorities from amending the constitution to allow direct election of a president, rather than having a prime minister selected from within parliament – the opposite of the concern in Mongolia. Ultimately, in 1999, the court rejected a demand for a popular referendum on the question of direct election of the head of state, again an attempt to entrench electoral rules in favor of momentary majorities. Although the court ultimately could not withstand the parliamentary rise of Prime Minister Viktor Orbán and the right-wing Fidesz Party in 2010, the court's early efforts

---

[27] See Kim Lane Scheppele, *Democracy by Judiciary Or, Why Courts Can Be More Democratic than Parliaments, in* RETHINKING THE RULE OF LAW AFTER COMMUNISM 25, 44 (Adam Czarnota et al. eds., Budapest, Hungary: Central European University Press, 2005).

[28] Alkotmanybirosag (AB) [Constitutional Court] Mar. 25, 1994, MK.16/1994 (Hung.), translated in 1 EAST EUROPEAN CASE REPORTER OF CONSTITUTIONAL LAW 245–46 (Anton van de Plas and Adrie Labrie eds., Den Bosch: The Netherlands, 1994); *see also* BÉLA TOMKA, WELFARE IN EAST AND WEST HUNGARIAN SOCIAL SECURITY IN AN INTERNATIONAL COMPARISON, 1918–1990, at 92–95 (Berlin, Germany: Akademie Verlag, 2004).

forced Hungary's contested democracy within the parliamentary framework, not outside of it by mass-driven claims for alteration of the electoral rules.

Romania provides another example of how constitutional courts preserve and refine the electoral machine of an emergent democracy.[29] In late 2009, the Romanian Constitutional Court made a crucial decision in the race for the presidency between Romanian Social Democrat leader Mircea Geoana and incumbent Traian Basescu.[30] After President Basescu was determined to be the victor of the presidential race by a mere 70,000 votes, the Romanian Social Democrats filed a complaint with the constitutional court, charging that the vote was riddled with fraud. Specifically, the party alleged that there were multiple ballot castings, vote buying, and voided ballots, which made the election illegitimate. Romania's constitutional court then ordered an examination of the 138,000 or so disputed ballots. This is reminiscent of the role played by the U.S. Supreme Court in resolving the Florida presidential vote controversies in 2000. In a weak state such as Romania, however, there was no institutional alternative that could step into the breach if the constitutional court did not serve as ultimate arbiter of proper electoral practices. Ultimately the court rejected the request of the Romanian Social Democrats to annul the election results, and found that the incumbent Basescu was indeed the rightful winner of the election – an orderly resolution to a serious contest for office in a fledgling democracy.

AVENUES OF ELECTORAL CHALLENGE

The combination of proportional representation and government subsidies for all political parties represented in the national parliament is a persistent source of constitutional ferment. If the threshold for participation in the election is set too low, the government is forced to underwrite the participation of marginal parties with little claim on popular support. Oftentimes these marginal parties are sources of antidemocratic ferment from the left or the right and the public subsidy is incommensurate with their role in contributing to democratic politics. On the other hand, a high threshold of exclusion, as the term is used by political scientists, insulates the established parties from

---

[29] *See, e.g.,* WOJCIECH SADURSKI, RIGHTS BEFORE COURTS: A STUDY OF CONSTITUTIONAL COURTS IN POSTCOMMUNIST STATES OF CENTRAL AND EASTERN EUROPE 216 (Dordrecht, The Netherlands: Springer, 2nd ed., 2014) (analyzing the constitutional court's decision that upheld a time-limited exclusion of police officials from entering into candidacy in the first post-Communist election).

[30] *Romania: Romanian Leftists Seek Re-run of Presidential Vote,* ASIA NEWS MONITOR, Dec. 9, 2009.

political challenge. In nascent democracies, where embryonic parties are still sorting themselves out in the electoral arena, political parties may emerge from a regional basis of support, or even out of exile. A stiff barrier to access to the parliamentary arena rewards the more established parties, including those that may enjoy direct lineage from the prior autocratic regime. The trick is to find the sweet spot between fragmentation and strangulation.

Across the new democracies, there are persistent claims by minority parties that the rules of the game are being manipulated to forestall new challengers for power. The jurisprudence in Europe invariably harkens back to the German Constitutional Court in the 1950s confronting a minor party challenge to the proposed increase in the threshold percentage for parliamentary representation from 5 percent to 7 percent.[31] In that case, the German court noted that the function of the minimum threshold requirement was an assurance against an overly fractious governing body that would be ineffective and impotent in decision making. The court decided to focus on a two-prong analysis in which the 5 percent threshold would not be replaced unless exceptional circumstances merited a change and found that, in the case at hand, there was no valid reason to increase the threshold. Over the years, the German court has continued to preserve a functional balance, noting that low thresholds risk stymieing effective governance while thresholds that are too high become hindrances to real political choice. Most significantly, the court deviated from the 5 percent threshold after the reunification of Germany based on a finding that the threshold would not allow adequate representation in office for the weak political organizations emerging from East Germany.[32]

The Czech Constitutional Court similarly upheld minimum thresholds in the face of two distinct challenges.[33] The first was a constitutional challenge by a small party, the Democratic Union, which had received roughly half of the 5 percent threshold for getting itself into parliament.[34] In rejecting the demand for liberalized access to parliament, the Czech court relied on the same balance between representational access and effective governance struck by the German court. Invoking the experience of the Weimar Republic

---

[31] Donald P. Kommers & Russell A. Miller, The Constitutional Jurisprudence of the Federal Republic of Germany 254 (Durham, NC: Duke University Press, 3rd ed. 2012).

[32] *See id.* at 255–59 (discussing and translating in part *National Unity Election Case*, Bundesverfassungsgericht (BVerfG) (Federal Constitutional Court), 82 Entscheidungen des Bundesverfassungsgerichts [BVerfGE] 322 (1990)).

[33] *See* Sadurski, *supra* note 29, at 213–14.

[34] *See* Nález Ústavního soudu ze dne 02.04.1997 (ÚS) [Decision of the Constitutional Court of Apr. 2, 1996], sp. zn. Pl. ÚS 25/96, *translated in* 5 E. Eur. Case Rep. Const. L. 159, 162 (1998).

and the French Fourth Republic, the Czech court posited that unrestricted proportional representation would lead to democratic instability. For the moment at least, 5 percent was neither too high a barrier nor too low for effective governance. When subsequently, in 2001, the rival Social Democrats and the Civic Democrats together sought electoral changes raising the minimum thresholds for coalition representation, the court allowed the modification as not excessively restrictive.[35]

The same is also visible in Romania. Prior to its elections in 1992, the Romanian Parliament introduced a 3 percent minimum threshold requirement to its electoral law.[36] If a coalition were formed, one percentage point would be added for each party that was included in the coalition, with a maximum electoral threshold of 8 percent. The Romanian Constitutional Court upheld the thresholds after a constitutional challenge, explaining that "too many small parties in parliament would hamper the democratic process, and thus a threshold is reasonable and constitutional."[37] The threshold was later raised in 2000 such that individual parties faced a threshold minimum of 5 percent.[38] The result was the same in Turkey, which operates under an electoral threshold of 10 percent.[39] That was challenged in the European Court of Human Rights after the 2002 parliamentary elections by the excluded People's Democratic Party. The ECHR upheld the high threshold, although in part on procedural grounds.[40]

ADMINISTERING POLITICS

The Council of Europe has devoted considerable resources to the question of how to stabilize democracies in contested terrains. Its Venice Commission helps to train new democracies not only in broad commitments to democratic

---

[35] *See* Zdenka Mansfeldová, *The Czech Parliament on the Road to Professionalization and Stabilization*, in PARLIAMENTARY ELITES IN CENTRAL AND EASTERN EUROPE: RECRUITMENT AND REPRESENTATION 36 (E. Semenova, M. Edinger, & H. Best eds., New York: Routledge, 2014) (explaining that before coalitions of two parties needed 7 percent, of three 9 percent and of four or more 11 percent and the new amendment raised the standard such that an alliance of two needed 10 percent, of three 15 percent, and of four or more 20 percent).

[36] Janos Simon, *Electoral Systems and Democracy in Central Europe, 1990–1994*, 18 INT'L POL. SCI. REV. 361, 366 (1997).

[37] Sadurski, *supra* note 29, at 154.

[38] Cristina Bucur, *In Romania, Electoral Reform Is Taking a Backwards Step, to the Benefit of the Ruling Parties*, London School of Economics EUROPP Blog (May 30, 2012), http://blogs .lse.ac.uk/europpblog/2012/05/30/romania-elections/.

[39] Sinan Alkin, Note, *Underrepresentative Democracy: Why Turkey Should Abandon Europe's Highest Electoral Threshold*, 10 WASH. U. GLOBAL STUD. L. REV. 347, 347, 350–51 (2011).

[40] *Id.* at 365, 365 n.115.

liberties but in the nitty-gritty of how to run clean elections. In taking up the fundamental question of how to ensure integrity in the electoral arena, the Commission begins with a few core premises. Thus, the Code of Good Practice in Electoral Matters begins its section on the implementation of democratic elections by stressing the importance of the separation of election administration from political power:

> Only transparency, impartiality and independence from politically moti-
> vated will ensure proper administration of the election process, from the
> pre-election period to the end of the processing of results.... [I]n states with
> little experience of organising pluralist elections, there is too great a risk of
> government's pushing the administrative authorities to do what it wants....
> This is why independent, impartial electoral commissions must be set up
> from the national level to polling station level to ensure that elections are
> properly conducted, or at least remove serious suspicions of irregularity.[41]

Focusing on the independence of election administrators highlights the outlier status of the United States. Alone among the world's democracies, the United States allows partisan officials (such as secretaries of state or attorneys general) to be in charge of election administration. These election officials are beholden to the very electoral contenders they are supposed to oversee. Typically in the United States, top election officials are either elected on a partisan slate or directly appointed by incumbent elected officials. To give but one example, in the contested Florida presidential election of 2000, what ultimately was resolved by the U.S. Supreme Court as *Bush v. Gore*, the top state officials responsible for election administration were the secretary of state and the attorney general. Florida Secretary of State Katherine Harris was also the co-chair of the state election campaign for George Bush, while Attorney General Bob Butterworth was the chair of the election campaign of Al Gore.

Latin America provides an alternative that utilizes judicial independence to oversee elections while trying to insulate courts from charges of partisan capture. The Latin American approach is to use independent electoral tribunals who assume control of all aspects of electoral governance, including the adjudication of disputed election outcomes. These tribunals are a special branch of the judiciary whose jurisdiction is limited to electoral matters, but which are the supreme tribunal for matters within their competence. This approach began in Uruguay in 1924 and was soon thereafter adopted in Chile and Costa

---

[41] EUROPEAN COMMISSION FOR DEMOCRACY THROUGH LAW (VENICE COMMISSION), CODE OF GOOD PRACTICE IN ELECTORAL MATTERS: GUIDELINES AND EXPLANATORY REPORT 26–27 (2002).

Rica.[42] These tribunals control election procedure, administer the preliminary vote tally, supervise election registration, adjudicate any electoral disputes, and have sole power to certify election results. Despite the notorious military regimes of the 1970s and 1980s in Uruguay and Chile, these three countries (especially Costa Rica) have been the most stable democratic regimes in Latin America.

In the post-1989 period, the Uruguayan model has been broadly adopted, with Brazil being the most notable example in South America. In Mexico, the emergence of an independent electoral commission and the creation of the Mexican Supreme Electoral Tribunal in the 1990s were critical developments in moving the country from the one-party stranglehold under the Partido Revolucionario Institucional (PRI). The Electoral Tribunal now hears upward of 8,000 cases a year on matters ranging from local electoral practices to disputes over campaign expenditures under Mexico's system of public finance.

The importance of the Tribunal was underscored not so much in the routine administration of Mexico's increasingly vibrant democracy, but when the integrity of the electoral process was under challenge. In 2006, Mexico experienced a variant of *Bush v. Gore*, a closely contested election that strained the frailties of the election counting system. There, candidates Felipe Calderón and Andres Manual López Obrador were embroiled in the tightest race for the presidency seen in modern Mexican history, one that public opinion polls before the election and the initial estimates of the outcome deemed too close to call.

López Obrador claimed that he had won the election by 500,000 votes, but that proved ill grounded. The Federal Election Institute (IFE), the independent administrative agency, declared Calderón the winner. López Obrador filed suit before the Federal Election Tribunal claiming all sorts of electoral misconduct including outright ballot stuffing. Unlike the seemingly ad hoc procedures in the United States after the Florida voting in 2000, the Mexican election challenges were funneled into previously established procedures

[42] *See* Fabrice E. Lehoucq, *Can Parties Police Themselves? Electoral Governance and Democratization*, 23 INT'L POL. SCI. REV. 29, 36 (2002) ("In 1924, Uruguayan parties formed an electoral court as an agent of the bicameral legislature. The Congress entrusted the court with the task of reviewing all election results before the Senate, and the Chamber of Deputies, in line with the constitution, certified final election results. Eight years later, a new constitution made the electoral court completely responsible for electoral governance."). On the relation of election administration to Uruguayan political history, see LUIS E. GONZALEZ, POLITICAL STRUCTURES AND DEMOCRACY IN URUGUAY (Notre Dame, IN: Helen Kellogg Institute for International Studies, 1991).

before a court dedicated to electoral disputes. The Tribunal ordered a recount in 10 percent of all the votes cast in order to sample for irregularities, a far different process than the selective recounts done in Florida in 2000 by partisans looking for pockets of likely additional votes. Based on that sampling, the Tribunal concluded that there was no evidence of fraud. On inspection of the ballots themselves, the Tribunal ordered that nearly 160,000 votes be voided, which did not alter the outcome of the election.

For the young Mexican democracy, this was a decisive moment. López Obrador claimed fraud in all the Mexican institutions and called on his supporters to take to the streets. Yet despite some initial protests in Mexico City, the Tribunal's decision was the final word. The independence of the electoral institutions from the government gave legitimacy to the certification of Calderón as the victor. As if to drive home the point, when López Obrador lost in the 2012 presidential election, he turned once again to the Electoral Tribunal for relief – and lost again.

GOVERNMENTAL BENEFITS

Countries emerging from authoritarian rule typically inherit a swollen public sector. Not only does the government control a disproportionate share of employment, but its economic weight is felt across the full range of seemingly private economic activity. Much of this book is devoted to the uneven and often arrested development of the political and governmental institutions necessary for the stabilization of a democracy. The same could be written of the economic domain as well. Private markets emerge slowly and access to capital or important commercial transactions often relies on some relation to state authority. Political competition may be the lifeblood of democracy, but economic competition is no less indispensable in the efforts to dampen the chokehold of the authoritarian state. Just as incumbent authorities can use the trappings of office to thwart subsequent political challenges, so too can they use the secondary powers of office to reward loyalists and to punish opponents. Any party in office that can credibly make clear that political challenge will be met with exclusion from governmental employment or any state-related contracts dramatically enhances its power.

The same process of purging the state of its authoritarian past can bleed over into giving the first democratic governments control over economic opportunity as a means to leverage their initial political advantage. These governments legitimately engage in some lustration of the state apparatus from its autocratic forebears. Yet, as we saw with the judiciary in postwar Germany, there is a tension between removing holdover political forces from the authoritarian era and retaining the knowledge and expertise of officials who have experience running an administrative state. Still, the picture is complication, even allowing for the legitimate desire to curb the influence and possible power consolidation of the former authoritarian politicians. Efforts to preserve a democratic state through lustration laws also introduce the capacity for far less noble ends. One may be the desire for revenge, while another may be an opportunity to reward political supporters.[43]

In Bulgaria, the first post-Soviet government enacted the Law on Banks and Credit and the Pension Law, which prohibited individuals who were high-ranking officials in the Communist Party from holding managerial positions in commercial banks. The direct relation between a role in the ruling Communist Party and a subsequent role in commercial banks was tenuous, and did not seem to correspond to the wrongful conduct of the ruling Soviet-backed leaders. The disconnect between the prior improprieties and the forbidden later activity led the constitutional court to strike down the prohibition as excessively punitive. A more extreme example comes from Albania, where a lustration law adopted in 2009 prevented any individuals who worked in the former secret police, the prosecutors' office, or the judiciary during the Communist period from holding any government employment at all. The Albanian Constitutional Court struck down the law as not supported by a compelling governmental purpose:

> As long as the purpose of the lustration law is to remove from their duties individuals with an undemocratic behaviour, the period over which this measure is applied must be finite, as activities carried out in the past cannot be considered final evidence of the current or future behaviour of an individual.[44]

Moreover, the court believed the law to limit the right to run for and hold office, which Article 17 of the Albanian Constitution guarantees. Limiting the basic democratic right of individuals to run for office against the incumbent authorities required satisfying a heightened burden of justification that the court sought to protect. Absent a greater level of individual-specific proof, a concept sounding in due process was invoked for the protection of the affected individuals, meaning that no such broad-sweeping lustration could hold.

---

[43] *See* Mark S. Ellis, *Purging the Past: The Current State of Lustration Laws in the Former Communist Bloc*, L. & CONTEMP. PROBS., Autumn 1996, at 181, 190–92.

[44] Jonilda Koci, *Albanian Lustration Law Criticised*, TURKISH WEEKLY (Feb. 5, 2009), http://www.turkishweekly.net/news/64198/albanian-lustration-law-criticised.html.

Poland provides a further example of the tenuous line between protection of democratic values and the silencing of opposition. An initial law in 1997 required public officials in sensitive offices to submit a statement declaring whether they had supported or worked with the Communist regime, and even created a special administrative court to handle claims of fraud in the submitted statements.[45] The law survived initial constitutional challenge based in part on the review offered through the administrative processes and under the Polish criminal procedure code. That decision was overturned by the European Court of Human Rights, which found the procedural protections insufficient under Article 6 of the European Convention on Human Rights.

Even while the challenge to the first Polish law was pending, the nastier side of lustration took hold. Under the increasingly authoritarian regime of the late President Lech Kaczynski and his identical twin brother, Prime Minister Jaroslaw Kaczynski, the Polish government adopted in late 2006 a new lustration law that broadened the sweep of targeted individuals through an ever widening definition of "persons 'performing a public function.'" The law would have imposed a ten-year ban on office holding for any individual who failed to submit a declaration explaining how his or her name came to be on any government "lists" from the Communist regime. Given the pressures and pervasiveness of totalitarianism, innumerable individuals would be compromised by such a loose definition of collaboration. Indeed, during the 2000 election, both famous Solidarity leader Lech Walesa and the winning candidate, Aleksandr Kwasniewski, were charged with having been collaborators because their names appeared on lists of persons who had spoken to Communist security officers – an almost inescapable fate for anyone of any public stature under the prior regime.[46] More bizarre was the fact that names might appear on the lists for having had conversations with undercover government agents, meaning that individuals often had no awareness of the circumstances that might land them on a list of police "contacts."

Coming in the wake of the ECHR's decision on the earlier lustration law, the new law sparked a good deal of criticism about the potential for witch hunting. This charge came from both EU officials and the foreign press, as well as the more direct accusation that the new lustration law was nothing more than a "generational bid for power," an effort by the Kaczynski brothers to see

---

[45] *International Legal Developments in Review: 2007–Regional and Comparative Law*, 42 INT'L L. 975, 1003–05 (2008).

[46] *See* Joanna Rohozińska, *Struggling with the Past*, CENT. EUR. REV. (Sept. 11, 2000), http://www.ce-review.org/00/30/rohozinska30.html.

their opponents "purged from offices and replaced by their own loyalists."[47] Opponents further claimed that the lustration law was part of a concerted effort by the Kaczynskis to root out any vestiges of contrary political authority in the country's democratic institutions.

Acting with the backing of the ECHR, the Polish Constitutional Court struck back. First, it limited the permissible scope of lustration laws: "[m]easures to dismantle the heritage of the former communist totalitarian systems may remain in agreement with the ideas of a democratic state ruled by law, provided that the measures, while conforming to the principles of a democratic state ruled by law, will be directed against situations threatening the fundamental human rights or the process of democratization."[48] To survive constitutional scrutiny, the court held, lustration laws should protect democracy from a return to authoritarian reign, not stymie political competition. Second, and even more suspect, was the lustration law's retroactive effect in removing elected public officials from office. There, the court stressed that such an influence on these rights would make "illusory" the right to vote and the right to run for office and would act as a dismantling of the "principle of the sovereignty of the Polish People."

The court's response was to caution the government that lustration was not an opportunity to settle political scores, but to serve the broader ends of justice. The court took pains to limit the reach of the law to those who were proven to have cooperated specifically with the state security agency (as opposed to other civil agencies that were not part of the security apparatus). More significant perhaps, the court limited the ability of the law to reach political opponents of the Kaczynski government – most notably, journalists were completely exempted from the requirement to submit a declaration. As a matter of compassion for life under authoritarian rule, the court further exempted those who acted "under compulsion in fear of loss of their life or health [or that of] closest persons."

Of greater significance here are the steps taken to protect against lustration being the opportunity for Poland to revert to one-party governance. The court held that officeholders who had been "elected in universal elections" prior to the entry in force of the new law were not obligated to submit declarations, deeming the application of the declaration requirement to incumbent

---

[47] *See* Wiktor Osiatynski, Op-Ed., *Poland Makes Witch-Hunting Easier*, N.Y. TIMES, Jan. 22, 2007, at A19.

[48] Trybunał Konstytucyjny [Constitutional Court of Poland], No. K. 2/07 of May 11, 2007, *translated in Judgment of 11th May 2007, file Ref. No. K 2/07*, at 6, TRYBUNAŁ KONSTYTUCYJNY, http://www.trybunal.gov.pl/eng/summaries/documents/K_2_07_GB.pdf.

officeholders a "legal trap" that is "inadmissible in light of the principle of protection of trust in the State and its laws." Like the Albanian court intervention discussed earlier, the court recognized the connection between due process rights for individual government officials and the rights of the individuals those officials serve and represent – giving the law retroactive effect, it held, "influences both the right to vote and the right to stand as a candidate in elections, hence the rights that are constitutionally guaranteed." If those who had been elected prior to enactment of the law could be forced out for failure to file a declaration or for making a false declaration, it would make "the principle of the sovereignty of the Polish people ... illusory." Despite internal divisions yielding nine dissenting opinions, the court went on to demand "'repair' activities on the part of the legislator" lest any further legislation be struck down as well. At the same time, the court took pains to indicate that lustration principles remained valid so long as there remained a threat of former Communist officials reestablishing their authority.

In the words of Poland's most significant democratic intellectual, Adam Michnik, "The Constitutional Court stood up to its responsibilities and, after repeated government efforts to postpone the court's session and to impeach its judges, it reviewed the new law and found it unconstitutional."[49]

The group culpability sweep of the lustration laws and their criminal-like quality stands as an invitation to broad removals of disfavored opponents from the political process entirely. The lack of individual findings and procedural protections for banned individuals has been a significant issue in the implementation of the lustration laws generally. But settling scores can yield even greater threats to democratic legitimacy.

In some cases, such as Moldova and particularly the Baltics, lustration quickly implicated critical ethnic divides between the local population and Russian speakers or ethnic Russians. In the Baltics, the latter group was a generations-long presence as part of the Soviet effort to establish control of the region, which included forcing Russian upon the occupied lands as the official language and filling the ranks of the security state with ethnic Russians. But over the course of Soviet control of the Baltics, the occupation became not only a matter of troops in barracks, but of a civilian population that knew no other home. In Estonia, for example, the ethnic Russians came to represent one-third of the entire civilian population by the end of the Soviet period.

---

[49] Adam Michnik, *The Polish Witch-Hunt*, N.Y. REV. BOOKS (June 28, 2007), http://nybooks.com/articles/archives/2007/jun/28/the-polish-witch-hunt (noting how the government attempted to strip Bronislaw Geremek of his parliamentary seat after he "refused to sign a declaration that he had been a secret police agent during the Communist years").

Efforts in the Baltic republics to eliminate Russian from public life – understandable after the removal of Soviet rule – nonetheless required judicial resistance lest they remove a large part of the population from participation in the new democratic order, including the ability to secure governmental employment or even stand for office.

Moldova presents a clear example of the use of official power over language to cement early incumbent party domination. Moldova is an unstable collection of four different peoples, tucked uncomfortably between Romania and Ukraine. The eastern part of the country is predominantly Russian speaking and did better under the long winter of Soviet rule. In the immediate jockeying for political power after 1989, the remnants of the Communist Party managed to reconstitute themselves as the first organized political force, with heavy support in the Russian ethnic parts of the county. In turn, the Communist-controlled government made plans to make Russian mandatory in all Moldovan school systems, aggravating and intensifying ethnic divisions that were already present in the country. The move had the predictable effect of provoking opposition protests, including large rallies by the opposition Christian Democratic People's Party (CDPP) in the capital Chişinău and mass marches into the central square of the city. The government, through the Moldovan Justice Ministry, then suspended all CDPP activity for one month after the party had "ignored multiple warnings" about their "unsanctioned rallies." Although the ban was ultimately rescinded under protest from the Council of Europe, the effect was to disable the only viable political opposition. The Moldovan government, dominated by the Communist Party, attempted to spring an accelerated election schedule to exploit the oppositional party's disorganization because of the ban that had been in place. The CDPP then filed a complaint with the constitutional court, which in turn declared the government's action unconstitutional. Here, the court asserted its independence and prevented the then-ruling parties from unduly trammeling on the rights of the oppositional party. The U.S. Department of State cited the decision as one example of "the Constitutional Court show[ing] strong signs of independence during the year," "balancing out several controversial initiatives of the Communist authorities."[50]

JUDICIAL ENGAGEMENT

To return to the opening themes, the ability of the South African Constitutional Court to insert itself forcefully into the heart of reconstituted political power

---

[50] See *Country Reports on Human Rights Practices – Moldova*, U.S. DEP'T OF STATE, http://www.state.gov/g/drl/rls/hrrpt/2002/18381.htm (last visited Oct. 28, 2010).

cannot be seen merely as a product of South African exceptionalism. Nor is the willingness of political forces to abide simply a tribute to the democratic vision of Nelson Mandela, much as that cannot be gainsaid. Rather in country after country of the new democracies, courts assume the role of checking majoritarian concentration of power. Generally, the issue is presented as a matter of protecting parliamentary authority vis-à-vis the executive, the first branch typically to consolidate power in the transition, although – as with South Korea and Mongolia – this is not always so. A review of the constitutional courts of Eastern Europe in particular reveals how large a portion of the docket concerns cases that involve the superintendence of the democratic process. As in South Africa, the bulk of these cases concern excessive prerogatives for incumbent political power that limit the ability of an opposition to mobilize and compete for political power. Rather than fighting the old authoritarianism of the autocratic past, these courts frequently engage the excessive consolidation of power in the hands of the first post-transition rulers. The threat is not an immediate recreation of the autocratic past, but a new species of one-partyism: the excessive consolidation of unaccountable power in the related realms of the political, the social, and the economic.

The forceful introduction of constitutional courts exercising supervisory power over the political process is the defining institutional innovation of the Third Wave of democratization. The persistence of the political questions before these courts is striking, even when the courts try to adjudicate the cases in the more familiar posture of individual rights claims. Viewed across the spectrum of the distinct national settings in which they arise, the pattern is nonetheless clear. Politics provides a central arena for the development of a constitutional jurisprudence in these nascent democracies, measured not only in terms of the number of cases but of the significance of the issues confronted.

Constitutional court power leaves open many questions about just how sustainable repeated judicial confrontations with incumbent power might be. Already, examples such as the Mongolian Parliament wearing down the constitutional court or the troubled history of Ukraine indicate that court ascendancy may not provide a stable end-state. Nor does the fact that courts assumed the role of arbiters of political authority explain why this occurred. The remaining chapters address these issues before attempting to draw a balance sheet of the experience of the first quarter century of strong-court constitutional rule.

10

The Constitutional Bargain

Constitutionalism in divided societies poses a core paradox. Why would rival social groups enter into any apparently constraining constitutional bargain with imprecise terms, and why would they expect the objectives of the bargain to be honored? Societies suddenly thrust into the proto-democratic arena (like the former Soviet republics) typically lack the civil society institutions that buttress democratic rule, the political parties that can organize democratic participation, and even the basic cadre of candidates groomed in the public demeanor of democratic politics.[1]

The immediate issue is why immature political movements in emerging democracies would look to resolve these basic constitutive problems of democracy through the creation of independent courts. This question is distinct from the more common one of what explains the long-term stability of relatively independent courts in successful democracies.[2] Where stability can be safely assumed, sophisticated political actors operate with an understanding that who will rule at any point in the future is uncertain and they should accordingly seek to limit the ability of one or the other to exploit momentary political favor.[3] As a result, "[e]nforcement of the constitution ... might be

---

[1] This point is made in the political science literature dealing with emerging democracies. *See,* *e.g.,* Lucan A. Way, *Authoritarian State Building and the Sources of Regime Competitiveness in the Fourth Wave: The Cases of Belarus, Moldova, Russia, and Ukraine,* 57 WORLD POL. 231, 232 (2005).

[2] For an example of this type of inquiry, see William M. Landes & Richard A. Posner, *The Independent Judiciary in an Interest-Group Perspective,* 18 J. L. & ECON. 875 (1975).

[3] For a simple example, during the negotiations leading up to Hungary's transition to democracy in 1989, the Communists sought a strong constitutional court that would strike down anti-Communist legislation. JOHN W. SCHIEMANN, THE POLITICS OF PACT MAKING: HUNGARY'S NEGOTIATED TRANSITION TO DEMOCRACY IN COMPARATIVE PERSPECTIVE 162 (New York: Palgrave Macmillan, 2005). The foundational article using this approach is Landes & Posner, *supra* note 2. For a counter argument focusing on the specific

understood as an equilibrium resulting from the tacit agreement of two or more social groups to rebel against a government that transgresses the rights of either group."[4] The key is that the parties believe they are participating in what may be termed a repeat game and that being ahead or behind at any point does not mean that the roles will not be reversed in the future.

Newly created democracies lack the basic confidence in the long-term stabilizing role of courts: untested democracies cannot vouchsafe that there will be rotation in office and that all political factions will ultimately benefit from some kind of arbitrated guarantee of a fair process. The first time in any exchange appears as the only engagement and the rules of repeat play only come into effect when there is a shared sense of the long term. At the moment of state creation, the only power that is likely to matter is control of the executive and, by extension, of the military. The struggle, therefore, is to be the first to hold office. Separation of powers and other institutional limitations are at best untested at the threshold stage of state formation, and the idea of judicial restraints on the exercise of power is an even more remote theoretical construct.

Yet all the transitional negotiations in the Third Wave of democratization have turned time and again to the creation of a constitutional court, most often with conspicuous specification as to the composition of that court. These emergent democracies appear to look to constitutional courts to serve as an "institutional barrier to majoritarian abuse."[5] From a theoretical perspective, there are two possible answers to the paradox of negotiating parties at the foundational moment of a new democracy creating an independent judicial authority and then believing that it will in fact continue to be independent and protect the democratic bargain. Neither construct can explain all the nuances of the state-by-state democratic experiences of the past twenty-five years, yet they provide some insight as to why the creation of a strong judicial power may help fill the void in legitimate power after the fall of autocracy.

The first construct is that the presence of an external authority might facilitate the ability of the contending parties for state power to realize an initial agreement that permits a government to be formed. On this view, the ability to turn to an arbiter to resolve complications in implementing the initial accord

---

case of Japan and the effect of one party having a long-term hold on political office, see J. Mark Ramseyer, *The Puzzling (In)dependence of Courts: A Comparative Approach*, 23 J. LEGAL STUD. 721, 722, 727–28 (1994).

4   Jack Goldsmith & Daryl Levinson, *Law for States: International Law, Constitutional Law, Public Law*, 122 HARV. L. REV. 1791, 1835 (2009).

5   Sarah Wright Sheive, *Central and Eastern European Constitutional Courts and the Antimajoritarian Objection to Judicial Review*, 26 L. & POL'Y INT'L BUS. 1201, 1221 (1995).

relieves the negotiating parties of the burden of hammering out all the details of how the new government will operate. To return to the South African example, it was easier for the difficult negotiations at Kempton Park to reach agreement on a limited set of 34 Principles than on an entire constitutional architecture. The key insight is that parties to any contract are better able to reach accord if they can reduce the difficulty of negotiating all details to completion. The presence of an external arbiter promotes efficiency in the bargaining process by allowing the parties more efficiently to reach a solution.

But that is only the first step. A second construct looks not to the question of whether a bargain can be reached, but whether the terms might be more just or enduring. The insight is that the presence of a future constitutional arbiter may improve the quality of the solution reached. For this purpose, the existence of a court to rule on imprecise issues concerning the bounds of state authority may promote a fairer initial bargain, and may lessen the advantage obtained by the first officeholders. Here the focus is not on the ability to realize *a* bargain, but on the actual terms contained in *the* bargain that is achieved. In the game theory literature, the ability to turn to an alternative trading partner or an alternative arbiter during the process of negotiation is known as bargaining with an outside option.[6] The term is used here slightly more expansively than in the technical economics literature and serves to denote an alternative process that might constrain the downside risk for the party that loses out on the initial selection for governmental power.

In examining the reasons that constitutional courts may facilitate the transition to democracy, the terms of inquiry look to both the likelihood of adverse parties realizing a constitutional pact, and to the equities of the terms of that accord. Accordingly, the question under examination is whether the presence of an outside option in the form of a constitutional court can be expected to promote efficiency in bargaining and fairness in the results.

THE CONTRACTUAL MODEL

The wave of newly constituted democracies allows reflection on the dynamics of creating a constitutional pact.[7] If we generalize across the many national

---

[6]   The classic paper on this is Avner Shaked & John Sutton, *Involuntary Unemployment as a Perfect Equilibrium in a Bargaining Model*, 52 ECONOMETRICA 1351, 1363 (1984); *see also* Ken Binmore, Avner Shaked, & John Sutton, *An Outside Option Experiment*, 104 Q. J. ECON., 753, 757 (1989) (testing the impact of an outside option on bargaining outcomes in a laboratory setting).

[7]   *See* MILADA ANNA VACHUDOVA, EUROPE UNDIVIDED: DEMOCRACY, LEVERAGE AND INTEGRATION AFTER COMMUNISM 11–13 (New York: Oxford University Press, 2005) (studying the reform trajectories of six post-Communist Eastern European states).

settings in which new democracies have emerged, certain common features stand out, even if the fit may be imperfect to any particular national events. First, the new democracies tend to emerge in countries bearing the deep fractures of prior, often violent divisions. These can take the familiar form of racial, ethnic, or religious strife, ranging from postapartheid South Africa and the explosive divisions in Iraq to the smoldering hatreds in Moldova and the Balkans. But these divisions emerge even in the seemingly more homogeneous populations of the Baltics, with their generations-old Russian population, which must now be integrated into a post-occupation role in a functioning democracy.[8]

Second, the process of constitutional negotiation is unlikely to yield a completely realized set of agreements. The romantic view of constitutional design assumes a Rawlsian baseline of dispassionate founders, deeply immersed in the political theory of the day, aspiring to the wisdom of the ages from a veil of ignorance as to how they would immediately benefit. But constitution making, the act of actually getting a political accord that will provide the foundations of a democratic state, is more likely a rhapsodic event. The moments of upheaval and uncertainty that put the foundations of a society at issue are precisely those that are least likely to sustain reasoned examination of political principles. The precommitment process of constraining future actors to an elaborated political design – termed Peter sober binding Peter drunk[9] – may get one critical detail wrong. Reviewing the political tensions and accompanying forms of social release that are at play in actual constitutional negotiations, Jon Elster provocatively claimed the precommitment to be Peter drunk binding Peter sober.[10] It may be that the passionate euphoria of the founding moment ill serves the more prosaic undertaking of later governance.

---

[8] This concern was already recognized in academic literature in the early 1990s, during the first experiments with democracy in the newly liberated Baltic states. *See, e.g.*, Eric Rudenshiold, *Ethnic Dimensions in Contemporary Latvian Politics: Focusing Forces for Change*, 44 SOVIET STUD. 609 (1992) (recognizing the challenge posed to the nascent Latvian democracy from ethnic conflicts within the mixed Russian and Latvian electorate).

[9] STEPHEN HOLMES, PASSIONS AND CONSTRAINT: ON THE THEORY OF LIBERAL DEMOCRACY 135 (Chicago, IL: University of Chicago Press, 1995); *see also* JED RUBENFELD, FREEDOM AND TIME: A THEORY OF CONSTITUTIONAL SELF-GOVERNMENT 176–77 (New Haven, CT: Yale University Press, 2001) (focusing on intertemporal cooling off as central to constitutional order).

[10] *See* Jon Elster, *Don't Burn Your Bridge Before You Come to It: Some Ambiguities and Complexities of Precommitment*, 81 TEX. L. REV. 1751, 1768 & n. 51 (2003); *see also* Jon Elster, Ulysses Unbound 159 (2000) (reciting historic examples of constitutions drafted against backdrops of social disruptions).

Even Elster's less ennobling account fails to give full force to the modern constitutional settings. In less divided societies, it is possible to ratify a constitution through relatively unrepresentative proceedings, or even by fiat, as with the American imposition of a new constitutional order on militarily defeated Japan.[11] But a constitution is fundamentally a social compact, one that has long been recognized as a political resolution of the competing claims for power in the particular society. As captured millennia ago by Aristotle:

> [P]olitics has to consider which sort of constitution suits which sort of civic body. The attainment of the best constitution is likely to be impossible for the general run of states; and the good law-giver and the true statesman must therefore have their eyes open not only to what is the absolute best, but also to what is the best in relation to actual conditions.[12]

The fractured settings for the newly emergent democracies require a process of negotiation that can create an enduring form of governance, but must do so through accommodation reached by parties or groups frequently bearing long-standing historic grievances against each other. This generally means two things. First, the process will take time, what Ruti Teitel terms the "fits and starts" of constitutional negotiation.[13] As a result, any rush to "premature constitutionalization" threatens the ability to form a political consensus over what can be agreed to, and just as centrally, what the parties are not able to agree to.[14] The two-stage process of constitutional negotiation in South Africa provides a helpful model, in which a preliminary constitution predicated on broad and relatively noncontentious principles of governance serves as an intermediate step in the process of constitutionalization. And, second – again as in South Africa – the resulting agreement is likely to leave critical issues unresolved.[15] Vicki Jackson

---

[11] *See generally* KOSEKI SHŌICHI, THE BIRTH OF JAPAN'S POSTWAR CONSTITUTION (Ray A. Moore trans., Boulder, CO: Westview Press, 1997) (1989).

[12] ARISTOTLE, THE POLITICS OF ARISTOTLE 181 (Ernest Barker trans., Oxford: Oxford University Press, 1948).

[13] RUTI G. TEITEL, TRANSITIONAL JUSTICE 196 (New York: Oxford University Press, 2000).

[14] Noah Feldman, Commentary, *Imposed Constitutionalism*, 37 CONN. L. REV. 857, 870–72 (2005) (chronicling the risks associated with imposed constitutional provisions in the context of multilateral negotiations in Iraq and Afghanistan). For a related argument on the necessity of a flexible amendment process for new constitutions, see Stephen Holmes & Cass R. Sunstein, *The Politics of Constitutional Revision in Eastern Europe, in* RESPONDING TO IMPERFECTION: THE THEORY AND PRACTICE OF CONSTITUTIONAL AMENDMENT 275 (Sanford Levinson ed., Princeton, NJ: Princeton University Press, 1995).

[15] An older example is the inability of the Israeli founding generation to agree on formal terms on such questions as the extent of religious influence in the new state. *See* GARY J. JACOBSOHN, APPLE OF GOLD: CONSTITUTIONALISM IN ISRAEL AND THE UNITED STATES 102–03 (Princeton, NJ: Princeton University Press, 1993).

refers to the resulting process as yielding either incremental constitutionalism or even an interim constitution.[16] In either case, the immediate task of the constitutional process is to signal a clear break from the prior regime, even if the precise terms of the new constitutional order are left to another day, or another actor. Most significantly, leaving some matters unresolved avoids forcing the parties "into a negotiation 'for all the marbles' in a zero-sum environment."[17]

Unfortunately, the incompleteness of the constitutional commitment can have fatal consequences for nascent democracies. Some 40 percent of proto-democracies in post-conflict countries revert to violence within a decade,[18] suggesting the fragility of these accords. The ability to create a paper constitutional accord lends a democratic air to an unresolved battle for a cruder form of domination. In such circumstances it is hard to avoid the conclusion of Paul Collier that the press for elections to consolidate democratic rule actually exacerbates the risk of violence, as competing factions see the chance of prevailing in an election as an opportunity to continue the civil war more effectively with the authority of state power. To give but one example, the early election in Burundi in 2005 witnessed an initial hiatus in political violence. The rival tribal-backed groups put their efforts into gaining formal office through the electoral arena, especially in the presence of international observers and peacekeepers. But after the initial electoral victory by the Hutu forces there was a return to political repression almost immediately, including the expulsion of UN forces who had been safeguarding the election process.

Here we may suggest that when viewed as a complex, cross-temporal compact, the incompleteness of constitutional accords and the need for institutions to fill the gaps in the underlying accords is not surprising. Indeed, this conception of constitutionalism shares much in common with conventional accounts of gap filling in private contracts, and with the use of courts as independent institutions tasked with honoring the generalized but incomplete intentions of the parties. Further, the typical incompletely realized constitutional compact will require separation of powers among different institutions of government in order to limit the reach of the first group to hold office. As political scientist Martin Shapiro notes, "[w]henever a constitution divides powers, it almost always necessitates a constitutional court to police the boundaries."[19]

---

[16] Vicki C. Jackson, *What's in a Name?: Reflections on Timing, Naming, and Constitution-Making*, 49 WM. & MARY L. REV. 1249, 1265–68 (2008).

[17] Feisal Amin Rasoul al-Istrabadi, *A Constitution without Constitutionalism: Reflections on Iraq's Failed Constitutional Process*, 87 TEX. L. REV. 1627, 1629 (2009).

[18] PAUL COLLIER, WARS, GUNS, AND VOTES 75 (New York: HarperCollins, 2009).

[19] Martin Shapiro, *The Globalization of Law*, 1 IND. J. GLOBAL LEGAL STUD. 37, 49 (1993).

Although Shapiro aptly captures the function of constitutional courts after a regime of divided powers is in place, his formulation fails to address the role that may be played by the prospect of constitutional courts serving as a condition precedent to the birth of democratic rule. It is not simply that the founding pact is likely to be incomplete; there is no guarantee that the first democratic choices will follow anything other than the former lines of division. In other words, the imprecise boundaries of democratic power will place state authority in the hands of one of the previously contending factions for political power. The presence of an independent court places an obstacle in the way of immediate, complete consolidation of power by the first electoral victors. The question then is whether courts serve as not merely a temporary distraction but as a significant obstacle, although hopefully not the only one, to the consolidation of unaccountable political power in the hands of the first officeholder.

Constitutions may well be the political equivalent of incompletely realized agreements, but that alone provides little direct guidance for courts charged with filling out the terms. Courts are unlikely to find fully satisfactory guidance within the four corners of the text or through the more common forms of contract interpretation. At the time of constitutional negotiations, particularly in societies quickly emerging from authoritarian rule, the participants in the constitutional bargain are unlikely to have long-standing relations of trust among themselves, nor much experience with what may be the difficult issues of implementation in the new constitutional order.[20] The result is likely to be a document that is in large part aspirational and that uses terms of broad ambition but little specificity (for example, "due process of law," "equal protection," or "privileges and immunities"). These terms serve as placeholders for a proper democratic order, even if the founding agreement could not concretize many of these features.

Textual ambiguity places a distinct institutional pressure on constitutional courts in new democracies. The need to fill in the meaning for underspecified constitutional commands forces implementing courts to act as common law rather than civil law institutions, ones attendant to the incremental realization of core constitutional objectives through the accretion of decisional law. For jurists largely trained in the civil law tradition of close-quartered exposition of textual commands, the transition is challenging. The divide between

---

[20] The problem of information asymmetries and the strategic withholding of information in constitutional negotiations is identified in ZACHARY ELKINS, TOM GINSBURG, & JAMES MELTON, THE ENDURANCE OF NATIONAL CONSTITUTIONS 69–71 (New York: Cambridge University Press, 2009).

the common law demands of constitutional adjudication and the civil law tradition for nonconstitutional cases reproduces the divide in the European Union. There, too, a largely common law set of practices has emerged in the European Court of Justice and the European Court of Human Rights, which in turn have to be translated into national law by national courts rooted in the civil law tradition.[21]

Viewed in this light, there is an inevitable tension in the role to be assumed by constitutional courts. Because the ultimate authority of these courts comes from the fact of a constitutional accord, courts will likely succeed in helping forge a constitutional order to the extent that they appear to honor the intentions of the parties. As a working assumption, the intention to be bound by the agreement is best revealed by the definiteness of the terms of the pact, in constitutions as in ordinary contracts.[22] But contract law teaches that for a variety of reasons, including imperfect knowledge of future conditions and strategic withholding of private information, parties to a contract frequently fail to specify all of the relevant terms, leaving the contract incomplete.[23] Modern contract law has generally abandoned formalist rules that would previously have rendered contracts unenforceable when significant gaps in material terms existed. Modern contract law, across many jurisdictions, has moved in the direction of favoring more liberal rules of interpretation that permit courts to serve a gap-filling role.[24] In the American context, for instance, the Uniform Commercial Code expressly accepts as enforceable a "contract with open terms" that allows gaps in the realized accord to be filled with reasonable or average terms.[25] Similarly, the *Restatement (Second) of Contracts* also favors

[21] For an examination of the encounter between the common law of EU courts and the civil law practiced in member nations, see Vivian Grosswald Curran, *Romantic Common Law, Enlightened Civil Law: Legal Uniformity and Homogenization of the European Union*, 7 COLUM. J. EUR. L. 63, 72–75 (2001).

[22] *See, e.g.*, RESTATEMENT (SECOND) OF CONTRACTS § 33(3) (1981) ("The fact that one or more terms of a proposed bargain are left open or uncertain may show that a manifestation of intention is not intended to be understood as an offer or as an acceptance.").

[23] *See, e.g.*, Randy E. Barnett, *The Sound of Silence: Default Rules and Contractual Consent*, 78 VA. L. REV. 821, 821–22 (1992).

[24] *See, e.g.*, Omri Ben-Shahar, *"Agreeing to Disagree": Filling Gaps in Deliberately Incomplete Contracts*, 2004 WIS. L. REV. 389, 389 (2004). Although there has been a general shift toward a lax application of the indefiniteness doctrine, the common law rule has not completely fallen by the wayside. *See* Robert E. Scott, *A Theory of Self-Enforcing Indefinite Agreements*, 103 COLUM. L. REV. 1641, 1643–44 (2003).

[25] U.C.C. § 2–204(3) (2002) ("Even if one or more terms are left open, a contract for sale does not fail for indefiniteness if the parties have intended to make a contract and there is a reasonably certain basis for giving an appropriate remedy.").

liberal application of incomplete contracts when it is clear that the parties intended to be bound by the agreement.[26]

There are at least two arguments for gap filling, sounding primarily in efficiency,[27] each of which has some implication for the role of courts addressing constitutional compacts. The first theory is based on the idea that it is inefficient for parties to invest in discovering and negotiating all of the details and contingencies that might arise in their agreement. If the transaction costs of forming a full contract exceed the benefits, it makes sense for some terms to remain open and to allow a court to fill in the gaps as the necessity arises. In these situations, the commonly accepted remedy is for the courts to fill in the missing terms as they believe the parties would do themselves under costless bargaining. This method of gap filling is described as "majoritarian" because it seeks to provide terms that most parties would have endorsed under the circumstances.

The second theory for efficient gap filling is based on informational asymmetries or other strategic obstacles to full disclosure between the parties that prevent the optimal contract from being formed.[28] In many contractual settings, parties to a contract may have private information that might be of use in adversarial negotiations. Courts may use information-forcing default rules to induce the contracting parties to reveal private information by providing terms that would be unfavorable to the better-informed party. This is the concept of a penalty default in which bargaining parties are given an incentive to reveal more information or face presumed acceptance of a suboptimal arrangement.

For instance, if one party values performance more than would be ordinarily assumed by the other party, it is efficient for this information to be communicated to the other party so that that party might take the necessary precautions to ensure performance. In its classic setting, a shipper of goods might not wish to reveal the unanticipated high value or delicate quality of the goods. Were the goods to be damaged, the default rule should be that any damages owing to the malfeasance of the shipper will be limited to the normal range of value or fragility of goods. In order to induce the shipper to assume the responsibility for non-standard goods, this kind of default forces the party with superior information to disclose, or risk not being compensated

---

[26] RESTATEMENT (SECOND) OF CONTRACTS § 33 (1981).

[27] *See* Ian Ayres, *Default Rules for Incomplete Contracts, in* 1 THE NEW PALGRAVE DICTIONARY OF ECONOMICS AND THE LAW 585, 586 (Peter Newman ed., New York: Stockton Press, 1998).

[28] Ian Ayres & Robert Gertner, *Filling Gaps in Incomplete Contracts: An Economic Theory of Default Rules*, 99 YALE L.J. 87, 91 (1989); *see also* Lucian Ayre Bebchuk & Steven Shavell, *Information and the Scope of Liability for Breach of Contract: The Rule of* Hadley v. Baxendale, 7 J.L. ECON. & ORG. 284, 286 (1991).

in case the goods are damaged. If the default rule sets damages at the average or ordinary cost of nonperformance, the party with the idiosyncratically high valuation will have the incentive to reveal his private information during bargaining.[29] Further, the knowledge that courts will enforce incompletely realized agreements itself provides incentives for the parties to negotiate as many terms as they can, knowing they may be held to a less desirable outcome by an independent adjudicator.

Translated to the context of constitutional bargaining, constitutional courts may facilitate the transition to democracy in two ways. The first is by permitting the parties a quick transition to basic democratic governance before they are capable of full agreement. Constitutions, by contrast to statutes, are notoriously open-textured in their commands. Imprecise but evocative terms such as "due process" carry forward the *soupçon* of commitment without the substance of the agreement. Oftentimes this is the product of the inability to resolve deeply contested issues.[30] At other times, vagueness may serve as an efficient mechanism to allow the parties to reach sufficient consensus to proceed in circumstances where either social norms or strategic considerations might overly tax the ability of the parties to reach express understandings.[31]

The second advantage offered by constitutional courts has more to do with the specifics of constitutional compromise, recognizing in the spirit of John Marshall that "it is a *constitution* we are expounding."[32] Unlike parties in conventional contracts, the harm in constitutional breach is not retrospective but prospective. Parties to a constitutional compact do not so much fear that their expectations at the time of contracting will not be realized as they fear that the powers they are creating will be used prospectively against them. At the heart

[29] *See Hadley v. Baxendale,* (1854) 156 Eng. Rep. 145, 9 Ex. 341.

[30] For example, Andrew Kull's review of the legislative history of the Fourteenth Amendment shows how the term "equal protection" was chosen because of fundamental disagreements on the rights to be afforded the freed slaves. ANDREW KULL, THE COLOR-BLIND CONSTITUTION 67–69 (1992).

[31] For a more formal account of how deliberately vague language can be welfare enhancing by mitigating conflict, see Andreas Blume & Oliver Board, *Intentional Vagueness,* 79 ERKENNTNIS 855 (2013) (providing numerous examples of commonplace uses of vagueness ranging from sexual innuendo to the famously inscrutable pronouncements of former Federal Reserve chairman Alan Greenspan). For an account of how vague judicial opinions might ease tensions over judicial intrusion on the political branches, see Jeffrey K. Staton & Georg Vanberg, *The Value of Vagueness: Delegation, Defiance, and Judicial Opinions,* 58 AM. J. POL. SCI. 504 (2008).

[32] *McCulloch v. Maryland,* 17 U.S. (4 Wheat.) 316, 407, 415 (1819) ("[W]e must never forget, that it is *a constitution* we are expounding" that is "intended to endure for ages to come, and, consequently, to be adapted to the various *crises* of human affairs.").

of any constitutional compromise lies the brutish fact that some of the parties to the pact will soon hold state power over their erstwhile fellow negotiators.

From this perspective, constitutional courts play the role of an "insurance policy" against forms of power grabs that cannot be specified or negotiated at the outset of the constitutional process. The term is from Professor Tom Ginsburg, who attributes to the courts the power both to cement the terms of the bargain and to provide for an acceptable response to conditions subsequent to the negotiations:

> [U]ncertainty increases demand for the political insurance that judicial review provides. Under conditions of high uncertainty, it may be especially useful for politicians to adopt a system of judicial review to entrench the constitutional bargain and protect it from the possibility of reversal after future electoral change.[33]

This argument may be pushed even further, perhaps by extension of Richard Pildes's caution against excessive rigidity in initial constitutional design,[34] to say that the prospect of active superintendence of the constitutional pact by courts may allow for greater experimentation and flexibility in the initial institutional design under the initial constitutional framework.

Although American constitutional law remains excessively focused on the justification for the power of judicial review, this need not prove a hindrance in new democracies. The prevalence of constitutional courts indicates at least a tacit recognition that judicial review may indeed be indispensable to establishing a functioning constitutional democracy. On this score, the legitimacy of these courts subsequent to the founding may turn on the degree that they reinforce the "democratic hedge" that accompanied the founding. This is a departure from the conventional debates, at least in the United States, about the source of legitimacy of constitution-based judicial review – the proverbial imposition of the dead hand of the past on the political will of the present majority. Rather than being tied to a narrow originalist vision of enforcing the agreed upon terms of the original pact, the contemporary

---

[33] TOM GINSBURG, JUDICIAL REVIEW IN NEW DEMOCRACIES: CONSTITUTIONAL COURTS IN ASIAN CASES 30–31 (New York: Cambridge University Press, 2003). A similar argument can be made in the context of more gradual democratization of autocratic regimes. For example, in Mexico, the emergence of strong challengers to the PRI's hegemony and the possibility of electoral reversals created an incentive for the ruling PRI to institute reforms granting real measures of autonomous judicial authority. See Jodi Finkel, *Judicial Reform as Insurance Policy: Mexico in the 1990s*, 47 LATIN AM. POL. & SOC'Y 87, 88 (2005).

[34] See Richard H. Pildes, *Ethnic Identity and Democratic Institutions: A Dynamic Perspective*, in CONSTITUTIONAL DESIGN FOR DIVIDED SOCIETIES 173, 173–75 (Sujit Choudhry ed., Oxford: Oxford University Press, 2008).

approach in new democracies imposes a broader duty on a constitutional court to reinforce the functioning of democracy more broadly. The original pact turns not only on the areas where agreement was reached – text, of course, is still central – but also on the areas where no agreement was possible save for the overall commitment to political accountability of the first set of rulers.

This idea that courts are integral structural parts of the moment of original constitutional creation is confirmed by the additional responsibilities over democratic accountability given to them. In most new democracies, the creation of these constitutional courts is accompanied by "ancillary powers" beyond simply the ability to subject legislation to judicial review.[35] Most common among these additional powers is some form of oversight over the electoral process itself, reaching in many cases to election administration, the subject matters of elections, the eligibility of parties to compete in elections, and electoral challenges. Indeed, 55 percent of constitutional courts hold specific powers of either administration or appellate review over the election process.[36]

The combination of constitutional review of legislation affecting the political process and administrative oversight of elections appears fortuitous. Both afford constitutional courts the ability to check efforts to close the political process to challenge. More centrally, both correspond to a vision of strong constitutional courts as a necessary check on excessive concentration of political power under conditions that are unforeseeable at the time of constitutional ratification or whose terms cannot be specified under the strategic uncertainties of the installation of democracy.

Here an American example may be helpful. In a fascinating critical account of the process of Iraqi constitutional formation, Ambassador Feisal Amin Rasoul al-Istrabadi recalls how the American Constitution was forged in the face of the Framers' inability to resolve the fundamental question of slavery.[37] Whether explicit (as in the recognition of a time limit for the slave trade)[38] or implicit (as with the absence of federal involvement in the internal political affairs of the states),[39] much of the constitutional structure was delicately balanced around a recognition that to address the question of slavery was to

---

[35] Tom Ginsburg & Zachary Elkins, *Ancillary Powers of Constitutional Courts*, 87 TEX. L. REV. 1431, 1440–41 (2009).

[36] *Id.* at 1443 tbl.1.

[37] *See* al-Istrabadi, *supra* note 17, at 1629–30.

[38] *See* U.S. CONST. art. 1, § 9, cl. 1.

[39] *See generally* Earl M. Maltz, *Slavery, Federalism, and the Structure of the Constitution*, 36 AM. J. LEGAL HIST. 466 (1992).

call the Union into question. Moreover, once the Supreme Court removed the capacity for further political accommodations of the slavery issue,[40] an explosive civil war ensued. The question for new constitutional regimes is whether the sources of political accommodation not available at the founding may be developed over time. Indeed, the question is whether under conditions of political accommodation and increased trust, the divisions may prove more tractable such that the American experience of a brutal civil war can be avoided.

Although the contract analogy helps explain how courts can fill the breach in nascent democracies, it is by its nature a limited analogy. There are inherent difficulties in fashioning any comprehensive theory of interpretation, even at the level of commercial contracts.[41] Once the move is made to the realm of statutes, the difficulties of interpretation are compounded by the institutional incapability of courts to apply any canons of interpretation consistently and accurately. As Elizabeth Garrett argues, many canons of statutory interpretation falter precisely because of the limited "institutional capacity of judges" to apply them.[42] Moved one step higher to the plane of constitutional interpretation, the difficulty is again compounded. Trying to figure out the shared objectives of parties to constitutional negotiations is not a simple undertaking. To begin with, there is no presumed universal set of values or beliefs that unite people across such fundamental divides as religion or race. Unlike in the case of commercial contracts, there is not a relatively accessible economic presumption that the parties seek to maximize their joint welfare. And, unlike statutory interpretation, the canons of construction do not operate against the customary presumption – even if difficult to realize in practice – that the legislature in its continuing capacity is free to override improper court interpretations of its objectives. Even in the context of legislation, there are critiques of the ability of courts to construct a "democracy-forcing statutory interpretation."[43] And, yet, that is the task with which constitutional courts are charged in trying to shore up the prospects for democratic governance.

---

[40] *See Dred Scott v. Sandford*, 60 U.S. (19 How.) 393 (1857).

[41] *See* Alan Schwartz & Robert E. Scott, *Contract Theory and the Limits of Contract Law*, 113 YALE L.J. 541, 543 (2003) (arguing that modern contract law has neither a descriptive nor normative theory that is sufficiently complete to apply across the spectrum of private contracts).

[42] Elizabeth Garrett, *Preferences, Laws, and Default Rules*, 122 HARV. L. REV. 2104, 2137 (2009) (reviewing EINER ELHAUGE, STATUTORY DEFAULT RULES: HOW TO INTERPRET UNCLEAR LEGISLATION (Cambridge, MA: Harvard University Press, 2008)).

[43] *See* ADRIAN VERMEULE, JUDGING UNDER UNCERTAINTY 132 (Cambridge, MA: Harvard University Press, 2006).

THE BARGAINING MODEL

Common sense would seem to dictate that it is easier to forge a constitutional accord if the parties have less over which they may disagree. An intuitively attractive insight is that the fewer the issues that negotiating parties have to agree upon, the more quickly agreement might be realized. In this sense, the presence of contractual defaults or a post-pact arbiter would serve to relieve the cost of bargaining, as recognized in the Uniform Commercial Code's approach to majoritarian defaults in private contracts.

Unfortunately, the picture is a bit more complicated. In some circumstances, the presence of what economists term an outside option may complicate the ability of the parties to resolve matters themselves. An outside option refers simply to the possibility that if parties cannot agree on a price for the sale of some good, both have alternatives. The alternative might be other buyers and sellers in the marketplace, or it may be some form of compelled arbitration of a reasonable price, a common practice in long-term commercial relations.

The availability of an outside option may distort the incentives the parties face at the bargaining stage. When the outside option takes the form of an arbiter empowered to resolve impasses between the parties, the result may be fewer rather than more agreements. The parties may become more reluctant to make concessions through bargaining because they may believe they will do better in the adjudication of the dispute. Thus, the models of game theory are quite equivocal on this score because what is termed a strong arbitration rule may compel the parties to turn to the arbiter and not to attempt to resolve disputes themselves.[44] The models typically consider the relative strength of the outside arbiter as a key variable in determining under which conditions the parties are likely to try to realize agreement among themselves and when they will push off the dispute onto the arbiter and not attempt private resolution.[45]

Like many models, however, the formal exposition starts to break down when applied to the real world. Most notably, the theoretical literature on

[44] *See, e.g.*, Marc J. Knez & Colin F. Camerer, *Outside Options and Social Comparison in Three-Player Ultimatum Game Experiments*, 10 GAMES AND ECON. BEHAV. 65 (1995). For an interesting analogy to the ability of laws governing marriage and divorce to alter the availability of divorce and, consequently, the divorce rate, see Abraham L. Wickelgren, *Why Divorce Laws Matter: Incentives for Noncontractible Marital Investments under Unilateral and Consent Divorce*, 25 J. L. ECON. & ORG. 80 (2009).

[45] *See* MERCEDES ADAMUZ PEÑA, ESSAYS ON BARGAINING WITH OUTSIDE OPTIONS: THE ROLE OF PROCEDURE (Saarbrücken, Germany: VDM Verlag, 2010), *full text available at* http://www.tdx.cat/bitstream/handle/10803/4059/map1de1.pdf?sequence=1 (arguing that the authority of the arbitrator influences the outcome between parties).

outside options starts from the assumption of a relatively static outside force (formally described as being "exogenous" to the actual negotiations) such that the conduct of the outside arbiter would not be affected by what happened in the course of negotiations. That assumption of independence of the outside option from the conduct of the parties in the negotiation has limited applicability to law. The most common outside option is a court or arbitrator, and no contract dispute could be analyzed without reference to the bargaining intent of the parties. In the theoretical literature that has tried to model the outside option as being dependent on what happens in the negotiations, the results are more complicated and may actually yield inefficiencies in bargaining depending on the costs associated with delay.[46] Put in plain terms, the problem is that the prospective future judges are not preordained but are an integral part of the negotiations themselves, producing a great deal more complexity than the more stylized economics models allow for.

The constitutional negotiations after 1989 depart from the theoretical models precisely because the parties in country after country devoted great attention to how disputes would be resolved under conditions of uncertainty or disagreement. The distinct feature of the often rapid-fire process of state formation after the fall of the Soviet Union was the need to consolidate a blueprint for elections and governance. Part of the negotiations between the parties was, in effect, over what form the outside option would take if constitutional courts were created to police the political pact and fill in its voids. Under such extraordinary circumstances, the theoretical literature does little beyond confirming the plausibility of the intuitive understanding that parties can more quickly reach agreement if they are able to leave some sticking points to be worked out over time.

Nonetheless, the literature on bargaining with an outside option may yield insights about the distributional outcomes of the negotiations. Most of the theoretical literature on bargaining with an outside option concerns whether the parties will bargain quickly to the midpoint of the differences between them, a variant of what is termed the Rubinstein alternating offers model.[47]

---

[46] *See, e.g.*, MARTIN J. Osborne & Ariel RUBINSTEIN, BARGAINING AND MARKETS 50–55 (Bingley: Emerald Group Publishing, 1990) (identifying outside options as one of the factors that may contribute to delay in reaching bargaining resolution).

[47] *See* Ariel Rubinstein, *Perfect Equilibrium in a Bargaining Model*, 50 ECONOMETRICA 97, 98–101 (1982). The basic insight is that, with perfect information, parties bargaining across a potentially infinite series of offers and counteroffers will quickly and efficiently converge upon the midpoint to resolve their dispute. In worlds of imperfect information, the results are more complicated and agreement may be reached only after some delay, and there remains some first-mover advantage. When there is a need to match offer and acceptance for either party to gain anything, the Rubenstein model becomes more of a coordination game, as well

The presence of an outside option should alter the focal point of the negotiations in such a way as to promote the substantive fairness of the outcome, even if the parties are unable to realize that in negotiations. Although the literature on this is thin, the argument to date is that the presence of a strong outside option, such as a strong arbitrator, results in the weaker party in the negotiations being better able to resist pressure toward an inequitable bargaining outcome.

The beneficial results that can obtain from an outside alternative in negotiations is again highly intuitive and can be understood apart from the formal models of game theory. The benefit in terms of fairness corresponds to the sensible result that the ability to seek a strong outside ally for the weaker bargaining party diminishes the power of the stronger party to cram down its desires. It is possible to think of the negotiation between a strong incumbent political power and its defeated rival as an ultimatum game in the absence of an external alternative actor, such as a constitutional court. In such an ultimatum game, the stronger party has a take-it-or-leave it power and the weaker party is hard-pressed to resist. The addition of an ability to turn to an outside ally, as with a court, gives the weaker party the hope that resistance might not be futile.

Without the outside option of turning to another institutional actor, the weaker party fears that subsequent political negotiations will take the form of a cram-down of the classic take-it-or-take-it sort, in which no alternative but recourse to full confrontation is presented. The defeated rival has the choice only of accepting whatever is doled out by the triumphant party, or else repudiating the entire agreement – in effect, either submitting to or rejecting democratic pathways, presumably by derailing the functioning of government or in extreme cases by insurrection. The presence of a court gives the weaker power an alternative avenue for seeking to vindicate its interests, although even this scenario is complicated if there are multiple parties and the bargaining process could yield coalition politics. Moreover, uncertainty over the actions of a powerful outside arbiter increases the likelihood that the parties will in fact reach a negotiated solution on mutually acceptable terms.

The importance of quickly and equitably realizing the initial bargain over governance is underscored if we think of the post-Soviet period not as the triumph of democracy but as a forum for the reassertion of autocratic rule.

---

summarized in Richard H. McAdams, *Beyond The Prisoners' Dilemma: Coordination, Game Theory, and Law*, 82 S. Cal. L. Rev. 209, 236–37 (2009). For applications of coordination strategies to explain similar structures in international accords, see Jack L. Goldsmith & Eric A. Posner, *A Theory of Customary International Law*, 66 U. Chi. L. Rev. 1113, 1127–28 (1999).

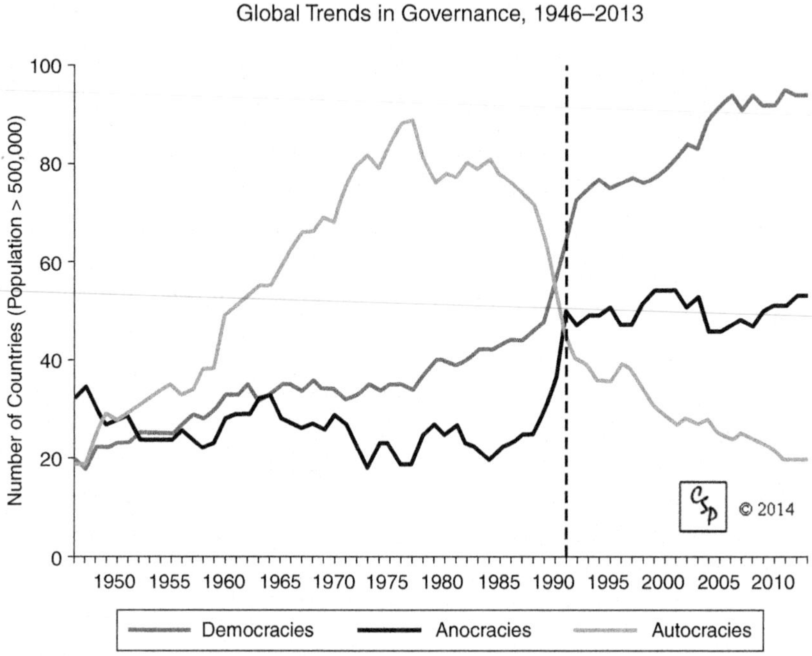

Global Trends in Governance, 1946–2013

FIGURE 10.1. Pre- and post-1989 democracies. © 2014, The Center for Systemic Peace.

It is all too convenient to imagine that there is no reversibility to the democratic gains after the fall of the Soviet Union. Posed as the story of democratic ascendency, the post-1989 narrative threatens to become a Whiggish tale of the eventual triumph of good over evil, certainly a curious claim for many countries manifestly lacking in the per capita income levels and the civil society institutions that characterize stable democracies. A snapshot of the Soviet orbit before and after 1989 certainly would tell a heartening story of the growth of democratic governance. But a more nuanced inquiry would reveal an initial period of democratic contestation across the former Soviet empire beginning in 1989 and then a gradual reemergence of autocratic authority in a number of the former Soviet states, most notably Belarus and Russia in the west, and virtually all the central Asiatic states in the east.

It is thus possible to invert the inquiry and start not with the story of democracy ascendant, but with the assumption that the natural state of affairs for these countries is some form of authoritarian rule or even collapse of central state functions – what in Figure 10.1 is termed an "anocracy" and what is more customarily referred to as a "failed state."[48] Framed in this fashion, political scientist Lucan

---

[48] The figure is from the Center for Systemic Peace, available at http://www.systemicpeace.org/

Way analyzes these countries not in terms of the lead-up to democracy, but as the failure of autocracy to take hold initially: "competitive politics were rooted much less in robust civil societies, strong democratic institutions, or democratic leadership than in *the inability of incumbents to maintain power or concentrate political control* by preserving elite unity, controlling elections and media, and/or using force against opponents."[49] On this view, democracy turns out to be the potential training ground for future oppression, and democratic governance becomes the organizational incubator for the tyrants in waiting. Following this decidedly less rosy view, the challenge is to safeguard the renewability of consent that characterizes the rotation in office of democratically elected officials. A constitutional court then becomes not only a facilitator of the initial bargain, but a central actor in its maintenance. The role of a strong constitutional court in the initial constitutional bargain can be seen as anticipating the need to enlist another institutional actor to constrain potential strong-arm rule by the first government in office. The constitutional bargaining anticipates this need: "Independent judicial review is valuable to political competitors when those competitors would prefer to exercise mutual restraint but the necessary monitoring and enforcement of restraint are not possible or are prohibitively costly."[50]

CONSTRUCTING THE COURTS

At the end of the day, someone has to man the ship. If the rapid democratic transitions were to rely on effective constitutional court stewardship, a cadre of judges would be needed who could resist the political pressures of the moment and, if needed, stand down the first consolidated political powers. Much would depend on the first generation of constitutional court judges and on how their new powers of constitutional oversight would be utilized.

Two important generalizations may help guide this inquiry. First, one needs to confront the legacy of the past in terms of the availability of judicial stalwarts. In countries with long-term authoritarian regimes such as Nazi Germany, Fascist Italy, the Soviet orbit, or apartheid South Africa, it is unlikely that there would be a large reservoir of individuals untainted by prior affiliation with the oppressive past who would be able to constitute an entirely new judiciary. As mentioned in the introductory chapter to this section, there simply were not enough trained judges in Germany or South Africa, or even in Eastern Europe, to structure a legal system comprised entirely of person who had not been Nazis, or apartheid officials, or Communists. One of the consequences of a modern

---

[49] Way, *supra* note 1, at 232.
[50] Matthew C. Stephenson, *"When the Devil Turns ...": The Political Foundations of Independent Judicial Review*, 32 J. LEGAL STUD. 59, 84 (2003).

authoritarian state is that professional training and advancement in politically freighted professions such as law, or the judiciary specifically, was impossible without some compromise with the ever-present state authorities. No one trained as a lawyer and judge in these systems could advance without some deep compromise, either by having to belong to the Nazi Party in Germany, or by being an overseer of the apartheid definition of limited rights to the vast majority of the South African population. This means that, absent a complete lustration of the court system, the ultimate responsibility for ensuring the democratic viability of the new system would have to reside in an institution whose selection and processes were outside the normal workings of the legal system.

This then led to a second reason for the impossibility of a complete lustration strategy. Countries like Nazi Germany or apartheid South Africa had a well-trained professional judiciary that continued to administer the everyday commands of a legal system for contract enforcement or tort claims, even while deeply tarnished by the commanding repressive political structure. Confidence in the judiciary to administer day-to-day legal affairs may have been lower in the Soviet bloc, amid complaints about "telephone justice" that allowed party bureaucrats to direct the outcome of even low-level disputes. But even there, it was inconceivable that an entire court system could be remade without the institutional presence of judges from the Soviet era, and the legacy of some legal entitlements and obligations that they would have to administer during the transition. For as much as these were oppressive societies, they also represented a range of sophisticated economic and social institutions that needed some measure of ordered legal process.

In the most sophisticated settings such as South Africa or the Czech Republic, to pick two well-established legal cultures, the task was to integrate the best of the prior judicial structures into a new democratic society, while structuring guarantees of their subservience to that democracy. Creating constitutional courts outside the normal command and promotion chain of the judiciary allowed both an incorporation of the former judges into the new democratic order, and the creation of a separate body of judicial power whose accountability was to democracy as such. The creation of new constitutional courts in Eastern Europe was "fuelled by a distrust of the judiciary and by the firmly held belief that courts and judges inherited from the Communist regime were (or would be) incapable of exercising the powers allocated to the constitutional courts."[51] Further, by isolating judicial review of statutes in new

---

[51] Renata Uitz, *Constitutional Courts in Central and Eastern Europe: What Makes a Question Too Political?*, Juridica International, 2007, at 47, 49 http://www.juridicainternational.eu/ public/pdf/ji_2007_2_47.pdf.

courts, the drafters of these new constitutions sent "a message of 'out with the old and in with the new.'"[52] The fresh faces on these courts counteracted the inherited distrust of all governmental institutions by offering a highly visible "institutional check" on state authorities for the generations that had grown up under Communist-dominated governmental institutions. These governmental institutions suffered from popular perceptions that under Communism they were under the thumb of a "less-than-legitimate Parliament and government," and rightfully so.[53]

Fortunately, the new democratic authorities were following a clearly demarcated path established in Germany, the home of the most visible and successful of the post-authoritarian constitutional courts. Germany was the wellspring for the emergence of the postwar model of using strong independent judiciaries to enforce the new democratic order, even against holdover institutions or state officials from the prior regime. More centrally for purposes of this account, Germany became the model for courts having institutional responsibility for the limits on democratic politics, lest political actors yield to the temptation of a return to a forbidden set of unacceptable outcomes. In Germany, the early role of the constitutional court was to enforce a notion of constrained democracy, what became the basis for "juridical democracies," under Donald Kommers' favorable account,[54] or more pejoratively, for what Ran Hirschl terms "Juristocracy."[55]

The German Court was not the product of internal agreements among rival social factions, as discussed earlier in setting forth the role of courts as a democratic hedge against excessive majoritarian power. Rather, the German court was created to institutionalize a bulwark against recurrent Nazism, serving at least as much of a guarantee to the occupying Allied powers against an engorged central state power as to internal political commitments. The role of the German court was to stand as the ultimate protector of civil liberties and to serve as the check on "arbitrary governmental action," as set forth in the West German Basic Law.[56] Toward that end, the initial selection of constitutional

[52] Sheive, *supra* note 5, at 1208 (quoting interview with Valerie P. Calogero, director of the Rule of Law Program at the Central and East European Law Initiative).
[53] Wojciech Sadurski, *Postcommunist Constitutional Courts in Search of Political Legitimacy* 10 (European University Institute, Law Working Paper No. 11, 2001).
[54] Donald P. Kommers, *The Federal Constitutional Court: Guardian of German Democracy*, 603 ANNALS AM. ACAD. POL. & SOC. SCI. 111, 126 (2006).
[55] RAN HIRSCHL, TOWARDS JURISTOCRACY: THE ORIGINS AND CONSEQUENCES OF THE NEW CONSTITUTIONALISM (Cambridge, MA: Harvard University Press, 2004).
[56] Taylor Cole, *The West German Federal Constitutional Court: An Evaluation after Six Years*, J. POL., May 1958, at 281–82.

court judges favored "persons who not only failed to join the Nazi Party but who went into exile or temporary retirement during the Third Reich," or even someone whose anti-Nazi credentials were burnished by involvement in the 1944 plot to assassinate Hitler.[57]

No set of formal requirements could cement the break from the past. Nonetheless, the composition of the constitutional court became an immediate concern of parliament as it drafted the Constitutional Court Act.[58] The parliamentary recruiters sought justices who were "clean" and "untainted by Nazism," and informally they sought to ensure that "a portion of the seats was to be assigned to persons of Jewish ancestry."[59] Ultimately, the twenty-four justices included individuals who had been in exile, or had resigned from official positions for unwillingness to embrace Nazism, or had eschewed public positions during the Nazi period, or held minor positions during that period. The message was clear: a constitutional court for a new democratic order needed to signal a clear break from the authoritarian past, a demand that could not be directed at the judiciary as a whole. A significant part of that signal was to be conveyed by the composition of the court itself.

Similarly, in South Africa, the negotiated transition rejected proposals from the National Party that the power of constitutional review be given to existing appellate judges, even though under the Westminster system of parliamentary sovereignty these judges had never exercised the power of judicial review. Rather, the ANC negotiators insisted that "most of the apartheid-era judges were unsuited to decide on constitutional issues,"[60] and that a new court be created, although they agreed that four of the eleven justices would be drawn from the ranks of the incumbent judiciary.

Under the negotiated procedure, President Mandela retained authority to appoint the president (later chief justice) of the court, and appointed one of South Africa's most prominent lawyers, Arthur Chaskelson, who had been Mandela's personal lawyer in the historic political trials under apartheid. The remainder of the court was made up by four sitting judges (including Richard Goldstone, whose role at the end of apartheid forced him briefly into exile under death threats) and six newcomers, nominated by the multiparty Judicial Selection Committee. In reality, all the appointees (of whom a majority was

[57] Glenn N. Schram, *The Recruitment of Judges for the West German Federal Constitutional Court*, 21 AM. J. COMP. L. 691, 701 (1973).

[58] DONALD P. KOMMERS, JUDICIAL POLITICS IN WEST GERMANY: A STUDY OF THE FEDERAL CONSTITUTIONAL COURT 120 (Beverly Hills, CA: Sage Publications, 1976).

[59] *Id.*

[60] Jeremy Sarkin, *The Political Role of the South African Constitutional Court*, 114 S. AFRICAN L.J. 134, 134 (1997).

white) had a record of opposition to apartheid, even among the judges who had served under the prior regime. The selection was sufficiently in keeping with the expectations of the original negotiations that the multiparty Government of National Unity (GNU) Cabinet, comprised on the basis of the first democratic election in 1994, agreed by consensus to President Mandela's choices of new judges.[61] If anything, the insistence on independence from apartheid led to some "charges that many [were] too close to Mandela's ANC."[62] But the key remained that the constitutional court would stand independent of the established and compromised judiciary, and would be the repository of a newly minted power of constitutional review of government action, including the right to strike down statutes or, as we have seen, even the constitution itself.

The scrutiny with which the initial cohort of constitutional justices was selected was just one aspect of the attention dedicated to designing these new courts. Country after country experimented with different institutional designs, adjusting factors ranging from the scope of the court's jurisdiction to the mandatory retirement age of its judges. Despite the broad range of possible variation, the structuring of constitutional courts can be understood as varying along three principal axes: first, how judges are selected to serve on constitutional courts; second, how issues are brought before the tribunal; and third, what effects follow from the court's adjudication. Although cataloguing all possible permutations is too long an endeavor for this review, a survey of prototypical and atypical examples sheds light on the importance of institutional design to constitutional negotiators, and the political benefits that can redound from a given arrangement. Each decision carries the potential to strengthen or weaken the constitutional court, and thereby to expand or shrink the bargaining parties' "political insurance" against a downturn in their electoral fortunes.[63]

Who becomes a constitutional court judge depends on several design choices. At the most basic, negotiators must decide the number of seats on the bench, the tenure of the judges, and the renewability of their appointments. Longer, nonrenewable terms maximize judicial independence, while shorter, renewable ones allow political organs to rein in the court. The most common outcome is for judges to serve a fixed term of nine years, with one possible reappointment. Although some states, such as Poland, explicitly forbid reappointments, others, like the Czech Republic, provide for renewable

[61] Princeton N. Lyman, *South Africa's Promise*, FOREIGN POL'Y, Spring 1996, at 105, 106–08.
[62] *Mandela Inaugurates South Africa's First Constitutional Court*, WASH. POST, Feb. 15, 1995, http://www.sfgate.com/default/article/Mandela-Inaugurates-South-Africa-s-First-3045708.php.
[63] Ginsburg, *supra* note 33, at 30–31.

terms.[64] The Constitutional Court of Bosnia and Herzegovina combined these options, with the first cohort of judges serving a five-year term and subsequent judges appointed until the mandatory retirement age of seventy.[65] Having nonrenewable terms was generally conceived of as a protection against political influence over judges who might fear offending their political overseers. Similarly, long tenures were also generally perceived as a mechanism to give judges greater independence and greater likelihood to develop an institutional élan separate from the political branches. Unfortunately, such formalized institutional practices cannot ensure the actual independence of the judiciary. In Russia, for example, a series of amendments from 1994 to 2005 extended the judges' terms from twelve years to life. This extension was criticized as "less a sign of respect for judicial independence and more a reward for political loyalty."[66] Notably, in Russia, the extension of the judicial terms in office coincided with the collapse of any meaningful judicial independent oversight powers over the Putin government.

A more complex design feature is the mechanism for appointing judges. Appointment represents "the point where constitutional justice and party politics intertwine in the most evident and manifest way. The members of the constitutional court are appointed by politicians at least in part in every constitutional justice model."[67] Wojciech Sadurski has categorized the appointment mechanisms as either "shared," "collaborative," or "parliamentary."[68] Under the shared model, different state bodies are assigned a set number of seats that each can fill. In the Constitutional Court of Italy, for example, five judges are appointed by the president, five more are appointed by both parliamentary chambers sitting jointly, and a final five are appointed by Italy's supreme

---

[64] *See* WOJCIECH SADURSKI, RIGHTS BEFORE COURTS: A STUDY OF CONSTITUTIONAL COURTS IN POSTCOMMUNIST STATES OF CENTRAL AND EASTERN EUROPE 27–34 (Dordrecht, The Netherlands: Springer, 2nd ed. 2014) (comparing examples in post-Communist Europe); *see also* VENICE COMMISSION, COUNCIL OF EUROPE, DECISIONS OF CONSTITUTIONAL COURTS AND EQUIVALENT BODIES AND THEIR EXECUTION (2011) 15–17 (comparing survey responses of forty-five states); Tom Ginsburg, *Constitutional Courts in East Asia: Understanding Variation,* 3 J. COMP. L. 80 n.2 (2008) (comparing examples in East and Southeast Asia).

[65] Sadurski, *supra* note 63, at 27.

[66] CARLA L. THORSON, POLITICS, JUDICIAL REVIEW AND THE RUSSIAN CONSTITUTIONAL COURT 149 (New York: Palgrave Macmillan, 2012).

[67] Katalin Kelemen, *Appointment of Constitutional Judges in a Comparative Perspective: With a Proposal for a New Model for Hungary,* 54 ACTA JURIDICA HUNGARICA 5, 6 (2013), *available in translation at* http://ssrn.com/abstract=2229184.

[68] Wojciech Sadurski, *Constitutional Courts and Constitutional Culture in Central and Eastern European Countries, in* CENTRAL AND EASTERN EUROPE AFTER TRANSITION 99–100 (Alberto Febbrajo and Wojciech Sadurski, eds., Surrey and Burlington, VT: Ashgate Publishing, 2010).

courts. A similar model is found in South Korea, where the president, parliament, and the high court each appoint three judges. Such divided appointments appear most likely when future political contests are unpredictable, and where "each faction believes it is likely to be *out* of power," as occurred when Korea was negotiating the composition of its court.[69]

A collaborative approach gives multiple bodies authority over the appointment of any given judge, as in the United States where federal judicial appointments require presidential nomination and Senate confirmation. Similar shared appointment powers exist in Albania, Austria, the Czech Republic, and Slovakia. Alternatively, a parliamentary model allows the legislature exclusive power to select judges. This model is used in Hungary, where a two-thirds majority is needed to appoint a judge, as well as in Poland and Croatia, which require a simple majority. Because only one body is responsible for selecting judges, the parliamentary model is generally seen as most vulnerable to political majority domination.

Beyond the mechanics of appointment, many states have enacted eligibility requirements for potential judges, as well as factors that would result in their disqualification. The requirements vary too greatly to chronicle here, although legal expertise is an unsurprisingly ubiquitous consideration. Certain systems require constitutional court judges to be appointed from another court; others are more flexible regarding which positions are eligible, but require a certain number of years of experience.[70] Bosnia and Herzegovina's court requires the inclusion of three noncitizen justices.[71] France's Conseil Constitutionnel requires no legal background whatsoever, and automatically includes all past presidents.[72] Thailand's court reserves two seats for "qualified persons in political science, public administration or other social sciences."[73] In addition to the *de jure* requirements, certain factual patterns have emerged in these appointments. Poland and Hungary, for example, showed an overwhelming

---

[69] Ginsburg, *supra* note 33, at 93.

[70] Italy's constitutional court, for example, has three routes to eligibility: "a judge (active or retired) on one of Italy's higher courts (ordinary or administrative); a full professor of law; or a lawyer with 20 years' experience in practice." Center for Constitutional Transitions at NYU Law and Democracy Reporting International, Constitutional Review in New Democracies 5 (Sept. 2013) [hereinafter CT & DRI], *available at* http://www.democracy-reporting.org/files/dri-bp-40_en_constitutional_review_in_new_democracies_2013-09.pdf.

[71] Sadurski, *supra* note 63, at 7.

[72] CT & DRI, *supra* note 69, at 5.

[73] *See generally* Venice Commission, Council of Europe, The Composition of Constitutional Courts 8–10 (1997); CT & DRI, *supra* note 69 at 5. *See also* Thai. Const., Aug. 24, 2007, § 204(4).

preference for law professors, at least in the early stages when there were no people who both had judicial experience and were without Communist backgrounds. In both countries, legal academics formed a majority of the early incoming judges, something that may have tied in to the notably aggressive judicial review in those two countries.[74] On the flipside, judicial disqualification is often premised on any engagement in overt political activities, a measure designed to ensure judicial independence and distance the new court from the old regime.[75]

Like the question of who decides, the question of what issues are to be decided provides a powerful lever by which to control the strength of a constitutional court. Negotiators over the court's jurisdiction can calibrate when the court can engage in judicial review, what type of review it will undertake, and who has standing to bring issues before the court. A more extensive jurisdictional grant can translate into a stronger guarantee against abuse by future political majorities, although it may also be more conducive to bringing the judiciary into more extensive conflict with the political branches. Judicial review of legislation may occur prior to its promulgation, afterward, or both. This decision is similar but not identical to what type of review to permit. Many constitutional courts review the constitutionality of legislative action in the abstract, either before or after its enactment, while some are limited to deciding concrete disputes that have arisen. The French Conseil lacked any *a posteriori* jurisdiction over enacted laws or concrete cases and instead acted as a constitutional advisor to the parliament, something that changed only recently with the expansion of its authority to include after-the-fact review.[76] The U.S. Supreme Court, by contrast, allows only for *a posteriori* concrete review brought in the context of a specific "case or controversy."[77] A *priori* review is rare in the post-Communist sphere, although many courts will adjudicate both concrete and abstract appeals.[78] In reality, neither the temporal element nor

[74] Catherine Dupré, Importing the Law in Post-Communist Transitions: The Hungarian Constitutional Court and the Right to Human Dignity 35 (Portland, OR: Hart Publishing, 2003); Kelemen, *supra* note 66, at 16 n.57 (24 out of 36 Polish judges appointed between 1985 and 2001 were law professors).

[75] *See, e.g.*, Open Society Initiative, Monitoring the EU Accession Process: Judicial Independence 38(2001),*available at* http://www.opensocietyfoundations.org/sites/default/files/judicialind_20011010.pdf.

[76] Tom Ginsburg & Mila Versteeg, *Why Do Countries Adopt Constitutional Review?*, 23 J.L. Econ. & Org. 1, 6 (2013), *available at* http://ssrn.com/abstract=2319363.

[77] U.S. Const. art. III, § 2, cl. 1.

[78] Sadurski, *supra* note 63, at 91, 102–03.

the type of review can be reduced to such neat dichotomies. Some systems modify the rules with carve-out exceptions.[79] Others allow for alternative techniques with quasi-judicial review, such as advisory opinions on early drafts of legislation or abstract constitutional interpretations not associated with any specific proposals.[80]

Courts differ in terms of who has standing to invoke the court's jurisdiction, with this right being assigned to various actors, including presidents, prime ministers, groups of parliamentarians, courts, prosecutors, ombudsmen, sub-federal political units, and even trade unions. Some systems allow individual citizens access to abstract review in the form of *actio popularis*. In Hungary, for example, even noncitizens have the right to initiate this process. Unlike Hungary, Estonia has established very strict standing requirements, where no member of parliament can challenge a law's constitutionality.[81] France is equally strict in an opposite direction, allowing only politicians to bring a challenge and only recently allowing referrals from other French courts.[82] Finally, some constitutional courts are empowered to raise a constitutional issue *sua sponte*, acting on their own initiative.[83]

Finally, there is considerable variation on the effect of constitutional court judgments. For example, national arrangements differ as to which state organs must defer to the constitutional court; whether the court can postpone the effective date of its own rulings; and whether the court can issue decisions with retroactive effect.[84] Some legislatures, as in Romania until 2003 and Poland until 1997, allow a parliamentary override of constitutional court decisions. The Canadian Charter of Rights and Freedoms offers a limited parliamentary override via the "notwithstanding clause," which allows provincial

---

[79] Moldova does not allow for judicial review of acts that came into force before the constitution. France does not allow review of laws passed by referendum. Hungary and Turkey allow for review of the constitutionality of constitutional amendments, although most other countries do not. Venice Commission, *supra* note 63, at 6.

[80] Although the former is rare in countries with centralized constitutional courts, it is more common in countries with decentralized constitutional review. Bulgaria, Hungary, and Slovakia all have the authority to issue binding abstract constitutional interpretations. *Id.* at 11; Sadurski, *supra* note 63, at 106–07.

[81] Sadurski, *supra* note 63, at 15.

[82] Alec Stone Sweet, *The Politics of Constitutional Review in France and Europe*, 5 INT'L J. CONST. L. 69, 71.

[83] This prerogative belongs to the courts of Hungary, Albania, Montenegro, and Serbia. Sadurski, *supra* note 63, at 19 & n.52.

[84] Venice Commission, *supra* note 63, at 12–21.

governments to enact legislation for up to five years notwithstanding a violation of certain rights enshrined in the Charter.[85] And, of course, no court is
ever completely immunized from political scrutiny entirely. Except with some
of the specific unamendable provisions of constitutional law, as in Germany,
governments can always override constitutional courts by passing a constitutional amendment.

---

[85] Tsvi Kahana, *Understanding the Notwithstanding Mechanism*, 52 U. Toronto L.J. 221
(2002).

11

Can Law Protect Democracy?

The argument of this book is unreservedly instrumental. There is no claim of "Herculean" wisdom in the judiciary, as per Ronald Dworkin, nor any attempt to engage at a first-order level the arguments for greater democratic legitimacy of the political branches, as per Jeremy Waldron. Instead the argument is that courts have emerged as the stopgap protections to two of the classic disabilities of democracy, particularly for young and untested regimes. The first challenge comes from without in the form of enemies of democracy who use the inherent porousness of democratic politics to undermine the core value of electoral legitimacy that underlies any form of democratic rule. The second comes from within through the suffocating command over the instrumentalities of government by a strong party or strong leader, no longer accountable to meaningful electoral contestation.

Despite the provenance for the new form of court-enforced constitutionalism in the need to watch over the democratic process, the reality is more complicated. In many instances courts back away from this role, fearing wisely or not that intervening in the name of democratic legitimacy threatens direct conflict with political powers. Wojciech Sadurski notes that, despite their strong constitutional mandate, "the dominant justification for the robust position of the constitutional courts of post-communist states in [Central and Eastern Europe] is based on the role of these courts in the protection of individual rights – in particular, those explicitly entrenched in the respective constitutions."[1] Sadurski attributes this reluctance to engage the preconditions for democracy as such to, at least in part, "the existence of reasonable disagreement about the processes and devices of democracy."[2]

---

[1] WOJCIECH SADURSKI, RIGHTS BEFORE COURTS: A STUDY OF CONSTITUTIONAL COURTS IN POSTCOMMUNIST STATES OF CENTRAL AND EASTERN EUROPE 145 (Dordrecht, The Netherlands: Springer, 2nd ed., 2014).

[2] *Id.* at 152.

But the reluctance to embrace democracy as the metric for court over-sight can hardly be explained by the complexity of the ensuing inquiry. Constitutional law abounds with topics such as abortion, affirmative action, hate speech, or same-sex marriage that are no less subject to disagreement for being framed in the language of rights. And Eastern Europe does not lack for structural interventions by courts that can ill be presented as matters of indi-vidual rights alone. Much of the burden of this book has been to unearth the jurisprudential logic of these cases. An individual rights enforcement strategy cannot capture what occurs in cases across the former Soviet empires, as with the Lithuanian ruling striking down a proposal that the minister of justice rather than an outside judicial college had the authority to nominate judges, or the Moldovan ruling preventing President Lucinschi from holding a refer-endum to expand the powers of the presidency at the expense of parliament.[3]

The question then arises of what happens when courts are not capable of assuming a protective role in nascent democracies, or lose the will to con-tinue doing so after the initial transition from authoritarian rule. Here South Africa again serves as an important illustration. In the transition from apart-heid and in the initial period under Nelson Mandela, South Africa provided an inspiring example of the process of constitutional formation and the hope for constrained democratic governance. Yet South Africa is unfortunately also the home to a sobering cautionary note. Having described that country's promising process of constitutional formation, let us now carry the story closer to the present day, by describing how South Africa is faced with the peril of constitutional retreat.

Of particular concern for present purposes is the difficult role for courts in the face of consolidated political power, particularly the one-partyism that emerges from the great authority of the heroic trailblazers battling autocracy. In South Africa, the historic role of the African National Congress (ANC) as the leaders of the antiapartheid struggle, combined with the tremendous per-sonal authority of Nelson Mandela, translated over time into a consolidation of party political authority. As with the Partido Revolucionario Institucional (PRI) in Mexico, the leadership of the revolutionary movement soon became the uncontested heads of the new political order. The ANC brand, as it were, became the shorthand for black-majority rule in an almost unquestioned manner. As expressed by one South African journalist, "[i]n the intervening years the ANC has grown into something of a religion; it is the only thing that several generations, old and young, associate with the liberation of blacks from

---

[3]   *Id.* at 79.

descendants of white settlers."[4] With that authority came the temptation to stifle political challenges, especially as time passed and the founding political generation yielded office to those more and more accustomed to the exercise of governmental power, and its accompanying perquisites.

The passage of time changes the role of constitutional courts as well. The account of the role of constitutional courts has focused initially on weak democracies facing the challenges of either antidemocratic forces that seek to use the openness of democratic politics to undermine democracy itself, or in the difficult process of the transition from autocracy. As democracies mature, however, the challenge shifts from the establishment of an electoral democracy to the maintenance of democratic accountability for the exercise of governmental authority. The example of the Colombian Constitutional Court confronting the threatened permanence in office of President Uribe well illustrates a different stage of judicial superintendence of the frailties of democracy.

An examination of the PRI in Mexico over much of the twentieth century or of the ANC currently in South Africa raises the distinct problem of democracy collapsing onto itself. From the American perspective, it is too easy to assume that the periodic turn to the ballot box is the critical dimension of democratic governance. After all, such periodic elections in which governments are selected by the citizenry are the most visible and recognizable features of democracies. But what confers legitimacy on the outcomes of such elections? Much of this book is about the problem of elections being reduced to a plebiscite on whether one social faction or another will deploy the arsenals of state power against its historic adversaries. Any meaningful commitment to democracy cannot stop at the point where the imagery of elections serves to cover over the absence of a tolerant social order. Winston Churchill may well have been articulating an irreducible bottom line when he quipped about democracy being the worst form of government except all the others that have been tried. But countries with weak democracies in which citizens have real little choice cannot rest satisfied by the claim that matters could be worse.

In reality, democracy is a more complex form of political organization than simply the fact of holding periodic elections for government. Behind the image of the voter at the polls stands a conception of civil liberties that allows for political organization and speech, and a series of institutional actors who provide the structure for political competition, most notably political parties. Both the tolerance for dissenting expression and the organization of

---

[4]   Bongani Madondo, *The Loyal Bunch*, N.Y. Times, May 14, 2014, at A27.

views into political parties exist to guarantee the ability to compete for power. Democracy is, first and foremost, the ability to contest established governmental authority and claim a mandate for a new ruling coalition, one that in turn will be subject to subsequent contestation by new rivals vying for the support of the electorate.

The dominant exposition of democracy as the perpetual competition for state authority comes with the work of Joseph Schumpeter, an Austrian economist who briefly served as minister of finance in Austria before ultimately settling into an academic career at Harvard. In his classic exposition, Schumpeter challenged all claims that democracy turned on either the aggregation of preexisting voter preferences or the participatory deliberation of the populace. Rather, representative democracy necessarily entailed a competition for office by political elites, who would in turn educate, cajole, and entice the citizens to vote for them. As Schumpeter defined the task, "the democratic method is that institutional arrangement for arriving at political decisions in which individuals acquire the power to decide by means of a competitive struggle for the people's vote."[5]

Two elements of democracy stand out in this theory. First, the key to legitimacy is the presence of a competitive struggle for support. It is the fact of competition that assures both accountability of the political elites and legitimacy in the subsequent exercise of state authority. Second, the judgments of the people are not based on a tabulation of their preexisting preferences, but on an evaluative assessment of the performance of those in power. The population emerges from a competitive electoral arena more educated, more engaged, and better able to assess the claim of incumbent officeholders to continue to be in power.

The exercise of the franchise is largely a retrospective assessment of government, rather than a prospective act of molding anticipated acts of state to set preferences among the electorate. That "collectives act almost exclusively by accepting leadership"[6] does not condemn democracy, but gives it vitality. The key to democracy is the retrospective ability of voters to "evict" the incumbents, and it is the ability to "throw the rascals out" that becomes the defining feature distinguishing a vital democracy from an authoritarian state whose governors may originally have been selected through election.[7] Elections in

---

[5] JOSEPH SCHUMPETER, CAPITALISM, SOCIALISM AND DEMOCRACY 241 (Abingdon: Routledge, 2010) (1942).

[6] *Id.* at 242.

[7] The formulation that this is the nub of democracy is from G. BINGHAM POWELL, ELECTIONS AS INSTRUMENTS OF DEMOCRACY 47 (New Haven, CT: Yale University Press, 2000). The underlying view holds that "the primary function of the electorate" in a democracy is not

a democracy are defined by the permanent insecurity of the rulers who may face displacement through competition for votes.

Competitive elections work like merchants at the market trying to procure a sale by explaining what is wrong with the offerings at the next stall. Individuals lack both the time and expertise to assess the attributes of all the products they may need to purchase, just as they lack the ability to master all the diverse undertakings of government. In any market where there is only one seller, the consumer is at great risk. But introduce a second merchant or a full market-place and the consumer is empowered.

I recall walking through the Grand Bazaar in Istanbul some years ago, determined to buy a rug at the stalls, an undertaking reported from the time of the Crusades and likely well before. I knew nothing meaningful about rugs, nor did I have any sense of what the real price of anything might be. A lamb ready for slaughter, no doubt. My sense of unease would likely have led me to abandon the enterprise had there been only one merchant. But there were dozens and over cups of tea, each would explain a little more how to assess the quality of rugs, what kind of price could be arranged. This was no act of educational generosity. They needed me to appreciate why they were offering a superior product to that of their rivals. Of necessity, they had to persuade all potential customers who then, imperfectly to be sure, would leave with a better sense of what separates the goods under consideration. Slowly but surely, the process of competition led them to educate me enough to make a purchase. Undoubtedly, I still paid too much (at some point the time value of additional education began to weigh in the balance) and undoubtedly there were many points I missed. Nonetheless, that rug is still a favorite, not only for its workmanship, but for the primary lesson in how markets incentivize the powerful to convey information to the weak.

Markets also reward repeat play. Were I to return time and again to buy rugs, then I would also have the benefit of testing my knowledge by assessing which of the merchants were more honorable, which really took extra care in the workmanship, and other details that would have allowed the next level of informed interaction. Or, with more time, I might turn to a trusted interme-diary, such as online surveys or *Consumer Reports*, to compare my evaluations with that of other consumers. But even with the limited investment available in a busy life, I could emerge a more informed decision maker from the sim-ple marketplace of exchange.

---

only creating "a government (directly or through an intermediate body)" but also "evicting it." Schumpeter, *supra* note 5, at 272.

Political markets operate in the same fashion. In the political market-place, the coin of the realm is the challenged claim of the incumbent powers to the wisdom of their stewardship. Countering that claim is another political merchant, the opposition, trying to give the electorate sufficient reasons to discharge the incumbents and vote in the opposition. That the information may be conveyed through invective, rhetoric, negative ads is simply a feature of how the consumers process information. Whatever the norms of campaigning, it is only in the competitive crucible of periodic elections that the claims of superior leadership are tested in a meaningful fashion. Further, because political parties are repeat players making claims and promises over the cycles of many elections, the voting public has the advantage of testing the claims over time and relying on these intermediaries to organize the issues in a digestible form. Political competition offers not only an incentive for the leaders to educate the public, but an opportunity for repeat play learning.

Unfortunately, this account of democracy assumes what may well be lacking in many newly constituted democracies: truly competitive elections. The emergence of a single dominant party, such as the PRI in Mexico or the ANC in South Africa, tests the vitality of democracy under the control of a single dominant party. In such circumstances, there are elections that decide who will assume governmental office, and the elections may fairly tabulate the votes cast by the citizenry. Further, such elections may be entirely or relatively free of coercion, chicanery, or efforts to deny the decision-making power to the voters themselves. Yet, such elections in reality may be desultory affairs in which there is only one real contender for office and in which the results are a foregone conclusion. Hollowed out democracy, devoid of electoral competition, introduces its own set of challenges.

South Africa well sets the stage. In the first instance, and focused primarily on the historic *Certification Decision* of 1996, the court enshrined a period of what Bruce Ackerman has termed "constrained democracy." In that role, the court was created as a central institutional guarantor of the orderly transition from apartheid to competitive elections open to all South Africans. As the ANC consolidated power, however, the constitutional court's role changed. The task of securing a peaceful transition ended, and in its place a new challenge was presented by the lack of political challenge to one-party rule. Increasingly, the key issues taken up by the court were presented as questions of broad interpretation of constitutional protections for minority parties or of the independence of prosecutors with authority over official corruption. In each instance, the South African court was called on to assume a role beyond enabling the transition to a multiethnic constitutional democracy.

Instead, the court confronted the effects of the stranglehold on power of the triumphant ANC.

Sujit Choudhry has soberly assessed the prospects for a democracy shorn of real electoral competition. What happens, he inquired, if a democratic system designed for vigorous dissent and electoral challenge is transformed by the will of the people into a one-party bazaar in which "one party enjoys electoral dominance and continues to win free and fair elections that are not tainted by force or fraud?"[8] The heart of the question is whether – in the absence of electoral competition – a tolerant constitutional order can be established and sustained. For Dean Choudhry and for myself, South Africa was long the most intriguing and compelling example of constitutional hope in the transition to democracy. More recently, however, that aspiration is increasingly shifting to concern.

Like many foreign observers, I was drawn to the emerging South African jurisprudence during the halcyon first stage of democratic transition. The promise of a pacted transition under the constitutional oversight of a sophisticated constitutional court made the South African court the most significant of the new judiciaries created by the post-1989 process of democratization. As democracy and majority rule consolidated, most commentary turned to the role of the judiciary in securing social rights under the capacious commands of the new constitution. At the same time, the deference to the policy initiatives of the ANC in the realms of the social and economic began to invite a worrisome deference as well to the consolidation of centralized political power. This prompted cautionary accounts of a different kind of threat to democracy, this time from an excess of majoritarianism. The question is now whether the court will be, and perhaps whether it can be, a restraining influence on excessive consolidation of political power.

This chapter now takes up the difficulties of post-transition constitutional democracy as power consolidates. The immediate question presented after the democratic transition was whether the court would serve as a check, even in the early days of postapartheid governance, against the possibility of one-party domination. As with all broad accounts of judicial relations to politics, the question rarely arises in the abstract. Rather, challenges are more likely presented incrementally in cases that often have more symbolic importance than centrality in the domestic political culture. For every case involving a direct challenge to the outcome of a presidential election there are likely to be dozens that test the rules of selection. In these more incremental challenges are

---

[8] Sujit Choudhry, *"He Had a Mandate": The South African Constitutional Court and the African National Congress in a Dominant Party Democracy*, 2 CONSTIT. CT. REV. 1, 3 (2009).

generally found the decisive confrontations between institutional actors seeking to define the political landscape. Yet it is precisely in these secondary cases that the constitution exercises vigilance over the democratic process and must protect democracy from the threat of being overwhelmed by consolidated political power.

THE PERIL OF CONSTITUTIONAL RETREAT

South Africa presents the next stage of the inquiry. Once more, the initial focus is on a relatively secondary provision of the democratic transition that is best understood as anticipating the risk of overly consolidated political power. All democracies face the risk that incumbent power will be used to diminish electoral accountability. The mechanisms vary widely and run the gamut from suppression of competing groups to subtle manipulation of electoral rules. The problem is most acute, however, where one party dominates electorally and faces no significant check on the exercise of its political will.

From the start of the negotiations leading to the transition to democracy, the prospect of untrammeled political control by the ANC was a source of concern. Most particularly, unrestrained black political power was a distinct threat to white interests, especially their property claims. As Machiavelli warned aspiring rulers in *The Prince*, "above all a prince must abstain from [taking] the property of others; because men sooner forget more easily the death of their father than the loss of their patrimony."[9] While formal constitutional guarantees against expropriation of white landholders were an essential ingredient of the ultimate political compromise, the formal legal protections were deemed insufficient without some political protection as well. To the extent that government power became centralized and unchallenged, so too would the vulnerability of disfavored minorities increase.

The result was an attempt to secure a competitive multiparty electoral arena by protecting all political parties from government domination. The intuition actually comports with the modern political insights of public choice theory. A consolidated majority powerfully threatens all others with the sheer dominance of its political will. But majorities invariably have to satisfy multiple constituencies and, as a result, risk fracturing. By contrast, in coalitional politics, smaller parties tightly organized around intensely held positions or interests will generally get more than their due, especially if they are necessary to

---

[9]   NICCOLÒ MACHIAVELLI, THE PRINCE 97 (George Bull trans., New York: Penguin, 1981) (1532).

forging the governing coalition. One antidote to the inherent risk of majoritarianism in democracies is therefore the preservation of independent political expression of minority interests. The hope is that the need to form coalitions over a series of issues allows for interests to be protected by the "obligation to pull, haul, and trade to find common political ground," as Justice Souter once described interest group politics in the United States.[10]

Under both the 34 Principles and the constitution, the concern for independent political actors took two primary forms. The first was securing representation of minority interests through proportional representation and avoiding the over-rewarding of cohesive majority constituencies that can follow from use of what are termed first-past-the-post, winner-take-all elections. In any single-peaked election, the majority or plurality wins that seat, as with a single congressional district election in the United States. If the majority is spread across the electoral districts, it can win a crushing supermajority, even against a significant minority. Two results from Canadian provincial elections illustrate extreme possible outcomes. In 2000, the Liberal Party won 52 percent of the popular vote in Ontario, but walked away with 100 of the 103 seats in the legislature. Similarly, in Saskatchewan in 2011, the Conservatives garnered 93 percent of the provincial legislative seats with 56 percent of the vote.

Proportional representation guarantees only access to office for the lesser parties, subject to the minimum threshold requirements in place. By themselves, the ability to gain office does not protect the minority parties as such once they are in office. Indeed, as part of the *Certification* decision, the constitutional court had to address various constitutional provisions affecting minority parties to determine whether they were sufficiently protective of the lesser parties in parliament. Once in office, there remains the risk that political side deals will compromise the meaningfulness of minority representation.

As glimpsed in the digest of the court's jurisprudence in Chapter 8, the constitution contained an "anti-defection" principle in addition to the protections of proportional representation, under which a member of parliament would have to resign if he or she attempted to switch parties.[11] In principle, there is a logic to anti-defection provisions in election systems in which voters choose a party slate and then seats are apportioned to reflect the votes each slate received. No individual legislator can claim an individual electoral mandate that could stand independent of the party slate that was the initial electoral vehicle. In the particulars of South Africa, however, the anti-defection

---

[10] *Johnson v. DeGrandy*, 512 U.S. 997, 1020 (1994).
[11] *In re* Certification of the Constitution of the Republic of South Africa, 1996 (4) SALR 744, 829 (CC) (S. Afr.) (considering whether the anti-defection principle was unconstitutional).

provision was something more. The provision was an express subject of negotiations in the transition from apartheid because of the perception from the
beginning of the transition process that the ANC might emerge too powerful. Anti-defection obstacles reflected the fear that the likely parliamentary
majority of the ANC could be used to woo minority legislators and overcon-
centrate political power. South Africa joined other countries that formalized
such anti-defection concerns through legal prohibitions on what is known as
floor-walking or floor-crossing.[12]

But that did not end the debate over floor-crossing in the South African
Parliament. Once in office, and once its political power was consolidated, the
ANC used its legislative supermajority to repeal the anti-defection provision.
Under the new law, defection was permitted so long as the defecting group
constituted at least 10 percent of the party's legislative delegation.[13] This apparent limitation did little to placate critics. In practice, a 10 percent threshold
would pose an insurmountable hurdle to defections from the ANC, given the
large number of legislators that would have to coordinate their floor-crossing.
But the 10 percent threshold would leave defection a matter of individual
choice for any party with fewer than fifteen members of parliament, and allow
the ANC to pick off individual legislators one by one.[14]

The floor-crossing constitutional amendment prompted a second constitutional challenge, this time a claim that the amendment would violate the
principles of party integrity and separation of powers inherent in the entire
constitutional structure.[15] No one would argue that the breakthrough question
in South African democracy would be whether legislators could switch party
affiliation. Nonetheless, the anti-defection question challenged the constitutional court's role in guaranteeing the structures of democracy at an early stage
in the ANC's consolidation of one-party control. The *Certification* decision
had been noteworthy precisely for its attentiveness to the problem of structural
limitations on the exercise of political power, something that was certainly in

---

[12] New Zealand similarly prohibited party switching by members of parliament in the
Electoral (Integrity) Amendment Act, 2001, but the prohibition was statutory and sunsetted
in 2005. *See* Mathew S. R. Palmer, *Using Constitutional Realism to Identify the Complete
Constitution: Lessons from an Unwritten Constitution,* 54 AM. J. COMP. L. 587, 610 & n.64
(2006).

[13] Loss or Retention of Membership of National and Provincial Legislatures Act 22 of 2002 §
23A(2)(a) (S. Afr.), *repealed by* S. AFR. CONST., Amendment Act of 2003.

[14] Charles M. Fombad, *Challenges to Constitutionalism and Constitutional Rights in Africa
and the Enabling Role of Political Parties: Lessons and Perspectives from South Africa,* 55 AM.
J. COMP. L. 1, 32 (2007).

[15] *United Democratic Movement v. The President of the Republic of South Africa,* 2003 (1) SALR
495, 510, 530–31 (CC) (S. Afr.).

the air in the immediate aftermath of the South African negotiations. The question was whether the court would continue to use the democracy-promoting metric as the analytic foundation for evaluating efforts by the ANC to consolidate power in ways that moved beyond the original constitutional design.

Viewed after the end of the struggle to overthrow apartheid, and after the first generation of leadership from the Mandela generation left office, the anti-defection question could have been a watershed moment in the history of South Africa under the ANC. The robust political exchange at the time of transition assumed that there would be black majority rule, that the ANC would emerge as the dominant political actor, and further that constitutional guarantees would serve as a bulwark against the overcentralization of power. The political shakeout of postapartheid politics had not yet occurred, and even the ascension of the ANC into increasing political hegemony was tempered by the calibrated leadership of Nelson Mandela. As the founding generation moved off the historic stage, however, and as less broad-minded functionaries took the reins of power, the heroic ANC was transformed into the self-conscious governing class of an increasingly one-party state, with all the attendant capacity for antidemocratic abuse.[16] South African democracy entered a period of what is termed "dominant party" democracy, a term that connotes the risk of imminent collapse of real democratic contestation.[17] From this perspective, the question of the day is whether the ANC will turn into the PRI, which was similarly the inheritor of a romantic revolutionary struggle, but which then imposed one-party rule to suffocate Mexico for almost the entire twentieth century.[18]

Translated into the context of constitutional adjudication, the anti-defection issue offered the court the ability to reassert the structural underpinnings of the *Certification* decision. The court could have found in the constitution a commitment to democratic pluralism that required institutional protections for minority political parties. Certainly the basic constitutional order could not have tolerated a constitutional amendment allowing minority political parties to be suppressed, to have their media silenced, or to allow the exclusion from office of their candidates. The question was how to assess a dominant party's aim of disrupting the minority's ability to maintain a parliamentary

---

[16] The extent of the threat posed by the ANC's electoral dominance is still uncertain. *See* Roger Southall, *The "Dominant Party Debate" in South Africa*, 39 AFR. SPECTRUM 61, 61 (2005) (arguing that although "the ANC's electoral and political hegemony does carry threats to democracy, the ability of the ANC to extend its dominance is subject to considerable limitations").

[17] The best account of this process in South Africa is found in Choudhry, *supra* note 8.

[18] I am indebted to Pablo de Greiff for the analogy to the PRI.

opposition. It may be that a prohibition on minority parties would be readily struck down, as would the jailing of minority political leaders. But what if the means of disruption were the carrot instead of the stick?

For the constitutional court, the constitutional question became whether the ANC could leverage its parliamentary supermajority into changes in the ground rules of democratic engagement. Unfortunately, the challenge of creating a substantive constitutional doctrine of democratic integrity proved a step too far, at least initially. Instead, the court retreated to a formalist account of the constitution as guaranteeing primarily procedural norms and individual rights and not a broader commitment to democratic engagement. Thus, the court rejected the challenge to the floor-crossing amendment both on the procedural ground that the mechanisms of constitutional amendment had been adhered to, and on the ground that no individual voter could claim a right of faithful representation after the election:

> The rights entrenched under s[ection] 19 [of the constitution] are directed to elections, to voting and to participation in political activities. Between elections, however, voters have no control over the conduct of their representatives. They cannot dictate to them how they must vote in Parliament, nor do they have any legal right to insist that they conduct themselves or refrain from conducting themselves in a particular manner.[19]

Perhaps the court could have drawn deeper structural authority not only from the negotiated history of South Africa's transition from apartheid, but from the text of the South African Constitution. The South African Constitution contains a unique provision guaranteeing some form of effective minority party participation consistent with the aims of democracy. As set out in the constitution, the rules and orders of the National Assembly must provide for "the participation in the proceedings of the Assembly and its committees of minority parties represented in the Assembly, in a manner consistent with democracy."[20] Within the sections establishing the structure of the legislative bodies at the various levels of the federal system, parallel language requires that the rules for the National Assembly, the National Council of Provinces,[21] and the

---

[19] *United Democratic Movement*, 2003 (1) SALR at 516.
[20] S. AFR. CONST., 1996 § 57(2)(b).
[21] *Id.* § 70(2)(c) (stating that the rules and orders of the National Council of Provinces (NCOP) must provide for "the participation in the proceedings of the Council and its committees of minority parties represented in the Council, in a manner consistent with democracy"). In addition, the allocation of delegates to the NCOP "must ensure the participation of minority parties in both the permanent and special delegates' components of the delegation in a manner consistent with democracy." *Id.* § 61(3).

provincial legislatures provide for minority party participation "in a manner consistent with democracy."[22]

The guarantee of minority participation consistent with democracy could have given the court a textual hook for a deeper inquiry into buffers necessary to maintain democratic integrity. The South African provision for rules "consistent with democracy" is reminiscent of the American republican guarantee clause. Each represents a constitutional commitment to a broader vision of a properly functioning political process, yet each is maddeningly vague about what that broader vision must be. The U.S. Supreme Court has relegated the republican guarantee to desuetude, finding its commands to be a political question outside the bounds of judicial enforceability. The South African court took a step in the same direction by placing the functioning of the parliament effectively outside the textual command of democratic consistency.

Instead, the upshot of the anti-defection decision was that the South African court deferred to the ANC to define the rules of governance, and the anti-defection provision was allowed to stand. The decision placed at risk all minority parties and found that to be outside constitutional purview. As it turned out, the anti-defection controversy ended only when the ANC itself decided that it had not yielded the hoped-for political benefits, and in turn decided to abandon it.[23] Paradoxically, the need to woo minority legislators with prized parliamentary positions disrupted the seniority ranks within the ANC and proved a source of dissension rather than consolidation within the ANC's parliamentary ranks.

Nonetheless, the potential raiding of minority parliamentary caucuses could have been the occasion for the articulation of a broader constitutional commitment to competitive democracy. This was the moment when the South African court might well have looked to the basic structures jurisprudence developed by the Supreme Court of India or to some variant of a substantive democratic vision of constitutional governance. A basic-structure approach, modeled on the Indian Supreme Court's doctrine, could potentially have provided the South African Constitutional Court a structural lever for evaluating the effect of single-party political consolidation resulting from the potential for floor-crossing. The textual guarantee of minority party participation, inherited

---

[22] *Id.* § 116(2)(b) (stating that the rules and orders of a provincial legislature must provide for "the participation in the proceedings of the legislature and its committee of minority parties represented in the legislature, in a manner consistent with democracy").

[23] For a fuller account of the efforts of the ANC to secure the right to woo opposing legislators and the role that floor-crossing played in ANC maneuvers at the provincial level, see Choudhry, *supra* note 8.

from the original 34 Principles, could have provided a stronger doctrinal basis for this assertion of a judicial guarantee over the democratic process than that existing in India. Although floor-crossing is no longer part of the political challenge to democracy in South Africa, the consequence of deference to a dominant party remains an act in progress.

ONE-PARTYISM IN PRACTICE

After a period of relative quiescence as to democratic governance, the constitutional court appears to be entering a new period, one whose progress is far from set, but meriting of notice. In South Africa, the floor-crossing case,[24] while interesting jurisprudentially, proved not to be a watershed in terms of ANC consolidation of power; indeed, the entire experiment with trading parliamentary blocs was abandoned once it did not yield the desired results in party-raiding.[25] If one were to judge by the cases that have reached the constitutional court in the past few years, the relation of consolidated one-party rule to the prospects for democracy has fully emerged as the defining constitutional issue in South Africa. Despite the limits of the empirical methodology, it is nonetheless striking that the court has repeatedly confronted attempts by the ANC either as a party or as the government – through the executive – to wall itself off from accountability and institutional constraints on its power.[26]

Political dominance by a single party places inordinate pressure on any top court unable to carve out a space for judicial independence amid political uncertainty. Parties that have indeterminate long-term horizons and must fear losing power to their rivals are less likely to confront the judicial authority head-on. In the United States, for all the concerns over "judicial activism" or judicial overreach, there are few political actors who shy away from seeking judicial relief when their political fortunes are in low ebb. Given the changes

[24] *United Democratic Movement v The President of the Republic of South Africa* (No 2) 2003 1 SA 495 (CC); 2002 10 BCLR 1086 (CC).
[25] *But see* Choudhry, *supra* note 8, at 37–44 (detailing the political backdrop and the court's decision in *United Democratic Movement* and stating that "floor-crossing enhanced the ANC's dominant status at the national level and in all nine provinces").
[26] *See Ramakatsa and Others v. Magashule and Others* 2012 JDR 2203 (CC) (S. Afr.); *Oriani-Ambrosini v. Sisulu* 2012 (6) SA 1 CC (S. Afr.); *Democratic Alliance v. President of the Republic of South Africa and Others* 2013 (1) SA 248 CC (S. Afr.); *National Treasury and Others v. Opposition to Urban Tolling Alliance and Others* 2012 (6) SA 223 CC (S. Afr.); *Premier: Limpopo Province v. Speaker of the Limpopo Provincial Legislature and Others* 2012 (4) SA 58 CC (S. Afr.) (*Limpopo I and II*); *Mazibuko v. Sisulu, Speaker of the Nat'l Assembly* 2013 (6) SA 249 CC (S. Afr.); *Glenister v. President of the Republic of South Africa and Others* 2011 (3) SA 347 CC (S. Afr.).

in fortune over time, no party can ever believe that it will never need recourse to the courts at some point in the future. Hence one source of legitimacy and protection for an independent judiciary.

A confident dominant party, by contrast, may readily jettison the hazy political legitimacy conferred by judicial independence for the hard-and-fast claims to power from leveraging its electoral mandate.[27] Many aspects of the one-party dominance of the ANC have commanded the attention of political scientists.[28] But only recently has attention turned to the jurisprudential implications of one-party rule for constitutional oversight of the democratic process.[29]

In South Africa today there is simply no escaping the fact that the ANC is now the established and dominant political force in the country and, thus far, faces no significant political opposition. As is often the case when electoral competition recedes, the dominant party becomes the center for all political and economic dealings with the government, and an incestuous breed of self-serving politics starts to take hold. In this period of political consolidation, the court is confronting some of the efforts of the ANC government to place itself beyond customary forms of legal and democratic accountability.

The political transcendence of the ANC limits the ability of the political system to correct course or, at the very least, has frustrated many efforts to date. In a case such as *Ramakatsa and Others. v. Magashule and Others*, for example, the court faced an allegation of internal ANC voting irregularities in the selection of delegates to the Free State Provincial Congress of the party.[30]

---

[27] This is the main argument advanced by Sujit Choudhry, who best explores the pressures from electoral mandates on judicial autonomy based on claims to constitutional authority. *See generally* Choudhry, *supra* note 8 ("This reflects the court's inadequate understanding of the concept of a dominant party democracy, its pathologies, the pressure it puts on what is otherwise a formally liberal democratic system because of the lack of alternation of power between political parties, and how this pressure is generating constitutional challenges.").

[28] *See, e.g.*, THE AWKWARD EMBRACE: ONE-PARTY DOMINATION AND DEMOCRACY (Hermann Giliomee & Charles Simkins eds., Amsterdam, The Netherlands: Harwood Academic Publishers, 1999); Roger Southall, *Opposition in South Africa: Issues and Problems*, 8 DEMOCRATIZATION 1 (2001).

[29] *See, e.g.*, Choudhry, *supra* note 8, at 32 (discussing the "characteristic set of pathologies" present in "dominant party [d]emocracies" and the effects of such on the constitutional court); HEINZ KLUG, THE CONSTITUTION OF SOUTH AFRICA: A CONTEXTUAL ANALYSIS (Oxford: Hart, 2010) (focusing on the problem of "unipolar" democracy); THEUNIS ROUX, THE POLITICS OF PRINCIPLE: THE FIRST SOUTH AFRICAN CONSTITUTIONAL COURT, 1995–2005, at 334–64 (New York: Cambridge University Press, 2013); *see also* Choudhry, *supra* note 8, at 34 ("[T]he domination of the ANC means that the Court cannot rely on the risk of losing power as a check on the abuse of public authority.").

[30] *Ramakatsa and Others v. Magashule and Others* 2012 JDR 2203 (CC) (S. Afr.).

At first blush, the issue appeared to be a matter of internal party affairs generally reserved for internal party resolution. In granting relief that included the dissolution of the Provincial Executive Committee, the court had to apply to the ANC party the constitutional guarantee of a right to participate in the activities of a political party as set out in Section 19(1)(b) of the South African Constitution. As a formal matter, *Ramakatsa* required treating the ANC as if it were the state itself and subjecting its internal processes to constitutional scrutiny as if it were the state itself that was charged with improper electoral practices. *Ramakatsa* and a series of other cases from the recent past signal a new constitutional jurisprudence emerging to address the threats to democratic governance, coming not from the history of apartheid but from the now established role of the ANC as the party of state. In the absence of meaningful electoral checks on the consolidation of power a new series of constitutional issues is presented.

Recent cases reveal that the South African Constitutional Court is still confronting the question of how to evolve a structural jurisprudence directed at the concentration of power, and that a more critical jurisprudence is emerging than that which marked earlier watershed cases such as treatment of floor-crossing in *United Democratic Movement*.[31] In *Democratic Alliance*, for example, the court addressed a matter of political appointment to office, what is generally outside the bounds of judicial review in most if not all democratic countries.[32] The particular issue was the appointment of someone with a compromised history on corruption issues to the post of National Director of Public Prosecutions. The appointment was a power grab by the executive, selecting a compromised administrator in order to erode one of the few checking sources on political power. The court lacked any doctrinal mooring for reviewing political appointments and in turn agonized over the appropriate standard of review for what were generally the discretionary actions of the political branches of government. Initially, the court sought guidance from other cases that dealt with the policy prerogatives of the government, such as *Affordable Medicines*, a case that established a wide measure of deference from the court to the policy decisions of the government. In *Affordable Medicines*, the court rejected a constitutional challenge to a government regulatory reform that required all persons selling or dispensing pharmaceuticals to be licensed by the state. In rejecting a claim that this would adversely affect

---

[31] See *United Democratic Movement v. The President of the Republic of South Africa*, 2003 (1) SALR 495, 510, 530–31 (CC) (S. Afr.).

[32] See generally *Democratic Alliance v. President of the Republic of South Africa and Others* 2013 (1) SA 248 CC (S. Afr.).

access to medical services, the court stressed the importance of holding policy decisions to limited judicial oversight. The doctrinal tool of highly deferential judicial oversight served to confine judicial interventions to policy choices that could not be reasonably justified, what is technically understood as a limited rational relations standard of review:

> The rational basis test involves restraint on the part of the Court. It respects the respective roles of the courts and the Legislature. In the exercise of its legislative powers, the Legislature has the widest possible latitude within the limits of the Constitution. In the exercise of their power to review legislation, courts should strive to preserve to the Legislature its rightful role in a democratic society.[33]

In *Democratic Alliance*, the court transported the limited scope of judicial review for government policy initiatives to questions of the organization of governmental power itself. The analogy to discretionary acts of governmental policy portended a limited role for any meaningful judicial oversight of the ANC. To an outside observer, the South African rational relations standard of review seems a poor institutional choice for addressing the distinct problems presented by the entrenchment of a dominant political party. The American version of rational relations review is designed to be deferential to the policy discretions of the modern administrative state. Although there have been recent examples of rationality review being used to evaluate the substantive merits of congressional enactments,[34] the basic role of rational relations review is to provide a wide swath of governmental power without judicial intrusion.[35] Put a different way, rationality review is designed to defer to the outputs of governmental decision making. Questions about the design of governmental institutions, the input side of the ledger, are ill suited to a deferential stance. The justifications for judicial deference to the policy expertise of the political branches in running the government cannot be extended in the same fashion to the design of the government itself.

The South African version of rational relations review seems designed to interdict a different set of concerns over misdirection of the policy aims of the

[33] *Affordable Medicines Trust and Others v Minister of Health and Another* [2005] ZACC 3; 2006 (3) SA 247 (CC); 2005 (6) BCLR 529 (CC) (*Affordable Medicines*) at para. 86.
[34] *See United States v. Windsor*, 133 S. Ct. 2675 (2013) (striking down the Defense of Marriage Act); *Shelby County v. Holder*, 133 S. Ct. 2612 (2013) (striking down the formula for administrative preclearance under Section 4 of the Voting Rights Act).
[35] The rational relation standard of review begins with "a strong presumption of validity" for governmental decision making, including the use of classifications necessary for legislation or regulation. *Heller v. Doe*, 509 U.S. 312, 319 (1993).

national government. Rational relations review is appropriate to detect sectional legislation, rewards to discrete groups of people that are disconnected from the broader aims of governmental policy. Hence, the South African case law imposes a higher burden of justification on legislative decision making than the American version. But the South African court is now pushing further in its scrutiny of the ANC. The justification requirement that is emerging from the court's application of rationality review appears designed to tease out impermissible benefits along classifications that are worrisome precisely because of the consolidated power of the ANC. This could give rise to a more exacting standard of judicial oversight, what in the American context would be termed a strict scrutiny standard of review. According to one well-known formulation of the South African test:

> In regard to mere differentiation the constitutional state is expected to act in a rational manner. It should not regulate in an arbitrary manner or manifest "naked preferences" that serve no legitimate governmental purpose, for that would be inconsistent with the rule of law and the fundamental premises of the constitutional state. The purpose of this aspect of equality is, therefore, to ensure that the state is bound to function in a rational manner. This has been said to promote the need for governmental action to relate to a defensible vision of the public good, as well to enhance the coherence and integrity of legislation.[36]

The court's rational relations jurisprudence distinguished the aims of government from the classifications used to get there, with a much broader swath given to the former than the latter. As Theunis Roux observes, the latitude given to the ANC government to evolve in the policy domain was critical to not forcing the court into a premature, and likely unwise, confrontation with the political branches.[37]

This core division between policy selection and actual implementation continues in recent decisions that have steered clear of involvement in outwardly policy questions involving the conduct of conventional governmental functions, something that would take any court beyond its area of expertise and legitimate authority. For example, in *National Treasury and Others v. Opposition to Urban Tolling Alliance and Others*,[38] a lower court injunction

---

[36] *Prinsloo v. Van der Linde and Another*, 1997 (3) SA 1012 (CC) at para. 25.

[37] Roux, *supra* note 29, at 3–11, 390–91, 392 (noting that the court was successful in "negotiating the law/politics tension to avoid political attack" in part by "defer[ing] to the ANC's primary policy-setting role").

[38] *National Treasury and Others v. Opposition to Urban Tolling Alliance and Others* 2012 (6) SA 223 CC (S. Afr.).

against the system of collecting highway tolls was reversed by the constitutional court, which instructed that courts must be sensitive to, "whether and to which extent the restraining order will probably intrude into the exclusive terrain of another branch of Government. The enquiry must, alongside other relevant harm, have proper regard to what may be called separation of powers harm."[39] As such, injunctive relief on clearly defined executive or legislative authority may be granted "only in the clearest of cases."[40]

As a general matter, this is a wise principle, avoiding a propensity for constitutional courts to get drawn into political skirmishes.[41] The risk of imposing unpopular or elite values on a recalcitrant democracy is always present.[42] The pure Kelsenian model of centralized review[43] of a fully independent constitutional court yields inevitably over time to greater and greater interplay between the political branches and a constitutional court,[44] as questions of appointments and independence become themselves political issues subject to democratic contestation.

It does not follow, however, that courts owe a duty of deference across all political dimensions, even to legitimate constitutional governments. Returning to the distinction between inputs and outputs, it is one thing to defer to the policy outputs of a government that is itself the product of a proper system of electoral choice and accountability. It is another to give deference to the powers that be over the mechanisms of how governments are selected and the powers they should hold while in office. In prior writings, I have looked to the law of corporate governance as clarifying the limits of policy deference. Under the laws of Delaware, the most developed corporate governance code in the United States, the business judgment rule insulates from judicial review

---

[39] *Id.* at para. 47.

[40] *Id.* at para. 65.

[41] *See* Victor Ferreres Comella, *The Consequences of Centralizing Constitutional Review in a Special Court: Some Thoughts on Judicial Activism*, 82 Tex. L. Rev. 1705, 1707–08 (2004).

[42] Ran Hirschl, Towards Juristocracy: The Origins and Consequences of the New Constitutionalism (Cambridge, MA: Harvard University Press, 2005).

[43] Alec Stone Sweet, *Constitutional Courts*, in Oxford Handbook of Comparative Constitutional Law 816 (Oxford, UK: Oxford University Press, 2012). According to Alec Stone Sweet, this comprises four distinct components. First, a constitutional court possesses a monopoly on the power to declare laws constitutional. Second, its jurisdiction is restricted to constitutional questions; it does not have the authority to preside over ordinary litigation. Victor Ferreres Comella refers to this feature of a constitutional court as its *purity*. Third, the constitutional court is formally detached from all other branches of the government. Finally, the constitutional court may review statutes "in the abstract."

[44] Sarah Wright Sheive, *Central and Eastern European Constitutional Courts and the Antimajoritarian Objection to Judicial Review*, 26 Law & Pol'y Int'l Bus. 1201, 1204–08 (1995).

almost all economic decisions of a firm absent fraud or some breach of fiduciary duties. At the same time, there is no such rule of deference given to the decisions of management about the organization or selection of management itself. On this score, courts and regulators must be vigilant lest the insiders insulate themselves from challenge, familiarly known as a lockup.[45]

Applied in the South African context, the question is whether the discrete problems presented by the risk of self-dealing by a dominant party are well addressed within the rational relations framework under the South African version of proportionality analysis.[46] The limitations of not having a robust theory of constitutional protection of democracy against democratic manipulation is perhaps best seen in the two recent court cases having to do with independent prosecutorial or anticorruption authority. Each of these cases addresses the problem of concentrated executive power, a power that is unlikely to be effectively constrained by a legislature controlled by the same dominant party. This is especially true given the unified executive in South Africa, in which the president is both head of state and head of government. Most critically, the South African president is elected by the National Assembly and thus is directly accountable only to the dominant legislative bloc, an unlikely source of strong limitations in the absence of parliamentary contestation.

In *Democratic Alliance*[47] and again in *Glenister*,[48] the issue before the court was first the appointment of the National Director of Public Prosecutions and subsequently the independence of the National Prosecuting Authority (NPA), a specialized prosecutor for political corruption cases. In each case, the court interceded to roll back executive conduct that would have further insulated the government from anticorruption checks on official misconduct. Strikingly, however, in each case the court tried to employ the same restrictive rationality review for the structure of government as it had used for the broader policy objectives that are properly the province of parliament.

---

[45] Samuel Issacharoff & Richard H. Pildes, *Politics as Markets: Partisan Lockups of the Democratic Process*, 50 STAN. L. REV. 643 (1998).

[46] *See First National Bank of SA Ltd t/a Wesbank v. Commissioner for the South African Revenue Services and Another* 2002 (4) SA 768 (CC); *First National Bank of SA Ltd t/a Wesbank v. Minister of Finance* 2002 (4) SA 768 (CC), 2002 (7) BCLR 702 (CC). The constitutional court elaborated the proportionality doctrine in the context of the highly contentious issue of land forfeitures. For a broader account of the role of proportionality in guiding apex courts through fraught confrontations with politically charged cases, see AHARON BARAK, PROPORTIONALITY: CONSTITUTIONAL RIGHTS AND THEIR LIMITATIONS (Cambridge University Press, 2012).

[47] *Democratic Alliance v. President of the Republic of South Africa and Others* 2013 (1) SA 248 CC (S. Afr.).

[48] *Glenister v. President of the Republic of South Africa and Others* 2011 (3) SA 347 CC (S. Afr.).

Democratic Alliance, as discussed, was the court's first tentative engagement with ANC efforts to forestall scrutiny on corruption issues, and the court took small steps toward imposing some form of overall accountability for governmental conduct in the context of the lack of any other institutional or political constraints. In that case, the court found that the president's decision to appoint a tainted candidate in the face of concerns over improprieties in earlier public charges represented a procedural failure to consider prima facie evidence of dishonesty. This was a tentative opening gambit, but it did render the appointment invalid.

Of greater significance is *Glenister*, the more far-reaching and interesting decision in addressing structural alterations by the ANC that threatened to further insulate it from challenge. The factual background was a reform under the National Prosecuting Authority Amendment Act that abolished a critical part of the NPA and placed control of anticorruption prosecutions in the hands of the police, rather than a special prosecuting body. Even as the ANC consolidates power, there remain parts of the government that are relatively independent of immediate ANC control and whose officials have a measure of institutional protection of their independence. This is all the more important in the context of anticorruption prosecutions as charges of cronyism and corruption against the central government abound. The existence of institutional checks on the executive through the NPA, or even the more generalized oversight of all branches through the public prosecutor, remains an important constraint as political competition ebbs in the face of ANC hegemony.[49]

The opinion in *Glenister*, while ruling against the government, shows the ambivalence of the court. The opinion emphasized that the anticorruption unit need not be formally independent, only that it retain "an adequate level of structural and operational autonomy."[50] That, the court found, was also a question of the reasonableness of the decision, and placing the unit within the police force was not per se unreasonable, nor was the decision to disband the Directorate of Special Operations (DSO). Still, the Act was deficient both in failing to provide "secure tenure" for employees of the Directorate of Priority Crime Investigation and in providing for "direct political oversight of the entity's functioning."[51] Previously, senior DSO personnel enjoyed

---

[49] For a discussion of the importance of the public prosecutor being able to shame officials into responsiveness and discharge of their tasks, see STUART WOOLMAN, THE SELFLESS CONSTITUTION: EXPERIMENTALISM AND FLOURISHING AS FOUNDATIONS OF SOUTH AFRICA'S BASIC LAW 246–48 (Cape Town: Juta & Co., 2013).

[50] *Glenister* 2011 (3) SA 347 CC, at para. 162 (S. Afr.).

[51] *Id.* at para. 213.

considerable protection – once appointed, they could be removed only in limited circumstances by the president, who was subject to parliamentary veto.[52] The court argued that the abandonment of the institutional buffer enjoyed by the DSO placed "significant power in the hands of senior political executives" who might "themselves ... be the subject of anti-corruption investigations."[53] This, the court insisted, was "impossible to square with the requirement of independence."[54]

When charged with the source of authority for its holding, the court hesitated. Notably, the court carefully steered clear of the broader principles of democratic governance as the basis for its ruling. Instead the court turned to the relationship between the domestic constitution and international law. Section 39(1)(b) of the constitution requires that courts "consider international law" in interpreting the Bill of Rights.[55] Section 231(2) provides that a ratified international agreement "binds the Republic." Finally, Section 7(2) "implicitly demands" that steps taken to fulfill the state's obligation to promote the Bill of Rights be "reasonable."[56] Reading these provisions together, the court concluded that an anticorruption program could not be constitutionally "reasonable" if it failed to honor South Africa's treaty obligations. South Africa is party to a number of international conventions that require member states to establish anticorruption agencies that are "independent from undue intervention" and political pressure, or at least that was the court's rendition of these accords.[57]

Placing responsibility for its decision on international law is an interesting judicial expedient. It has the effect of avoiding a direct confrontation with the constitutional underpinnings of democratic authority and instead turning attention to the commands of foreign engagements. The court could sidestep any engagement with the hard questions of the one-party weight of the ANC and instead purport to act as the simple messenger of international law. It was the South African government that entered into the international covenants and the court could act as if its hands were tied. Yet the purportedly compelling international commitments are far too abstract to carry the weight of the exact institutional framework for locating government anticorruption officials. To begin with, how anticorruption authority is vested is something that no

[52] *Id.* at paras. 225–26.
[53] *Id.* at para. 232.
[54] *Id.* at para. 236.
[55] *Id.* at para. 192.
[56] *Id.* at para. 194.
[57] *Id.* at paras. 184, 183–86.

doubt varies tremendously within the signatories to an international covenant, to the extent that it is not in fact honored in the breach by most signatories. But again, the court was able to avoid a head-on collision with the power grabs of the ANC.

On the other hand, when Section 8(a) of the Judges' Remuneration and Conditions of Employment Act, which authorized the president to extend the chief justice's term of office beyond the twelve-year constitutionally pre-scribed term, the court did show it had to reach deeper to protect its own insti-tutional integrity from executive overreach. In *Justice Alliance of South Africa v. President of the Republic of South Africa*,[58] the court relied more heavily on first-order principles of controlling concentrated executive power: "The term or extension of the office of the highest judicial officer is a matter of great moment in our constitutional democracy," and by permitting the president to ask the chief justice to stay on for an additional term of years, "the Act threatened judicial independence by implying that the Chief Justice serves at least to some degree at the pleasure of the President, and is thus subject to Executive influence."[59] At least in the context of protecting its own institu-tional independence, the court was willing to invoke first-order considerations of proper democratic governance.

In other cases, the court has come back to the concentration of leg-islative power in the hands of the ANC, the issue that previously came to the fore in *United Democratic Movement*. The most significant of these is *Oriani-Ambrosini, MP v. Maxwell Vuyisile Sisulu, MP & Speaker*,[60] a leg-islative challenge to an Assembly rule that no bill could be brought to the floor without the prior approval of the Speaker. In effect, the new procedure for bringing cases to the floor could eliminate the ability of a minority party even to force debate on an issue that the ANC wished to keep off the polit-ical agenda. The restriction would serve as a legislative parallel to the shut-ting of internal party deliberations presented to the court in *Ramakatsa*. The court struck down the legislative-screening rule based on "the principles of multi-party democracy, representative and participatory democracy, respon-siveness, accountability and openness."[61] While these principles are abstract, the court came to the heart of the matter: Forcing debate "facilitates mean-ingful deliberation on the significance and potential benefits of the proposed legislation" and is "designed to ensure that even those of us who would, given

[58] 2011 (5) SA 388 (CC) (S. Afr.).
[59] *Id.* at paras. 65, 67–68.
[60] *Oriani-Ambrosini v. Sisulu* 2012 (6) SA 1 (CC) (S. Afr.).
[61] *Id.* at para. 46.

a choice, have preferred not to entertain the views of the marginalized or powerless minorities, listen."[62]

Together, these and other cases addressing the concentration of power in
the absence of political challenge appear to be defining a new agenda for the
constitutional court. It is by no means an easy role for a court to engage concentrated political power if for no other reason than the inherent weakness
of the judiciary before the political branches. The Indian court developed its
basic structures jurisprudence in the face of repeated Congress Party attacks
on the judiciary, including using popular antipathy to the Supreme Court as
part of the dominant party's electoral platform. The same political backlash
occurred in Hungary. The Indian court survived and plays an important role
in Indian democracy; the Hungarian Constitutional Court is, by contrast, a
much weakened institution. Already there are ominous signs in South Africa
of political attacks on the constitutional court as an institution, a disturbing
trend no doubt. But the court remains the only significant institution not
under direct ANC control and, for better or worse, that is beginning to define
a significant part of its judicial role.

COURTS IN THE CROSSFIRE

The recent confrontation of the South African court with the ominous des-
potic trends of the ANC raises a further question about the proper judicial
approach to confrontations with the political branches. In repeated engagements with entrenched political power, a confrontational judiciary is at grave
risk of emerging as the loser. While there are certainly occasions of principle, the nature of the cases that come before courts generally have the feel
of incremental alterations of government relations. As with the institutional
placement of the prosecuting agency for public corruption, the lines of judicial principle rarely appear quite so clear-cut.

At the same time, there is a failure to stake a claim of principle when judges
rely on strained procedural rulings or on questionable claims of international
law to mask the nature of the real issues at stake. My late colleague Ronald
Dworkin invoked the concept of "law as integrity" to try to impose upon the
judiciary the obligation to reach for compelling accounts of principle: "Law
as integrity ... requires a judge to test his interpretation of any part of the
great network of political structures and decisions of his community by asking whether it could form part of a coherent theory justifying the network

---

[62] *Id.* at paras. 59, 43.

as a whole."[63] Few courts could, or likely should, seek to achieve this level of principle in the face of unsettled societal commitments to the rule of law. Yet, the flight from principle in the face of consolidating political power appears a path fraught with peril. If judges do not have claim on a broader principle for confronting the political branches, then why should they not stand down in the face of the political will of the majority?

In Colombia, the constitutional court successfully derailed President Uribe's attempt at a third term in office, despite the inability to articulate a well-fashioned constitutional principle in defense of its actions. One must suspect that a court would be unsuccessful if it repeatedly tried to overturn procedurally proper constitutional amendments. That the South African court chooses to engage the ANC's consolidated power through legal incrementalism does not come close to exhausting the range of possible judicial responses.

Another alternative approach to judicial intervention is found in Thailand, in what is probably the most currently unsettled democratic setting outside Ukraine. Trying to give a nutshell account of Thai politics is impossible. For present purposes, the central divide is between the Pheu Thai Party, which at the time of the conflict controlled an absolute majority of the Thai House of Representatives, and the opposition, led by the Democrat Party. The Pheu Thai government was headed by Prime Minister Yingluck Shinawatra, the sister of former prime minister Thaksin Shinawat, who had been forced into exile after being removed by a military coup in 2006 and convicted of corruption in 2008. With the return of civilian rule, the Pheu Thai Party was elected back into power, supported by its associated United Front for Democracy against Dictatorship – together colloquially known as the "Red Shirts."

The Pheu Thai government pursued populist policies that no doubt benefited the Thai poorer classes, particularly the rural poor. The Thaksin government was also widely perceived as deeply corrupt and increasingly autocratic, but an expanding economy and expansive clientelist policies, such as subsidies to rice farmers, built up a loyal constituency outside the more educated, middle-class sectors of Bangkok and the urban parts of the country. Urban uprisings, led by the "Yellow Shirt" opponents of the government, ultimately brought down the Thaksin government and set up the constitutional conflicts that engulfed Thailand in 2013–14. These uprisings possess the "Tahrir Square appeal" of Westernized, educated protesters claiming the public arena with iPhones, Twitter, and all the trappings of modern cosmopolitan engagement. The difficulty remains that while these urban protestors

---

[63] RONALD DWORKIN, LAW'S EMPIRE 245 (Cambridge, MA: Harvard University Press, 1986).

readily capture what may be termed the "CNN moment," they operate at a political and social distance from the poorer and generally more conservative rural mass of the population.

Two legislative initiatives sparked the crisis that consumed Thailand as this book was being completed. First, the Yingluck-dominated House of Representatives, in an odd predawn special session, initially approved and then subsequently passed an amnesty provision that would have cleared Thaksin of his conviction and permitted his return to Thailand, and presumably to political office.[64] Of greater significance was the adoption of a constitutional amendment providing for direct election of the upper chamber of the parliament, the Senate. Prior to the 2006 coup, the entire Senate was elected, but after the return to civilian authority, only half the Senate was elected from regional constituencies, with the remainder filled by a complicated form of appointment by a select committee outside direct governmental control. As a result, the Senate remained outside the control of the electorally hegemonic Pheu Thai Party even as that party built up its base of support.

The opposition sought to invalidate the Senate-selection constitutional amendment before the constitutional court. Unlike the third term for President Uribe, the proposed constitutional change did not trigger any immediate democratic objection at the level of general principle. Other than the American Tea Party's curious obsession with the direct election of senators as a result of the Seventeenth Amendment to the U.S. Constitution,[65] it is hard to think of any mass democratic movement that has mobilized in support of an appointed branch of the national legislature. At the same time, the move to a directly elected senate would remove an important institutional bar to consolidated rule of the sort that had prompted earlier street riots and military intervention. The question was whether any constitutional principle could really prevent a procedurally proper constitutional amendment that did not have any of the obvious hallmarks of being a fundamental attack on the constitutional order.

In a landmark opinion, the Thai Constitutional Court nonetheless struck down the proposed constitutional amendment. Uniquely among the constitutional courts that have had to engage the issue of democratic majoritarian

[64] Thomas Fuller, *Amnesty Bill that Would Clear Ousted Premier Stirs Thai Anger*, N.Y. TIMES, (Nov. 3, 2013) http://www.nytimes.com/2013/11/04/world/asia/amnesty-bill-stirs-opposition-in-thailand.html (describing the backlash against the amnesty bill).

[65] U.S. CONST. amend. XVII; *see also* Keith Johnson, *Anti-Washington Ire Kindles Old Debate*, WALL ST. J. (Nov. 1, 2010, 12:01 AM), http://online.wsj.com/news/articles/SB10001424052702304879604575582192395853212 (describing the resurgence of the idea of repealing the Seventeenth Amendment due to the rise of the Tea Party).

excess, the court spoke openly about the need for vigilance against the risk of what it termed a "majority dictatorship":

> There must be measures to prevent ones who gain the position to exercise people's sovereign power not to arbitrarily abuse the power for personal or for the particular group's benefits, by holding the principles of division of sovereign power.... If any party is left with absolute authority without being checked and counterbalanced, it would be highly tempted to cause damages and lead the country to ruin because of a stray indulgence of the state power holder.[66]

While the Thai decision is the most elaborately reasoned engagement with the problem of dominant party democracy, it also exposes the vulnerable nature of a judiciary getting too close to the live wire of electoral politics. The court clearly aligned itself with one faction of Thai society, moving closer to the argument of Ran Hirschl that a cosmopolitan "juristocracy" assumed the power of constitutional review to hold at bay the more conservative impulses of the poorer and less worldly sectors of the society.[67] The Thai setting does not have the central religious narrative that was central in Hirschl's narrative, but it shares the fundamental conflict of more traditional and more cosmopolitan world outlooks.

Whatever the gain in judicial reasoning, the Thai court's intervention did little to alleviate the building conflict. Within two months of the court's ruling, street riots consumed Bangkok and the government declared a sixty-day state of emergency. Protesters then turned their wrath on the next scheduled elections and called on their followers not only to refuse to participate, but also to block the electoral process. In the final judicial pieces of the puzzle, the constitutional court invalidated the electoral results, further inflaming the political unrest. The court then ordered the prime minister removed from office altogether in an act that seemed a prelude to civil war. A military seizure of power then followed in May 2014, resulting in the suspension from office of all the elected branches, hardly a testament to any democratic aspirations.

The three national settings under review illustrate the problem rather than prescribe the remedy. The Colombian, South African, and Thai courts differed both in terms of how confrontational to be with regard to entrenched political authority, and in terms of how expansive to be in providing a rationale for judicial engagement as a matter of higher-level principle. The results are not yet clear in any of the three, but to the extent that Thailand appears

---

[66] My thanks to Siranya Rhuvattana for translating the Constitutional Court's decision.

[67] Hirschl, *supra* note 42, at 11–12.

poised for civil war, or that South Africa is at risk of descent into the excesses associated with strong-arm rule, it is unlikely that any of this has much to do with the tactical decisions made by courts along the way. Perhaps strong judicial opposition, as in Ukraine during the Orange Revolution, can galvanize or embolden political oppositions. But, as recent events in Ukraine show, there is little that can be guaranteed in fragile democracies still struggling to develop the institutional predicates for competitive elections. Constitutional courts may be best positioned to incubate nascent or fragile democracies; ultimately they cannot substitute for the full array of institutional commitments to democratic governance.

12

Constitutionalism in the Time of
Fragile Democracies

History rewards cautious judgments. Had this book been written a half-century earlier, at the height of the postwar consociationalist experiments, a certain triumphalism would no doubt have accompanied the description of negotiated power sharing among rival ethnic or religious groups. That enthusiasm would no doubt have waned as civil wars ravaged Cyprus, Sri Lanka, Ivory Coast, and other bastions of negotiated accommodation of coordinated political solutions.

Twenty-five years have now passed since the fall of the Berlin Wall and a renewed period of democratic euphoria. The historic end of the Cold War brought with it a heralding that the epochal wars of the twentieth century had at last been concluded. Democracy was triumphant. Its ideological challengers of fascism and communism were defeated. The market was ascendant in China and the few outliers in North Korea or Cuba were simply rogue states that were ill suited to resist the demands of their populations for freedom and improved material standards of living.

With the fall of the Soviet Union, the proxy wars of the great powers ended, leaving the client states of East and West vulnerable to popular demands for liberty and democratic rule. In short order, apartheid fell in South Africa, democracy took root in the Pacific Rim, and Mexico recovered competitive elections. Entire regions were transformed, as with the stabilization of civilian rule in Latin America. Even in sub-Saharan Africa, long the bastion of strongman rule, there was actual rotation in office for the first time in the postcolonial period.

History was on the march, and this was a glorious Whiggish account, with perhaps a touch of Dr. Pangloss thrown in for good measure. The Hegelian unfolding of events had revealed the "end of history," as proclaimed by Francis Fukuyama: "What we may be witnessing is not just the end of the Cold War, or the passing of a particular period of post-war history, but the end of history as such: that is, the end point of mankind's ideological evolution and the universalization of Western liberal democracy as the final form of human government."[1]

Perhaps the rapid collapse of the Soviet Union invited such broad claims. The new democratic period seemed to spark popular upheavals in the name of democracy and its associated liberties. The Rose Revolution in Georgia led to the Orange Revolution in Ukraine, which led to the Cedar Revolution in Lebanon, and ultimately to the most improbable democratic gain, the Arab Spring itself. Surely, China was next.

What a heady time it was. Democracy was both inevitable and easy. Just hold elections for head of state – the visible touchstone for any regime claiming democratic legitimacy – and, poof, democracy ensues. Once elections were held, democracy was secure. Every post-Soviet country held at least one election, as did Afghanistan and Iraq after foreign intervention. And upon election of a government, mission accomplished.

Certainly there were cautionary signals along the way. Resurgent Islamic parties in the Middle East and Turkey presented uncertain commitments to democracy, even as they enjoyed the benefits of electoral politics to compete for state power. Terrorism complicated the picture as the demands for national security compromised the liberal openness associated with the robust give-and-take of electoral politics. Economic crises provoked an anti-liberalization backlash in Latin America even before the Eurocrisis and the global economic downturn of the post-2008 period. But these could all be considered exogenous to democracy itself. Religious identity, even religiously motivated terrorism, and perhaps even poorly managed fiscal policy, all were matters of statecraft to be managed by democratic governments. Surely, they could not – or must not – call into question the fundamentals of the great *fin-de-siècle* democratic legacy.

Would that it were so. A quarter-century retrospective confirms what should have been apparent all along. Democracy is a complicated interaction between popular sovereignty, political competition, stable institutions of state, vibrant organs of civil society, meaningful political intermediaries, and a commitment to the idea that the losers of today have a credible chance to reorganize and perhaps emerge as the winners of tomorrow. Elections are the end product of democratic selection, but not the definition of democracy as such. The great challenge, particularly for the constitutional courts that are the focus here, was how to ensure that the first election was not the last election.

---

[1] Francis Fukuyama, *The End of History?*, NAT'L INTEREST, Summer 1989, at 4.

In countries emerging from authoritarian rule or violent conflict, the multiple institutional pillars of democracy are slow to emerge and invariably are unlikely to appear all in tandem. Indeed, in the disorganization that followed the sudden collapse of the Soviet Union, to take but one example, the easiest component to organize was formal elections. Foreign experts, like the Venice Commission of the Council of Europe, could provide oversight and a reasonable integrity to the election itself. The most difficult to realize, and likely the key to any long-term democratic stability, would be the proven ability to have rotation in office. No new democracy could possibly have a track record of peaceful surrender of power to an electoral challenger. Yet, as discussed throughout this book, that is what wise observers, such as Adam Pzreworski and his colleagues, have come to define as an operational core of genuine democratic governance.

Too often in retrospect, early elections appear as a contest not over democratic governance but over which political or ethnic faction would seize the instrumentalities of the state. In the worst cases, such as the former Soviet republics of Central Asia, the elections were simply a prelude to the consolidation of new strong-armed power. In some instances, as in Belarus, a weak electoral system was overtaken by the former Communist Party, ill disguised in its resumption of power. It is hard to credit that any real democratic moment occurred in these countries, simply an interregnum in a cycle of autocratic rule.

Of more interest are the countries that emerged from the post-1989 period with incomplete institutions of democratic transition. Some of these, like Poland and the Czech Republic, are the success stories of Europe. Their counterparts are found in South Korea, in Mexico, in Colombia, in countries that struggle through the creation of a responsible political system, often in the face of economic dislocations and severe challenges from sinister forces such as narcoterrorism.

In yet another paradox of history, many of these post-Soviet-era democracies, Samuel Huntington's famous Third Wave of democratic surges, face an unexpected threat. The threat is not the stifling of democracy under the autocratic ancien régime, but the excess of democracy. Better put, the risk is the excessive consolidation of democratic power by an increasingly dominant party. The obstacle to electoral competition and rotation in office is not the fraud or violence associated with tyrannical regimes, but the suffocating control by the party that manages to consolidate its political apparatus in office. Worse yet, these parties claim the mantle of democratic legitimacy from the fact of electoral success.

Democracy without electoral uncertainty is precarious. Wise constitutional designers have built on Madison's basic insight that institutional ambition must be made to counter other ambition. Excessive consolidation of power is impeded by periodic elections, mixed constituencies for upper and lower chambers of bicameral legislatures, and federalist constraints on centralized command. Each introduces an entry point for the political opposition to mobilize and to resist an all-or-nothing claim to authority by a numerical majority at any one point in time. By contrast, authoritarian rule is often accompanied by plebiscitary approbation, as in Germany and Italy in the 1920s and 1930s, or in the Crimea in 2014. The plebiscitary model short-circuits any role for political parties, legislative processes, or intermediary organizations. In the strong-party state, the plebiscite is the acme of form over substance: a formal democratic choice without any meaningful contestation for power.

Elections under a completely controlling party, even if untainted by rampant fraud or violence, are in substance no different from the plebiscite. With only a strong party seeking election to the formal offices of the executive and legislative branches, the elections are really nothing more than an up or down vote without a genuine alternative. In the absence of meaningful forms of electoral competition, the single-party elections are, in effect, plebiscites on complete control by one institutional actor.

There are exceptional moments when even just the formalities of elections do matter. In Sri Lanka, for example, an increasingly dominant United People's Freedom Alliance attempted to secure a third term for President Mahinda Rajapaksa by holding early elections against a largely unformed opposition. The history looks much like Colombia's, as Rajapaksa had tremendous popular appeal after militarily defeating the Tamil Liberation Tigers insurgency. Tranquility led to the consolidation of power, which led to a constitutional amendment allowing a third term in office. Yet, unlike Colombia, Rajapaksa was defeated at the polls in early 2015, a reminder that there is a democratic reservoir of popular authority that emerges from the electoral process itself.

For every Sri Lankan account, however, there are too many instances of elections with little prospect of constraining political power. The post-1989 democracies introduced a distinct source of constitutional authority that could withstand, in many instances, the initial concentration of political authority. A defining feature of all the new democracies is the creation of a strong form of constitutional court review of the political process. Where political competition lags or fails, these courts are often the only institutional actor capable of challenging an excessive consolidation of power. But constitutional courts facing consolidated political power are themselves terribly handicapped by their absence of independent levers of power. Once power is truly consolidated, courts are capable of being bypassed as irrelevant institutions, as in Russia today, or subject to replacement of their leading jurists, as in Hungary – or perhaps simply disregarded.

Russia provides an important cautionary note on the limited prospects for the judiciary to prevail in a direct conflict with the executive. From the end of the old Soviet hierarchy in 1989 until 1993, the Russian Constitutional Court was one of the striking examples of the rise of a judicial power in the post-Soviet era. The court handed down a number of significant constitutional decisions on such high-profile matters as the dissolution of the former Communist Party and the terms for the reconstitution of local political parties, including those representing former Communist policies.[2] In 1993, the court staked itself on a direct confrontation with President Boris Yeltsin over presidential decrees suspending parliament. In a dramatic series of events, the court ultimately ruled that not only had Yeltsin exceeded his powers, but that he was subject to impeachment for his improper exercise of presidential authority. In response, Yeltsin claimed the authority of a referendum supporting his reforms and dissolved not only parliament but the court as well. By the end of 1993, Russia had a new constitution and no constitutional court. A constitutional court was reestablished only in 1995, and remained a diminished institution, now even further subordinated under President Vladimir Putin.

As the Russian example shows, courts may be forced to decide how to confront consolidated political power, particularly where they are left as the only institutional buffer against complete one-party hegemony. There is a strong element of judicial self-interest at stake, as it is only in the context of contested political power that courts can play a dependable role in ensuring the constitutional boundaries of democracy. Courts are at their strongest when there is uncertainty among rivals for political power, and at their most precarious when all the other institutional levers are under the unitary control of a single dominant party. Yet it may be necessary for courts to intervene precisely when institutional checks on incumbent governmental power are limited, and when political competition is weak or nonexistent.

If there are risks associated with both excessive confrontation and passive inaction, how are courts to act during periods of brewing constitutional confrontations? This difficult question necessarily leads to an inquiry into the means by which courts should respond when facing serious challenges to democratic contestation coming from an elected dominant party. In such

[2] See Yuri Feofanov, *The Establishment of the Constitutional Court in Russia and the Communist Party Case*, 19 REV. CENT. & E.EUR. L. 623 (1993).

circumstances, courts are unlikely to have secure support from strong institutional actors that can rival the dominant party. The problem is in creating a basis for judicial challenge to legislative or constitutional initiatives that have the form of democratic legitimacy but threaten the capacity for democratic contestation; in shorthand form, this is the problem of the democratic threat to democratic transitions.

To the extent that courts highlight the central threat to democracy posed by concentrated power, they can typically invoke the highest aspirations of the constitutional order. But such appeals to first-order principles put them on a stronger collision course with the governing authorities. Paradoxically, the more certain the need to confront excesses of political power, the more isolated the courts will be. Judicial intervention is most manifestly needed when there are no other political institutions capable of confronting consolidated power. But the absence of allies should prompt caution in a judiciary that cannot easily withstand the powers of mobilization of the political branches. On the other hand, to the extent that courts evade the central questions of constitutional limits on power, they risk rendering trivial judgments that may be circumvented as lacking any sustaining legitimacy. The prudent course of nonconfrontation may simply postpone the inevitable reckoning with excess power, likely at a time when dominant party authority is even more entrenched.

These are the questions previously addressed in discussing the doctrinal efforts of the Colombian and South African courts, and contrasting them with the basic structures jurisprudence of the Indian Supreme Court. We can further illuminate the risks associated with first-order confrontations with political authority by looking to the extreme intervention of the Thai Constitutional Court and how that risks bringing courts directly into the political fray. While each of the judicial responses is likely the product of nuanced local circumstances, it is still possible to examine the judicial interventions as products of a similar reaction to the failure of other institutional checks on single-party dominance. It would be fanciful to claim that there is a single judicial response that must be taken, or even that is more likely to work in any given national arena. But the question of how to respond to dominant power is becoming a defining issue for courts in the period after the initial democratic transition.

In previous chapters, much of the focus has been on the ability of constitutional courts to develop a jurisprudence that matches the democracy-reinforcing role that they must play. Inescapably, however, the need for the judiciary to police close to the core of the democratic process risks compromising any claim to institutional independence. Constitutional courts in South Africa or Colombia or Thailand, or the Supreme Court in India, walk a necessarily fine line in trying to match a doctrinal justification for their interventions into the political process with attentiveness to the consequences of interceding too directly in politics.

The potential political consequences are twofold. Judicial intervention may prompt a premature confrontation with the consolidated power of a dominant party regime. Judicial intervention is most likely successful in a climate of political uncertainty where rival political actors may buttress the rulings of a constitutional court. A fraught political rivalry as in Ukraine in 1994 provides a good example for a court ruling that is effective and enforceable precisely because there is not a single, unassailable source of political power. Second, direct confrontation with the ruling authorities will necessarily be high profile and may thrust the courts into the role of partisan actors.

While the causal relations are complicated, the developments in Thailand raise a serious concern about the ability of courts to survive as independent institutions. There are obvious threats when a dominant political figure, such as a President Yeltsin or a President Putin in Russia, forces a court into submission by sheer force or political power. But a court that engages too directly in the exercise of governmental power also risks getting drawn into the political battlefield far too directly. Thailand may be a paradigm of a highly principled form of judicial decision making being deployed in the service of suspect nonjudicial aims. Whatever the principles invoked by the Thai court, ultimately its intervention looks like the prelude to the seizure of power by the Yingluck regime's opponents.

COURTS IN THE CROSSFIRE

The constitutions of the late twentieth century institutionalized an aggressive power of judicial review as a constitutional check on the political branches. Almost invariably, these constitutions give express textual protection to democratic processes and to the institutions of democratic politics, first and foremost political parties. Further, these constitutions frequently impart to the judiciary a direct administrative role in ensuring the integrity of the electoral process, even apart from controversies presenting themselves in the form of litigation.

Purely as a matter of self-interest, courts should seek to promote political balance and electoral contestation as giving more space to judicial authority. Uncertainty about who the officeholders of tomorrow might be provides a powerful incentive to all political actors to have a judicial intermediary to hedge the downside potential of a lost election.[3] Yet all this leaves open the question about how courts are supposed to act in furtherance of that function. Most specifically, and at the most basic level, how confrontational can or should constitutional courts be in challenging the hegemonic aspirations of a dominant political party?

Much of the scholarship dealing with the role of courts in the post-1989 period has addressed the establishment of a rule of law in the early stages of democratic transition. This makes sense because it was in the first opinions of the South African Constitutional Court,[4] or the far-reaching efforts of the Hungarian Constitutional Court,[5] or the early confrontations with strong-armed efforts to defeat democracy that the new era of strong court constitutionalism was most fully and most proudly on display. Key to the transitional period was the maintenance of democratic rule in order to stabilize civilian authority against efforts to restore the autocratic rule of the past or simply to overthrow weak democratic regimes. Issues of human rights and minority protection necessarily loomed large, as did the protection of the separate institutions of government.

Shift the time horizon, however, and courts still confront issues of stabilization. Now a new source of concern emerges not so much from the past as from the present. Courts are in a more precarious situation because their claim to authority is not the importance of constitutional democracy against vestiges of an autocratic past, but of a superior set of constitutional values against democratic claims to power. Courts are not simply a central part of the transition to democracy, but are the enforcers of limits on majoritarian prerogatives, of what in contemporary European debates is referred to as "constrained democracy."[6] The difficulty inheres in that these cases pit the branch with the

---

[3]   *See* Tom Ginsburg, Judicial Review in New Democracies: Constitutional Courts in Asian Cases 30–31 (New York: Cambridge University Press, 2003) (arguing for an insurance model of constitutional courts); Jodi Finkel, *Judicial Reform as Insurance Policy: Mexico in the 1990s*, 47 Latin Am. Pol. & Soc'y 87, 88 (2005) (making a similar argument about PRI's willingness to empower courts as it confronted the prospect of removal from office).

[4]   *See generally* Theunis Roux, The Politics of Principle: The First South African Constitutional Court, 1995–2005 (New York: Cambridge University Press, 2013) (exploring the context and decisions of the first South African Constitutional Court).

[5]   *See* Kim Lane Scheppelle, *Guardians of the Constitution: Constitutional Court Presidents and the Struggle for the Rule of Law in Post-Soviet Europe*, 154 U. Penn L. Rev. 1757, 1773–90 (2006) (discussing the achievements of the first president of the Hungarian Constitutional Court).

[6]   Jan Werner-Müller, *Beyond Militant Democracy?*, 73 New Left Rev. 39, 44 (2012) (speaking of the "post-war European understanding of constrained democracies"); *see also* Jürgen Habermas, *Constitutional Democracy: A Paradoxical Union of Contradictory Principles?*, 29

least democratic authority against the popularly elected political branches, generally over matters within the confines of formal legality.

Alexander Hamilton warned of the limits of judicial power, possessed as it was with neither the purse nor the sword.[7] In repeated confrontations with entrenched political power, a confrontational judiciary is at grave risk of being the loser. While there are certainly occasions of principle, the cases that come before courts generally have the feel of incremental alterations of government relations. As with the institutional placement of the prosecuting agency for public corruption, the lines of judicial principle rarely appear quite so clear-cut.

UNCERTAIN PROSPECTS

An old saw has it that two economists were stranded on a remote island lacking in food. To their amazement, a can of food washes up on the shore. Lacking any kind of implement to open it, one posits, "assume a can opener ...".

Unfortunately, much of the advice given to embattled democracy takes the form of the economists' assumptions. It is one thing to posit the importance of civil society, the autonomy of political parties, the liberties of press and speech, and the commitment to rotation in office following contested elections. It is quite another thing to create institutions capable of preserving a democratic political space when the associated commitments to liberty and political competition have not taken hold. One does not last long in post-authoritarian or post-conflict environments by invoking the economist's hypothetical, "assume a properly functioning democracy ...".

Ultimately, the question presented is one of institutional design. It is not a question of the optimal arrangement for all democratic societies at all times, but a matter of survival for democracies confronting the task of stabilizing contested claims to power. Recall that most of these democracies are created in countries that fail John Stuart Mill's admonition that democracy must presuppose a common language and culture. To the contrary, democracy in the modern era does not follow from the creation of common national enterprise, but often is the effort to establish what would more properly be the preconditions for democratic governance.

POL. THEORY 766 (2001). For a broader application of the importance of constraints on democratic prerogatives, see DARON ACEMOGLU & JAMES A. ROBINSON, ECONOMIC ORIGINS OF DICTATORSHIP AND DEMOCRACY 33–34 (New York: Cambridge University Press, 2006).

7   THE FEDERALIST No. 78, at 465 (Alexander Hamilton) (Clinton Rossiter ed., New York: The New American Library, 1961).

The new and weak democracies of the late twentieth century turned to a new institutional design to shore up their vulnerable rule. A quarter century after the new wave of democracies hit the world stage, the historical account remains incomplete. In some areas, such as the former Soviet republics of Central Asia, democracy had little traction and the attempts ceded to authoritarian rule relatively quickly. In other parts, such as Ukraine and even Russia itself, the history was more contested, even if the prospects look poor.

Even so, there remain more people living under some form of democratic rule than a quarter century ago, and certainly more than at any time before that. Contested elections for power are found in previously unwelcoming places, including Africa, Central America, and the Pacific Rim. Characteristically these are countries without strong civil society institutions, without a developed sense of national solidarity, and without a tradition of core liberties of speech or association. These were hardly the optimal conditions for democracy to blossom.

Not surprisingly, the historical ledger reveals mixed results. Whether courts can ultimately stabilize democratic governance in fragile democracies has yet to be determined. The key role assigned to a new institutional actor, the constitutional court, is one of the signal innovations of the post-1989 wave of new democracies. While the final accounting is yet to be written, the lesson thus far is that entrusting these courts with stewardship over the democratic enterprise was certainly a valiant experiment.

Epilogue: Democratic Objectives

Across many national settings, the recent history of constitutional courts shows the need for these courts to handle politically freighted issues on which democracy depends, and the surprising willingness of diverse political systems to accept court intervention. Particularly in the case of newly minted apex constitutional courts, the customary concern in the United States with the countermajoritarian difficulty should not and does not detain these courts. These courts were created for the express purpose of checking legislation against a constricting constitutional template.

In concluding this book, it is important not to lose sight of the overriding objective. The goal of constitutional review is not so much jurisprudential as the enabling of democratic self-governance. Constitutional judicial review is a way to keep the politically powerful from derailing the experiment in democracy. As expressed by my colleague Stephen Holmes in an early assessment of democratic transitions after the fall of the Soviet Union, democracies cannot function if the core objectives of the polity are not entrenched beyond immediate political challenge. This is the constraining role of the constitutional compact. Such constitutional constraints are "enabling" in the sense that public confidence against tyranny allows positive authority to be vested in government institutions because they are less likely to be captured for illegitimate ends.[1] But like all institutional arrangements, constitutional limits are imperfect. A constraint is not an absolute prohibition, and risks remain.

Democracies may succumb to passion, to the momentary whims and desires of majorities, to forces not readily controlled within the normal majoritarian processes of governance. Understanding the frailties of democratic governance goes back to the remarkable accounts of Thucydides regarding

---

[1] STEPHEN HOLMES, PASSIONS AND CONSTRAINTS: ON THE THEORY OF LIBERAL DEMOCRACY 6–8 (Chicago, IL: University of Chicago Press, 1995).

the inability of classical Athens to resist popular demands for ill-fated military adventures, including the doomed attack on Sicily.[2] Modern constitutional scholarship has picked up the theme well formulated by John Hart Ely as a matter of institutional distrust.[3] The role of constitutionalism is to provide security against downside risk if state power fails to conform to democratic expectations.[4] As expressed by Adrien Vermeule,

> [C]onstitutional rules should above all entrench precautions against the risks that official action will result in dictatorship or tyranny, corruption and official self-dealing, violations of the rights of minorities, or other political harms of equivalent severity. On this view, constitutional rulemakers and citizens design and manage political institutions with a view to warding off the worst case.[5]

Constitutionalism is a safeguard for democracies, but it is not a substitute for democracy as such. We may conclude by asking how courts should navigate the difficult boundaries between democratic choice and constitutional limits. Where courts review the exclusion of extreme views from the political arena, there is necessarily a diminution of democratic choice. That tension is even more pronounced when the subject of judicial vigilance is the strong, often overwhelming choice of the voting public. Courts are unlikely to find a fixed polestar in either established jurisprudence or in political theory to guide them through these difficult decisions. Yet the creation of strong constitutional courts in emerging democracies and the corresponding expansion of judicial oversight by established supreme courts is an indication that these courts are expected to play a more direct role in superintending the institutions of democracy and, particularly, in defining the limits of democratic decision making.

The ability of constitutional courts to frustrate democratic preferences gives rise to a more fundamental challenge than the generic anti-majoritarian concern identified by Alexander Bickel. As most forcefully articulated by Ran Hirschl in his 2004 book *Toward Juristocracy*,[6] these new courts draw on a set of elite values that are framed in the language of constitutionalism as against the presumably baser impulses of the broad masses. Constitutional courts

[2] THUCYDIDES, HISTORY OF THE PELOPONNESIAN WAR (Rex Warner trans., New York: Penguin Books, 1972).
[3] JOHN HART ELY, DEMOCRACY AND DISTRUST: A THEORY OF JUDICIAL REVIEW (Cambridge, MA: Harvard University Press, 1980).
[4] JON ELSTER, SECURITIES AGAINST MISRULE (New York: Cambridge University Press, 2013).
[5] ADRIAN VERMEULE, THE CONSTITUTION OF RISK 11 (Oxford: Oxford University Press, 2014).
[6] RAN HIRSCHL, TOWARD JURISTOCRACY: THE ORIGINS AND CONSEQUENCES OF THE NEW CONSTITUTIONALISM (Cambridge, MA: Harvard University Press, 2004).

frequently speak in the name of universal values and cite each other as authority for their oversight of domestic democracy. For Hirschl, this is an invitation to the secular as opposed to the religious and oftentimes sectarian will of the masses, it is pro-market rather than populist, and it defies the revealed preferences of the voting majority.

Turkey is a good example of the clash for much of the twentieth century between a Kemalist constitution that sought to impose Western, secular values, and an increasingly religious population that wanted a greater role for Islam in public life. Yet the secular elite versus religious masses division is too schematic to capture the limitations on a third term for President Uribe in Colombia, or the efforts to prevent electoral appeals to religious incitement of Hindu versus Muslim in India, or the limits on accountability for the increasingly corrupt and autocratic tendencies in the ANC in South Africa. In each case, the apex courts were protecting democracy from a structural frailty internal to the country itself, and turning on a complex set of historical considerations that defy easy characterization as cosmopolitan elites versus religious masses.

There is no escaping the inherent conflicts in courts trying to enforce the sober reflection of long-term constitutional commitments as against the momentary give-and-take of democratic politics. By their nature, constitutional courts assume an oversight role with regard to the political process because, typically, they have no jurisdiction to consider the operation of ordinary legislation.[7] The need to invoke democratic authority against the democratic processes requires delicacy in application and a guiding set of principles in the supervening courts.

So long as democratic political institutions retain their flexibility to respond to internal domestic pressures, courts are invariably hard-pressed to assess the desirability of any particular accommodation. The natural inclination is to move to higher levels of principle, often found in the form of categorical rights claims, and to apply those in rather formalistic fashion. To give just one example, the German Constitutional Court found itself perilously close to upholding a claim that the Maastricht treaty somehow violated individual voting rights in Germany.[8] It is hard to imagine a more difficult political

---

[7] For a critical assessment of the tendency to turn quickly to constitutional principle by specialized constitutional courts, see Victor Ferreres Comella, *The Consequences of Centralizing Judicial Review in a Special Court: Some Thoughts on Judicial Activism*, 82 TEX. L. REV. 1705, 1730 (2004) ("[A] constitutional court is not likely to earn its own space in the institutional system if it regularly upholds the statutes that are challenged before it.").

[8] *Maastricht Treaty Case*, Bundesverfassungsgericht [BVerfG] [Federal Constitutional Court] Oct. 12, 1993, 89 Entscheidungen des Bundesverfassungsgerichts [BVerfGE] 155 (F.R.G.), *translated in* DONALD P. Kommers & Russell A. MILLER, THE CONSTITUTIONAL JURISPRUDENCE

decision than to cede some of the historic badges of sovereignty by entering a Europe-wide political and monetary union. Whatever the arguments
on behalf of European integration – and there are many – it would be sheer
folly to view such a historic move through the distorting prism of individual
voting rights.

Of necessity, many claims of democratic engagement are presented, properly, as matters of fundamental rights. The ability to participate regardless of
race or gender or ethnicity is the most obvious. These claims are almost invariably addressed by reference to higher authority at the national level or even
at the supranational level. But it is important not to confuse these claims with
those that address the structure of governance. The former are framed primarily in terms of the relation of individual citizens to the state, whereas the latter
are concerned with the structure of governmental power. Drawing this distinction should serve as a caution against the easy adoption of a collectivizing
template under the mandate of generalized rights jurisprudence.

Democratic politics needs and deserves a wide berth, with all the messi-
ness and interest group battles that ensue. Excessive constitutionalization of
policy risks debilitating rather than promoting democratic self-government.
The hard question is to find a zone of proper political disagreement that is
not subject to being commandeered by a too ready recourse to constitutional
principle. To give a concrete illustration, an example from Canada, a decidedly non-fragile democracy, provides a useful counterweight to the central
account of the era of strong constitutionalism under the direction of strong
constitutional courts.

QUEBEC REFERENCE ON SECESSION

In 1998, at the height of one of the periodic upsurges in separatist sentiment
in Quebec, the Canadian Supreme Court was presented with a question as
direct as it was bedeviling: "[W]e are asked to rule on the legality of unilateral secession 'under the Constitution of Canada.'"[9] The matter was admittedly one of first impression and, because the existence of Canada could well
have been in the balance, the court faced the daunting prospect of ruling
on a matter of last impression. The court quickly discovered that the constitutional structure of Canada did not explicate the exact source of popular
consent to governance; rather, "[t]he representative and democratic nature of

OF THE FEDERAL REPUBLIC OF GERMANY, 238–42 (3rd ed., Durham, NC: Duke University
  Press, 2012).
[9] Reference re Secession of Quebec [1998], 2 S.C.R. 217.

our political institutions was simply assumed."[10] Without a clear mandate on the central question of the democratic premises of the state, the court had to acknowledge the compelling claim of Quebec, at least initially: "The argument that the Constitution may be legitimately circumvented by resorting to a majority vote in a province-wide referendum is superficially persuasive, in large measure because it seems to appeal to some of the same principles that underlie the legitimacy of the Constitution itself, namely, democracy and self-government."[11]

The general appeal to democracy could not resolve the question of separation without first resolving the problem that "there may be different and equally legitimate majorities in different provinces and territories and at the federal level."[12] There were no mediating principles in Canadian constitutional law or in general democratic principles that could resolve the apparent conflict should a majority of the Québécois opt for independence while a majority of the broader Canadian constituency (including the Québécois) vote to preserve the territorial integrity of Canada. Rather, Canadian politics had long subsumed a form of Québécois separate representation through the reigning Liberal Party requirement that the leadership of the party alternate between French and English speakers and the party's practice of setting informal quotas for cabinet seats between the two groups.[13] Not only does Canadian politics strongly recognize the need for regional representation, but Quebec has greater representation in the Senate than do other provinces; moreover, one-third of the justices of the Supreme Court are from Quebec.[14] In addition, given the strong concessions toward regionalism on matters such as language, and given that overall economic benefits flowed to rather than from Quebec, there were no readily credible claims of oppression of the sort that may have sustained independence demands in the Baltics under the Soviets or in the broader regions of Kurdistan, for example.[15]

---

[10] *Id.* at 253.

[11] *Id.* at 259.

[12] *Id.* at 255.

[13] Brendan O'Leary, *Debating Consociational Politics: Normative and Explanatory Arguments,* in FROM POWER SHARING TO DEMOCRACY: POST CONFLICT INSTITUTIONS IN ETHNICALLY DIVIDED SOCIETIES 3, 16 (Sid Noe ed., Montreal, Canada: McGill-Queen's University Press, 2004).

[14] Twenty-two of the 105 Canadian senators represent Quebec and three of the nine sitting Canadian Supreme Court justices are members of the Quebec Bar.

[15] By and large, the international law consensus on the right of self-determination, to the extent there is one, is limited to situations of conquest or colonization. *See* Patrick Macklem, *Militant Democracy, Legal Pluralism, and the Paradox of Self-Determination,* 4 INT'L J. CONST. L. 488, 505 (2006).

A formalist resolution could have been crafted by focusing narrowly on the mechanisms of constitutional amendment. The Canadian court could have construed the dissolution of Canada as a form of constitutional amendment requiring the full mandates accompanying any constitutional alteration. The effect would have been not only to move the level of decision making to the national level but to trigger the supermajority requirements for constitutional change.[16] That presumably would have answered the challenge presented in a particularly unsatisfactory way: a minority constituency feeling aggrieved and unable to achieve its aims at the majoritarian level of national politics could only have appealed to the supermajoritarian constraints of the larger body politic. Such a course may have resolved the constitutional question but not the broader question of democratic legitimacy.

At the end of the day, the Canadian court found a halfway measure that relied on the political debates of democracy rather than the first-order principles of constitutionalism. The court's intervention granted separatist claims the right to initiate a dialog on dissolution of the country. In what is known as the "clear majority/clear question" requirement, the court mandated that a majority of the Québécois would have the right to initiate a process of political renegotiation whose outcome could be secession, although those terms remained unspecified:

> A referendum undoubtedly may provide a democratic method of ascertaining the views of the electorate on important political questions on a particular occasion. The democratic principle identified above would demand that considerable weight be given to a clear expression by the people of Quebec of their will to secede from Canada, even though a referendum, in itself and without more, has no direct legal effect, and could not in itself bring about unilateral secession.[17]

The effect was to create a species of "Canadian secession clause," to use Sujit Choudhry's formulation,[18] although one that was not judicially enforceable.

---

[16] Formal mechanisms of constitutional amendment are a relatively new process in Canada. Prior to the constitutional reorganization in 1982, amendments of the Canadian Constitution were formally made by the U.K. Parliament as amendments to the British North America Act. Such amendments were typically approved only upon request endorsed by concurrent majorities of the House of Commons and the Senate, generally after obtaining a substantial degree of provincial consent. *See generally* PETER W. HOGG, CONSTITUTIONAL LAW OF CANADA 61–76 (3rd ed., Toronto, Canada: Carswell, 1992).

[17] 2 S.C.R. at 265.

[18] This formulation is from Sujit Choudhry, *Popular Revolution or Popular Constitutionalism? Reflections on the Constitutional Politics of Quebec Secession, in* THE LEAST EXAMINED BRANCH: THE ROLE OF LEGISLATURES IN THE CONSTITUTIONAL STATE 480, 487 (Richard W. Bauman & Tsvi Kahana eds., New York: Cambridge University Press, 2006).

The Supreme Court's gambit of subgroup rights to dialog over a process of dissolution was never put to the test. The last referendum in Quebec occurred in 1995 and lost by less than a percentage point. Even here, there was considerable debate over the outcome because the referendum prevailed strongly among the francophone Québécois. The margin of electoral defeat came from the overwhelming opposition of the anglophone minority in Quebec, many of whom were recent arrivals from other parts of Canada, together with those known as allophones, namely, recent immigrants to Canada whose native language is neither English nor French and who then represented more than 10 percent of the population of Quebec.

In the aftermath of the failed referendum, the issue of Canadian dissolution has receded from that country's political life. For the past two decades, while the main secessionist force, the Parti Québécois, has been a constant presence in Canadian politics, its political fortunes have dwindled. The Canadian Supreme Court's gambit succeeded and its restrained constitutionalism allowed the process of democratic engagement and negotiation to find a political resolution.

Although it has not been put to the test in a genuine effort at secession, the Canadian court's analysis is significant for another reason, one with greater pertinence for this assessment of the relation between court constitutionalism and democratic politics. The question referred for judicial review was whether there was a right in either Canadian constitutional law or, at a higher level of authority, in international law that mandated the ability of a regional majority to compel secession. Rather than turn to a rights claim abstracted from politics, the court turned to the nature of Canadian political institutions, finding an inextricable link between democracy and federalism. Claims of right regarding the political process must necessarily be mediated through the institutional structures of governance. At the very heart of a constitutional framework is the ability to "provide for a division of political power that allocates political power amongst different levels of government."[19] In rejecting the narrow rights claim, therefore, the court concluded that the ultimate principle of constitutional settlement "would be defeated if one of those democratically elected levels of government could usurp the powers of the other simply by exercising its legislative power to allocate additional political power to itself unilaterally."[20]

Canada provides a useful and highly influential example of courts respecting the boundaries of democratic politics in a non-fragile state. Rather than

[19] 2 S.C.R. at para. 74.
[20] *Id.*

leap for the constitutional brass ring, the Supreme Court channeled a political resolution through the clear statement on clear question rule of demand, followed by political negotiations. The court sagely defused the sense of Quebec being aggrieved and used its constitutional authority in the service of democracy. At no point, however, in the disputes over Quebec was Canada at risk of descending into civil war or massive bloodshed. This was the primacy of politics in a decidedly mature and decent democratic society. The challenge for the many new fragile democracies is to find an equilibrium in which constitutional stewardship similarly reinforces the democratic virtues of popular sovereignty.

CONCLUSION: JUDICIAL OVERSIGHT AND POLITICAL EXPERIMENTATION

The cases under consideration in this book present in extreme form the conflict that emerges whenever courts confront the basic institutional arrangements of national politics. They are extreme because judicial intervention is not conditioned by easy recourse to precedent or to an organizing theory of what is the proper allocation of political responsibility among different potential levels of governance.[21] In the absence of readily distilled principles either in law or political theory, courts should be guided by a proper appreciation of the role that judicial oversight can play in the political arena. There are four key justifications for judiciaries to override local political arrangements, which may be applied in cases of high consequence that nonetheless lack clear doctrinal moorings. This is not the place to develop at length the justification for each of these grounds for judicial intervention. Summarizing them together provides some concluding principles and a useful buffer against the easy imposition of the one-size-fits-all approaches that disrupt functioning political arrangements.

First, there are, of course, actual claims of rights violations. While this book focuses on the structural deficits of democracy, simple rights to the franchise remain at the heart of the democratic enterprise. The denial of the ability to participate on the basis of race or gender or religion falls within the sort of individual entitlement readily recognized and addressed by courts. There is no

---

[21] Some have tried to fill in this gap by relying on principles of citizen engagement in possible decision making, thereby drawing on a view of democracy that promotes participation and the generation of information from local bodies. *See* Roderick M. Hills Jr., *Against Preemption: How Federalism Can Improve the National Legislative Process*, 82 N.Y.U. L. Rev. 1 (2007).

shortage of cases from around the world upholding the basic elements of the franchise against discriminatory exclusions. Nevertheless, precisely because individual right-to-vote cases provide the path of least resistance, there is the unmistakable tendency for courts to package complex political questions in the ready formula of rights claims. In the United States, a presumed individual right extended to everyone to equally effective votes became the vehicle of choice for the court to overcome the political question barrier beginning with the reapportionment cases of the 1960s. As the German Constitutional Court's willingness to consider a rights challenge to the Maastricht treaty indicates, however, the temptation to see fundamental political arrangements through the prism of individual rights is by no means limited to the United States.[22]

A second source of judicial authority to disrupt settled political arrangements lies in the obligation to ensure accountability of the process to the electorate. Ultimately, elections in a democracy "must provide the opportunity for genuine contestation, and their outcomes must not be preordained by the design of institutional structures."[23] The key insight is a skepticism toward the problem of "self-interest in institutional design,"[24] a likely result when insiders are able to realize substantial protection by altering the rules of the game to their benefit. This issue has been at the heart of the arguments about legal regulation of the political process as well as central to the academic debates over the law of democracy for more than a decade.[25] The overall question of the competitive vitality of the electoral system increasingly has instructed judicial inquiries into such critical matters as the threshold of representation in proportional representation systems,[26] or the impact of party finance regulation

---

[22] Another noteworthy example from the ECtHR comes with Bowman v. United Kingdom, 26 Eur. H.R. Rep. 1 (1998), a challenge to the entire British system of financing of political parties and election campaigns, also handled from the limited perspective of individual rights to participate. *See* Jacob Rowbottom, *Access of the Airwaves and Equality: The Case Against Political Advertising on the Broadcast Media, in* PARTY FUNDING AND CAMPAIGN FINANCING IN INTERNATIONAL PERSPECTIVE 77 (K.D. Ewing & Samuel Issacharoff, eds., Portland, OR: Hart, 2006).

[23] Guy-Uriel E. Charles, *Democracy and Distortion*, 92 CORNELL L. REV. 601, 609 (2007).

[24] Elizabeth Garrett, *Who Chooses the Rules?*, 3 ELECTION L.J. 139, 139 (2005).

[25] The opening gambit in this inquiry was Samuel Issacharoff & Richard Pildes, *Politics as Markets: Partisan Lockups of the Democratic Process*, 50 STAN. L. REV. 643 (1998).

[26] In Germany, for example, the Constitutional Court upheld a 5 percent threshold for representation as a reasonable political accommodation, particularly in light of the postwar need for stability. *See* Kommers & Miller, *supra* note 8, at 254 (discussing the *Bavarian Party Case*, BVerfG Jan. 23, 1957, 6 BVerfGE 84). Subsequently, after reunification, the court struck down efforts to expand the scope of newly integrated parties to "piggyback" on coalitions in order to achieve the 5 percent threshold. *Id.* at 255–59 (translating, in part, the *National Unity Election Case*, BVerfG Sept. 29, 1990, 82 BVerfGE 322).

on the overall accountability of elected representatives,[27] or even the proper application of protections against minority vote dilution in the United States under the Voting Rights Act.[28] The core insight is that courts remain important institutional actors standing against the manipulation of electoral institutions to the advantage of incumbent officeholders.[29]

Third, and relatedly, courts may intercede as a backstop against institutional desuetude. The unresponsiveness of an electoral system can be a matter of a lock up of power by self-interested incumbents or of the calcification of institutional arrangements when there is insufficient political will for change. The problem of malapportionment in the United States, the predicate for the *Baker v. Carr* line of cases, is an example of both the self-interest of the overrepresented rural constituencies and the inertial difficulties of political reform. By contrast, where political arrangements are more recent and reflect a genuine compromise, there should be a much greater presumption of legal tolerance of experimentation. Certainly this was a focus of the ECtHR in *Mathieu-Mohin and Clerfayt v. Belgium*,[30] in which the court upheld complicated Belgian local arrangements. For the ECtHR, the fact that the voting rights of the linguistic groups in local communities were the product of recent negotiations was one of the grounds to permit experimentation and not to impose a simplistic rights command – and properly so.

Finally, judicial oversight may serve as a protection against opportunism, particularly when political boundaries serve to isolate those who bear the costs from any realistic ability to challenge political decision making occurring elsewhere. Evidence for this may be found in the American Constitution's prohibition on interstate compacts that potentially burden nonparticipating states.[31] But the same problem can arise independently of a formal agreement between two states to privilege themselves at the expense of others. The

---

[27] *See McConnell v. FEC* 540 U.S. 93, 247 (2003) (Scalia, J., concurring in part, dissenting in part).

[28] *See* Ellen Katz, *Reviving the Right to Vote*, 68 Ohio St. L.J. 1163 (2007).

[29] The basic instinct here was well captured by John Hart Ely, who viewed elections cases as "[involving] rights (1) that are essential to the democratic process and (2) whose dimensions cannot safely be left to our elected representatives, who have an obvious vested interest in the status quo." Ely, *supra* note 3, at 117.

[30] Eur. H.R. Rep. 1 (1988).

[31] "No State shall, without the Consent of Congress, … enter into any Agreement or Compact with another State." U.S. Const. art. I, §10, cl. 3. "The Founders were acutely aware of the need to protect states and their citizens from sister-state aggression; that is why they adopted the Compact Clause … [to protect] comity and equality among the states." Michael S. Greve, *Compacts, Cartels, and Congressional Consent*, 68 Mo. L. Rev. 285, 293 (2003). *See generally* Joseph Francis Zimmerman, Interstate Cooperation: Compacts and Administrative Agreements (Westport, CT: Praeger, 2002).

simplest manifestation of this may come with pollution, as when any state in the Midwest of the United States has the power to permit the burning of high-sulfur coal for power, subject only to a requirement of tall smokestacks to send the fumes aloft. For the citizens of the Northeast, by contrast, the consequences of acid rain are not susceptible to any political form of self-protection. To provide such protection, therefore, is a task that some courts, such as the U.S. Supreme Court and the European Court of Justice, have read into the role of ensuring economic integration through doctrines such as preemption.[32]

In more recent constitutional arrangements, such as that of South Africa, there may be a direct commitment that all spheres of governmental authority must "exercise their powers and perform their functions in a manner that does not encroach on the geographical, functional or institutional integrity of government in another sphere."[33] Almost invariably, the increased scope of market activity as it reaches national and international levels is a strong factor in the push toward the use of higher-order legal authority when dealing with regulation of economic activity. But in countries where political power has consolidated in the hands of President Uribe or the ANC, regional authorities may be as powerless to resist political exploitation from the center as they would be unilaterally to counter the effects of distant emissions or the centralizing force of markets.

In sum, even a brief look at the court decisions reviewed in this book shows that it is becoming commonplace for courts to confront questions that were long deemed beyond the realm of possible judicial competence. Simply as a descriptive matter, courts now routinely engage the complicated world of political power in ways unimaginable a few generations back. In some cases, extreme perhaps, this new state of affairs requires a confrontation with the first-order question of what is the proper form of governance for a nation of multiple peoples living in overlapping lands. Little in either the common law or civil law traditions prepares the field doctrinally for the resolution of such questions. This book is ultimately about some of the difficulties in confronting an area without clear markers in either legal or political theory, and yet the importance in helping protect democracy against its inherent frailties. At the same time, it is necessary to conclude with a word of caution against courts being swept along too easily by the tide of rights claims that were, in many cases, the initial impetus for the courts to enter the political domain. The world of politics is too contested and too precarious for such a simple template.

---

[32] For an extended discussion of this theme, see Samuel Issacharoff & Catherine M. Sharkey, *Backdoor Federalization*, 53 UCLA L. Rev. 1353 (2006).

[33] S. Afr. Const. 1996 § 41(1)(g).

Index

in new democracies, 9–12, 191, 197,
200, 214–20
institutional desuetude as justification for
intervention by, 288
judge selection in, 231–38
jurisdictions of, 238–39
lustration laws and, 207–11
in mature democracies, 214, 243
minimum electoral threshold requirements
and, 202–4
political exploitation from center as
justification for intervention by, 288–89
political leaders acquiescence to, 189–90
rights violations as justification for
intervention by, 286–87
separation of power and, 191–96
U.S. model for modern, 152, 158
underspecified constitutional commands
and, 220–21
constitutional formation, 178
bargaining model of, 227–31
contractual model of, 216–26
underspecified constitutional commands
and, 220–21
constitutional negotiations, 217, 218, 219,
220, 226
bargaining with an outside option model
and, 227–29
political violence and, 219
constitutional retreat, South Africa and, 242
constitutionalism, 8–12, 14, 191, 214
defined, 11, 11n21
popular constitutionalism, 189
South Africa and, 170–72
constitutions, 46, 48, 122, 197, 220, 275, *See
also* by specific country
unamendable provisions and, 48
constrained parliamentarianism, 104
corruption, 135, 158, 260–62
Costa Rica, 206
Cromwell, Oliver, 199, 199n23
cronyism, 158
Czech Republic, 271
Czech Republic Constitutional Court, 197–98
minimum electoral threshold
requirements, 203–4
Czechoslovakia, 57, 166
Czechoslovakian Constitutional Court, 49

Delaware, 259
democracy
defined, 11, 11n21, 121, 134

electoral competition and, 243–47
post-Soviet collapse, 166
rotation in ancient concepts, 128
Democratic Alliance (South Africa), 256,
257, 260
democratic constraints, 38–42, 124, 136, 276,
279, *See also* banning of political parties
liberal theory on, 39–41
questions on parameters of, 42
democratic integrity, 41, 98, 104, 157n55,
252, 253
democratic intolerance, 35
democratic tolerance, 3, 5, 32, 33, 39, 124
censorship and, 32–34
right to insult and, 33
democratic transitions, 1, 196, 276, *See also*
constitutional formation; South African
constitutional formation
from authoritarian regimes, 136, 138–39,
178, 207
Denmark, 32–34
Dennis v. United States, 21–23, 60, 94
Dorr Rebellion of 1841–42, 153
Dworkin, Ronald, 33, 40, 40n35, 241, 264

ECtHR, 288
Egypt, 1, 52
elections, 271, *See also* U.S. Presidential
elections
antidemocratic groups in U.S. and, 23–25
antidemocratic threats and, 34–38
Athenian view of, 128
in Botswana, 135, 136
in Burundi, 219
election administration, 204–7
election tribunals in Mexico, 206–7
electoral participation banning, 97–99
ethnic conflict and, 3–4
in fractured new democracies, 2–6,
122n69
minimum electoral threshold
requirements, 202–4
paramilitary groups and, 36
political violence and, 219
renewability of consent and, 122–23, 135
rotation in office and, 127–29, 132–34, 136,
151, 198
second elections, 3, 128–29
stability of in U.S., 26
electoral accountability, 287–88
electoral challenges, 12
Czech Constitutional Court and, 203–4

CPSIA information can be obtained
at www.ICGtesting.com
Printed in the USA
LVOW13s0309160917
548879LV00013B/136/P

9 781107 654549